D1174091

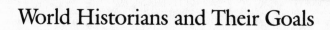

World Historians and Their Goals

WORLD HISTORIANS

AND THEIR GOALS

Twentieth-Century Answers to Modernism

Paul Costello

Northern Illinois University Press

DeKalb 1993

© 1993 by Northern Illinois University Press
Published by Northern Illinois University Press,
DeKalb, Illinois 60115
Manufactured in the United States using acid-free paper
Design by Julia Fauci

Library of Congress Cataloging-in-Publication Data
Costello, Paul.
World historians and their goals : twentieth century answers to
modernism / Paul Costello.
p.   cm.
Includes bibliographical references and index.
ISBN 0-87580-173-0
1. Historiography—History—20th century.   I. Title.
D13.C674   1993
907.2—dc20   92–15134
CIP

For Rachel

CONTENTS

PREFACE

THE CRITICISM OF CYCLICAL METAHISTORY since the Second World War may obscure its predominant place in the historiography of world history in the first half of the twentieth century. The purpose of this study, an intellectual history of world historical paradigms in the twentieth century from H. G. Wells to William H. McNeill, is to explore the way in which these paradigms have evolved to digest Spengler's cyclical view to save a progressive movement in history.

The writings of the world historians of our century have sought to articulate and answer the crisis of their own civilization by putting it into the context of a universal history. The formulation of each of these paradigms has entailed an elaborate dialogue between the historian's prospect on the future, his philosophical or religious sense of the ends of man, and his confrontation with historical evidence. Each has attempted to educate modern society toward the resolution of current macrohistorical dilemmas.

No one has yet drawn together an exhaustive exposition of these paradigms. Pitirim A. Sorokin's *Social Philosophies of an Age of Crisis* (1950) may still be the best survey of the world historical systems of the first half of our century. Sorokin evaluated the works of Danilevsky, Spengler, Toynbee, Shubert, Kroeber, and Schweitzer, but he was interested in them as social theories and not as world historical systems per se. His focus was further clouded by his own religious agenda and the fact that his own work was at the center of the cyclical tradition both philosophically and temporally in the twentieth century. He was therefore unable to discern the conclusion of this movement of cyclical social philosophies in the works of, among others, Dawson, Mumford, and McNeill.

Other historians have written sweeping surveys of metahistorical theory from the Bible and Augustine. John Barker has written in *The*

Superhistorians (1982) a study of those historians who have created a sense of the past within their contemporary mentality. Barker encapsulates his world historical paradigms neatly but does not bring his analysis past Toynbee and Wells. Frank E. Manuel's *Shapes in Philosophical History* (1956) may be the best short survey of the continuity of cyclical and progressive theories in world history, but his long-range perspective does not allow him to elaborate broad analyses of the range of cyclical themes in the twentieth century or the closing of this tradition. Karl Löwith's *Meaning in History* (1949) begins with Nietzsche and works backward chronologically to argue against him by demonstrating the essential role of telos (purpose) in Western conceptions of history. After Wells and Spengler, each of the writers to be evaluated in this text—Toynbee, Dawson, Mumford, McNeill, and Sorokin—has made an analysis of his historical place in answering the paradigms of his predecessors.

No one outside this tradition has written a summary and analytical survey of their work that includes Wells's warnings of catastrophe and the problem posed by Oswald Spengler, that examines the religious premises inherent in the early formulation of Toynbee's history of civilizations, that exposes the roots in and influences upon this tradition of Dawson and Mumford, and that evaluates William McNeill's place in symbolically closing out the tradition of the history of civilizations. This study undertakes these tasks while focusing on the confrontation of the world historians with the crisis of the West, their utopian or religious perspectives on the transformation of humanity essential to its resolution, the continuity of their reaction to technological growth and bureaucratic agglomeration, and their fears of a mechanized, totalitarian social order.

The present analysis examines each author's work separately as an architectonic scheme that attempts to answer the central problems, the "crisis," of the twentieth century and embodies his goals for the future. In doing so the author relies on the sense of eschatological motive inherent in the writing of metahistory that has been described and analyzed in broad historical surveys by Rudolf Bultmann, John T. Marcus, Robert J. Lifton, Frank E. Manuel, and Karl Löwith.[1] These authors share a common belief that world history serves a psychological function in providing a ground or sense of place in an age of rapid change and apocalyptic potential.

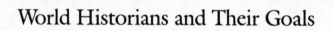

World Historians and Their Goals

CHAPTER ONE

World History in the West

An Interrupted Dialogue with Providence

From Death and dark Oblivion (near the same)
The Mistress of Man's Life, grave History,
Raising the World to good, or evil Fame,
Doth vindicate it to Eternity.

High Providence would so: that nor the Good
Might be defrauded, nor the Great secur'd
But both might know their ways are understood,
And the Reward and Punishment assur'd.
                                        —Sir Walter Raleigh[1]

The world beneath the moon its shapes doth vary
And change from this to that; nor can it tarry
Long in one state; but with its self doth jar,
Kills, and is kill'd, in endless Civil war.
New form'd again, 'tis but to dye. The frame
Neither of *Bodies* nor of Minds the same
But that above the Spheres, the Heavens on high,
In which God reigns in Glorious Majesty,
Free from old Age, unchang'd, and of one face,
Alwaies presents it self in equal Grace.
                                        —G. Buchanan[2]

T HE PERSPECTIVES of western world historians in the twentieth century are dominated by an overwhelming sense of crisis, a feeling that Western civilization may be doomed to destroy itself in a cataclysmic suicide or fall into a degenerate stagnation where "the machine" will supersede the highest aspirations of humanity and society will sink into depersonalized automatism. In the study of world history one confronts civilizations or unified cultural systems made up of habitual patterns of symbols and material life—as wholes—that live and progress, or die and disintegrate, in rhythm with a hidden underlying reality. To grasp this reality is essential to the resolution of the crisis of the twentieth century, where old symbols have broken down, old faiths have been lost or betrayed, where God is dead and progress becomes a fearful passage of Faustian striving toward ends that lose their attraction with our approach, where the old utopias become prisons and asylums.

To most of the major world historians of the twentieth century, modern man has lost his connection with a unity beyond his own self-interest; through progress he has broken his connection to a meaningful cosmos. The modern individual's vision of the world is distracted by his concern for detail; the mechanical increment is taken for reality as a whole and consequently he cannot come to grips with the ultimate issues of his time or the eternal ones of his nature. To the world historians there is a crisis in modern man's epistemology; as the frame of reference is constricted so is the possibility of any meaning in the world beyond a narrowly circumscribed sensate experience. As reality is broken down to its constituent data nothing can be known except the quantitative, and the person becomes a fragment.

According to Henry Adams, "unity is vision; it must have been part of the process of learning to see."[3] History, for the world historian, is a projection of this unity on the past. In his mind's eye the historian orders events; he attributes meaning to them, assigns importance, coordinates them chronologically and adapts received evidence in line with a psychological *Weltanschauung*. This world view guides him in the selection of meaningful fact; it is in a perpetual dialogue with his study of history, both formed by what he learns of the past and simultaneously producing that past through selecting from the discreet elements of historical data. This implies a relativism of the historian toward his times as well as a breakdown in the division of subject and object, as the internal psychological and even religious disposition of the writer infuses his view of history as a whole. This is inherent in the writing of any history to some extent. It is magnified in the writing of world history which, in its attempt to grasp the pattern of the past as a unity, is least amenable to bare empirical investigation.

According to Christopher Dawson, "metahistory is concerned with the nature of history, the meaning of history and the causes and significance of historical change."[4] While it is possible to approach metahistorical issues in the abstract, questions of the meaning of history lead logically to the observation of the patterns of the whole, and to speculative forecasts on the future direction and outcome of these trends. World historians are metahistorians par excellence. For the purposes of this study world historians are defined as schematic students of the past who have attempted to specify the pattern of the past from earliest recorded time to the present. An evolving idea of world history in the West originated in the biblical tradition and has developed since the Renaissance in an increasingly secular direction.

Despite this secularization, the idea of world history has retained fundamental elements of continuity through the interruptions and transformations that it has undergone.

• • •

The appeal of world history to the general public in the twentieth century is closely connected to the faults that academic historians find with it. Its apocalyptic and moral themes and tone, the grand generalizations that seem magnificent in the abstract but horrify the specialist, the organicism and anthropomorphism in its study of cultures and civilizations, its moral imprecations and speculative predictions, and its claims to empirical validity and scientific method while describing nebulous supersensual abstractions, all offend the scholar who declaims, "Mais ce n'est pas l'histoire!"[5] even as it draws an avid reading public. Despite errors in the particulars, and the contradictions and absurdities inherent in some of the theories themselves, world history has articulated elements common to the modern world view where history has come to provide psychological grounding for life in an age without a common faith in any cosmic setting or supernatural drama.

Even those historians who have rejected the globalizing attempts of the metahistorians retain, if unconsciously, unexamined assumptions and analogies with which they place their sector of the past within a general field. In the attempt to make this field explicit and to enlarge it from the nineteenth-century scheme of the ancient, medieval, and modern history of Europe, the macrohistorian takes a step that, whatever its drawbacks, must be considered courageous given the epistemological predilections of modern Western academic culture. Such attempts ultimately are doomed to failure, and models of world history are fated to perpetually give way to one another, for they can only approximate reality from a relative position and express it only through the use of grand metaphor rather than perceive and express the thing in itself that is world history. "Progress," "challenge and response," the "*Volk*" or historical people, the life cycle of civilizations or conceptions of "unified cultural supersystems" unify the "natural history" of the human species and reify demonstrable but perhaps isolated occurrences and unilateral patterns by enlarging them into hermeneutic models. The analogical media that the world historians select act the same way in which Freud employed his concept of the "instincts" for universal explanation: they are "mythical entities, magnificent in their indefiniteness."[6]

Clearly what William McNeill has called "mythistory" differs from the work of more empirically restricted regional and period histories. The difference, however, is one of degrees on a continuum; the same epistemological problems are inherent for the specialist in expressing any interpretation of (or indeed even in the selection of) his historical data. But it is the broad myth-making propensity of our grand theorists that arouses the ire of their professional colleagues even as it ensures their popularity with the general reading public. World historians reflect and contribute to the collective symbols of their times, articulating world views that find a ready market especially in ages when the myths of the past are questioned and the symbol systems discredited. The power that world historical faiths exert in our time can scarcely be exaggerated—one need only think of the fascist manipulation of the past, the Marxian faith in future destiny that guided revolution and empowered Stalin and Mao Tse-tung, and the perennial, if at times unexamined, progressive liberalism of the modern West.

Ultimately, world history is employed as predictive. If one can ascertain the imperatives of the past, the causal chain that has produced the present, then one can extrapolate to the future by extending one's perspective forward to the ends of this pattern. Inherent in this technique is the possibility of the historian consciously or unconsciously extending his own goals for the future into the past, of finding a progression in the long duration of history that will inevitably bring his desired future into being or will do so if certain actions are taken. This warning is not to denigrate the real historical and hermeneutic value of world historical models; it is only to recognize the continuous and almost innately human dialogue that occurs between one's sense of the ends and goals of history and the patterns of the past.

An obvious example of this propensity is Marx, whose view of the progression of the economic relations of classes and the means of production is predicated at least in part on his preconceived historical goal of a classless Communist society. As Robert Nisbet has put it, "long before Marx thought in terms of the science of society, he was consecrated to the transformation of society."[7] Here the revolutionary comes before the historian in turning to the past to describe the stages leading, with the hard logic of economic inevitability, to a personal vision of utopia. While the violence of class struggle is still essential for the success of the transformation to communism, history is on "our side." The historian, having found the key to the future, becomes a prophet of the new order; the writing of history becomes both an expression of his goals and a polemical tool toward their realization.

Action in line with the deep pattern of the past becomes a moral duty. For Marx, while this scientifically discerned progression was inevitable, each individual had to do what he could to further it. The moral imperative is to act in accordance with the movement of history, not simply to struggle for one's class interests but to strive to be in harmony with destiny rather than to pursue a reactionary line that would leave one by the wayside or under the steamroller of progress. This same sense of historical imperatives is integrated into each of the models of world history examined in this volume; in an age they perceive as one of crisis, the world historians' projection of a future is essential to their task and motivates much of their writing.

Modern world historians pursue one form or another of world unity in history. They project a future world united by crisis, by the evolution of mind and technics, by revolution or dictatorial force. Like William McNeill they study progressively enlarged hegemonies or, like Pitirim Sorokin and Nikolai Berdyaev, look back to a Medieval unity that must be recaptured.

• • •

Each of the authors we will examine is motivated by a sense of crisis. Each notes a loss of faith in the traditional religious dogmas of the West and in the secular creed of progress. Each is concerned with the increase of humanity's power without a corresponding growth in its capacity for wisdom or tolerance; each also fears the influence of a technology, seemingly beyond social control, on the liberty of the individual and on social mores and values. Twentieth-century world historians prophetically warn of social decay and at the same time evoke images of enslavement to the machine and ultimately the possibility of the destruction of the human personality or of the world itself.

From Burckhardt and Henry Adams to McNeill, macrohistorians warn of the end of the world as an incipient possibility with the rise of human power. They reiterate the eschatological prophesies of the Christian millenarians and, like Old Testament prophets, they call on individuals to mend their ways, to recognize historical imperatives in the present and thereby save the world as well as their souls. For most of the authors examined, the crisis of the West requires for its resolution the institution of a new man, a new mentality, and a new social organization based upon a fundamental shift in values and morality. This cannot occur without a connection beyond individualism, either to an idealized humanity as in H. G. Wells's Comtean religion or in the recognition of a supreme being external to, but in contact with, human beings. Until William McNeill's *The Rise of the West*, the world historians of our century have tended to emphasize the religious implications and origins of macrohistorical patterns. Their visions of the future have included millennial utopias to be achieved in the

successful passage of the ordeal of modernity; in an age of individualism they have held that this requires the internal conquest of self in
a sublimation to a transpersonal, even transcendent, unity.

These observers of world processes manifest an antimodernist and
to some extent antirationalist conception of history; they have rejected
naive views of progress under the successive hammer blows of twentieth-century events, especially the two world wars, which mark major
shifts in their perspectives on the destiny of modern civilization. Not
until the work of William McNeill did the central trend in the writing
of world history revert to a strictly linear and progressive view of time
and human development, and even then this has not been without
serious qualification and moral admonition.

The histories that follow are examined as paradigms, as architectonic
structures. Each is briefly outlined, then evaluated in relation to each
author's views of the present and the future. Critical, here, are the
expressed goals of the historian. This study concentrates on the interface between the historian's perception of the dilemma of his time and
his view of history as providing analogous periods that can show the
way out or give the consolation that in the long run a phoenix will
arise out of the ashes.

The purpose of this study of world history is not to judge how
closely the world historians come to reality, how universal their theories are, or how well they accommodate known facts. This volume is
less concerned with the accuracy of the facts collected by the metahistorians than with the underlying world view that guides their
selection. The "truth-value" of a particular world history is relative to
the reader and to the use to which it is put. This study examines these
histories from another tack, as mythistories that reflect their authors'
personal sense of purpose, historical necessity, and human destiny.
Instead of developing exhaustive psychobiographies of the authors,
the texts of their writings will be employed as the primary key and
test of their intentions. Obviously, there is no one historian who fits
all the generalizations the field as a whole prompts one to make.

The epistemological crisis in the modern West is clearly reflected in
the struggle to put together a view of the history of the world that
could act as a meaningful sense of place after the breakdown of a
consensual and unifying world view. The world and history for these
authors take the place of, or in some cases demonstrate, Providence,
and thereby assert a destiny in a world where beneficent progress has
gone from being an unquestioned faith to a central question and
problem. For the world historians under study, the rejection of world
history itself registers the blindness and defeatism of the modern age.
To avoid the challenge of a global perspective is to abdicate in the face

of the historian's central task—to decipher the meaning in history. To reject world history in a time of crisis is to renege on the historian's ultimate responsibility of confronting society with its past in a meaningful and useful way, as a dialectical step toward the resolution of its fundamental historical problems.

• • •

This introduction provides only a brief and selective view of particular world historical models as they have evolved in the West. One must not assume that each model gives way smoothly before its natural descendant, nor accept Pitirim Sorokin's belief that there is a rhythmic recurrence of cyclical and linear perspectives. While there is an essential continuity in Western conceptions of the history of the world, it has always been subject to interruptions. Individual authors have emphasized progress or Providence, the sacred or the profane, linear patterns or combinations of cyclical rise and fall along with underlying directional movements. Even when progress in one form or another has been the dominant world view of a period, cyclical perspectives have emerged, like Vico's at the outset of the Enlightenment, Ferguson's at its height, and Danilevsky's in the mid-nineteenth century. A brief and by no means inclusive overview of pre-twentieth-century models of world history in the West will be useful in exposing the themes, goals, and trends that repeatedly crop up and serve as foundations for the problem that world history has become in our century.

The Bible comprises the first world history in the West. Though creation myths have been formulated since before the dawn of historical time, the Jewish people were the first to go beyond their genesis of the world and of man to delineate a complete chronological history from these origins to the covenant with their God and to the contemporary lives of the Chosen People. This was a linear and ecumenical history—the known world was that of the People bounded by their contacts in space with the peoples surrounding them and, in time, by the creation and fall of humanity and the ends of history in the reunion of the tribes of Israel, the rebuilding of the Temple, and the coming of the messianic kingdom. Later Christian eschatological speculation would grapple with Daniel's interpretation of Nebuchadnezzar's dream of the four metals, which he saw as four earthly kingdoms beginning with Babylon. Otto of Freysing in the twelfth century was one of those who employed Daniel to predict the imminent end to the fourth age of the world and the Second Coming. From the Bible arose a belief in a linear movement of time that is the essential prerequisite for any progressive ideology and thus a primary source of the modern Western world view.

Robert Nisbet has convincingly repudiated J. B. Bury's thesis that the idea of progress is a recent invention of the West by pointing out the pervasiveness of the idea among the Greeks.[8] Hesiod's world history incorporated an inverse, though linearly progressive, movement from the Age of Gold to those of Silver, Bronze, and Iron. Protagoras produced a sketch of progress. Aristotle, while holding to a cyclical sense of history, also believed that knowledge increased like the "links of a chain." Polybius employed historical cycles even as he claimed that the history of the world pointed to the development of the Roman Empire as its culmination. Zeno, Democritus, Epicurus, Lucretius—atomists, skeptics, stoics believed in progress. Seneca held that progress occurs but is in some ways negative, as intellectual progression breaks human bonds and increases wars and other disturbances; he predicted an end in world destruction.[9]

Augustine's *The City of God* (426), aside from the Bible perhaps the most influential expression of a Christian world historical system, was inspired by the capture of Rome by Alaric in A.D. 410. Critics of Christianity attested that the city had fallen because it had turned to the worship of Christ and the God of the Jews. Augustine's apologetic in response to these critics established a fundamental pattern for Christian world historical thought that would dominate the field of metahistory for more than a millennium and has been retained by many to this day. To Augustine the city of Rome was but a state in this world, subject to the vicissitudes of mundane struggles for power and to the evil inherent in the world after the Fall, while the City of God was eternal and inviolable in heaven. The earliest Christians were nearly ahistorical in their conception of the future. The Gospel of John had claimed that the Day of Judgment was now at hand; Paul likewise proclaimed its imminence. The New Testament, and particularly the Revelation (a history of the future), is replete with assertions that the end was near. "Behold, I am coming soon, bringing my recompense, to repay everyone for what he has done."[10] Augustine rejected the vestigial cyclical element in Christian metahistory held by Origen (of the accumulation of evil and periodic cleansing by God) to posit a seven-stage world history with periods ending with Noah, Abraham, David, the Babylonian Captivity, and the coming of Christ. The present age, the sixth in world history, was passing; it would be followed by a final epoch. He became the first philosopher of the Church by defining the current stage of history as that designed for the universal extension of the Church so that all men would be ready for the end of history in the Second Coming. Augustine held that this progressive City of Man intersected historically with the City of God;

in this he left a legacy of conceptualizations of eschatology and Providence.[11]

Augustine's seventh stage acquired an increasingly millennial cast with the passage of time. Rudolf Bultmann has documented the way in which the Christian sense of time became increasingly historical with the distance from the events of the New Testament and the continual delay in the Second Coming.[12] Otto of Freysing's *History of the Two Cities* (1146) marked out cycles for secular progress alongside a Providential movement in the sacred realm. With Joachim de Fiore, a Cistercian abbot who lived from 1132 to 1202, Augustine's seventh stage was definitively tied to the Revelation of Saint John in an "Eternal Gospel" of history. The seventh stage was equated with the millennium of Jesus on Earth. Joachim developed a Trinitarian doctrine from his study of the Old Testament and the Gospels; the three ages of history, Before Christ, After Christ, and the Millennium, corresponded to the three persons of God. Each was accompanied by a sacred dispensation; the first one of married people led by the Father, then that of the clergy led by the Son, and finally a communistic heaven on earth of monks inspired by the Holy Spirit. The existing Church, founded on Christ, would give way to a new messianic leader who would institute the Kingdom of Christ in this world, after a final crisis in the second age.[13] Nisbet has also documented that the High Middle Ages were not exclusively concerned with the spiritual but had already conceived an earthly view of progress.[14] John of Salisbury held to a cumulative sense of progress; "we are on the shoulders of giants." Roger Bacon's writings on material progress and his role as a founder of the scientific method are well known; his work exemplifies the interpenetrating dualism of Western thought as he holds to a progressive naturalism alongside a forward-looking belief in the coming of the Antichrist and millennium.

With the Renaissance and its dominant tendency to look back to a Golden Age of antiquity, millenarian questions in the writing of world history were de-emphasized and progress was questioned. The rediscovery of classical knowledge included a revival of the popularity of Greek and Roman cyclical formulas. Machiavelli's world historical perspective noted the cyclical passage of empires through six forms of government. The rule of a prince degenerated to tyranny, which gave way to the rule of an aristocracy that decayed to an oligarchy, which was succeeded in its turn by a democracy that fell to anarchy. Each progressive downturn in the pattern marked a loss of virtue in series, first by the prince, then by the aristocracy and, finally, by the democratic citizenry.[15] Sir Walter Raleigh's *The History of the World* (1614), despite the author's genuflections to Providence at the outset and end of his history, traced a tragic pattern of meaningless change in this world, warning that those who sought to break balances of power ended in precipitating their own falls.[16]

With the Reformation came a revival of sacred history. John of Sleidan revived Daniel's view of the four successive monarchies in his *De Quatour Summis Impiris* (1558).[17] Jean Bodin wrote his *Method for the Easy Comprehension of History* (1583) as a deliberate "sacred history," a "means of inculcating piety to God, reverence to one's parents, charity to individuals and justice to all."[18] Even so, Bodin sought a "history of the activities of men only," which could avoid the confusion of human and divine affairs to see "bare history" without judging moral and philosophic values. His system turned to the dynamic and determinative effects of latitude on human society and a nascent evolutionary perspective along with a secular sense of progress; races and hence civilizations were determined by their respective distances from the equator.

Bodin held the theory that men of historical accomplishment presently resided between the forty-fifth and seventy-fifth parallels where "men grow increasingly warm within, while southerners, since they have more warmth from the sun have less from themselves."[19] Temperature, humors, and "biles" were the critical factors in history; the progressive movement of civilization from south to north corresponded to the dominating humor of each latitude in three historical periods. The south, where civilization originated, had a religious predominance. Men of the mid-latitudes excelled in practical matters and leadership. The northern peoples dominant in the present had acquired their power through their natural talents for invention and their proclivity to skill in warfare.

While Bodin attempted a natural, even ecological history, he soon moved beyond natural forces to posit relationships of climatic regions with the rule of planets; Saturn and Venus ruled in the south, Jupiter in the mid-latitudes, and Mars in the north. He also found that the cyclical "change of empires" in history, where each gave way progressively to an order at a higher level, could be calculated through the manipulation of Pythagorean numbers.

Bodin's attempt to form an ecological perspective ultimately was bounded by a sense of the universal hand of Providence. The study of the numbers in the dates of history showed "divine wisdom," and the cosmos was ordered by God in a harmonious balance wherein no event, no quantity, escaped a universal significance.[20] Bodin is most famous for his assertions of the divine right of kings; he demonstrated that royal power was both historically the most stable system of government and the most natural, that is, in correspondence to God's will. He closed his history of the ecumene with a stirring argument for tolerance, against ethnocentrism and for the unity of all men as common descendants of Noah, and he claimed that those who professed a more ancient origin or nobility of descent than other men had faced divine retribution again and again in history. The Greeks were so punished for their sense of separateness and superiority, and the Latins for their pride.[21] In the end Bodin was unable to extricate divine from human action in history; world history remained an evolving matrix of ecological processes, human decision, and divine intention and chastisement.

Nearly one hundred years after Bodin's *Method* Bishop Bossuet wrote his *Discours sur l'histoire universelle* (1681) as a last-ditch defense of the Bible as a literal world history, a progressive revelation that, in the New Testament, embraced the ecumene as a whole. The *Discours* was written as a moral and humanistic tract for the education of Bossuet's former pupil, the Christian Prince Louis XIV, "to explain the history of religion and the change of empires." Bossuet's was a history where the God-fearing were the victors and where idolaters and immoral leaders were punished, and their people with them.[22] When the good bishop looked back from the rightful rule of Louis XIV and Pope Innocent XI he found a clear chronological line to Peter, then to Aaron and Moses, the Patriarchs, and to the origins of the world. In the last analysis, the two testaments told the essential story of world history: "The relationship between the two testaments prove both of them to be divine . . . the former lays the foundation and the latter finishes the structure; in a word, the former foretells what the latter shows fulfilled. Thus all ages are united, and an eternal scheme of Providence is revealed to us."[23]

Clearly Bossuet, despite his extensive knowledge, was a preacher and educator first and a historian second. In an age still reverberating with Reformation and Counter-Reformation and bitten by a rising and pervasive skeptical detachment, Bossuet was a defender of the true faith who championed the central historical "continuity of church" to the king; he proclaimed a moral maxim that whatever interrupted this continuity "ought to be abhorrent to you."[24] Empires had fallen in the past, after all, from idolatry, injustice, liberty carried to an "excessive and intolerable degree," jealousy between the natural estates, and the consequential breakdown of a solid sense of the place and duty of each citizen before God and his monarch. "God reigns over every nation," rewarding justice and chastising immorality. When this has been realized in our perception of the whole of history it all will come clear: "All things concur to the same end; and it is only because we fail to understand the whole design that we see the coincidence or strangeness in particular events."[25]

Looking from Bossuet to Giambattista Vico one has a sense that in forty years a corner has been turned; we are confronted by the central themes and motifs of the systematic exposition of world history that anticipate in large measure those of primary concern to the twentieth century. Where Bossuet's popularity reached its peak in the romantic reaction to the French Revolution, Vico was largely unappreciated in his own day; his work has received its greatest acclaim in our century. Vico's *The New Science* (1725) was a brilliant condensation that took up the questions of the origins of gentile civilizations in religious myths, the providential commonality of natural law, and the ages of nations with their accompanying languages, epistemology, mores, myths, views of nature, and patterns of thought. Vico's analysis of the unity of each age foreshadowed Sorokin's systematic and quantitative exposition of these periods and the cyclical perspectives of Spengler and Toynbee. His emphasis on the manner in which cultures have originated in myths dramatically anticipated the views of Burckhardt, Nietzsche, Adams, Dawson, and Mumford.

Vico turned from the study of the City of God in the history of the Jews and the Christians to that of the other world cultures, to the "science of institutions" and "common nature of nations." In doing so he deliberately avoided a world history based, like that of Bossuet, on the Judeo-Christian tradition of Providence as one of unique actions by God among his Chosen People. Instead, Vico's *New Science* investigated an immanent providence that was revealed in the universal similarity of human customs and historical patterns and could be studied through systematic science. Providence here was like Hegel's "cunning of Reason." Vico held that "there is a divine providence and . . . it is a divine legislative mind." It certifies natural laws; "uniform ideas originating among entire populations unknown to each other must have a common ground of truth."[26]

In Vico's system each gentile nation passed successively through three eras, each with an accompanying order. Each age, from the Age of Gods to the Age of Heroes and the Age of Men, had an associated language, character, civil nature, form of government, authority, and jurisprudence. These aspects of cultural life were united by a general solidarity of phase.[27] Each nation had a foundation in a religion, a system of marriage, and a burial of the dead. Religion was present at the dawn of every nation and even at the foundation of humanity itself—"every gentile nation has its Jove." The first taming of man to humanity occurred through an archetypal thunder god, who turned the eyes of childlike primitive men to the skies and, through an anthropomorphic projection like that later postulated by Ludwig Feuerbach, populated the heavens.[28] In the Age of Gods nature was perceived as a world of divine immanence, one interpreted by theological poets by means of a divine language. At the dawn of the Age of Heroes, "every gentile nation had its Hercules." Heroic poetry emerged from the theology of the first age, and heroic kingdoms, or Patria, rose out of theocratic governments. Vico argued against Bodin's theory that states were first and by nature monarchic to assert that monarchies emerged in the late Age of Heroes to unite the dominant aristocracy, whose members are the only people considered as citizens, against the multitude of rebellious common people. In the end, the Age of Men is inevitable as the common people demand a God in their image and the extension of a system of sacred marriage to their unions. The civil stage recognized human nature as "benign and reasonable, recognizing for laws conscience, reason and duty."[29]

The rule of reason, however, gave way to a barbarism of reflection and led to a "*recourso*" that was manifested in a return to the "pure and pious wars of the heroic period," a "second barbarism." Vico looked, predictably, to the Fall of Rome to document this *recourso*; he found a movement with the decline to a new Age of Gods, and then, with the heroic raids of the Germanic barbarians, a root of a nascent Age of Heroes that finally coalesced with the origins of the feudal period. This sense of traveling the same stages in the same order, following a disintegration through oversophistication and overreflection, is one that pervades the cyclical formulations of twentieth-century theorists, most precisely in Sorokin's three-beat dialectic of cultural orders and *Weltanschauungen*.

From Carl Becker's study of *The Heavenly City of the Eighteenth Century Philosophers* to Bury's *The Idea of Progress*, it has become almost axiomatic that the theory of and faith in progress replaced that of Providence by the end of the eighteenth century.[30] Voltaire, who coined the phrase the philosophy of history and as much as any other figure of his day contributed to a relativistic perspective on civilizations, wrote his *Essai sur les moeurs et l'espirit des nations* (1756) as a story of the intermittent "progress of the human spirit." Voltaire isolated four ages of the world that exemplified human greatness and sought a Newtonian axiom that could explain their success. He found one in the idea that progress never occurred without enlightened leadership and toleration.[31] For Voltaire progress became antithetical to Providence; it occurred through the application of enlightened reason by leaders to the affairs of men and consisted in part in the erasure of the shibboleths and superstitions of the past, including the idea that God actively interfered in human history.

Other Enlightenment philosophes held a wide variety of progressive stances, from an ecstatic faith in the future evolution of human consciousness to a mechanistic determinism. While Diderot turned to an agnostic materialism and apotheosized Posterity and, with Helvétius, sought an education toward perfection, Baron d'Holbach produced a *System of Nature* (1770) that excluded any sort of deity or free will in favor of a strictly deterministic social movement of progress in nature that foreshadowed the evolutionary views of the second half of the nineteenth century. Turgot self-consciously blended a study of the progressive "advances of the human race" with a belief that the growth of nations, Enlightenment, and increased human happiness all "contributed to the designs of Providence."[32]

Adam Ferguson, a friend of David Hume and Adam Smith and a leader in his own right in the Scottish Enlightenment, wrote his world history in *An Essay on Civil Society* (1767). Ferguson held that progress occurred through the division of nations, the balancing of power, and the diffusion of civilization from its origins in Egypt to all the nations.[33] Ferguson foreshadowed modern evolutionary perspectives and the "challenge and response" themes so prevalent in the twentieth century by claiming that when competition between nations was stifled public virtue likewise declined. Where Greek independent city-states in mutual competition were "the nurseries of excellent men," Rome became monolithic to a point where the stimulus of division was lost, along with public interest in the state and the martial virtues that accompany it—"National vigor declines from the abuse of that very security which is procured by the supposed perfection of public order." Anticipating another modern theme Ferguson asserted that advanced civilized nations fall from the moral decay of their members, the result of a corrupting despotism, a decay that issues from too much success.[34] Ferguson was not really a progressive. To him, "every age hath its consolations, as well as its sufferings." He felt that the progress involved in the advance of a civil society was balanced, in the end, by its corruption and decay; "the progress of societies to what we call the heights of national greatness, is not more natural, than their return to weakness and obscurity is necessary and unavoidable."[35]

The secularization of Providence into progress reaches what might be considered a culmination in Condorcet's *Sketch for a Historical Picture of the Progress of the Human Mind*. This optimistic work was written, ironically, while Condorcet was in hiding from the Jacobins between July 1793 and March 1794, just before his death in prison. It elaborated nine stages in the progress of humanity in the past and asserted that "perfectibility is indefinite" and would follow from the rational calculation of human happiness, welfare, and government.[36]

Condorcet's world historical sketch is an open expression of faith in a posterity released from the terror of his immediate situation: "How consoling for the philosopher who laments the errors, the crimes, the injustices which still pollute the earth and which he is often the victim, in this view of the human race, emancipated from its shackles, released from the empire of fate and from that of the enemies of its progress, advancing with a firm and sure step along the path of truth, virtue, and happiness!" The enlightened man knows that his strivings are "part of the eternal chain of human destiny."[37] Surely in this vision of posterity one might find one's immortality!

There is no sharp dividing line between philosophies of history based upon a divine plan and those that emphasize a strictly secular progressivism. Lessing echoed Joachim de Fiore (and foreshadowed Saint Simon and Comte) in his anticipation of a third age of the world, one with a "new eternal gospel." He held that education was the key to the progress of humanity, that "education has its goal, in the Race, no less than in the Individual."[38] The education of the race, to Lessing, was a reciprocal process between Providence and human development where reason, trained through progressive revelations, was now able to turn back and understand revelation: "Revelation has guided their reason, and now, all at once, reason gave clearness to their Revelation." Now, "that which Education is to the individual, Revelation is to the Race."[39]

Herder maintained a dualistic sense of human character embedded in a particular historical and geographic place that provided an ecological conditioning to it. At the same time he claimed that "God is in all his works"; He was immanent in nature and in history, too. Man's destiny was suspended as the highest link in creation, in a middle state between the two worlds of the divine and the material, partaking of both and tending always, through a "golden chain of improvement," toward the "throne of Providence."[40]

Kant, Herder's mentor, also held that history was teleological; there is a purposive movement toward a destination for human history, which "Nature has as her ultimate purpose," the rule of reason and moral law and a "universal cosmopolitan condition" of social and political organization.[41] Auguste Comte, in founding his System of Positivism, delineated three world historical stages from the Theological to the Metaphysical and up to the Positive era, when the rule of reason would prevail. Ironically the progressive rule of reason and science would lead to a new age of unity in a rationalized Religion of Humanity.[42]

Hegel took the sense of the immanence of Providence in history to some of its logical conclusions. Reason, the "concrete representation" of God, actualized itself in history. Through the "cunning of reason" humanity was led progressively to the consciousness of the divine Idea of Freedom and, as it is manifested in the world, the State. Providence and progress are here so closely wedded as to be inextricable from each other; "the present stage of spirit contains all previous stages within itself."[43] When Marx 'turned Hegel on his head' in an atheistic rejection of the actualization of "spirit" in history, he retained the functional equivalent of Hegel's view of the "cunning of reason" as "the law of the world."[44] While Providence was rejected an underlying logic was apotheosized as historical process; progress was an inevitability predicated on the nature of the evolution of modes of production, their accompanying organizations of productive labor, and their inherent class contradictions.[45]

Even as Marx found in history a material process—class struggle—that contained its own progressive imperatives, others turned to the mundane world of humanity's relationship to its environment and of human racial strains in competition. The influence of Darwin on paradigms of modern world history will be examined in some detail in later chapters. Herbert Spencer's "synthetic philosophy" equated progress with the absolute freedom of individuals to compete in the evolutionary "survival of the fittest."

George Perkins Marsh wrote of the downfalls of historical civilizations and the threat to his own because of humanity's misuse of the natural environment. History to him was the story of "natural revolutions," where the emergence of civilizations naturally gave way to their degenerations as a result of the disruption of ecological balances. Marsh held that nature tended always to revert to a balanced steady state; his call to his contemporaries to act toward the "restoration of disturbed harmonies" was an early root to the conservation movement in the United States.[46]

Others, like de Gobineau, Houston Stewart Chamberlain, and Alfred Rosenberg, employed naturalism to produce a racist world history. In his *The Inequality of Human Races* (1853), de Gobineau postulated that "all civilizations derive from the white race, that none can exist without its help, and that a society is great and brilliant only so far as it preserves the blood of the noble group that created it."[47] To de Gobineau "civilization is incommunicable"; the ten historical civilizations that he recorded were products of a pure racial strain, most often the Aryan one, that have all inevitably degenerated with their intermixture with the blood of the "inferior races."[48] At the turn of the century Houston Stewart Chamberlain echoed de Gobineau's racism in an enormously popular and influential world history, *The Foundations of the Nineteenth Century* (1899). Chamberlain wrote with the clear and calculated mission of the "awakening of the Teutonic peoples to the consciousness of their all-important vocation as the founders of a completely new civilization and culture."[49] As George Mosse notes in his introduction to Chamberlain's work, the *Foundations* gave Nazi racism an academic respectability of a sort; his world history was a coherent base used to demonstrate the deep historical "truth" of racist doctrines.[50] Chamberlain's perspective was more optimistic than de Gobineau's; degeneration of race was not inevitable; closed civilizations that are born and decline are but a part of history. Chamberlain felt that universal history contained a pattern transcending declines, that of the rise of a "master builder" race, a practical people who, presumably through Chamberlain himself and the "sun of his life," Richard Wagner, would realize their racial ideal and, in this confluence of practicality and vision, produce a Teutonic world order.[51]

Toward the end of the nineteenth century world historians increasingly questioned the optimistic ideal of progress. Jakob Burckhardt expressed fears of "the despotism of the masses" and predicted the rise of "terrible simplificateurs" who would lead in a renewed barbarism as culture was "flooded by waves of majority from below." He argued that the West was in a late stage of civilization, without "natural" moral and political authorities, where the calculation of interests and the rational organization of society suppressed man's highest attributes. To him, "greatness" can only "appear at moments when mere calculation ceases and a way of thinking, a feeling, overwhelms everything."[52] Leopold von Ranke foreshadowed major twentieth-century concerns in his multivolume *Universal History* (1888) by dividing progress into a moral and cultural category, and one of material advancement. According to Ranke, "we can assume in the areas of material interest an absolute progress, but we cannot find a similar progress in moral affairs."[53] Ranke eschewed eschatological forecasting. He noted that history itself contains no clue to its end and that "every epoch is immediate to God and its value consists, not in what follows it, but in its own existence, its proper self."[54] Lord Acton was confronted by the same dilemma as he sought unsuccessfully to extricate a world history of the progress of liberty from a parallel pattern he discerned in the rise of an increasingly centralized, and ultimately corrupting, political power in the state and the modern bureaucratic organization of society.[55]

While observers from de Gobineau to Burckhardt noted the parallel downfalls of civilizations of the past and warned of a similar fate for the modern West, Nicholai Danilevsky, in his *Russia and Europe* (1869), revived a systematic view of cyclical processes in the rise and fall of civilizations that foreshadowed those of Spengler, Toynbee, and

Sorokin in our century. Danilevsky's identification was with a nascent Slavic civilization in the East; he condemned the "pernicious delusion of Westernism" that held that Western civilization was a world historical culmination to which other peoples might rise.[56] He felt that the West was in a decline that anticipated its imminent downfall. Modern European civilization was corrupted, first of all, by a Protestantism that relied on personal, rather than collective, authority; second, by an all-embracing naturalism that took the place of a unifying religious faith; and third, by a "socio-political anarchy" resulting from the unresolved contradiction between political democracy and economic feudalism. In Danilevsky's view the Slavic peoples bore a religious élan that made them the chosen people who would overcome the Germano-Roman world and dominate the next era of world civilization.[57]

Danilevsky foreshadowed Spengler's closed cycles and his belief that the future belonged to a Slavic civilization; Nietzsche's philosophy acted for Spengler as a death knoll to Western culture, an impetus to his elaboration of the crisis in world history that he articulated in *The Decline of the West*. In the first of his books, *The Birth of Tragedy* (1872), Nietzsche set the problem that would dominate modern world history. His argument has become almost a truism of twentieth-century modernism and deserves to be quoted at length:

> Every culture that has lost myth has lost, by the same token, its natural healthy creativity. Only a horizon ringed about with myths can unify a culture. . . . The images of myth must be the daemonic guardians, ubiquitous but unnoticed, presiding over the growth of the child's mind and interpreting to the mature man his life and struggles. . . . Let us consider abstract man stripped of myth, abstract education, abstract mores, abstract law, abstract government; the random vagaries of the artistic imagination unchanneled by any native myth; a culture without any fixed and consecrated place of origin, condemned to exhaust all possibilities and feed miserably and parasitically on every culture under the sun. Here we have our present age, the result of a Socratism bent on the extermination of myth. Man today, stripped of myth, stands famished among all his pasts and must dig frantically for roots, be it among the most remote antiquities. What does our great historical hunger signify, our clutching about us of countless other cultures, our consuming desire for knowledge, if not the loss of myth, of a mythic home, the mythic womb? Let us ask ourselves whether our feverish and frightening agitation is anything but the greedy grasping for food by a hungry man.[58]

Ironically, even with his profound passion over the fate of culture, Nietzsche can be considered perhaps the most potent of the Socratic enemies of the predominant surviving myths of Western culture: Christianity and progress. Nietzsche recognized this contradiction but claimed that any movement toward a true culture required an absolute sincerity toward the idols of the time that would shatter any system, like that of his own day, of merely "decorative culture." His analysis of the relationship between the "death of God" and the conjoined downfall of all forms of progressive faith, ideology, and positivistic "truth" has become a commonplace notion in understanding modernism. His "revaluation of all values," of morality, of the sense of time and world view, promoted a nihilistic elimination of progress, perhaps (as he himself saw it) the central and final key remaining to the "fixed and consecrated origin" and goal of Western culture. Nietzsche's perspective on the necessity for this and his view of alternatives will be examined further in evaluation of Spengler's attempt to apply a Nietzschean revaluation to world history as a whole. Whereas history, as exemplified by works from Turgot to Marx, was of a universal progress based upon a Judeo-Christian linear sense of time, Nietzsche celebrated the Dionysian moment, which overcame individuality, time, and Becoming in an experience of primal Being. He rejected the entire Western *Weltanschauung* with its teleological perspective on man's temporal position, for one where the eschaton (end or goal of time) is experienced in moments and life is not lived through regret, guilt, and anticipation. To Nietzsche this was a "superhistorical" view: where the world is seen in the moment, "the past and present are one and the same . . . a picture of eternally present imperishable types of unchangeable value and significance."[59] His sense of the "eternal recurrence" of times led him to look toward the great men on mountain peaks of culture in the past and future and to speculate on the cyclical pattern of history.[60]

It would be hard to overestimate the importance of Nietzsche's impact on the writing of world history in the twentieth century. Throughout the century, the idea of progress has been described problematically by world historians; the cycles of history predominated in the world historical writings of the first half of the century, and the problem of the destruction of historical myths and their reformulation have been central. The writing of twentieth-century world historians has been governed by the attempt to reanimate a meaningful myth of history, to reestablish a historical ground as a purposeful setting for modern life, as a basis for some sort of progress. Historians have been forced to answer Nietzsche and to do this in part from within a Nietzschean perspective. His "eternal recurrence" combined with the classical training of Spengler and Toynbee to guide metahistorians back to a reexamination of Greek models of historical cycles as opposed to the Christian outlook of linear progressivism.

When Spengler articulated the crisis in world historical thought with his abstract analysis of tragically closed historical cycles, he believed that he was completing the work of Nietzsche in history. Toynbee's work relied on a Nietzschean cyclicism and a perspective on the overman-saints who created civilizations and provided the continual élan that spurred their growth. Berdyaev, Sorokin, Mumford, Dawson, and Kroeber all have relied on cyclical metahistorical patterns. After Spengler's "hard pessimism" of closed cycles of independently doomed cultures, however, modern world historians have been driven to find a progress that answers Nietzsche and that transcends meaningless recurrence to revitalize a hopeful teleology in history.

CHAPTER TWO

Evolutionary Ethics and the Rise of the World State

The Universal History of H. G. Wells

From being a premature, he became a forgotten man.

—H. G. Wells[1]

The power my brother calls God proceeds by the method of Trial and Error; and if we turn out to be one of the errors, we shall go the way of the mastodon and the megatherium and all other scrapped experiments.

—George Bernard Shaw[2]

WELLSIAN WORLD HISTORY is founded on an ideology of threatened progress. The utopias and anti-utopian societies of Wellsian fiction serve either as guiding ideals or as warnings of possible dehumanization—in the literal sense of racial degeneration—if certain negative trends in the present are not reversed and if historically residual patterns and practices from nationalism and factory specialization to class differentiation are not left behind. The study of history, for Wells, was also an exercise in the articulation of human goals and warnings. In his view, the full realization of humanity's progressive potential could only occur when individuals recognized that their private destinies were wedded to the destiny of the race as a whole, with the "identification of the interests of each with the interests of all," as Condorcet expressed it.[3] In subsuming their egotistical, class, ethnic, and nationalistic ideologies to a faith in the common advance into the future, individuals would complete the current task of evolution by creating a collective mind and will. This moral goal is the primary thread connecting all of Wells's historical discourse. Individuals are encouraged to renounce greed and privilege in favor of the common good and in the face of the cataclysmic potential that Wells evoked all too clearly in his anti-utopian fiction. He left his readers with a choice between self-sacrifice or degeneration, the God-man or the man-ape, the World State or Armageddon.

Wells set out to write a world history as a means of educating his society toward a new enlightenment. To Wells, "all history is the history of ideas"; like Condorcet, he believed that governmental organization and practice would follow inevitably from the "progress of public opinion."[4] Wells closely followed the prescriptions of the Enlightenment philosophes who sought progress to cosmopolitan unity through the application of rational principles to all aspects of human society. In his *Outline of History*, Wells charted the progress of life from its inorganic roots toward the present evolutionary task of world unification. He conceived the *Outline* as an element in a new model of Diderot's *Encyclopedia* that would fill the needs of an age on the brink of unity but also confronted by new apocalyptic possibilities.[5] With Voltaire, Wells rejected Panglossian views, such as those expressed by Condorcet in his *Sketch* on progress, and instead retained a qualified optimism like that affirmed by Turgot in his essay "On Universal History."[6] Turgot sought a history written as the "advances of the human race." In his essay on "The Progress of the Human Mind," he argued that "progress, although inevitable, is intermingled with frequent periods of decline as a result of occurrences and revolutions which come to interrupt it."[7] Wellsian world history charts just this path but marks the shift in Western universal history to the modernism anticipated earlier by, among others, Burckhardt and Henry Adams, who warned that the progress of the race could result in its self-destruction.

The most important difference between Wells and the Encyclopedists, in his own mind, was in the philosophes' hostility to religion. According to Wells, "they believed that man was naturally just and politically competent, whereas his impulse to social science and self-forgetfulness is usually developed through an education essentially religious."[8] He deplored Rousseau's romanticization of Nature, which flew in the face of post-Darwinian biology. While his own enlightened elite of Samurai were in part modeled on the philosophes and their idea of enlightened despotism, their duties toward mass education and social progress through self-subordination were directly opposed to the romantic conception of man as naturally good.

To Wells it was only in transcending nature through self-control that humanity could progress. Nature, red in tooth and claw, enjoins untamed competition, which, in the modern setting, leads to brutalization and the selective survival of outmoded and essentially destructive animalistic attributes. Wells endorsed the evolutionary theories of his mentor at the Kensington Normal School, Thomas Henry Huxley, and spent the greater part of his life writing both fiction and propaganda to popularize and extrapolate the implications of Huxley's view.

In *Evolution and Ethics* (1893), Huxley articulated his perspective on the progress of human organization, which is driven and maintained by ethics and proceeds at a faster rate than purely biological change. Human evolution has shifted from the "organic stage" to the "social stage," from the competitive struggle of each against all to the cooperative realization of the duties of members in a community. To Huxley, at this stage, "the ethical progress of society depends, not on imitating the cosmic process [as Spencer held], still less in running away from it, but in combatting it."[9] Evolution, left to itself, can lead to no "millennial anticipations"; any perfectibility of man will occur in the pursuit of humanity's highest sublimations of instinct: justice and cooperation. The process of civilization is one of taming the adaptive traits acquired in the competitive struggle for survival. Social order becomes a struggle of human will against nature, of the tended garden as opposed to the jungle, and of human self-direction against accidental variation and "natural selection." To Huxley, only the repudiation of the struggle for existence through the application of the golden rule to society as a whole could lead to the realization of humanity's highest aspirations.[10]

Huxley rejected altogether the Victorian optimism such as that voiced by Spencer which assumed evolution would proceed toward ever higher forms of humanity. To Huxley, the first law of nature was change without finality; this precluded human perfectibility. The infinite mutability of nature occurs in a universe subject to the second law of thermodynamics: Under conditions of universal entropy, the cosmos is steadily winding down and humanity's fate, however interrupted by moral affirmations and noble achievements in civilization, is ultimately doomed, in the end, to follow the downward course of the cosmic processes of matter and energy.[11]

The threat to human growth, which Huxley along with the Adams brothers saw as an inexorable entropic degeneration, is the bête noire of Wellsian progressivism, a challenge answered by the evolutionary metaphysics of Henri Bergson and Teilhard de Chardin, and a universal motif in Western literature from George Bernard Shaw to Arthur C. Clarke. Shaw was largely justified in predicting that "creative evolution . . . is going to be the religion of the twentieth century."[12] The common theme in the creative view of evolution is the rejection of Darwin's perspective on blindly accumulative causation through accidental variations, and the assertion (which leads into a twentieth-century existentialist cliché) that man must make himself: humanity must seize upon its evolution and consciously interpret and then direct its path.

Even in his first large-scale literary success, *The Time Machine* (1895), Wells rejected unplanned natural evolution and the positivistic conception of inevitable progress by demonstrating the degeneration that he felt would follow from the present trends of class division and economic specialization.[13] The sense of progressive evolution being threatened by the disunity of humanity is the central theme around which Wells wrote his fiction, his history, and his socio-moral treatises throughout his career.

• • •

Wells was born the fourth and last child of a lower-middle class family in Bromley, Kent, in 1866. His mother, a lady's maid, was the daughter of an innkeeper. Wells was supposed to have been a girl. Mrs. Wells, a pious Episcopalian, had lost a beloved daughter, Possy, to appendicitis in 1864 and sought to replace her with another but was chagrined when God sent a third son instead.[14] Wells's ambivalent relationship with his mother and what she stood for in his eyes hinged upon his extended emotional and material dependence on her coupled with an almost total rejection of her system of values: her smothering sensitivity to keeping one's "place" in society, her malicious and violent God, her domestic inefficiency, and her worship of Queen Victoria. In the cynicism of his last years Wells lightly testified (in the third person) that his relationship with his mother was "embittered by a positive hatred for his own deceased sister whose death preceded his birth by a couple of years." Little Possy's virtues and charms were a constant reproach to a less-than-perfect little boy; "a more normal nature than Wells' would certainly have responded to these pathetic appeals to be a little Possy en Pantalon, but the diabolical strand in his nature raised him into an unconcealed hatred of this rival, who had, he felt, ousted him from his mother's heart."[15] Despite this admission, Wells denied any Oedipal conflict in himself and asserted that he blasphemed the pious conformity that Possy represented and defied his mother's deepest convictions for his faith, his life-style, and especially for his adult vocation.[16]

Mr. Joseph Wells, little Bertie's father, was a failed gardener from a family of gardeners, "born as it were for bankruptcy."[17] He owned an insolvent china and crockery shop, the Atlas House, and made money on the side as a champion, semiprofessional cricketer. Joseph was something of a local hero: he was the first player ever to take four wickets in successive balls in a county match.[18] Mr. Wells's popularity led to the first of many fortunate accidents in Bertie's life. When Wells was seven, the son of a local tavern keeper, in laughing celebration of Joseph's skills, threw Bertie up in the air next to the postgame beer tent asking "Whose little kid are you?" and failed to catch him on his second descent. Wells landed on a tent stake. The broken leg that resulted saved him, in his own view, from being a shop assistant for life: confined to bed, Wells acquired a habit for reading that became the key to his escape from maternal dominance and class position.[19] Mrs. Wells maintained the fixed conception that Wells, despite his lack of interest and an increasingly vociferous protest, should be a draper; toward that end he was sent to Morley's School until the age of thirteen, when he was old enough for his first apprenticeship.

It has been said that Wells's socialism was a quasi-religion formed in the image of his mother's faith.[20] While his eventual religious constructions retain a fundamental dualism, the person of God separate from man and his evolution was rejected by Wells in his childhood. When he was about twelve Wells had a terrifying nightmare that featured his mother's God "basting a poor sinner rotating slowly over a fire built under the wheel." He woke up full of hate and horror for such a being and lost all semblance of faith.[21] Even as he rejected his mother's creed, Wells embraced an inspiring vision of Britannia that included a faith in the ultimate triumph of the empire and, in his own words, "ideas about Aryans extraordinarily like Mr. Hitler's."[22] This nascent inspirational racism can be seen as the foundation of his later deification of the species as a whole; over time, and with education in the Darwinian view of the common origins of races, Wells extended his perception of racial identity to include all varieties of homo sapiens in a "patriotism of humanity."[23]

In 1877, in what may have been a suicide attempt, Joseph Wells fell from a ladder while pruning grapes and broke his leg, thus ending his career as a cricketer. In the poverty that ensued for the family, young H. G. Wells was apprenticed to a draper and his mother resumed her premarital occupation as a lady's maid at the local Up Park Estate. Wells inwardly rebelled against his mother's goals for him and against the deadening drudgery of shop routine; he was soon fired for his inattentiveness. In the wake of this disgrace, Wells found a position as a teacher-pupil in Wookey, Somerset, where he could further his own education while supervising students in the lower grades. To his utter dismay, the school became insolvent and collapsed after he had been there only three months.[24]

Between positions, Wells stayed with his mother at Up Park, whose master gave him free run of the library. Wells devoured Voltaire, *Gulliver's Travels*, and Plato's *Republic*.[25] In 1881 Mrs. Wells was able to arrange a new apprenticeship for her son, this time with Samuel Cowap, a chemist at Midhurst. To function effectively in the shop, Wells needed to acquire a knowledge of Latin, so he worked nights at the Midhurst Grammar School under headmaster Horace Byatt. He also studied sciences and literature for state examinations. Once he was established at Midhurst, it became evident that his mother could not afford to pay his employer for his training, so again Wells lost his post. He moved into the Midhurst Grammar School to continue as a teacher-pupil, only to be pulled out against his wishes by his mother and apprenticed to the Southsea Drapery Emporium. Despite Wells's entreaties for release, his mother refused to allow him to quit and he stayed for two years at the emporium as an "inattentive and unwilling worker."[26]

Finally, out of desperation Wells ran away from the draper's position, thus forfeiting his mother's £50 investment. He was able to secure a student assistant position at Midhurst and then, after some excellent examination returns, a scholarship to the Normal School of Science at South Kensington under Thomas H. Huxley.[27] Here his atheism was confirmed by Huxley's Darwinian perspective of man in nature, his rebellion against his mother's confining conception of class and place was corroborated by a new exposure to the socialist movement, and his racial prejudices were put into the larger context of the species struggle for survival. Wells began to come of age: his adult opinions began to crystallize and his autodidacticism grew more systematically directed. By his second year Wells was lecturing his fellow students on evolutionary socialism, progress, and the coming scientific age. He became more interested in social theory, literature (especially Ruskin's writings), and polemics than in the nuts and bolts of scientific investigation. Reverently Wells led his classmates to William Morris's house at Hammersmith to hear Morris, G. B. Shaw, and Graham Wallas address meetings and debate the ways and means of the coming transformation of British society.[28]

In his first year at Kensington, with Huxley as his lecturer in biology, Wells did quite well, but in his third year, bored by inferior lecturers and the spadework of geological experimentation, he failed to make the grade. In the wake of this reverse, Wells secured employment in Wales at the Holt Academy in Wrexham, a miserably unstimulating situation after the social and intellectual life at Kensington. Once while fulfilling his extrascholastic duties by playing football, one of his more malicious pupils delivered a violent knee to Wells's back while he was down, crushing his kidney. As he recovered from the bleeding, Wells had the first of a series of possibly tubercular lung hemorrhages, which were to wrack him over the next five years and scar his lungs for life.[29] He thought he would die and was horrified to end his life without ever having experienced sex. Death and sex, Wells said in 1934, were henceforth intimately paired in his imagination; sex became "maddeningly desirable" for the rest of his life.[30]

Wells's illness forced him to give up, without regret, his work at the Holt Academy. After four months of recuperation at Up Park and three more with friends in the country, he made his way, despite his lingering illness, to London—again penniless and in pursuit of employment. This time, after a struggle, Wells received a position teaching science at the London Tutorial College, a knowledge factory aimed only at expeditiously cranking out pupils who could pass, by rote, the certificatory examinations for professional employment of London University. At the same time he began writing light, short pieces for the *Pall Mall Gazette* to a formula modeled on J. M. Barrie's fiction. His finances improved enough for him to marry his cousin Isabelle in 1891.[31] Despite relapses in health, dissatisfaction with his wife's level of sexuality, subsequent infidelities, and some continuing poverty, Wells began a relatively stable period, developing his writing skills in numerous stories, reviews, essays, and even a biology textbook. By 1893 he was able to support most of his extended family. He left Isabelle and moved in with one of his students, Amy Catherine Robbins, soon to be Jane Wells. In 1895 Wells's writing began to attract critical acclaim and widespread popularity with the publication of *The Time Machine*. From this point on, Wells produced an average of two books per year. In his lifetime Wells wrote 156 volumes, and his bibliography includes more than 3,000 citations.[32] Eventually Wells was able to support his parents, his mistresses (some with children), and his own family in solid comfort. He recognized the financial imperative that drove him to write rather carelessly, noting that "the larger part of my fiction was written lightly and with a certain haste."[33]

Wells's life is a rags-to-riches story. Like many of Horatio Alger's characters, he was proud of his successful money-making ability and was prone to worry over his fiscal security; even early on, however, his writings established the principle of the ascendancy of message over style and polish. In a sustained controversy with Henry James in the early twentieth century, Wells defended the use of literature toward a purpose, an idea antithetical to James's refined definition of artistic purity as its own end.[34] From Wells's point of view, James, along with Shaw and Conrad, erred in the importance that he gave to each discrete impression in literature relative to the underlying system that gave it meaning. Wells felt that these artists were "uneducated minds," that they wrote to catch the vivid imprint of perceptual detail, while he wrote to pull detail together into a system; the singular percept was meaningless to Wells as an isolated artistic impression; it only gained power as an element in a schematic plan.[35] Wells, on the other hand, in his anticipation of Socialist Realism, was criticized, especially in his latter work, as a polemicist and propagandist whose art was sacrificed to his prophetic delusions.[36] Yet, in consciously choosing the didactic novel, Wells provided one model of literature for the modern era, that of fiction written toward social change and a new social order in the utopian tradition of Plato, Thomas More, Roger Bacon, Swift, Butler, and Morris, but in an age whose speed and scale demanded social reorganization at a level beyond that of the island or city-state. Warren Wagar is quite correct, in his study of the prophets of world union in the twentieth century, to place Wells's "biological historicism" at the cornerstone of this modern intellectual movement.[37] Jack Williamson, in his intellectual biography of Wells, concluded that his ideas of world crisis, world economy, and world government were essential to the foundation of much of modern thought on these subjects.[38] In his writings Wells is a "man with a mission"[39] whose central guiding ideas remained remarkably stable throughout his adult life. His work can be viewed as a whole; the varying emphases and topics that he elucidated reflect various aspects of his world vision and the impact of events throughout his life, but the fundamental guiding principles of his thought underlie all. By 1934, Wells could say "My life, in the fact that it has evolved a general sustaining idea has become, at least psychologically, a religious life; its persona is dissociated from the ego. My essential purpose is world vision."[40]

The "system" in Wells's writing was "scientific," based on a Huxleyan evolutionary perspective, including an underlying, and mostly de-emphasized, dehumanizing entropy, and utilizing the close observation of present trends as a base for the scientific prognostication of future possibilities. Wells worked toward the development of a new discipline that he called "Human Ecology." The new science would take as its point of departure the point at which "Analytical Science" left off—with the requirement for synthesis—and would aim at the evaluation of what Teilhard de Chardin was to call the "phenomenon of man": humanity taken as a whole scientific phenomenon in the context of an extended perspective of natural history.[41] The new science would be studied by professors of "Analytic History."

This science is a sociology. While Wells rejected the sociology of statistical reduction, he believed that literature could serve a large part of the sociological purpose by projecting utopian models for human organization.[42] The other side of sociology, in his view, was the schematic interpretation of history closely tied to present social trends and the needs of social planning.[43] Wells's first application of his new science, outside of his fictional predictions, was in his *Anticipations* (1900), where he articulated the key themes of his subsequent work. *Anticipations* called for a "New Republic," modeled on that of Plato, in response to the "change of scale" and the collapsing of distances in modern life. A new social movement would originate in a select group of like-minded men and women who recognized the failure of democracy and the contemporary state system and foresaw the inevitable coalescence of a World State. *Anticipations* also prophesied an increasing rate of technological change in the twentieth century and included projections on the future importance of air transport, the tank, the submarine, and the machine gun, as well as the threat of "total war" and the increased power that humanity would gain in the exploitation of new sources of energy.[44]

In *A Modern Utopia* (1905), one of his earliest formulations of the shape of the World State, Wells predicted the rise of a class of Samurai, an elite meritocracy of the enlightened who would lead society beyond its petty nationalism into a new world order. Like Plato's Guardians, Comte's elite of technicians and priests, and Veblen's managerial class, a new technocratic and philosophical nobility would take its place in the leadership of a corporate hierarchical society.[45] A planned social order would arise where the machine would eliminate the need for physical labor, the security of the individual would be guaranteed by social insurance, and the work that was done would be accomplished out of pleasure and an instinct for workmanship like that conceived by Morris and Veblen. The Samurai were to be "an aggressive order of religiously devoted men and women who will trace out and establish and impose a new pattern of living upon our race."[46] Originally, Wells hoped that the British Fabian Society would be able to serve this purpose.

Wells was accepted as a member of the Fabians in 1903 with the sponsorship of G. B. Shaw and Graham Wallas after being courted by Beatrice and Sidney Webb at the "Co-efficients" lunch club they had formed together. He had attracted the favorable attention of the Webbs with the socialistic future he portrayed in *Anticipations*. Wells soon became a disruptive influence in the group, however, as he attempted to turn the Fabians to his Samurai ideal. He sought to enlarge the membership of the group from its limit of seven hundred up to ten thousand members, to discipline the membership to its leadership role, and to "sexualize socialism" by sponsoring a program aimed at the legal emancipation and sexual liberation of women.[47] The influence of the Wellsian platform is evidenced by the growth of a Wellsian faction and his election as a Fabian executive in 1907.

To Wells, as to Marx and Engels, the family was an extension of property to sex relations. He felt that jealousy was akin to Veblen's view of pecuniary emulation.[48] *Anticipations* had advocated birth control, and Wells was a long-time propagandist for its free use as a member of England's Neo-Malthusians and a supporter (and lover) of

Margaret Sanger of the United States. In 1906 Wells read a paper before the Fabians on "Socialism and the Middle Classes," where he argued that marriage must go with the downfall of competitive capitalism, private finance, and large-scale private property. In the same year he published *In the Days of the Comet*, which advocated free love. His Samurai, in *A Modern Utopia*, had a communal marriage. Wells's goals translated into a program for the Fabians that centered on the transfer of land and capital to the state, equality for women, and an endowment for the public support and education of all children. This latter goal would, in his view, provide child care by the community and free women economically and sexually.[49] Part of this emancipation was toward the alleviation of the petty jealousies of sexual life as a step in the development of people who would identify with the larger group and not with the individual possession of objects or other people. The utopia in *Men Like Gods* (1922) "had not abandoned the family. It had enlarged and glorified the family until it embraced the whole world."[50]

In the heat of the battle among the Fabians over Wells's radicalization program, the "Stop Wells" contingent learned that Wells, practicing what he preached, had impregnated Amber Reeves, the daughter of a Fabian couple split by their respective opposition and support of Wells. Wells was ostracized by the subsequent scandal and his enemies employed it effectively against him.[51] In the end, "the order of the Fabian Samurai perished unborn" and Wells resigned from the group in September 1908. The old guard, led by Sidney Webb and Shaw, made light of Wells's militant utopianism even as Lenin, from Wells's perspective, was evolving "an extraordinarily similar scheme" of centralized organization by a revolutionary elite.[52]

By the beginning of World War I, Wells had shifted his focus from British politics and the wranglings of Fabian socialism to the international battle to preserve democracy. He coined the phrase "the war that will end war" even as Lenin sought to "turn the international war into a civil war" toward the same end. Like Lenin, Wells anticipated the imminent arrival of world socialism in reaction to the crisis—the war would end as national states were swept into the dustbin of history to be replaced by a world federation of socialistic peoples.[53] Wells alienated many of his leftist associates, however, with his view that Germany must be defeated for this transition to occur and in his consequent support for the Allies. He was no pacifist; he visited the front and was active in research into technology that could assist the British war effort. War, in any case, was an essential step toward his envisioned new epoch: "I remain persuaded that there will have to be a last conflict to inaugurate the peace of mankind."[54] In 1918, Wells worked at Crewe House as the chairman of the Policy Committee for

Propaganda in Enemy Countries but resigned when he was informed that any promises of a "just peace" made for propaganda purposes were in no way binding on postwar governmental policy.[55]

At the outset of the war, Wells hoped that the conflict would establish a new world order; his millennial expectations prompted him to write *God the Invisible King* (1917), a deification of the system of evolution. Wells later called this his "theocratic phase" where, under the stresses of a "war for civilization," he sought a "captain of the World Republic" to unite the aspirations of humankind. In his autobiography, Wells disowned this religious evangelism as a regressive "falling back of the mind towards immaturity under the stress of dismay and anxiety" to regain the "reassurance of a child."[56] Aside from the personalization of a redeeming God, however, his "deistic humanism" is retained throughout his subsequent works. God is the "racial consciousness" or "collective mind," a synthesis of the "cells" of men and women, "an immortal being arising out of man" whose purpose is the "attainment of clear knowledge as a means to more knowledge and of knowledge as a means to power. For this he must use human hands and brains."[57]

In his autobiography Wells regretted his wartime religious enthusiasm for leading his supporters to think that they could rely on an external power. While the "Invisible King" is "external to the individual man," his first task is the "maintenance of the racial life" toward "ends that he is only beginning to apprehend."[58] This God evolves with humanity, is finite, and is gradually coming to consciousness in the "mastery of the blind forces of matter."[59] Wells, even in his chagrin over the false optimism of his war writing, always considered the World State his "religion and end" and continually asserted that the individual was but a member of the "mind of the species," which would eventually realize itself.[60] While his faith was less open for show after the war, and employed less ecstatic and transcendental imagery, most of the underlying tenets of Wells's creed were retained.

To Wells, God was not an external "being" as in Christian theology, but a process in human development. In 1929, Wells posited that "we may be but parts of a larger whole, as the quivering cells of our living bodies are parts of us," which may, at death, merge again into the "universal stream."[61] In *The Open Conspiracy* (1928), Wells argued that "our immortality is conditional [on our behavior] and lies in the race and not in our individual selves."[62] In his 1934 depiction of *The Shape of Things to Come*, Wells forecast that humanity would become "a colonial organism as any branching coral or polyp." "A confluence of wills" would lead to a "common consciousness."[63] What Wells objected to most was the idea of a "power beyond your own which excuses you from your duty. Utopia says, Do not leave things at all." To Wells, since the eye of God is given sight by the progressive adaptation of humanity and is actualized in evolution, man cannot leave things to God but must realize God in himself. Evolution is a blind process until the mind of man comes to realize itself and to direct its self-education.[64]

• • •

The "change of scale" that Wells foresaw in his *Anticipations* led to the "race between education and catastrophe," which he invoked and hoped to ameliorate in some small way in *The Outline of History* (1920). The interwar period for Wells was dominated by this race. Humanity's power to destroy civilization and ultimately itself as a species had outstripped its social evolution—the change in scale of warfare alone demanded a corresponding shift in the scale and intensity of social organization. In his 1903 story, "The Land Ironclads," Wells exposed some of the implications of tank warfare; in *The War in the Air* (1908), he foresaw massive air bombardments; and in 1914, with *The World Set Free*, the bombardment became nuclear and prompted a "Parliament of the World" and the abolition of war in a startling anticipation of the notions of the nuclear umbrella and deterrence.

From the onset of the war up to the year of his death, Wells preached the religion of world unity and the politics of the World State. His anti-utopian novels had earlier presented the prospective result of the failure to educate humanity to cooperation; they are genre catastrophes in which man does not adapt to the new conditions. Wellsian utopias also contain the catastrophic crisis, as in *The World Set Free, Men Like Gods*, and *The War of the Worlds*, where the cataclysm, when surpassed, leads to a utopian denouement.[65] The challenge to humanity is essential to its evolution, it demands an adaptive response—without the hurdles that confront progress, social degeneration would occur as it did for the Eloi in *The Time Machine*. Wells has been called a precursor of existentialism for his extension of the Darwinian perspective on pain and struggle as the selective mechanism by which evolution proceeds for both the individual and the collective; man makes himself in struggle.[66] Catastrophe, often blind and accidental like the dialectical impetus behind Darwinian evolution, provides a unifying challenge and a catharsis of natural, instinctual responses leaving civilized adaptations in place as the foundation of a new order. Psychologically, for the writer of the catastrophic tale with a utopian ending, the shattering of the old society may be very satisfying as an artistic expression; it makes all the struggles and frustrations of mundane existence petty and provides a millennial outlook that pulls one out of present angst in a forward-looking postponement of action—everything will be resolved in the end. Wells identified with Roger Bacon in his prevision and impotence: "I play at being such a man as he was, a man altogether lonely and immediately futile, a man lit by a vision of the world still some centuries ahead, convinced of its urgency and powerless to bring it nearer." In the face of harsh attacks by literary critics, and a general lack of popular enthusiasm for his later works, this perspective must have been comforting for Wells.[67]

In *The Outline of History* Wells applies challenge and response to history as a whole, as well as to the civilizations that make it up. While Arnold Toynbee employed his challenge-and-response paradigm to the specific rise and fall of his twenty-six independent civilizations, and then to the world as a whole in its present crisis, Wells began with the concept of racial unity and emphasized the diffusion of adaptations throughout the species. He took the foreshortened view of the apocalyptic challenge to the species as a whole as his starting point and the particular challenges to societies as incidents in that total evolutionary process. To Wells, civilization has occurred more in specific periods than in distinct units. The evolution of civilization as a whole culminated for both the species and societies with the challenge to the modern West, which would determine the fate of the world as a whole.

Evolution, again, shifts to social evolution with civilization and occurs through education in a common belief system. For Wells, modern knowledge, particularly in the physical and biological sciences, made earlier thought obsolete. The common cosmology that had united the West, the Bible, had served as a "general history of Mankind" but it had "lost hold . . . [and] nothing has arisen to take its place"; therefore, "our modern communities are no longer cemented."[68] While this expresses a general malaise of modernity, clearly Wells in his *Salvaging of Civilization* (1921), *The Outline*, and subsequent works is responding to postwar despair. As a vigorous proponent first of the "war to end war," and then of the League of Nations, which he felt was born disfigured by nationalism, Wells sensed that the accomplishments of civilization were threatened by dissolution and reversion to barbarism. The revolution to socialism and the biological adaptation required at this stage of evolution were one and the same; the means of transition would be universal education for world citizenship. What was required, in Wells's view, was a "Bible of Civilization," a new "idea of place in the world," a "new story of Genesis," with "rules of Life," and "Books of Conduct and Wisdom," as the basis for a new global enlightenment. Toward this end of a common history for humanity and a patriotism for world citizenship, Wells wrote *The Outline of History*.[69]

Wells shared the hope that Kant expressed in his "Idea for a Universal History from a Cosmopolitan Point of View" (1784), that "after many reformative revolutions, a cosmopolitan condition . . . will come into being as the womb wherein all the original capacities of the human race can develop."[70] Kant held that a universal history was an essential means to this end. Any schema of history is a construction of man and not a final truth, which is ultimately unknowable. Because of this it is inevitable that the historian aims his work toward the achievement of his goal and includes the goal as an integral thread through his scheme.

> It is strange and apparently silly to wish to write a history in accordance with an Idea of how the course of the world must be if it is to lead to certain rational ends. It seems that with such an Idea only a romance could be written. Nevertheless, if one may assume that Nature, even in the play of human freedom, works not without a plan or purpose, this Idea could still be of use. Even if we are too blind to see the secret mechanism of its working, this Idea may still serve as a guiding thread for presenting as a system . . . what would otherwise be a planless conglomeration of human actions.[71]

The phrase "even in the play of human freedom" is key to Wellsian faith in educational progressivism. The play of freedom is Platonic: "Justice is Wisdom."[72] As man realizes the Good, is educated to it by a Samurai class, he will act in it. The union of wills, all acting in mutual recognition of the common good, is to be the foundation of the "collective mind"; in its realization of the history of human progress and the present threats to its continuance, it will act in unison to choose the correct (necessarily progressive) path into the future. Human freedom, in this sense, is the freedom of the morally educated to choose in accord with a reasoned truth or to follow a General Will, like that of Rousseau.

A universal history, according to Kant, must be essentially teleological; in exposing a progressive thread in history it provides a guide to the actions of the enlightened toward a hoped-for future. In this sense universal history is predictive; it establishes a line of development that extends indefinitely into the future and by which one can judge one's actions. Wells attempted to make his world history a history for all people of all races and locales; he sought to coordinate a vision of past unity and the interdevelopment of the human race; he sought to promote into the future an ever-increasing consciousness of this unity as a guide to personal and political action. His visions of the past and future interact in the present as a Kantian moral imperative.

The Outline of History charts the origin of the species and presents a Freudian perspective on the childhood of the human race. The origins of consciousness and the foundation of society lie in the recognition of a power outside the self, the primal father.[73] The fear of the wrath of the tribal father instills taboos in avoidance of his anger that prove to be the origin of religious consciousness. While Wells deals at some length with the movement of peoples and the development of social and political structures, his history repudiates the nation-state and its "battles and kings" as the primary locus of development. From the first, Wells aimed at grasping the evolution of a religious consciousness as the fundamental element of human progress. Beginning with the advent of primitive religion, "the history of mankind . . . is a history of more or less blind endeavors to conceive a common purpose in relation to which all men may live happily, and to create and develop a common consciousness and a common stock of knowledge which will serve and illuminate that purpose."[74] In the development of a civilization, a "community of obedience" to the will of the primal father or an elite, be it of king and aristocracy or of a priestly class, gives way to a "community of will" as the externally imposed compact is internalized or socialized, and a rational understanding of the common social interest comes to dominate. A community of will, in the end, makes most state functions unnecessary due to the broad social consensus that comes to reign in the behavior of the citizenry.[75] In *The Outline*, Wells depicts the rise of social consciousness and the crystallization of the communities of will as the unifying foci of history.

A major awakening of the "free intelligence of mankind" occurred in the Classical Age in Greece where Plato first conceived of the idea of "willfully and completely recasting human conditions." Henceforth, thought—freed from a subservience to historical conditions, dogmas, and the current social hegemony of ideas—could orient itself to the future.[76] Wells claimed that earlier thought was embedded in images akin to dreams; thought was "undirected" like that of primitive men according to Jung's psychology of the unconscious. Post-Platonic thought was freed as "directed thought," which aimed at education in self-knowledge and, from there, conscious social construction. This awakening thus marked, for Wells, the shift to the evolutionary movement that Huxley saw as possible in civilization.[77]

At the same time the Hebrew mind "awoke suddenly to the endless miseries and disorder of life, saw that these miseries and disorders were largely due to the lawless acts of men, and concluded that salvation could only come through subduing ourselves to the service of the one God."[78] While the Greeks approached the problem of self-knowledge and the community as a rational inquiry into right living, the Jews employed monotheism to the same end. Wells's history rings with evangelism over this shift to self-subordination—one never yet fully realized historically but the essential duty of man. In the upward movement from the unconsciousness of the animal world to the racial and tribal self-consciousness of primitive man and then to the individual consciousness, there was a sense of the "inevitable tragedy of self-seeking" and the inadequacy of mere individuality, which ultimately provoked the subordination of self to law for the Hebrews and to the polis for the Greeks.[79]

Equally significant in the advancement of consciousness and in "closest harmony with modern ideas" was the rise of Buddhism in India. Wells argued that Buddhism closely reflected the findings of modern biology; it certainly mirrored his own religious point of view. Wells rejected the "immortality religions" of the West as faiths for the modern era; the immortality found in Buddhism, however, fit well with his own ideas on the relations between the self and the whole, "the merger of the narrow globe of the individual experience in a wider being."[80] This, of course, was his goal for evolution, the loss of the personal pronoun to something greater than self. The other advantage of Buddhism over traditional Western faiths was its lack of a jealous God—the zealous torturer he had feared and hated in his youth.[81] An interesting irony surfaces in Wells's one major objection to Buddhism: the religion was "stagnated and corrupted" by its cyclical conception of history.[82] This feature of Eastern religious thought would prove to be particularly attractive to later world historians such as Toynbee and Sorokin. One could argue that the Buddhist seeks Wells's end goal of evolution in the present as an internal evolution; in Wells's mind the transformative loss of self must be historical and firmly tied to a vision of humanity's technological progress to an age of material plenty.[83] This belief may be the result of his early deprivations, his Western cultural bias, and again, of the pattern of his own life. Clearly he embraced Freud's use of ontogeny recapitulating phylogeny and the cultural legacy of Judeo-Christianity, especially the linear conception of time. Only in the final adulthood of the human race would reason and religious self-subordination rule in the relations between men. As Wells put it, "the history of our race and the personal religious experience run so closely parallel as to seem to a modern observer almost the same thing. That . . . is the outline of history."[84]

To Wells, Jesus the Nazarene was a man who preached the renunciation of self as its own reward; self-sacrifice and doing for others *were* the Kingdom of Heaven, in process, in the world. Jesus was a progressive! Like Wells he struck out at narrow patriotism and the bonds of the nuclear family in favor of the brotherhood of mankind. He did so in the face of the priestly dogmatism of the Pharisees, who ultimately crushed him just as his own priestly followers would distort and undermine his message. The major advance of Christianity, its catholicism, its open universalism, its idea of self-subordination without regard for polis, nation, or people, mark it as the first nascent and fumbling conception of the Universal State.[85] Wells wrote sympathetically of the idea of the "peace of Christ on Earth" coordinated by the early church and aimed, in his view, at world government. This idea was distorted from the start, however, by Paul's invocation of the messiah and the priestly machinations of conservative dogmatists culminating with the abortion of Christianity at the Council of Nicaea.[86]

While humankind's evolution of consciousness was essentially toward the subordination of self to ever larger unities under religious systems, a parallel development took place politically as the hegemony of political organization enlarged with the progress of technology and the techniques of social organization. Wells bucked the popular opinion of his day in his low judgment of the "great men," the conquerors, empire builders, and heroes of history. He pointed to Alexander to illustrate the impediments in the sustained expansion of civilized hegemonies. Ever since Alexander, "human thought has been haunted by the possible political unity of the race."[87] His reason for the failure of the West and the world in general to achieve this unity is predictable. Alexander acted as an egotist and not in subordination to any perception of collective will.

The Fall of Rome is another example of the failure of a social organization to successfully adapt. According to Wells, Rome's prostration occurred because of the degeneration of its mental life; the inventions of the Greeks, like Hero's steam engine, were ignored or forgotten; there was no knowledge of life beyond the empire, of lands beyond the frontiers, of the patterns of migrations of the Germanic tribes. And again, Caesarism in a community of obedience rather than a general will predominated.[88] In addition, the empire was "saddled by a class of rich men who were creditors" but, like Veblen's pecuniary class, had no relation to production, invention, or any gainful activity but acted as parasites on the system who could call up capital and disrupt economic arrangements.[89] Directed intelligence by the leaders of society into these areas of ignorance was the appropriate but neglected means of maintaining the empire as a universal state. Wells repudiated Gibbon's complacent optimism that such an outcome could not recur in the modern West. Waste, ignorance, and economic inefficiency on an analogous pattern existed in the present "deflection of the profits of progress" to warfare and business competition rather than to education for citizenship. Moreover, Wells's attitude toward evolution contained the possibility of the reemergence of barbarism, now from within.[90]

The Outline charts the idea of the unity of mankind through Chinese, Arabic, and Christian cultures as a progressive realization of common humanity, paralleling Wells's life experience and culminating in Enlightenment rationalism and the rise of modern science, especially Darwinian biology. *The Outline of History* maps the progress of an idea in the past but clearly aimed to be an outline for the future: a common realization of the central theme of history that would lead to its actualization in the unified World State.

• • •

Wells's subsequent work was dominated by attempts to lead in the development of his self-conscious Samurai class through an "open conspiracy" of scientific and functional men in alliance with a world-wide intelligentsia of those who could perceive and orient themselves to the common goal of humanity. In *The Open Conspiracy* (1928), Wells attempted to summarize his mature perspective and to present a "scheme for all human conduct." The conspiracy was to result in the awakening of mankind from the "nightmare of the struggle for existence and the inevitability of war"; as such it would directly counter the fascist ideology growing on the continent.[91] In addition to producing a "Bible" for the future civilization and eventually a complete encyclopedia to provide the common "mental background of every intelligent man in the world,"[92] the conspiracy would reconsecrate daily life. It would adapt old rituals and invent new ones for the new binding religion. Wells proposed "meetings for mutual reassurance, confession and prayer, self-dedication sacraments, and seasons of fast and meditation"; all old patterns of worship must be "modernized or replaced by modern equivalents."[93]

This religious conspiracy is inherently undemocratic; the World State would not be voted into being. Only a few people realize "scientific" truth and are willing to dedicate themselves to the realization of historical ends. These individuals form a "natural elite."[94] Wells's elitism and pessimism over the future of liberal democracy mirrored the views of continental fascism. Sovereignty, to Wells, did not rest atomistically in the arithmetical calculation of the will of the people but in "that common impersonal will and sense of necessity" that is best recognized scientifically. It lies in the racial mind, a "merger of sovereignty" to be interpreted by the most intuitive, insightful, and scientific members of the social body.[95] Liberalism, at any rate, has failed to respond to modern imperatives. The old-style democratic rise of freedoms has contributed to a "world wide detachment of individuals from codes and controls, subjugation and responsibilities, functions and duties. I suggest that this process of dissolution is at an end, and that mankind is faced—is challenged—by the need for reorganization and reorientation." Liberal capitalism is not a defensible system, it is the "absence of a system"; it has reached a point of disorder that demands resolution and the only solution is a religious one.[96] Wells believed that the Communists and fascists were driven by an essentially "religious passion," one that he shared with them. Even as he affirmed antidemocratic principles and millennial anticipations of a new scientific social order in common with the fascists and Communists, he sought a middle way, a pre-Marxian socialism that would avoid class war, and racial and national divisions, through the evolution of the rule of an international Comtean elite.[97]

The Samurai discipline of this elite would be that of self-immersion. The members would work rigorously toward the sublimation of ego to the race, and their devotion to this task would justify them to act as the mouthpiece of the racial consciousness, as the interpreters of the needs of the race at each evolutionary juncture. The shift to the World State would be a shift in religious consciousness, like that which occurred in the spread of Christianity or Islam. "The World State must begin, it can only begin, as a propagandistic cult."[98] Trained as educators toward the common good, the Samurai would systematize this education for all, they would "catch and domesticate the ego at an early stage and train it for purposes greater than itself."[99] In the end, the educational system would, ideally, make government superfluous. In *Men Like Gods* (1922), the state has "withered away" and "our education is our government . . . there is no rule nor government needed by adult utopians because all the rule and government they need they have in childhood and youth."[100]

By the late 1930s, Wells was growing increasingly pessimistic of the World State ever coming into being. His Manichaean invocations to "adapt or perish" became harsher as he noted the extinction of other species owing to human mismanagement and the rise of new and restrictive conceptions of the "chosen people," especially that of the Nazis. The "change of scale" and "abolition of distance" of man's technological progress in unrestrained capitalism threatened the world ecosystem as a whole. Wells noted increases in deforestation, desertification, the exhaustion of resources, and the "killing off of whales, seals and a multitude of rare and beautiful species, [which ends in] destroying the morale of every social type and devastating the planet."[101] Until the crisis was resolved, Wells predicted the increased use of drugs, a refusal of some people to procreate, increases in suicides, and eventually a new "Dark Ages" in the "coming barbarism."[102] Wells felt that he was drowning unheard in a "sea of unconscious ignorance" that must be overcome or else "we shall destroy each other."[103]

Even as he grew more pessimistic as to humanity's ability to adapt and avoid extinction, Wells worked toward the organization of the

United Nations and in 1940 called for a new worldwide *Declaration of the Rights of Man* to be recognized as central to the Allies' war aims. Wells was instrumental in the development of the "Universal Declaration of Human Rights," which was ultimately adopted by the U.N.[104] As in World War I, he hoped that the Second World War would be the fulcrum for a new world order; this was tied to a dualistic sense that if the World State failed to be implemented, the war might be a step toward the end of humanity.

Wells's last work, *Mind at the End of Its Tether* (1945), is a desperate restatement of his main theses written in the pessimism of his illness in the last years of his life. He believed that the human race truly approached its doom. There was, he said, a mindless evil in human nature that had yet to be conquered and that threatened the dissolution of civilization.[105] David Smith has interpreted the work differently than most scholars. He concluded that Wells believed the ordinary man of the past was indeed at the end of his tether, only the new man could adapt to the new age and the World State and survive this "age of confusion."[106] Smith's position is attractive when one grasps the overall coherence of Wells's intellectual life, but the tone of the work is decidedly one of bleak pessimism about man's future prospects. Wells died of cancer in 1946, soon after the publication of his last volume.

• • •

H. G. Wells was not a historian in the academic sense of the term. No professional historian would have the audacity to write an outline of universal history based upon such a limited use of secondary source material, a complete lack of formal training, and minimal study of earlier attempts. Wells's perspective on world development was that of a bold pamphleteer; he was first and foremost a propagandist whose unstudied use and contortion of fact followed the thread of his millennial anticipations. His religious dualism prompted him to propound evolutionary imperatives to such an extent that even before the publication of *The Outline* he was rightly criticized for his "Messianic delusion."[107]

As Jack Williamson has noted, Wells, despite his inadequacy for the task, was the first writer to consistently apply the science of organic evolution, ecology, and social Darwinism to a chronologically developed world history and as a prospectus on future development. He also defined the realm of discourse for modern science fiction.[108] In the first half of the twentieth century, this discourse was in good part a reaction to a perceived Wellsian optimism about the new world order. Authors like Orwell, Zamyatin, Aldous Huxley, E. M. Forster, and

William Golding reacted against Wells's prospect of a scientific bureaucracy, which they saw as technocratic totalitarianism. As Orwell
put it in 1941, "much of what Wells has imagined and worked for is
physically there in Nazi Germany."[109] Despite his early distopian
works, including *The Time Machine*, *The First Men in the Moon*, and
When the Sleeper Wakes, Wells was condemned for a naive Victorian
progressivism, in which he never really believed, by those most in his
debt.[110]

Wells was an enormously popular public figure in his day. He
maintained a wide network of relationships with many of the most
important British and American intellectuals and political leaders of
his time, from Arthur Balfour and Lord Beaverbrook to Leonard and
Virginia Woolf, Joseph Conrad, G. K. Chesterton, William James,
Walter Lippman, Bertrand Russell, Maxim Gorky, and Charlie Chap-
lin. Malcolm Cowley argued in 1934 that "by the time he was forty his
influence was wider than any other living English writer."[111] Wells met
with four U.S. presidents and maintained a friendly correspondence
with Franklin Delano Roosevelt. He toured the world. He debated
with Lenin in the Kremlin in 1920 and with Stalin in 1934 on the
World State, the common interests of all mankind, particularly of
the United States and the Soviet Union in the upcoming age, and what
he saw as the Soviet errors of class struggle, and under Stalin, the
repression of dissent.[112]

William McNeill has called Wells a "brilliant amateur" for his *The
Outline of History*.[113] The work was never meant as a text for the
professional or the specialist; Wells saw himself as an "outsider" who,
because of his distance from the minutia of scholarship, could encapsulate the breadth and meaning of history in a way that the insider
could not.[114] *The Outline* was meant to replace national histories as the
basis for education in the schools; it was written as a history for the
common man. As such, *The Outline* reads like a *Reader's Digest* of
world history; deliberately popular in tone, the work in no way matches
the scholarly level of other studies to be reviewed in this volume.[115]
John K. A. Farrell, in a thoughtful evaluation of Wells as a historian,
noted that while his "conception is magnificent, his history is suspect,"
"subject to telescoping distortions" and an "inability to distinguish
prejudice from fact."[116] This observation is incontrovertibly true. Not
only is Wells's emphasis skewed by the dominance of his thesis and his
lack of detailed knowledge of his subject, but *The Outline* is full of
gaps through the omission of some of the essential personalities of
history. Shakespeare and Erasmus, for instance, are not mentioned,
and the origins of modern socialism are found exclusively in Robert

Owen—Saint Simon, Comte, and Fourier did not rate inclusion. Farrell also noted that Wells was "indifferent to documentation."[117] He wrote with the *Encyclopaedia Britannica* at his elbow and relied extensively on Gibbon, Carlyle, Plutarch, the Bible, and popular works of the day. Despite Wells's omissions, errors of detail, and inappropriate use of sources, Arnold Toynbee hailed the grand conception of *The Outline* as a "magnificent intellectual achievement"; to Toynbee the main flaw in the work was in its lack of connection between the macrocosm, of progress, and the microcosm of individual personalities, details, and events.[118]

Wellsian world history prefigures in many ways the perspective demonstrated by the neoprogressivism of William H. McNeill in his tour de force, *The Rise of the West* (1963). In 1934 Wells called his outline a "story of communications and increasing interdependence";[119] clearly this is also the central theme in McNeill's work. Both emphasize the progressive development of mankind as a whole—the race is on from day one. Both have a primary concern with the history of human and environmental ecology, as in McNeill's *Plagues and Peoples*.[120] Both chart the progress of technological and cultural diffusion in space, between peoples, and in time, in the cumulative nature of human invention and culture—the main theme in *The Rise of the West*. Both find a cultural juncture in the rapid development of technology, a change in economic scale, and a corresponding growth of governmental organization in response to these conditions. They depict the emergence of the military-industrial complex tied to an outmoded nationalism and warn, as McNeill does in *The Pursuit of Power* (1982), of its potential for mass destruction. Both Wells and McNeill emphasize the horizon point that these developments produce in the twentieth century and argue that their resolution can only be along international lines. Both write history as the progressive consolidation of human units through the spread of technology and education, and both qualify this process by documenting potential catastrophes in the future, and horizon points in the past. Admittedly their progressivism is poles apart in many ways: McNeill's liberalism resists the imposition of any Wellsian technocratic Samurai; he would celebrate the virtues of cultural pluralism and in his later work repudiate Wells's invocations of religious community.

Despite its inadequate scholarship, the importance of *The Outline* lies in its introduction of so many now commonplace elements to broad numbers of people who had not been exposed to them previously. *The Outline of History* was the most popular work of history written in the first half of the twentieth century, selling a million copies by 1931 and over two million in all.[121] John Barker claims that *The*

Outline was the most popular and one of the most influential works of history ever written.[122] Wells introduced for many people the notions of the World State, and the "abolition of distance" and "change of scale" implications of modern technology. He presented the ideas, first of a League of Nations and then of a United Nations with a universal bill of human rights. He exposed a historical view of Jesus, the importance of Eastern religion, and a Malthusian view of modern population dynamics along with the then-controversial advocacy of the free use of birth control and family planning toward the sexual emancipation of women. As Warren Wagar has pointed out, what was radical in Wells has been so thoroughly digested by the modern West as to seem "platitudinous" in retrospect. Wagar asserts that Wells "conditioned early twentieth century minds to think in terms of catastrophe."[123] The other side of potential destruction was of course the long-term education Wells delivered that conditioned his contemporaries to think in terms of international organization.[124] Wells typifies many of the themes and trends confronted by the majority of twentieth-century world historians, from the need for education toward international order to his religious conception of humanity's destiny and the challenges it must overcome to realize itself. What appears to us as platitude in Wells was once startlingly new to many; perhaps that so many of his ideas became clichés testifies to the tenacity of their influence as well as our own lack of distance in examining their ultimate historical significance.

The Problem
of Oswald Spengler

My friend, the times that antecede
Our own are books safely protected
By seven seals. What spirit of the time you call
Is but the scholar's spirit, after all,
In which times past are now reflected.
                                    —Goethe's *Faust*[1]

Every idea that is possible at all is a mirror of the being of its author.
                                    —Oswald Spengler[2]

The whole of history is the refutation by experiment of the principle of
the so-called "moral world order."
                                    —Friedrich Nietzsche[3]

FOR OSWALD SPENGLER historical truth was but an intuited abstraction. History was a personal realization of the a priori essence of culture. More than any other historian examined in this volume Spengler saw himself as an artist and a philosopher as well as a naturalist. His epochal world history of culture was his expression of a grand symphonic tragedy and his articulation of this tragedy was to him but an echo of the last climactic notes that presaged the silence of a doomed culture-soul. *The Decline of the West* (1918, 1922) reads like an epic poem: there is virtually no consistent narrative of any history; there is no recourse to empirical fact to evaluate perceived patterns or to define the reality of intuited cultural wholes. Instead, *The Decline* is an artistic articulation of despair and a violent attack on civilization in the West. Spengler's closed cycles of cultural emergence and downfall contain the frozen fascination of compelling tragedy, where an inevitably unfolding destiny prescribes the actions of the players toward the dramatic glories of their deaths. Alone among the important world historians of the twentieth century, Spengler anticipated the fall of the West without issue, survivors, or any contribution toward a meaningful future.

However one may criticize Oswald Spengler's morphology of cultures, it was he who set the principal problems in the discourse of world history for the twentieth century to which all subsequent world historical paradigms had to respond. Spengler's definition of the identity of culture has been of cardinal concern throughout the century. To him culture was a self-contained monad whose internal rhythms provided the central dynamic of world history and to which external influences could only be ephemeral and incidental. His distinction between civilization and culture, based on the widely held belief that any civilization in its later stages is decadent, overcivilized, limited by the achievements of its youth, and corrupted by its own overrefinement, provides a paradigmatic vehicle that either acts in the staging of future theories or must be actively opposed. And all this proceeds from Spengler's cyclical metahistory and the parallel between the course of culture and that of the seasons of nature or the life cycle of the individual person. Spengler confronted progress head-on and rejected it, thereby setting the central dilemma for meaning in the study of world history for the century. By disavowing any teleology in world history other than that within isolated cultures, he made the history of the world as a whole a senseless recurrence. Spengler concurrently made positive contributions to a "Copernican" view of world history in his perspective on the viability of earlier civilizations and his view that the modern West was not the single end product of historical development but a contemporary example of human development that paralleled previous examples and was philosophically contemporary with them. Finally Spengler set up a determinism of the whole in which the central idea or "soul" of any culture underlay and decided the phenomenal expressions of that culture; culture here takes on the part of the noumenal ground, of the invisible being whose life course is revealed to the poet and historical artist in the play of epiphenomenal events.

Ironically, for Spengler as for so many other political and metahistorical philosophers, this determinism of the whole does not preclude moral conduct by individuals, whose actions are so deeply conditioned by time and place, but posits a sociopolitical morality in relation to the deep currents of historical progression. One must act in accord with the laws of history and, in particular, according to the imperatives of the particular time and place of the culture that supplies one's destiny. According to Spengler, in this context freedom means "the necessary or nothing."[4] The consciousness that Spengler sought to impart to modern Faustian man was essentially tragic in its implications. One had no choice in one's destiny any more than one chose one's time; the only future is death, for the individual soul as well as the culture. One must remain at the gate, like the Roman legionnaire at Pompeii, and fulfill one's duty in the face of the inexorable annihilating future.

Spengler's metahistory was a modernist antidote to the positivist faith in historical progress and the documentation of the past by its broken shards and fragmented data. In this his rebellion paralleled that of the neo-idealists, Croce and Dilthey, except that he rejected their belief in the possibility of truly reexperiencing the inner life of earlier peoples or cultures. In any examination of history our perspective is conditioned by the Faustian lens embedded in our way of seeing, it is inherent in our cultural disposition, and at the core of our psychological development as individuals. Spengler's Copernican history is impossible except to Faustian man, who bears the mental equipment to grasp gestaltic cultural phenomena and whose sense of infinity allows him to accept a relativistic perspective. Our understanding of history then can be true only for us, true for our time and true only in this period between the realization of our cultural essence, beginning in the early nineteenth century, until the ultimate dissolution of our cultural integrity, in the centuries to come.

At the risk of being tautological one can claim that metahistorians share a particular frame of mind. They apply a wide-angle lens to the past most often in response to what they see as the death of a myth; the metahistorian attempts to consolidate a new world perspective or schema as a new ground for understanding and for action in the world. World history in the twentieth century is a sometimes desperate response to the crisis of modernism, attempting to find in history a replacement for the faith in progress of the nineteenth century positivists, which received such a setback at Nietzsche's hands and a shocking blow in the First World War. Spengler is himself both a symptom of this loss of faith and a destroyer of the progressive view of history. His *The Decline of the West* is a challenge that in some measure dominates the world systems of the next two generations of world historians who seek to rebuild a meaningful past.

In Spengler's case, despite the fateful implications of his philosophy, there is sense that Lewis Mumford has called "religious consolation"[5] in the eternal recurrence of the cycles of birth and death and in Spengler's postulation of a soul of a culture to which the individual's spirit and destiny are inextricably united. Though Spengler nihilistically posited cycles without human advance or meaningful legacy from one to another, he did not adopt a fellaheen or oriental passivism before the cyclical rise and fall of cultures as one might expect. Instead, he upheld a further solace in the present cycle by claiming that it was a period in which Faustian striving must be channeled into the ardor and passion of conquest for the last struggle of the West, that for world domination. In so doing he justified and affirmed his own personal and Germanic aggressive drive for power; he asserted a highest moral good for this twilight culture in the expression of his own violent hatreds and resentments as well as those of his contemporary national culture. Spengler provided key elements of mental equipment toward a historically embedded salvation in this last stage by taking on the prophetic mantle as the voice of destiny. This destiny required a sense of spiritual unity, found in part in Spengler's sense of culture-soul and "race-ideal," and his calls for a Napoleonic leader, a führer who could manifest the collective will and fulfill a role demanded by nature itself.

Brilliant as his insights and his manipulation of historical patterns could be, Spengler's scholarship was shoddy, his grasp of the historical record inadequate, and his designs contorted by his guiding ideas; *The Decline* is torturously convoluted, repetitive, and opaque. To review Spengler's ideas one must adopt a corresponding, if inhospitable, abstractness.

The cosmic pessimism of Spengler's world historical system was founded on the sense of destiny, fate, and *Weltangst* in his own experience; Spengler defined historical truth in the preface to his morphology of culture as the author's "being expressed in words."[6] To Spengler, fate applied to the single soul as well as to cultures; in his case fate provided a "miserable, joyless youth," a self-perpetuating psychological isolation, a reactive antiworld of fantasies of personal grandeur, power, and destiny, and a profound yearning for the saving heroes who could overcome civilization—and his own alienation—by actualizing a new anti-intellectual, aristocratic, Germanic barbarism.[7] Spengler projected a title to his proposed autobiography, of which we have only fragments, as the "Life of a Rejected One" or "Loneliness"; clearly Spengler saw himself as a man born out of his time, an outsider whose works could only be understood by the future.[8] To Spengler the downfall of the West was no great tragedy but an antidote to the bourgeois mediocrity of decadent modernism and even a projected wish fulfillment for the destruction of the external world that had conditioned his own life course and had cut him off from the sources of culture in emotion, community, and myth. In the place of this rejected world Spengler envisioned the actualization of the antiworld of his childhood, a noble world of virtue in the face of tragedy where heroic action was its own justification.

• • •

Oswald Spengler was born in 1880, the eldest of four children and the only son of a minor postal official at Blankenburg in the Harz Mountains. Bernard Spengler was a cold and repressive father, a close-minded "anti-literary man" who despised recreations of all sorts, and books with a special fervor; Oswald claimed that from his father he inherited his hatred, and his abiding sense of duty. In reaction to his father's overbearing dominance of his home Spengler affirmed that he could never accept imposed schedules or external authorities. In his autobiographical fragments Spengler continually asserted that as a youth he had no positive role model; he could only feel a silent hatred and pity for his father. Yet he had an almost desperate need for a "great man" who could lift him up; without one, Spengler felt, a man could only be an "inner cripple." He claimed that "I have such a strong urge to adore someone, not just Goethe or Shakespeare but a contemporary." Spengler later considered Goethe and Nietzsche as his "spiritual fathers" and dreamed that his life would have been fulfilled if Nietzsche had lived to be a model for him.[9]

Spengler's mother was a stifling hypochondriac who bitterly chastised her husband and daughters but spared her only son. She was from a musical family, her sister Adele was a virtuoso ballerina, and she herself painted and played music and so passed on to her son an enduring love of the arts, especially of poetry and music. Disabled from birth and subject to intermittent headaches—which Oswald inherited—Pauline Spengler modeled for the boy, especially after the death of her sister, an almost boundless anxiety. Frau Spengler taught her son that existence was a "walk of repentance . . . through the desert of life." Oswald clung to her and, later as a bachelor, to his three younger sisters, against his inherited *Weltangst*. He felt "limitless feelings of fear as a child in the world" and claimed that "I wanted to die because of the terror of life."[10] Spengler's *Weltangst* was so powerful that he founded his world historical system upon it; he held that life itself was founded on "dread," the fear of mortality, and "the thing become." In *The Decline of the West* Spengler asserted that "world fear is assuredly the most creative of all prime feelings"; in the last analysis, it is the inspiration of myth and symbol itself.[11]

In the face of his loneliness Oswald invented imaginary countries with detailed histories of wars, massacres, and natural disasters; at sixteen he made up an imaginary continent called Afrikasien.[12] Although he was never really rejected at home or in school, Spengler felt isolated and outside the normal relationships with the people and institutions around him; he created what he called "antiworlds" to his home, to his father, and later to university. Even as a child these included obsessions with power, with changing the map; in his daydreams Spengler took on the part of a Napoleon or a great statesman. In his fantasies he felt that he had to be a new messiah for a "new Germany" with a new sun worship; "that was nine tenths of my dreams." Spengler was confirmed, but already religion per se had ceased to be an issue for him; the attempt to make him a Christian through rigid training at home and school had turned him into an "anti-Christian" who read Nietzsche behind a prayer book and later lectured his family on the importance of Zarathustra.[13] As an autodidact in an antiliterary family, Spengler turned to an "inner world" that was "closed to everyone else." He asserted that he owed this fantasy world of poetry, knights, and angst to his father and that he retained it as "waking dreams" in his adulthood; his adult insights were the result of this youthful training in inwardness as an escape from his father's repressiveness.[14] Nonetheless, Spengler realized that the pattern of withdrawal he underwent in relation to his parents, his schoolmates, and teachers had scarred him deeply; he later understood that he had withdrawn from life into thought, the very fate of the "last man" of civilization, and he thoroughly regretted it.[15] In the end, however, one is not able to choose one's time or one's message to the world: "That which one . . . wills to express is in him *a priori*."[16]

It does not seem contradictory to describe Spengler's personality and world view in terms that he himself applied to human nature. Spengler claimed that the expression of personality was a "protest against humanity in the mass."[17] Like Haeckel, his vehicle to a Darwinistic perspective on the evolution of humanity, Spengler believed that "man is a beast of prey."[18] History is a battle in a universe that goes on with "godlike unconcern" where the individual, "a very solitary soul," is a "foe to everyone, killing, hating, resolute to conquer or die," who "stands in irreconcilable opposition to the whole world," who feels exultation in plunging a knife into another. World history is a "tragedy" of man, who, by his own creativity, breaks irreconcilably from nature; it is "the history of a rebel who grows up to raise his hand against its mother."[19]

Spengler started school in 1889 at the gymnasium at Soest but moved in 1891 to Halle where he studied mathematics, philosophy, and history. He graduated in 1899 and then as a postgraduate studied natural sciences until 1901, when his father died. He then went to Munich and Berlin. With the death of his father Spengler claimed that he felt freedom for the first time; "my father died at the right time."[20] At Munich Spengler was frustrated not only by his own alienation and anxiety, which made him a "spectator" of life rather than an actor, but by the fragmentary nature of the university curriculum, which taught truth in details and fragments, or *Fachwissenschaft*, rather than as a whole. He believed that he had acquired his own method of observation, which he modeled on that of Goethe.[21]

Spengler received his doctorate in 1904 at Halle with a dissertation on the classic heroic-vitalist Heracleitus, whose dictum that all was in flux and that "war is the creator of all things" foreshadowed Spengler's later perspective, and with a scientific work on the physiology of the eye in animals that echoed Goethe's research into the nature of light and presaged his later philosophic interest in ways of seeing. Most of his training was in math, physics, and the natural sciences but he had discovered Shakespeare and Nietzsche while still in his teens, and finally Goethe when he was twenty-two. His interest in philosophy and literature threatened to dominate his scientific perspective, and in the end he was a poorly motivated and unhappy teacher of mathematics and science. Spengler flew into tears when he saw the school building at his first assignment; he suffered a nervous breakdown during his first year teaching.[22] He then spent the next two years in various teaching roles, traveling to Paris, and holding temporary positions until he received a regular schoolmaster position in 1907 in Hamburg. In 1906 Spengler had been rejected for military service at Düsseldorf because of a heart condition. His youthful dreams of glory seemed headed for frustration in a teaching career that left little room for his imagination, much less heroic action. When his mother died in 1910 she left him a small inheritance, which enabled him to quit teaching and to settle on a vocation as a free-lance writer. Spengler moved to Munich, where he would remain for the rest of his life, and over the next few years lived in an intellectual vacuum; in his isolation he wrote a number of uncompleted plays and novels.[23]

In 1911 Spengler was inspired by the crisis at Agadir, where Wilhelm II's colonial aims in North Africa were frustrated by the French, to see a new era approaching the West. A "period of contending states" presaged a new Caesarism and the eventual downfall of Western civilization, a decline that paralleled those of earlier civilizations. By the end of the next year he had arrived at the title to his magnum opus after seeing Otto Seecks's *Geschichte des Untergangs der antiken Welt* in a bookstore window.[24] In 1911 Spengler's intention had been to deal primarily with current problems and entitle his work "Conservative and Liberal," but as he wrote he felt that he approached the "single and comprehensive solution" to the problem of modern history and philosophy that Nietzsche (who "had dared to look strict reality in the face") had articulated and that awaited final solution.[25] Spengler's brooding megalomania evinced itself in his view that his new intuitive and "provisional expression of a new world picture . . . will (I repeat) be accepted without dispute."[26]

Ironically *The Decline of the West*, written in Spengler's wartime optimism over the short-term victory of Germany tempered by his despair over the long-term benefits of this victory, achieved popular success in defeated Germany. Spengler asserted in 1921 that he had directed his work in "instinctive opposition to the prevailing mood," as a rebellion against the softening effects of the optimism of the progressive world view that gave people "a moral excuse for their timorousness."[27] Yet in 1914 Spengler had claimed that he was "a thorough optimist. We shall win and in such a way that the great sacrifices will be richly compensated." He believed that Germany would acquire an African empire, invade England, and retain Belgium. Spengler also believed, however, that in her victory Germany would degenerate into a "soulless Americanism" that would "dissolve art, the nobility, the Church, the world outlook" in a megapolitan materialism.[28] During the war Spengler lived in isolation and a sometimes dire poverty as he hunted for a publisher for the *Decline*. When the book finally came out in 1918 it was a huge and immediate success. Spengler went from being an unheard and isolated man to an international celebrity overnight.

He actively engaged in politics beginning in 1919 with the publication of his *Prussianism and Socialism*, which promoted a corporate view of society bound to a Prussian discipline and united in the nascent Caesarean age by a heroic leader, a führer. During the winter of that year he debated Max Weber in the Munich City Hall for a day and a half, and then a few weeks later locked horns with Moeller van den Bruck.[29] Spengler opposed the Weimar Republic and considered forming his own party to work against it. Later he looked to Stresemann and General Von Seect and even later to Gustav Von Kahr to overthrow the democracy. Kahr attempted to use Hitler and his S.A. to accomplish this task but Hitler's putsch was a ridiculous failure; as Hitler stood trial on February 26, 1924, Spengler lectured on "the political duties of German youth," ridiculing the flags, slogans, and parades of the Nazis.[30] After a period of writing similar political tracts Spengler moved away from politics and immersed himself more deeply in his "scientific" work. In 1927 he suffered a stroke that interfered with his memory. Spengler projected further great works in the later years of his life, such as a narrative of the "History of Man from His Origin," which he was never able to complete.[31]

• • •

When Spengler characterized his philosophy of history as "a German Philosophy" and even as "the philosophy of our time," he evinced his ambition to unite the various strains of German philosophy to produce a unified "morphology of world history."[32] This was the Faustian task par excellence: to express the true form of world history as the "mirror image of our own inner life," to understand all becoming in line with the eternal recurrence of being, to locate the striving for infinity that is our substance in a realistic approach to nature that demonstrates its very hopelessness.[33]

Spengler approached history as the "marvelous waxing and waning of organic forms," rather than as a progressive "tapeworm industriously adding on to itself."[34] These forms are Liebnitzian monads whose plantlike life courses proceed along a thousand-year life span, each in line with its prime symbol. "Cultures are organisms and world history is their collective biography."[35] Each culture has had its "own image . . . own idea . . . own passions . . . own life, will and feeling, [and] its own death." To Spengler the emergence and passage of the prime symbol of a culture disproves any progressive ideology.[36] He believed that his "Copernican discovery" of the morphological equivalence of world cultures overturned the Eurocentric myopia inherent in the traditional division of history into the mal-descriptive categories of ancient, medieval, and modern.[37]

To Spengler, there is a "morphological relationship that inwardly binds together the expression forms of all branches of a culture"[38]; any cultural attribute or action can only be understood from an intuitive experience of that unifying ground. This can also be expressed in terms of the "destiny idea" of a culture, the "true existence mode of the prime phenomena," which is the "organic logic of its existence." Like Herder, Spengler believed destiny inhered in all natural forms; once conceived they followed a course immanent in their autochthonous essence.[39] Any expression of a culture is relative to that symbol and can only be understood, according to Spengler, by a member of that culture—although in this he makes allowance for his own intuitive apperception of the symbols themselves as a means of realizing the central meaning of cultural movements. All "truths" are relative "established" realities since all knowledge of the world is relative to a particular culture and serves as its axioms and myths; part of Spengler's task then is to provide a "comparative morphology of knowledge forms."[40] For example, no mathematics are true in the abstract, there are only the mathematical expressions of particular peoples in various ages.[41] For the historian then the task was to isolate the prime phenomenon or the cultural essence and not to elaborate "facts."

In Spengler's cyclical metahistory, which he patterned on those of Polybius, Joachim of Floris, Goethe, and Nietzsche, cultures pass through four stages that correspond to the seasons in nature. The spring of a culture sees the birth of its prime symbol and the union of its social order in a myth. Spengler envisioned this symbol much as Hegel had, as the "soul" of a culture; it is "the possible" as opposed to the "world," which is the actual. Life—the emergence and growth of culture through spring, summer, and into fall—is the actualization of the possible. In his words: " 'Soul' is the still to be accomplished, 'world' is the accomplished, 'Life' the accomplishing."[42] The realization of the symbol in the world is the apex of a culture's development; the point is reached where the 'becoming' of the culture-soul in life is translated to the 'become' now expressed in the world, and the living process of culture is translated into a hardening and devolution of forms in civilization. "The Civilization is the inevitable *destiny* of the Culture."[43]

To Spengler civilizations are "conclusions, the thing-become succeeding the thing-becoming, death following life, rigidity following expansion . . . petrifying world city following mother earth and the spiritual childhood."[44] Spengler's use of the terms *Kultur* and *Zivilisation* has roots in Kant and is employed by thinkers as divergent as Houston Stewart Chamberlain, Thomas Mann, who sought a return to *Kultur* as a means of Germanic revitalization, Moeller van den Bruck, who shared much of Spengler's perspective without his pessimism, and Hitler, who in *Mein Kampf* recognized the distinction and called civilization the "enemy of true spiritual and living levels."[45] Central to the life process is the death of the myths that provided a unifying ground at the dawn of the culture's existence; like Vico (whom he did not read until later), Burckhardt, and, more directly, like Nietzsche, Spengler held that the loss of myth in a society marked the end of its health and creativity.[46] Again, "Pure Civilization, . . . consists in a progressive *taking down* of forms that have become inorganic or dead."[47] This petrification of soul occurs as cultural growth reaches its apex and is replaced by democratic, religionless, traditionless, megapolitan existence that centers on the intellection of the "fact men" and the competitive striving for power in the world of Caesars.[48] There is a nihilistic "de-souling" that takes place, a "spiritual extinction," as cultural values are transvalued under the skeptical eye of the fact men, and the mythical foundations held unconsciously by the culture are subjected to a corrosive rationality.[49] Spengler quotes Goethe to this effect: "The Godhead is effective in the living and not in the dead, in the becoming and the changing, not in the set fast; and therefore, similarly, the reason (*Vernunft*) is concerned only to strive toward the divine through the becoming and the living, and the understanding (*Verstand*) only to make use of the become and the set fast"; Spengler felt that this epigram comprised his entire philosophy.[50] In Nietzschean language, Spengler claimed that in the end, the "transvaluation of all values is the most fundamental character of every civilization."[51] The sterility of the end product of a cultural cycle leads men to a "metaphysical turn toward death"; "the last man of the world-city no longer wants to live," he breaks with nature, does not marry and reproduce or he plans for few children in an indolent treason to his blood.[52] There is a simultaneous regression in the whole of culture toward its founding myths and religious roots as an antidote to the decay experienced; this movement of "second religiousness," however, is a degeneration to stasis rather than an active and positive development or even a seed to a new phase of cultural growth as we will see envisioned by Sorokin and Toynbee. For Spengler in this last stage the coherence of the civilization disintegrates into a nonhistorical irrationalism, a mysticism in escape from the skepticism that is the only enduring result of the enlightenment period of the culture.[53] On the political front the reversion to primitive religiosity is paralleled by the regression to an ahistorical formlessness where the only valid mode of action is that of the pure striving for power and the hopelessly tragic attempt to preserve cultural forms in the twilight of the civilization. This is done by Caesars, whose destiny it is to compete for a final hegemony of civilization before the long night ahead. "The way from Alexander to Caesar is unambiguous and unavoidable, the strongest nation of any and every culture, consciously or unconsciously, has to tread it . . . the last race to keep its form, the last living tradition, the last leaders who have both at their back, will pass through, onward, victors."[54] Spengler's own state of mind is revealed in his concentration on the decline into civilization and a de-emphasis of the other stages in the life cycle. The angst he experienced was projected into his interpretation of Nietzsche's "last man," whom he recognized as himself, a fulfillment and desperate reaction to the end of culture, and at once a prophet of war who could overcome despair only by foreseeing a violent overcoming of the present decadence through the rise of a conquering savior.

Spengler did not fully develop the factors that give rise to culture in the first place, only approaching the problem in depth in the second volume, and then in response to racist views of world history—especially those of Houston Stewart Chamberlain—which he saw as making a romantic error in mistaking the effect for the cause. Chamberlain, in his *Foundations of the Nineteenth Century*, followed his mentor Gobineau; he held that world history was not a tale of the general progress of man as a whole but a record of the accomplishments of "a definite, individual racial type."[55] Following Herder, Spengler held that the environment, the way of life, and the history of a group provided them a character, an identity, that was bound by language and a consciousness of the group as a "we."[56] Herder rejected racial terms of description. To him, man is "formed in and for society"; people are "naturalized" to the areas of earth that they inhabit through an organic growth that is influenced by the forms of the land, the climate, and the traditional means by which a people adapt to an environment including the most important adaptation and distinguishing characteristic of a people, its language.[57] Herder's view of the "genetic spirit and character of a people," which "pertains to its region," is the model for Spengler's perspective of the unitary character of culture as a development rooted in a particular mother landscape and his notion of the central role of language in defining the "linkages of waking-being," as opposed to the racial aggregate of physical characteristics, of a people.[58] For Spengler the origin of culture is in this plantlike process of the organic development of a people, which reaches a critical threshold in language, the vehicle of categorization and naming, and which is accompanied by an inextricable religious development or spiritualization as language provides metaphors for the world.[59]

To Chamberlain the geniuses of a culture are the flowers of its racial being, they manifest race as its product.[60] To Spengler "peoples" themselves are the products, not the authors, of culture. Culture emerges, first, in its highest exponents who, as a nobility, articulate a sense of identity for the spring culture. These geniuses supply the "deepest foundations of spirituality" that serve as the basis for a cultural style.[61] Like Bergson, whose work he was not exposed to until after he had finished volume one, Spengler held that this elite manifested an élan that gave it a natural leadership role in cultural development. The sense of "we" that emerges around this cultural style is not the product of race but its foundation, as in time the autochthonous landscape, identification, and mutual "comradeship" act together to unite a people in "a yearning for its destiny." The "race-ideal" is at bottom a metaphysical feeling that has no necessary physical basis. Spengler further states that "in race there is nothing material, but something cosmic and directional, the felt harmony of a Destiny, the single cadence of the march of historical being."[62]

Cultures emerge in their springtime through the development of language, myth, and identification; their life is the actualization of the compendium of these three developments in a prime symbol through summer and fall, and their death is in the hardening and decadence of this actualization in the winter of civilization.[63] The articulation of the prime symbol centers on the perspective of space or the type of extension of each forming culture. Spengler held, contrary to Kant, that the mental concept for space was environmentally and culturally determined and not an a priori pattern in the mind. "The choice of this prime symbol in the moment of the Culture-soul's awakening into self-consciousness on its own soil—a moment that for one who can read world history thus contains something catastrophic—decides all."[64] The destiny inherent in this choice is exemplified for Spengler by the Egyptian culture, whose symbol of 'The Way'— the straight course through life to the judges of the dead—originated with the Fourth Dynasty (2930 B.C.) and dominated the cultural style of the Egyptiac civilization throughout its course.[65]

Spengler never really developed a detailed morphology of world history. Although he classified eight historical cultures—Egyptian, Babylonian, Indian, Chinese, Classical or Apollonian, Arabian or Magian, Mexican, and Western or Faustian—he concentrated his attentions on the Classical, the Magian, and the Faustian cultures. Of the eight cultures he depicted, all were dead or in decline. Spengler broke from any adherence to the Hegelian perspective of the dialectical path of history by presenting his cultures as wholes unto themselves. He recognized no real cyclical spiral to history within which individual cultures progress and give way to one another. Instead a culture exists in a closed circle; it emerges sui generis and follows a terminal circle in its self-actualization. Like Flinders-Petrie, however, Spengler adopted a naturalistic perspective that emphasized the contemporaneous stages of cultural progression.[66] So that, while history has no unity in itself, cultures progress homologously within their own closed life cycles. In this Spengler seems relatively shortsighted when compared to his predecessor Vico, whose theory of historical returns did not preclude the dialectical movement of world history as a whole.

As one might expect from his propositions concerning the centrality of the cultural symbol and the destiny of its expression, Spengler did not write a world history of events or even personalities but of abstracted images, from their inception to their dissolution. The Classical or Apollonian Greco-Roman culture had as its prime symbol the strictly self-contained body; this was expressed throughout the range of its cultural forms from statuary and architecture to Apollonian "mechanical statics" and geometry, to a sense of bounded time, of living in the instant, to the cult of the Greek gods exclusively bound to particular localities, the Doric column, and the self-contained city-state.[67] While the world picture of Apollonian culture was of a pure present with no direction or goal in its sense of time, to Magian or Arabian culture world space and world time were cavernlike, having a surveyable history bounded by creation and a known future. God acts within history, within the battles of light and darkness, between angels and devils; in the end the cavern may be destroyed, as Jesus prophesied or as the Chaldeans envisioned, as a series of cavern universes being born and dying. In the Magian cave, duty is in a "will-less resignation," as in "Islam" ("submission"), of the I to the we.[68] Magian culture had its first premonitions in the inchoate rise of mystery religions of the Near East around 700 B.C. By 300 B.C. a metaphysical current of "last things" had entered the Magian consciousness based on the prime symbol of the cavern and maintained by the apocalyptic myths of the end of the world, the last judgment, heaven and hell, and a belief in resurrection. The spring of Magian culture occurred in a third period, one of almost unbelievable religious intensity, homologous to the Faustian Gothic period or the Vedic period in India, where Christianity formed and broke into an efflorescence of movements such as those of the Monophysites, Roman Catholics, and Nestorians. By A.D. 200 the Magian soul had coalesced into a "dualism of two mysterious substances, spirit and soul"; this dualism was the basis for the Magian accomplishments of the Neoplatonists, the Gnostics, the Manichaeans, and the Jewish authors of the Talmud.[69] By A.D. 500, with the reign of Justinian, Magian religions had frozen into their characteristic forms and springtime was over; the last significant formation, Islam, was but an "outward" religion. Although in Islam Magian religion finally shook off classical forms and influence, having occurred when the spring was over it could not create anything appreciably new or "inner" but only follow and harden into earlier forms.[70]

The Faustian soul is of the north, of the dark, endless primeval forests of Germany. Western man is keyed to time, he lives in becoming, in the striving of the will to infinity; this figures in the clock and bell tower of his cities, the teleology of his religion and science, his quest for salvation and the ethic of psychological analysis that goes with it, his mathematical sense of the infinitely small and large, his artistic expression of perspective, distance, and depth. The prime symbol of Faustian culture is that of infinite extension; it reaches its highest expression in chamber music but is integrally entwined with all its artistic, philosophic, and political aspirations and even in the psychological aspirations of individuals as the " 'I' becomes the center of force in the Faustian sentence."[71]

Each civilization, in Spengler's view, has its own morale, an intellectual interpretation of life that assigns good and evil into particular categories; the modern Western morale was a socialistic one, in an ethical if not an economic sense—it becomes economic only with the 'last men' of culture. This socialism is inherent in the basic premise of the culture that "everything is in motion with an aim," and the very sense that action in the world can be ameliorative. Spengler sees this sense even in Nietzsche whose command, through the voice of Zarathustra, was for a reform of man according to *his* image: it is only the

Faustian who can have any moral imperative; there are no classical reformers. In his call for a "general transvaluation" Spengler holds that even Nietzsche acted in terms of the cultural idiom of "ethical mono-theism" that in practice is socialism—"All World Improvers are Socialists."[72]

Following Nietzsche, Spengler held that modern men live in a sea of becoming as opposed to the ahistorical Greek immersion in being; to him, by about A.D. 1000 the "mother becoming" was symbolized in art and religion as woman par excellence; she is time and destiny.[73] From this Gothic springtime, Faustian culture proceeded along the course of all cultures into the realization of itself in the world; it achieved a progressive actualization in the movements of the Renaissance, the Reformation, and the Baroque to reach its culmination and end point in the music of Bach, Handel, Haydn, Mozart, and Beethoven. Spengler posited 1800 as the "frontier of Civilization," where culture gave way to colossalism and theatricality within the old forms but lacked the creative spark of historical life inspiring it. The last Faustian arts died with Wagner's *Tristan* at Bayreuth, after which art could only be symbolism put in a pot and boiled all together and then "recast in wholly inorganic forms."[74]

Even now, however, as the West approached its period of Caesarism and its decadent "second religiosity," the Faustian man had an original task to perform; the hallmark of Faustian culture is its ability to discern the direction of its history. In Spengler himself there is a culmination as, for the first time, the entire cycle is envisioned by a "Faust-eye." We can see inevitable destiny as it approaches, and, with a "strong pessimism," act out our tragic roles to the last.[75]

Like Nicholai Danilevsky, whose sense of organic cultural life cycles was remarkably similar to Spengler's, he held that each culture was unique and could not be transmitted to another people, but he claimed that by "pseudomorphosis" a culture's phenomenal expressions could be distorted into the patterns of another culture.[76] This is the very antithesis of any theory of progress by diffusion. In historical pseudo-morphosis an older culture overlapped with a younger culture, and as a result the emergent culture failed to achieve its own self-consciousness.[77] The classic examples of pseudomorphosis that Spengler used were those of the Magian culture, which was distorted for most of its existence by the elements of Classical culture suffused in it, and that of the nascent Russian culture, which was presently suspended under the influence of the dominant West.[78] Russian Petrinism was a distortion of its destiny; Spengler saw the Bolshevik Revolution as the final straw of this pseudomorphosis, of Western social philosophy in its civilization phase. Marxism was to Spengler a "weapon for decaying megapolitan souls, an expression for rotting blood," which, he predicted as early as 1919, would be replaced by a new form of tsarism. Like Danilevsky, however, Spengler thought that the future, after the downfall of the West, belonged to the Slavs; he believed that Dostoyevsky's mysticism epitomized the autochthonous symbol of the boundless plain of Russia, and he forecast that "to Dostoyevsky's Christianity the next thousand years will belong."[79] He later warned, however, that the pseudomorphosis of Bolshevik nihilism might be retained and Russia not achieve its religious destiny as a "Third Rome"; it might instead turn outward, against the West, in response to Western (most likely German) aggression—but this would be "disastrous" for both sides.[80]

In the interim between the breakthrough of authentic Russian culture and the dissolution of the West, Spengler forecast a period of contending states in the West for the last struggle of Faustian universalization, that of world conquest. The Western tendency to infinite expansion in all realms of culture turned to the economic realm with the exhaustion of its other cultural channels, seeking to turn the whole world into a "single colonial and economic system"; this is a final product of the Faustian sense of infinity, first transposed into will, force, and deed.[81] In the end, success goes to the people or nation that can hold onto its cultural unity, its inheritance, and its native will to conquer. The victor will be the state most "in form," able to unite and maintain itself in tune with its essence. "Good form" is the replication of "the beat of a given species of being" and the maintenance of a living tradition of nobility.[82] It is also action in tune with the times; to Spengler all possibilities of Faustian philosophy, metaphysics, active religion, music, and the arts had been realized, and there was no avenue left for the will except that of the pursuit of power through technics and militancy.[83] As society turned away from reason and men sought faiths, new charismatic leaders—Caesars—would overthrow the powers of the monied interests and usher in a last glorious epoch of war or, through politics, "the continuation of war by intellectual means."[84]

In *The Decline of the West* Spengler's perspective on the ominous development of technology and economic growth was similar if more fateful to that in the work of Lewis Mumford. Both included in their definition of technics not simply human technology but also the human intentions behind it, its use in practice, and the system of thought upon which it was built.[85] Spengler felt that, historically, "true belief has regarded the machine as the devil." In the twilight of the West, Faustian civilization was dominated by a cancerous growth, a product of the machine, which had its own imperatives.[86] Modern culture had reached an unprecedented level of activity, and the earth trembled beneath it. The Faustian extension of the will to power over nature would cause future generations to see this as an era when nature was tottering and mankind modeled himself on his tools, a "slave of his creation." The dominance of the machine for Spengler, as for Henry Adams, symbolized the "deposition of God"; Faustian secular progressivism after the destruction of all of its sacred myths conceives "the idea of the machine" as a vehicle to Godness![87] The Faustian bargain with technological and economic growth, so familiar in current ecological parlance, was for Spengler a last result of the Faustian drive to infinite extension in all areas; it was inevitably doomed to failure. In time he believed that even the high priests of technocratic culture, the engineering elite, would come to see a "Satanism" in their creation; in some future generation these leading minds of society "will find their soul's health more important than all the powers in this world," and the mysticism of second religiosity would bring on an abrupt collapse of the intellectual and economic will of the Faustian culture-soul.[88] In his later work Spengler took the apocalyptical image of mechanized civilization further by pointing out the result of the mechanized order on the environment. He described species and productive land loss and claimed that Faustian civilization was destroying the organic world; "an artificial world is impermeating and poisoning the natural."[89] There is a sense here that the tragedy of Faustian decline somehow culminates the tragedy of the race as a whole; machine dominance of modern life is unprecedented. This idea is furthered in his examination of how technics developed in the West were being appropriated by the "colored world revolution" of rising peoples in precivilized areas on the periphery, who in the end would rise up against their former exploiters and shatter the last bastion of Faustian culture, the economic system. Then, according to Spengler, Faustian technics, rooted in the now-spent culture-soul, would be cast aside and forgotten—this again is destiny.[90]

After the enormous success of the first volume of *The Decline* Spengler wrote a manifesto for the future that expressed his ideals in political terms. In "Prussianism and Socialism," a work that was to be more popular than *The Decline*, Spengler defined the Germanic soul as one dominated by a "Prussian instinct" wherein "power belongs to the totality" and "each citizen is assigned his place in the totality. He receives his orders and obeys them. . . . This is authoritarian socialism."[91] This Germanic destiny would roll over any who opposed it; socialism would fulfill the German destiny even as it manifested itself in a hierarchical order of the all-powerful *Staat* ruled by a new class of "socialistic mastertypes."[92] Clearly his call resonated strongly with other Germanic voices of the period as diverse as Hitler and Rosenberg, Langbehn and Moeller van den Bruck.

Spengler voted for Hitler in April 1932 and then again in July; he and his sisters hung flags with swastikas from their windows. In 1934

Spengler claimed that no one detested the revolution of 1918 with greater fervor; at the same time "no one can have looked forward to the national revolution of this year [1933] with greater longing than myself."[93] He wrote *The Hour of Decision* as a "danger signal"; the times demanded action, "through the living example and moral self-discipline of a ruling class, not by a flow of words or force." Germany was the key country in the world, it must lead in the new age of contention, it must be the foundation of the coming *imperium mundi* that would rise out of the present world war age of transition.[94] While he criticized the Nazi party for its racism and the vulgar mass politics in which it engaged, Spengler's call for a führer was unequivocal.[95] He felt that "Hitler is a fool, but one must support the movement."[96]

Spengler's relations with the Nazi party were ambiguous. With the Nazi accession to power, Spengler was recognized as an intellectual predecessor of the party and was offered a chair at the University of Leipzig. He refused it. As early as 1927 Spengler wrote to a friend that he had stood aloof from the Nazis and had attempted to prevent the Munich putsch. He condemned Nazi tactics claiming that "politics should be based on sober facts and considerations and not on a romanticism of the feelings."[97] While he agreed with a good part of their program and arguably had contributed to their success with his negative views of parliamentary government, his assertions of the inevitability of a new Caesarism, and his call for a "Prussian Socialism," Spengler was averse to Nazi racism and the romantic emotionalism of the movement. He believed that the Nazis, particularly Hitler, were not aristocratic enough; they were voices from the mob. After a meeting with Hitler at Bayreuth in July 1933 (where he was overwhelmed for an hour and a half) Spengler felt that Hitler was a "very decent fellow, but . . . one doesn't feel for a second that he's significant."[98] Spengler sent Hitler his *The Hour of Decision* three weeks after their meeting: with its condemnation of plebeian politics, flags, and slogans, the book could not, if it were read at all, have pleased the Führer. In February of that year Goebbels had written to Spengler asking him for a preelection article "to be handed by me to the Press for further circulation" on the Germanic struggle for honor and position that the Nazi party was leading. Spengler replied: "I have never yet taken part in election propaganda and neither shall I do so in the future"—though he agreed that he would write what *he* thought if the government would cease its "unmeasured attacks on him."[99] In March Spengler was again courted by the Nazi hierarchy. He refused Goebbels's invitation to go on the radio on the evening of the ceremony at the Garrison Church in Potsdam, which symbolized the Nazi reconciliation with the Prussian past.[100] In October Goebbels worked out a late and poorly organized banning of *The Hour of Decision*. Ultimately it was difficult to reconcile Spengler's deterministic cycles and his postulate that a period of two centuries of Caesarism was all that was left for Western culture with the more optimistic Nazi premises that echoed Moeller van den Bruck's perspective on the Germans as a young people who had a long future ahead.[101] In 1934 Gunther Grundel voiced the party's sentiments in *Jahre Der Überwindung* (Years of Overcoming), which condemned Spengler's fatalism as "laming" the people's minds and will even as the Nazis led a Germanic "Resurrection."[102] That same year the Rohm Purge of the S.A., led by Himmler and Goring, devastated Spengler; friends and acquaintances whose political views were relatively congenial to his own, like Gustav von Kahr, Gregor Strasser, and Willi Schmidt, were assassinated.[103] His allegiance now clear, Spengler took the symbolic step of breaking his ties with Nietzsche's sister and the Nietzsche Archive over their support for the regime. Elizabeth Forster-Nietzsche wrote to Spengler with an irony and a sense of implied responsibility that must have infuriated him: "Does not our sincerely honored Führer have the same ideal and values for the Third Reich, as you have expressed in *Prussianism and Socialism*?"[104] In the end Spengler's name was banned from the radio, he was effectively silenced, and he died in 1936 of a heart attack, at home in Munich, a lonely and embittered man.

• • •

In criticizing Spengler's work one must start with his claim that he fulfilled the work of Nietzsche and applied Goethe's system of thought to world history: in his words, "Goethe gave me method, Nietzsche the questioning faculty."[105] Spengler was what Walter Kaufmann referred to as a "hard Nietzschean";[106] he held that history was a long tragic struggle; "this battle *is* life—life, indeed, in the Nietzschean sense, a grim, pitiless, no-quarter battle of the Will to Power" in which "ideals are cowardice."[107] To Spengler, the fight for existence in the face of this struggle, even though an essentially meaningless and hopeless task, is ennobling, it is the "*amor fati*" of Nietzsche. To him, the overman in a late cultural period can only be an amoral power seeker and not a seeker of truth or explorer of consciousness.

In an address on "Nietzsche and his Century" given on Nietzsche's eightieth birthday in 1924 at the Nietzsche Archive, Spengler put himself forward as a successor whose vision of history acted as a completion of Nietzsche's thought. He asserted that before Nietzsche "no one knew of the tempo of history" and no one had exposed the "rhythmic sequence of ages cultures and attitudes" that have no logic or goal. No one had recognized the universal causal principle in

history, the Will to Power.[108] Along with his praise Spengler commu-
nicated a sense that Nietzsche only needed a Spengler to fulfill his
vision of history as a "symphony." Clearly, Spengler did begin with
the questions that Nietzsche articulated. Yet even in his rejection of
progress and "scientific history" with its supposed objectivity and
"will-less knower" and his attempt to circumvent or forget the meaningless data of history in favor of a perspective on the essences of his
eight specific cultures, Spengler confused Nietzsche's historical categories of the monumental and the unhistorical and fell far short of
what Nietzsche meant when he sought the superhistorical as an antidote to historicism. Ultimately, Spengler mixed his metaphors and
erred in blending Goethe's physiognomic perspective on Nature with
Nietzsche's superhistorical perspective on being as opposed to becoming to produce a historical work that abused the best ideas of either
man.

Arguably, Nietzsche applied his sense of eternal recurrence metaphorically in maintaining an eternal repetition of historical events, but
he envisioned through this symbolization a superhistorical level of
being, outside of history, a Dionysian moment that the historical
perspective makes pass. From this perspective one can view Spengler's
effort as a bastardization of Nietzsche's essentially personal and experiential sense of time. A look at Nietzsche's understanding of the
superhistorical is helpful:

> By the word "unhistorical" I mean the power, the art, of *forgetting* and of
> drawing a limited horizon round oneself. I call the power "super-histori-
> cal" which turns the eyes from the process of becoming to that which
> gives existence an eternal and stable character—to art and religion. Sci-
> ence—for it is science that makes us speak of "poisons"—sees in these
> powers contrary powers; for it considers only that view of things to be
> true and right, and therefore scientific, which regards something as
> finished or historical, not as continual and eternal. Thus it lives in deep
> antagonism toward the powers that make for eternity—art and religion—
> for it hates the forgetfulness that is the death of knowledge, and tries to
> remove all limitation of horizon and cast men into an infinite boundless
> sea whose waves are bright with the clear knowledge of—becoming![109]

Surely Spengler has not gone beyond recurrent becoming! His sense
of destiny can hardly serve as ground in place of Nietzsche's eternally
unfinished art and religion. His history would have been abhorrent to
Nietzsche, both in its fatalism, which by its deterministic (if relativistic) sense of time and place restricts individual possibilities of "overcoming" history, and in his misplaced perspective on overcoming itself

as a process of political, and in the Faustian context, Germanic empow-
erment. According to Ernst Stutz, Spengler's metahistory is a projection of his personal political intentions upon the history of the world
as a whole covered over by a patina of naturalistic determinism.[110] In
spite of the transformations of Nietzsche's work accomplished by
Elizabeth Förster-Nietzsche and the proto-Nazi Nietzsche Archive that
so colored Spengler's view of Nietzsche, we know that Nietzsche had
no faith in a particularly German destiny but was a "good
European."[111]

While Spengler asserted that human beings must act in accordance
with their destiny, Nietzsche held that man must justify himself aesthetically, he must "say yes to life" through art, and further, he must
do this throughout the movement of a culture; decadence is eternally
recurrent in that it crops up as a feature of *all* times. Nietzsche
condemned the conscience that supplies a false dichotomy of good and
evil—to him this rose out of a sense of a fixed past and a fixed future.
While Spengler's moral invocation is to act in terms of one's time and
place, or destiny, Nietzsche's call is to act ahistorically in the artistic
expression of one's nature.[112] Nietzsche condemned Christianity as
dominated by the "will to deny life" and the "will to destruction," "a
secret instinct" that foreshadowed Freud's death instinct; surely, from
Nietzsche's perspective this instinct is the dominant motif in Spengler's
cultural eschatology.[113] Spengler has no place for Nietzsche's Dionysian joy; as Hans Barth has put it, after reducing Nietzsche to the
historical and the political, "nothing remained of the promise of a new
salvation through a life-affirming ethic."[114]

Spengler's sense of cultural morphology is, as we have seen, modeled
on Goethe's perspective on scientific morphology. While Spengler was
able to apply the morphology of Goethe's study of plants almost
directly as a dominant metaphor in his world history and relied on
Goethe's morphology of Epochs of the Spirit, he differed in his
orientation from Goethe who, like his mentor Herder, saw cosmic
processes as essentially teleological.[115] Spengler's Faust is more like
Marlowe's than Goethe's; in the end he is damned. Whereas Nietzsche
opposed ceaseless Faustian striving (in time) with his perspective of
ahistorical being, Spengler accepted Goethe's perpetual becoming but
desacralized the process and damned it to ultimate historical
disintegration.

Over the years Spengler's metahistory has been attacked on all
fronts. Christopher Dawson has convincingly demonstrated that the
origins of a civilization embrace myths and epics from a variety of
cultural sources; modern civilization is not just Germanic.[116] The
obvious corollary to this criticism is that cultures cannot exist as

watertight compartments that spring out of nowhere by spontaneous parthenogenesis; this perspective abstracts culture out of a wider world historical process.[117] Hans Barth has rejected Spengler's epistemological perspective of taking his prime symbol as a mythical substructure that leaves intellection as merely a reflection, or as a superstructure. He believes that Spengler simply invented an abstraction from discrete units of evidence and then used it to locate and judge these same bits and pieces of evidence.[118] R. G. Collingwood was an early critic who ridiculed Spengler's organicism, his "unsound" perspective on pseudomorphosis—which holds that one culture can only impact another to its detriment—and his attempt to "characterize a culture by means of a single idea or tendency" and, even worse, to make baseless predictions from such pseudoscientific premises.[119] According to another early critic, Don August Messer, it is absurd to posit that cultures are bound to a mother landscape and cannot spread or move to other environments. Messer also argued that people can use their intellects to solve problems that are important beyond their own cultural circle and times. Messer concluded in 1922 that Spengler's predictions of cultural decay were unfounded but that they could contribute to such a decline.[120]

Spengler is also criticized for his nihilistic perspective on the nature of man. Heller condemns Spengler as a "false prophet": "The image of man which lurks behind Spengler's vast historical canvas is perverted, and could only be accepted by a hopelessly perverted age."[121] Alfred Kroeber has called Spengler an "Expressionist" whose temperament "verges on the pathological." To him *The Decline* manifests "needless exaggerations, dogmatism, vehemence of conviction, blind spots, [and an] inability to balance evidence."[122] Martin Brauun noted that Spengler gave the Nazis "historical credentials" and was in active league with the irrational and destructive forces of his time.[123] Vermeil noted how Spengler's sense of pseudomorphosis and the need for renewal of good form for Germanic culture fit well with the Nazi effort to eliminate Magian corruptions of Faustian culture, particularly those of democracy, egalitarian socialism, and the corrupting Magian peoples, especially the Jews; in the end Spengler's "cultural anti-semitism" gave way before Hitler's materialistic and Darwinian view.[124] Adorno condemned Spengler's surrender to fate (*Schicksal*); he attacked Spengler's error of inventing an absolutist conception of nature that "he was prepared to defend against the elements of reason and enlightenment."[125] Clearly Spengler's perspective on nature and history as a single process of physiognomic rise and fall is a naturalistic myth modeled unconsciously on the Teutonic myths that Spengler, like Wagner, found at the source of Germanic culture. In the end Spengler prophesied *Götterdammerung*, an apocalypse without a millennium or salvation, not only for Faustian culture but for world history as a whole.[126]

Spengler's cyclical perspective on civilizations and their homologous contemporaneity can also be seen, however, as a positive contribution to dialogue. Seen as a heuristic device, the theory broadened the contemporary view of world history; Spengler is correct in claiming that he made a Copernican revolution by opening a discourse into the parallels between world cultures and shattering the complacent linear model of ancient, medieval, and modern continuity. As Ernst Stutz points out, Spengler also laid the foundation for a broad and interdisciplinary perspective on politics and the social sciences by demonstrating that politics, religion, art, and history are interrelated parts of an integrated cultural whole rather than isolated systems.[127] His insightful if pessimistic perspective on the machine of the modern social order and its technics is a central concern of world historians up to the present. Spengler's relativism, extreme though it was, opened a broad perspective on alternative ways of seeing among world cultures and to some extent established the inherent validity of other cultural perspectives. To Spengler, one could only understand a people by seeing it in its own terms.

In the end, Spengler's attempt to produce a Nietzschean world history failed. He erred in retaining a holistic pseudoscience alongside a determinism of human action that left room in the future for only the lowest common denominators of human action. In his pontifications on the future tragic glories of the German nation, Spengler reverted to the antiworld of his childhood fantasies and the waking dreams of his adult life. His apocalyptic predictions, accurate as some of them proved to be, were based as much on his own *Weltangst* and anger, even hatred, against a world in which he felt he had no place as they were on actual historical events. In an age of Caesars, Spengler was a misplaced metaphysician, an epic poet in an era that, according to his theory, could only grasp facts. His deterministic predictions were projected wishes, expressions of the author's "being expressed in words," more than they were results of careful historical scholarship.

Even his detractors have recognized the accuracy of some of Spengler's forecasts, and as penetrating a reviewer as he is, H. Stuart Hughes has called the *The Decline* the "nearest thing we have to a key to our times."[128] Spengler took heroic vitalism to an end point from which he could envision no hopeful future except in escapist mysticism and the glories of war. His nihilism reversed Schopenhauer's pessimism to make it active, directional, Germanic. Not only did he typify the pervasive groundlessness and despair over civilization in interwar Germany, he also embodied the antihistory of modernism with its relativism, its experiential and anti-intellectual biases, and its fundamental rejection of the positivist world system and the ideology of progress. As works of destruction Spengler's writings have acted as a fundamental challenge to any meaningful world perspective in the twentieth century. After Spengler, world historians were forced to rebuild world history, to rescue continuity, direction, and an ideology of progress. *The Decline of the West* demanded an answer, and much of the writing of world history in our century has been an attempt to provide one, by the resacralization of the world and the reaffirmation of meaning beyond the determined individual and the Will to Power.

CHAPTER   FOUR

The Religious Premises
and Goals of Arnold Toynbee's
World History

Tous les grand empires que nous avon vus sur la terre ont concouru par
divers moyens au bien de la Religion et la gloire de Dieu, comme Dieu
même l'a déclaré par ses prophètes.
—Bishop Bossuet[1]

When we are investigating the relations between the facts of history, we
are trying to see God through History with our Intellects.
—Arnold J. Toynbee[2]

THE FUROR HAS DIED DOWN. The intellectual and religious
passions that inspired vituperative condemnation, sarcastic ridicule,
and even occasional cultish mythicizing have all withered with the
death of Arnold Toynbee in 1975. His massive opus, *A Study of History*,
is rarely read with the enthusiastic immersion of the inspired or
converted but remains like a bombed-out cathedral shell, a monument
to his faith. Toynbee's goals in writing his epic began with the ideal of
a "synoptic view of history" and grew into an effort at regrounding
historical consciousness in the sacred to educate and inspire individuals
in the selflessness of the saints and thereby lead civilization through
the 'shadow of death' of modernism into a new age unified by an
integrated world religious faith.[3]
    Toynbee's importance in the field of twentieth-century thought can
scarcely be exaggerated. There has been perhaps no other historian in
the century able to master as extensive a wealth of historical detail from
such a far-flung variety of civilizations, no more cohesive and thorough
an applied paradigm of universal history, no more dramatic expression
of the present crisis facing the world and the West, and no more
ambitious study of the interrelationship between religious and secular
history. As much as any other single historian of the twentieth century,
Toynbee contributed to the modern view of cultural relativism and to
our conception of civilizations as independent historical entities living
out their own valid cultural experience rather than as people to be
enlightened in civilization by the modern West.

Toynbee's ambitions took him into the metaphysical, the metahistorical, as his field of study progressively opened up to include all of God's
creation. Even as the scope of his search for historical laws widened,
however, Toynbee sought to root the ultimate responsibility for the
creative action that determines historical destiny in the free will of
individuals to make moral decisions. To Toynbee, the human community progresses in mimesis of the macroscopic whole of God's universe,
and the locus of this motion is in the individual human soul reaching
toward a bridge between the two. In his explication of his empirical
epistemology, Toynbee affirmed that meaning preceded his enumeration of historical specifics and, in effect, made details into useful facts.[4]
Toynbee sought to break through modern relativism by testing a priori
intuitively conceived patterns through the multiplication of historical
instances that seemed to document them. In this way he could discover
universals in the behavior of civilizations and, more important, reveal
the evolving relationship between the lower world of civilized men and
the higher realm of truth perceivable "through a glass darkly" by
"mystically inspired personalities" who are the natural leaders in the
advancing movement of human civilization.[5]

Early in the writing of his *Study* Toynbee held that the relativity of
all things pursued by humanity in time governed all action, "including
the study of history itself," yet it masked "an underlying unity."
Civilizations are "philosophically equivalent"; they are "all representatives of a single species and are engaged upon an identical enterprise."[6]
Through yang action in the world, they advance to a new stage of
synthesis in a dialectical reversion to the yin and so climb ledge by
ledge up a common cliff. Each resting point is ephemeral; by leading
to a new challenge each ledge will provoke a new effort, or, in failing
to do so, will lead to the ossification of a death-in-life arrestation or an
abortion of its "birthright" ending in a reversion to insectlike order
and animalism. Despite the variety of challenges that face particular
peoples in particular environments, the unity of their response is "to
create something Superhuman out of primitive Human Nature."[7] In
his first three volumes of *A Study of History* (1933) Toynbee articulated
the "true goal" and universal goal of all peoples, which would "only be
attained when the whole of society has come to consist of individuals
of the new species which is represented by the Saints alone in human
history up to date."[8] In fact, the sainthood of humanity at large
through the mimesis of past and future examples is humanity's only
salvation in a disunited age with increasingly apocalyptic possibilities.
Toynbee's eschatology is seemingly left in the muddle of this endless
progression of cliffs and ledges alongside his cyclical view of the rise
and inevitable decline of civilizations and his ecstatic pronunciations,

which became increasingly emphatic in time, on humanity's progressive spiritual destiny.[9] Perhaps the only way to see through his mixture of ends is to separate, rather arbitrarily as he did, humanity's religious ends, which are progressive and hold the hope of some final salvation, from the historically cyclical path of secular civilizations. Civilizations can then be seen as the vehicles of religions in this world that can only approximate a transcendental order. They are always left challenged by the necessity to follow an eternal model against the vicissitudes inherent in mundane existence, which will overcome them in the end.

Toynbee's personal goal in his intellectual life and in the writing of the *Study* corresponded to what he proclaimed to be "human nature's goal":

> Its goal is to transcend the intellectual and moral limitations that its relativity imposes on it. Its intellectual goal is to see the Universe as it is in the sight of God, instead of seeing it with the distorted vision of one of God's self-centered creatures. Human Nature's moral goal is to make the self's will coincide with God's will.[10]

In taking this position seriously in the final definition of his field of study, Toynbee overstepped human intellectual limitations. After elimination of the city-state or nation-state as an "intelligible field of study," Toynbee first chose civilizations and their cycles of birth and decline as meaningful objects of study. In time, Toynbee found this level inadequate, as but a step toward a view of the role of civilizations as vehicles for the progression of the 'higher religions,' which, in a world unifying under the auspices of the now dominant Western civilization, could result in a unified religious world order—clearly an ultimate goal of Toynbee's eschatology. Behind these historical aspects of "God's Commonwealth" are the actions of God Himself in history. Ultimately, the "intelligible field of study" for Toynbee must include the actions of the Creator; "Man's Oikemene only becomes intelligible when it is recognized as being a fragment of God's universe," as a progressive reflection, in the historical dimension, of the City of God.[11] Toynbee's effort is unprecedented in the twentieth century. He not only sought to define the historical cycles of all civilizations to date, but in the end he transcended them with his view of religious progress and attempted, in an analysis that employed a vast wealth of both cross-cultural mythological illustration and erudite empirical compilation of historical detail, to resurrect an Augustinian historical view of the worldly mimesis of the heavenly city through the mystical apperception of the eternal by creative individuals. Toynbee presented this vision as a challenge, a moral call to action, and as an imperative that might offer the only hope for the salvation of individual souls in the modern world and indeed for the survival of the City of Man itself.

• • •

Arnold J. Toynbee was born in 1889 in London and was named for his uncle Arnold Toynbee, whose fame as a historian of the "industrial revolution," social efforts toward bridging the classes, and early death at the age of thirty provided a legacy to young Arnold.[12] The dominant influence on Toynbee's youth was his mother; a staunch Anglican and patriot, she was also a historian. Her Scottish tales and stories of ancient adventure gave Toynbee an early appreciation for the historical narrative of exotic peoples and places. Toynbee's father was employed as a social worker for the Charity Organization Society and earned too meager an income for the family to afford to rent a home independently. They had no choice but to live with Arnold's uncle Harry, a retired sea captain who had written a tome on the idolization of self as the "Basest Thing in the World." In this household Toynbee was raised an orthodox Anglican, "soaked in the bible at an impressionable age," and consequently, "the biblical view of history, stayed with me throughout my life."[13]

The family's financial limitations left any possibility of a higher education for Arnold dependent upon his own scholastic merit. Toynbee was something of a prodigy; he avoided sports and, in what his biographer William McNeill has called a "desolate loneliness," applied himself vigorously to his schoolwork at Wooten Court in Kent to achieve an extraordinary school record and, in 1907, a Balliol scholarship.[14] At Oxford Toynbee questioned his inherited faith and found it wanting; he could not accept the intolerant doctrine of a jealous God and what he saw as the religious accretions on a spiritual vision. He never regained a faith in any one church but remained a religious outsider who converted from his collegiate atheism by 1930 to a view of "Love is God," where love, though divine, was not omnipotent but must battle forever in a Manichaean dualism against evil and death.[15]

In his time at Oxford, Toynbee was confronted by some of the grandest experiences of his life, as well as some of the most painful. In 1909 Toynbee's father went insane and had to be hospitalized—he was to remain in an institution until he died in 1940. His father's breakdown left Toynbee with a lifelong fear for his own sanity; he left the duties of visiting and overseeing the care of his father almost entirely to his sisters and his mother. In 1911 Toynbee won the prestigious Jenks Prize, which allowed him to escape his books and family troubles to travel in Greece and Rome for most of a year. In his travels he tramped over three thousand miles through Greece and had three experiences of "visionary communion with the past." At Cynocephalae in Greece, Toynbee saw in his mind's eye the 197 B.C. battle between Macedonia and Rome. Then, coming upon an abandoned Venetian villa in Crete, he experienced a transcendental feeling for the passage of empires and an inspiration that a similar fate must unfold for Britannia. Again, at the Morcote Citadel of Momenvasia, Toynbee felt the presence of a living past and an equivalent present meeting. Toynbee's Greek wanderings ended when he contracted dysentery, which in his later writings he always claimed saved him from death in the First World War.[16] On his return from Greece in 1912 Toynbee received the high honor of a position as a Balliol Don in ancient history. Back at Oxford, Toynbee renewed his acquaintance with Rosalind Murray, the daughter of one of his mentors, Gilbert Murray, and married her not long after the onset of World War I.

When the war came Toynbee, immersed in the history of ancient Greece, came to an intellectual insight through reading Thucydides that echoed the mystical impressions he had in Greece. He suddenly realized that Thucydides had "anticipated our experiences," that somehow the two eras were contemporary, that the internecine warfare of parochial sovereignties that occurred in the Peloponnesian War and in the modern Western world war contained equivalent historical patterns. Toynbee later claimed that out of the "binocular vision" that resulted from these reflections, the "patterns and regularities which you find in my *Study* emerged empirically."[17]

Toynbee's experiences during wartime provided a survivor guilt that suffused his later writings. In his autobiographical works, Toynbee continually referred to the fact that fully half of his schooltime contemporaries were killed in the trenches of France.[18] The real suffering that his memories of those dead caused him acted as a personal challenge that spurred his life's work. In later life he claimed that World War I made the abolition of war his primary goal. William H. McNeill has documented that Toynbee, to evade military sevice in 1914, obtained a doctor's certificate stating that he would probably have a recurrence of dysentery if he were to serve in combat. Toynbee took this certificate when he volunteered knowing that it would prevent him from enlisting. In 1915 Toynbee again went to a doctor for similar documentation; when that doctor refused to give him such a certificate, Toynbee went for a second opinion in order to obtain it. Later, in 1916 and 1917, Toynbee got further exemptions from service by persuading his superiors at the propaganda unit where he was employed to certify that his work on Turkish atrocities was vital to the war effort. The contradiction between the heroic ideal that he espoused in his teaching on Greece and the deaths of those who did serve gave Toynbee a deep sense of survivor's guilt that, McNeill plausibly speculates, led to his obsessive work habits, first in the propaganda department and later at the Chatham House and on his *Study*.[19] Toynbee admitted to a compulsion to work, to the exclusion of his personal life; he was unhappy when he was not employed on a project, and his work was driven, at least in part, by an anxiety of conscience.[20]

Like H. G. Wells, Toynbee saw World War I as a forerunner of a cataclysmic struggle leading to a World State or to a future apocalyptic self-destruction. He dedicated his life to the prevention of future wars: "I must do all that I can to save my grandchildren and great-grandchildren from being overtaken by the fate that has criminally cut short the lives of so many of my contemporaries."[21] The war shattered Toynbee's faith in the unitary progress of civilization, and the peace process— which he observed as an advisor to the Political Intelligence Department—alienated him from the British political establishment in the short run and from nationalist parochialism in the long. After the war Toynbee returned to academia to take the Koraes chair in modern Greek and Byzantine history at King's College, but he never really took to teaching as a profession. After being forced to resign because of his criticism of postwar Greek atrocities against the Turks, he found his place in 1924 as the writer of the annual *Survey of International Affairs* put out by the British Institute of International Affairs at the Chatham House. The staff of the Chatham House conceived of its mission as working against the incidence of future wars through the education of public opinion.[22] Here for thirty-three years, Toynbee was responsible for a digestive exposition of each year's world history as it happened.

At the same time, inspired by the models of Polybius, Herodotus, Ibn Khaldun, and Augustine, Toynbee began his analytical elucidation of history as a whole.[23] Toynbee had conceived the outline of the *Study* in 1920 and had jotted down his major headings then much as they would be organized over the next thirty-four years. He was brought up short, however, when he discovered Spengler's efforts, which seemed to anticipate his own view of historical cycles. He quickly realized that Spengler's view of destiny did not explain either the growths of culture or their cyclical passage and he believed that the application of English empiricism to the growths and declines of civilizations would be more revealing and scientific.[24] By 1933 he was able to publish the first three volumes of his *A Study of History*; the next three volumes followed in 1939.

In the interwar years Toynbee was terribly disappointed with the failure of the League of Nations to take strong steps against the Italian invasion of Ethiopia in 1935–37. He came to see contemporary politics in increasingly eschatological terms with this failure of nerve of the league and with the rise of fascism and nazism culminating in the "natural epilogue" of Munich. Toynbee met with Rosenberg in 1934 and then with Hitler in February 1936, when he was lectured for two-and-a-quarter hours on the German needs for the unity of the Germanic peoples and lands, and on Hitler's role as a savior from the communist menace.[25] For a while he believed that war could be avoided; if only England made some positive move toward Germany Hitler would respond as a "Good European." William McNeill develops Toynbee's equivocations at length in his review of this period, demonstrating that Toynbee was neither the "intellectual ally of Hitler" as Trevor-Roper later claimed, nor an unequivocal appeaser. Instead Toynbee can be seen as subject to emotional and intellectual fluctuations. He anticipated a war that might bring the historically necessary World State, even as he was haunted by his memories of World War I and his pledge against war.[26] When the war finally came, Toynbee felt that it marked the end of the nationalistic epoch and the coming of the World State, either through force, in a Nazi victory, or by the united rising of the West to defeat Hitler. The war seemed likely to "sweep away barriers between classes and nations that looked, only a year ago, immovable."[27]

The period of the Second World War was one of great personal suffering for Toynbee, marked by health concerns, the suicide death of his eldest son, Tony, and the breakdown of his marriage. In the war Toynbee served as the head of the Foreign Research and Press Service, which condensed world news into a digested summary to fit the hectic schedules of policymakers. During the war, Toynbee worked harder than ever; in the tensions of his personal difficulties with Rosalind, he developed a facial tic and sleep disturbances. The war also led him into a deepened search for a sustaining faith, which drew him toward the security and authority of the Catholic Church and his friend Father Columba Cary-Elwes at the Ampleforth Abbey.[28] Rosalind had converted to Catholicism in 1932, and religion had been a central focus of their progressive estrangement. At the same time, the Church was a potent temptation to Toynbee during these years of suffering and uncertainty. In 1939 Toynbee's son Tony committed suicide by shooting himself. Rosalind had grown colder and more distant from Toynbee and his "nonsense book" over the years, and in 1942 she left him. Toynbee's concern for bringing Rosalind back subsequently became a single-minded obsession until he was able, partly through the aid of a psychoanalyst, to put aside all hopes of reconciliation. He finally divorced Rosalind in 1946 to marry Veronica Boulter, who had labored in his shadow as his indispensable aide in the production—and increasingly as a contributory writer and editor—of the *Survey of International Affairs*.[29]

Soon after the war, D. C. Somervell negotiated with Toynbee to work out a one-volume abridgment to his *Study* that summarized volumes 1 to 6. The abridgment came out in 1947 and was a tremendous hit, especially in the United States, where it was a best-seller. Toynbee became a world celebrity; Henry Luce put him on the cover of *Time* magazine, touting him as a prophet of a new world order, which he attempted to mesh with his own millennial vision of an 'American Century.' After the publication of volumes 7 to 10 in 1954, Toynbee retired from the Chatham House and went on a world tour in 1956–57. Public speaking engagements, controversy over the final four volumes of the *Study*, and the often harshly negative criticism he received after 1954 made Toynbee a figure of almost mythic proportions.[30] After the completion of the *Study* with his *Reconsiderations*, volume 12 (1961), Toynbee continued to write extensively; he produced several volumes on the crisis of the West and in defense of his paradigm of world history; he wrote period historical studies, such as his analysis of Hannibal's Legacy; he analyzed international relations, especially those between Russia and the United States. He also published several travel narratives and autobiographical sketches of places and people that he had known in his life. After the *Study* was complete, his religious concerns continued to dominate his work, although he became more pessimistic about the prospects of any immediate spiritual renewal. He continued to address himself to what he considered the central issues of the day; in the sixties these centered on the threat of nuclear confrontation, and by the seventies he was one of those who voiced concern about global ecology. In both these areas Toynbee saw crises of catastrophic dimensions in the making that could be avoided only through the spiritual transformation of individuals. Toynbee's views on the modern West will be examined in more detail, but first it is necessary to discuss his architecture of the long duration.

• • •

Only the bare-bones framework of the argument in Toynbee's massive theodicy will be examined herein, leaving aside almost entirely the wealth of historical documentation and mythological and poetic illustration that makes up much of the greatness of *A Study of History*. For our purposes, an outline can be more illuminating than a complete exposé, since our goal is to grasp Toynbee's evolving religious vision of history, rather than the enumeration of the historical details of particular civilizations, which he fit into his framework with varying degrees of success. Critics have emphasized the significance of Toynbee's religious shift in his 1954 publication of volumes 7 through 10. Clearly these works express a heightened religious passion and prophetic impulse. In the context of the work as a whole, however, these discontinuities are less essential than an evolving continuity; Toynbee's *Weltanschauung* was founded from the outset on a profound sense of spiritual dualism. This is clearly manifested even in the first three volumes of the *Study* in Toynbee's concern for the sacred and revelatory, in the way he multiplies his examples from world mythology to enumerate what are to him archetypal and underlying universal truths, in his apocalyptic and millennial anticipations and, most profoundly perhaps, in his perspective on the mystical process of human creativity. When Toynbee closed volume 3 (1933) with the injunction, "To Him return ye every one," he clearly was *not* consciously calling for a return to Christ and His Church, but he *was* closing on a note that expressed, for him, a universal truth and need, probably one for withdrawal and resacralization. If he did not express his final, full-blown vision of Christian and world religious syncretism, Toynbee did express a foreshadowing perspective of these later elements, sometimes recessively and at other times in the fore, as he propounded his theory of the geneses and growths of civilizations rooted in mystical creativity and the goal of human evolution of saintly supermen in ecumenical unity.[31]

Toynbee sought to exhibit the "life spans" of societies; to do so his first task was to define the living units of history, "the intelligible field of study," whose life would "resemble the successive experiences of a single person."[32] In a brief perusal of national histories Toynbee found them to be unintelligible as units outside of the larger "wholes" of which they were a part: civilizations.[33] After defining civilizations loosely as integral cultural wholes, Toynbee dramatically surveyed the history of the world to discover a total of twenty-one distinct representatives of this class: Western, Orthodox Christian (along with its Russian offshoot), Iranic, Arabic, Hindu and Far Eastern (broken into the discreet civilizations of Korea and Japan), Hellenic (including Roman), Syriac, Indic, Sinic, Minoan, Sumeric, Hittite, Babylonic, Andean, Mexic, Yucatec, Mayan, and Egyptiac.[34] As gestalts, these entities were originally seen as sufficient unto themselves; their geneses were, though in some cases affiliated, for the most part independent creations, and their progress toward an eventual disintegration followed internal imperatives and was not caused by external influences.

Toynbee rejected the then-current explanations of the genesis of civilization as due to racial or environmental determinism, like the diametrically opposed views of Houston Stewart Chamberlain and Ellsworth Huntington.[35] He insisted that causation was not to be found in the "Non-psychical domain of Nature" but went beyond the total geographic and social environment to include the directive force of the human will and intelligence in response to environmental or social challenges.[36] In this, Toynbee self-consciously aimed to supply a holistic pattern for world history that could respond to Marx; he claimed that "my outlook is the reverse of historical materialism."[37] The determinative factor in historical progression was not the impetus provided by the physical challenges and social readjustments inherent in the mode of production but in the psychological responses individuals made to material conditions. At the interface between physical conditions confronting a people and their response are psychological, even spiritual, variables that determine the nature of their responses in the end.[38] Toynbee disavowed determinism even as he sought historical "laws"; "Man is the master of his own destiny" and hence is morally responsible for the state of his society.[39]

Civilizations are formed in this encounter between "Challenge and Response," a dialectical yin/yang pulsation that runs throughout all nature. Toynbee insisted that he did not take the concept of challenge and response from the Darwinian view of the struggle for existence and the survival of the fittest or from Hegel's conception of the progressive dialectic, but from their common source in the Old Testament where Yahweh presented a series of challenges to his Chosen People to which a core of the enlightened responded in advancing God's purpose in the world.[40] Toynbee dramatized the challenges that disturb the yin immobility of primitive peoples by the use of myths that analogously illustrated the process of creation as he saw it. The challenging element in the world is compared to the serpent in Genesis, Satan in Milton and the book of Job, and Mephistopheles in Goethe's *Faust*, who identifies himself as "part of the force which would do evil evermore, and yet creates the Good."[41] God, being perfect, must accept the challenging foil of evil in the world in order to create.

In surveying the geneses of his original twenty-one models of civilization, Toynbee began with those he called the first generation of civilizations, which included the Sumeric, the Egyptiac, the Sinic, and later isolates like the Mayan and Andean civilizations, which came into being without precedent, "unaffiliated" with other cultural hegemonies. His classic paradigm for the rise of these civilizations is the Egyptiac case. The Nilotic civilization developed in response to the post–Ice Age challenge of the desiccation of the North African steppe, which left the choice of an adaptive nomadism or the conquest of the swamp and jungle environment of the Nile Valley to the North Africans. The response of the Egyptians, cultivating crops, using the Nile's periodic floods, and channeling the Nile in dry seasons for irrigation, marked their breakthrough into civilization. The problem of large-scale environmental management demanded a corresponding large-scale social organization.[42] The same pattern independently occurred on the Tigris and Euphrates in the genesis of the Sumeric civilization and on the Yellow River for the later Sinic civilization. For the Minoans, the challenge was that of the Aegean; the North African desertification prompted the *Volkwanderung* which, confronted by the sea, accepted its challenge.[43] The Mayans responded to the tropical rain forest while the Andeans had a poverty of soil and a bleak climate to stimulate them to a large-scale social order.[44] For the "second generation" of civilizations, those who had some previous model to respond to, the challenges combined environmental difficulties with those of the human environment in the breakdown of an old civilization or in the affiliative contact with a live one, to prompt a new model of cultural adaptation.

Toynbee used challenge and response as an almost universal explanatory metaphor both of the macrocosm of civilizations and the microcosm of individuals. The hard winters and rocky soils of New England toughened the men who conquered the American West. The swamps of Rome made it a stimulating environment. The penalization of slavery in North America provoked a positive black response in a revitalized Christianity (which may yet prove a model for a dying civilization). Religious repression stirred solidarity and deepened the faith of the Puritans and Mormons. Even "the long Hellenic intrusion on the Syriac domain" provoked a belated response, one no less powerful for having simmered unconscious for hundreds of years, in the Arab Islamic invasions.[45] The range of the activity of challenge and response can be categorized by the stimuli of "hard countries," of "new ground," of "blows," of "penalizations," and of "pressures," especially those of the marches, where a general rule holds that "the greater the pressure the greater the stimulus."[46] Toynbee relied here on the questionable assumption that challenges can be philosophically identical, varying only in the degree of severity, which will determine whether a civilization is capable of surviving them. His notion of the "Golden Mean of Challenge" is rather tautological: if a civilization survives then it has by definition met its challenge and been "stimulated to fulfill its nature" or birthright.[47] If it has not, then it may well leave no record of its failure except perhaps that of an unconquered jungle, mountain slope, or river and a primitive people stagnating in yin equilibrium.[48]

For individuals, and by generalization, in Toynbee's anthropomorphized civilizations, "suffering is the key to salvation, as well as to understanding."[49] The challenge to a civilization as a whole creates the suffering for individuals within it that activates them spiritually toward both secular and religious solutions. Challenges must be perpetual and pulsate recurrently within the spiritual lifeblood of the civilizational cliff climber to prevent the arrestation that follows a tour de force response that leaves no challenge unanswered.[50] The tour de force of the Eskimos to their environment, and of the Spartans and Osmanlis in their social organization, eliminated the impetus that makes societies human and ended in reversions to animalism. "In forcing the human mind into the similitude of animal morphology, the Eskimos, the Nomads, and the Osmanlis and the Spartans have betrayed their own humanity."[51] By the rejection of continual adaptation, and the conservative retention of patterned responses, these peoples rejected the implications of creative evolution. In a successful, progressive civilization, the rhythm of consecutive challenges and responses produces a corresponding élan in the spirit of the civilized people to overcome further obstacles. The first three volumes of Toynbee's *Study* are suffused by an encompassing biologism and anthropomorphism of civilizations modeled at least in part on Spengler's use of the life cycle to describe the rise and fall of cultures. In these volumes civilizations live through four main periods: birth or genesis; growth; breakdown; and disintegration, corresponding to Spengler's spring, summer, fall, and winter analogy. By volume 3, however, Toynbee had already moved away from the deterministic view of society as a vast leviathan superorganism following a predictable life course, toward one that conceived of society as a "relation" whose growth is found in progressive steps of self-determination or "self articulation" through the creative acts of individuals.[52] To Toynbee, all creativity occurs at an individual level and is not a result of the suprapersonal force of an inevitable destiny.[53] Toynbee went beyond the anthropomorphism of the macrocosm (as in Spengler) by turning to the study of the microcosm, of the individual role of creative leadership, and the subsequent mass mimesis in society of these individual creations that fulfill a civilization's response to challenge and overcome the inertia of cultural equilibrium.[54]

Early in his *Study* Toynbee broke with Spengler's view of the historical inevitability of a fixed pattern of the birth and death of civilizations both by equivocating over the fate of modern Western civilization and by hinting that a saving grace might allow him to retain a progressive view of history in the end. Toynbee mixed his metaphors about the ends of civilizations, sometimes positing his cyclical pattern as a universal "law" and at other times tentatively infusing a view of an ultimate end to history as when he suggested in volume 3 that the final product of an élan in a civilization may be to make "something superhuman out of primitive Human Nature," or when he asserted that "the differentiating Yang movement of growth is leading towards a goal which is a Yin-state of integration."[55] In either case, Toynbee's history, despite its cycles, is teleological from the beginning. The progression of a civilization proceeds toward a final dissolution, or toward an end, which becomes increasingly predominant as the *Study* goes on, in ecumenical religious and social unity.

To recognize the central role of religion in Toynbee's work—even in his first volumes—one must confront Toynbee's sense of the transcendental element in the process of creativity. In the development and growth of civilizations, social change occurs through the leadership of "creative minorities" or "mystically inspired personalities," who provide leadership in the transformation of the macrocosm of culture through the recreation in themselves of the internal image of man. These "supermen" disrupt the social equilibrium by their creativity and so give rise to human conflicts that are essential to the "creative mutation of human nature."[56] Toynbee held that "the individuals who perform this miracle of creation and who thereby bring about the growth of society in which they arise, are more than men. They work what to men seem miracles, because they themselves are supermen in a literal and no mere metaphorical sense."[57] The Nietzschean element in these "supermen" is obvious but Toynbee took them more from Bergson, especially from his *The Two Sources of Morality and Religion*, where Bergson claimed that "it is the mystic souls who draw and will continue to draw civilized societies in their wake."[58] Toynbee agreed that these Bergsonian mystics are his own "superhuman creators par excellence," and he described the process of their growth: "In the souls of certain human beings, a new spiritual species—a veritable Superman—emerges. The mystically illumined Personality evidently stands to ordinary Human Nature as civilizations stand to primitive societies."[59] This mystical illumination seems to imply a divine or at least transcendental source of inspiration at the foundation and growth of civilization. Toynbee took from Bergson this notion that mysticism provided the "vital impetus" that drove creative evolution, through the mechanism he called "Withdrawal and Return."[60] Here again, an archetypic yin/yang movement of internal intuition and creative inspiration occurs in a physical, intellectual, or spiritual withdrawal from the known world and a return from the internal to the external world to manifest the gains of the creative experience. Essential to the withdrawal is some sort of mystical reception of truth from an external spiritual force.[61] Percival Martin has described this process in terms of Toynbee's favored Jungian psychology as a withdrawal into the depths of the collective unconscious to acquire solutions to a current dilemma from a transpersonal timeless source.[62]

While civilizations come to birth and grow out of the creative impetus of a minority or series of minorities in response to challenges through withdrawal and return, the breakdown of civilization occurs

in the moral failure of the leading minority and the consequent
secession of their potential successors. "Breakdowns are failures in an
audacious attempt to ascend from the level of Primitive Humanity
living the life of a social animal, to the height of some superhuman
kind of being in a Communion of Saints."[63] When they do fall,
civilizations fall from within; they die from suicide rather than murder.
Toynbee categorically rejected Gibbon's thesis that the Fall of Rome
was due to the "triumph of barbarism and religion." Civilizations do
not collapse because of technological breakdowns, external violence,
or the rise of new religious movements; these are but symptoms of
their internal disorganization. A civilization that is conquered by
another is nearly always already in a state of internal decay; such a
"moribund civilization has [already] been thrown on the scrap heap by
an iconoclastic revolt on the part of its internal and external proletariat,
in order that one or the other of these insurgents may obtain a free
field for bringing a new civilization to birth."[64] Once again, these
proletarians are defined in terms of their internal psychological state
rather than by any materialist premise; they are spiritually "in but not
of" society and include, often as leaders, an intelligentsia of alienated
intellectuals who were nurtured at the meeting places between civilizations but remain outside any tradition, "born to be unhappy."[65]
Their sufferings stir them to psychological adaptations, which may
lead to a new wave of growth within a civilization, or act as a seed of a
new social order that may replace it.

As a creative minority successfully overcomes a challenge and inspires a society by its example, it may assume the position of a
"dominant Minority." Toynbee believes in general that each group can
resolve only *one* challenge: the dominant minority thus maintains, in
the wake of its accomplishments, a conservative inertia that prompts
the reactive secession of internal and bordering groups who may be
creative or come to be creative in the face of the challenges to which
they are exposed.[66] Toynbee describes the collapse of civilization as a
result of the breakdown of relations between individuals. The breakdown occurs in the failure of a cultural hegemony; under an uncreative
dominant minority the social cement of mimesis becomes mechanical.
In the lack of a mimesis of aspiration, internal and external peripheral
members of society withdraw psychologically and spiritually to conceive alternative values, life-styles, and patterns of social order.[67]

A moral breakdown, then, is at the core of this cultural schism and
disintegration. The creative minority, in its shift to the status of a
dominant minority, succumbs to the "nemesis of creativity"; it is
"resting on its oars." After its adaptive response to challenge it makes
an idol of its accomplishment, which orients it to the past rather than

to the future. The "Idolization of the Ephemeral Self" is a worship of the psychological integration of the last societal creation of personality.[68] In much the same way, the "Idolization of the Ephemeral Institution" conveys a reverence for past political and social accomplishments that limits further progress under the then-current dominant minority. The Greek idolization of the polis, for example, led to the Greek breakdown of 431 B.C. and left the integration of the larger ecumene to a power who could see beyond local patriotism, as the Romans did through their solution of dual citizenship in city and empire.[69] A third idolization, that of the "Ephemeral Technique," results in a blind overspecialization like that of the arrested civilizations of the nomads and the Eskimos, whose real achievements forced them into technological and ecological dead-end niches that they rigidly adhered to in sacrifice of future adaptations.[70] Another form of idolization, the "Intoxication with Victory," eventually spells the downfall of the militarized society, whose exaltation of past military glories prompts excesses on its part that lead to reactions by its neighbors and ultimately to its undoing.[71] In the last analysis, he who lives by the sword dies by it, and the pride of the dominant minority leads to its downfall. In the first six volumes, these Christian watchwords underline Toynbee's fundamentally biblical outlook and remain alongside a tolerance of other religious traditions in the last volumes. To Toynbee, the worship of humanity in any form, or of human deeds or institutions, was a repetition of the original sin of pride and a blasphemy against God. "Idolatry may be defined as an intellectually purblind worship of the part instead of the whole, of the creature, instead of the Creator, of Time, instead of Eternity; and the abuse of the highest faculties of the human spirit and the misdirection of its most potent energies has a fatal effect upon the object of idolization."[72]

The pattern of disintegration of a civilization in history, which Toynbee documented 'empirically,' was a rhythm of "Rout-Rally-Rout": first there is a breakdown; then the civilization spreads and coalesces politically as a universal state; a second and cataclysmic rout follows and there is a total collapse. This pattern was imprinted in Toynbee's mind through his analysis of Hellenic civilization: he located the first rout, the breakdown, at 431 B.C., in the failure of democratic ecumenical unification; the Augustine state was the rally; and the denouement was, of course, the *Volkwanderung* waves of barbarian conquest and plunder. The early breakdown here strains the imagination but hardly as much as that in the Sinic civilization, which occurred in 634 B.C., or in Russia in A.D. 1478, and in Western civilization, which, when he was not evading the issue, Toynbee dated from the wars of religion starting in the sixteenth century.[73] Toynbee most often left the modern West in a state of suspended animation, by withholding his final judgment, presumably somewhere close to its universal state on the road to its final disintegration. The universal state can play a redemptive role in the decline, however. It acts as a conduit for cultural, linguistic, technological, and spiritual transmissions between the peoples united under its hegemony, and also with those who surround it, which can plant the seed of a new cycle of civilization, through "apparentation," or affiliation, or even a religious synthesis. While the dominant minorities of universal states tend to seek stability and order above all else, their increasingly alienated internal and external proletariats may act as seeds that will shoot forth from its decomposition, making universal states "creators against their own wills."[74]

In the chaos of the disintegrative stage of civilization, individuals, under Toynbee's system, have three possible orientations available to them. The two "defeatist solutions" are to turn to a mimesis of past leaders and glories in "Archaism" or to look forward to utopia in "Futurism." These "forlorn hopes" may lead to violence in the degenerative schism that occurs with the decay of a civilization. In contrast to their this-worldly hopes of revival and transformation, Toynbee posited a third type of response, one motivated by a "yearning after a harmony that is not of this world [that] inspires the sublime failure of Detachment and the miraculous triumph of Transfiguration."[75] The inescapable worldly evils inherent in the degeneration of a civilization are analogous to Augustine's view of the timelessness of Original Sin; only a leap into the spiritual can succeed in surviving the downfall once it is underway.[76] There is a "schism in the soul" of individuals in the period of disintegration, a painful sense of spiritual drift accompanied by a profound sense of moral failure akin to the sense of sin. This spiritual homelessness leads individuals to a religious and cultural "promiscuity"; they absorb the customs and faiths of others to bolster, supplant, or complete their own. In the resulting syncretism, again led by exceptionally intuitive individuals, "higher religions" are born, as in the syncretic union of Judaism, Mithraism, and Greek philosophy into Christianity in the disintegrative phase of Hellenic civilization.[77]

A civilization is born and grows with the withdrawal and return of its creative minorities, it dies and disintegrates in "Schism and Palingenesis" where society divides into a conservative dominant minority, an external proletariat of "barbarians" and an internal proletariat that may turn to religious solutions. In volume 5 of the *Study* (1939), on the disintegration of civilizations, Toynbee reconsidered his definition of the "intelligible field of study" and realized that at the meeting points between civilizations the internal proletariats were stimulated to the creativity that led to the downfall of the dominant minorities and the rise of a transfigured religion out of the death of the old order.[78] Civilizations could no longer be conceived as complete fields unto themselves but must be examined in terms of their interactions and especially the palingenesis by which their key spiritual elements passed on, in metempsychosis, at their deaths to their affiliates and successors. In this light, civilizations as a category became as limited a field of study as the parochial nation-state had proved to be in the initial survey. Civilizations can only be discreet fields in their birth and growth, because, with the universal state, the civilization receives alien sparks that stimulate the production of higher religions.[79] The progress of these religions, then, becomes the only essential intelligible field.[80]

Stepping back from the study of civilizations, Toynbee envisioned the progressive pattern of their births and deaths as turns on a chariot wheel bearing higher religions toward an ordained destiny in the final unification of the ecumene. To see religions historically, Toynbee followed a scheme similar to that Bergson had employed in his *The Two Sources of Religion and Morality*, where he posited a religious evolutionary progression from "closed" static religions to "open" or dynamic religion, which is universal, open to the ecumene. It is mysticism that allows the step of turning static primitive religions toward dynamic all-embracing religions. Mysticism also gives its practitioners the vision to reject the sin of man-worship found in the primitive religious practices of the worship of ancestors and anthropomorphic spirits, or in their modern equivalents of the worship of the *Volk* in Nazi racism or the elevation of mankind as a whole in a Comtean religion of humanity. For Toynbee, mysticism points to the existence of a transcendental being not of this world.[81]

If civilizations were initially "philosophically equivalent" to Toynbee, religions clearly are not; there has been a progressive expansion in the realization of religious truth. By volume 7 (1954), Toynbee was prepared to assert consistently that "the history of higher religion appears to be unitary and progressive in contrast to the multiplicity and repetitiveness of the history of civilizations."[82] In coming to this conclusion, however, Toynbee shed a new light on the role of civilizations that undermined their equivalence as well. The "second generation" civilizations, those parented by the initial set of civilizations, came into existence, "not in order to perform an achievement of their own, and not in order to reproduce their kind in a third generation, but in order to provide an opportunity for fully fledged higher religions to come to birth"; their breakdowns are therefore their *raison d'être*.[83] The primary civilizations are meaningful only in providing seeds for the secondaries. History becomes, for Toynbee, a fully wrought progressive and syncretistic growth through the vehicles of civilizations. Humankind has a common destiny toward which all these elements progress; each civilization and religion has received a different ray of light from a common source, which is observable to the historian through the "eye of faith."[84]

In palingenesis a transformed culture rooted in a new religion is reborn from the ashes of the old society. The creative minority can be seen in this context as "saviors" whose renewed spiritual vision allows a fresh response to the challenges of psychological dislocation, moral chaos, and spiritual groundlessness.[85] This creation is, like Bergson's mystical epistemology or Berdyaev's God-Manhood, a revelation of sorts that, in Toynbee's view, comes out of tribulation. The suffering inherent in the down-turning wheel of civilization promotes spiritual growth.[86] Toynbee poses a general law that the circumstances favorable to the progress of religion are antithetical to those essential for secular growth, since it is in times of political and social defeat and disruption that new religions emerge. "This truth, that Man's failure, sin and suffering in This World may serve Man through God's grace, as a chariot on whose wings the Soul can soar heavenward is an apocalypse in which History works together with Theology to lift a corner of the veil that shrouds from human vision the mystery of Human Nature and Destiny."[87] The positive gains that suffering can provide are deeply etched into Christianity and Toynbee's other favored higher religion, Mahayana Buddhism, which grew out of the breakdown of their respective civilizations. For both of these higher religions, the realization of suffering is a first step in the path to overcome self-centeredness.[88]

Toynbee's eschatological side surfaces in his description of how the process of palingenesis may work in the future, leaving the impression that the West, in its turn, verges on disintegration. The escape from the coming "City of Destruction" will be found in "enrolling ourselves as citizens of a *Civitas Dei* of which Christ Crucified is King."[89] The Kingdom of God is the ultimate expression that human nature seeks in the alienating breakdown of civilization; it is "in but not of" this world. In the present, the "last stage of all, our motley host of would be saviors, human and divine, has dwindled to a single company of none but gods," and "only a single figure rises from the flood and straightway fills the whole horizon. There is the savior." When this savior comes, he does not seek to save society but to save people from it by opening the "way into the Other World."[90]

By volume 7 of the *Study* Toynbee had wrapped himself fully in the mantle of an evangelical prophet. He claimed that there was no future for a wave of "civilizations of the third generation," but in the downfall of the present civilization, after the unification of the rally of the

Modern West, the future will belong to a religious culmination that will include the victory of religion over science and a world spiritual unification led by Christianity.[91] According to Toynbee, however, this new religious unanimity can never bring the City of God fully to earth; humanity will always be subject to the original sin inherent in human nature.[92] Though there can never be a perfect, worldly utopia, "Salvation is to be sought in a transfiguration of This World by an Irradiation of the Kingdom of God—an intellectual paradox which is an historical fact." Toynbee resurrected Augustine's sense here of the participation within the two realms and also viewed progress in this world as a result of the received radiations of the other, digested and approximated into religions and institutions, manifest in civilizations in the world. Progress then, becomes the process of the opening of spiritual opportunity with the incremental expansion of religious institutions and spiritual exercises as a result of the mystical accretions of successive religious incarnations.[93] In the end, Toynbee follows Bergson's view of the end of progress through the worldwide expansion of mystical apperception and the mimesis of saints to a point where all people worship a common God. This would unite all people, end war, and provoke a shift in psychic energy from that now set upon economic goals to religious ones.[94] In Toynbee's words, "History is a vision of God's creation on the move, from God its source towards God its goal."[95]

In the last two regular volumes of the *Study* (volume 11 is a historical atlas and volume 12 a reply to Toynbee's critics entitled *Reconsiderations*), Toynbee turned his analysis almost completely over to arguments against the "antinomianism" of modern historians: the *Study* became an answer to the challenge of scientific agnosticism.[96] We have seen how Toynbee conceived of the process of creation as a mystical act and later described it as the will of God; in these last volumes Toynbee hinted at his own self-perception in writing his creative epic. "Prophets, poets and scholars are chosen vessels who have been called by their creator."[97] Modern liberalism and the antinomian spirit of modern science deaden the spirit, and when combined with the apocalyptic potential of modern technology and the "morally perilous leisure" that it supplies, they leave a void in the collective soul of the modern West that threatens catastrophe. New saviors are required on the model of the bodhisattvas of the East who can experience mystical union with the universe, but rather than withdraw permanently into the Atman, return to act, to bring along the mass of humanity.[98]

Toynbee undoubtedly saw his role as a world historian in the mythic terms of withdrawal and return, and in doing what he could to point the way out of the twentieth-century spiritual crisis. Toynbee shared his mystical experiences with his readers, like the dream he had of clinging to the cross at Ampleforth Abbey and hearing a voice call "Amplexus Expecta," "Cling and Wait."[99] The dream illustrates Toynbee's perception of himself as a sort of bodhisattva, as well as his self-conscious resistance to any religious orthodoxy despite his strong leanings toward Catholicism. In a letter to Father Columba at Ampleforth as early as 1938, Toynbee confessed that he felt his role was to bring his "fellow pagan 'intellectuals' " toward faith in the one true God. To do this he had to remain outside of any church, to hold fast as a bodhisattva rather than an arhat.[100] In the last four volumes of the *Study* he sought to instill the "Indian standpoint" of recognizing the unity of multiple paths to the truth.[101] In the last analysis, however, even the "higher religions" were not considered to be philosophically equivalent: Christianity was seen as the highest in that it was completely oriented toward God rather than collective human power, and the Mahayana was the highest in its "world-mindedness" or openness to the spirit as opposed to being cornered in mundane institutional structures.[102]

Clearly, Toynbee saw himself as a member of a new "creative minority" who could help guide modern Western civilization through its final stages and show the way to the necessary religious transfiguration. Toward this end he espoused a purified and opened Christianity combined with the highest features of other religious traditions. Perhaps his recognition of himself as an "outsider" both religiously and scholastically helped him to accept the sting of his attackers' vilification and to suffer in the righteousness of a patient martyrdom. The following passage summarizes Toynbee's conception of the necessity of suffering and the self-sacrifice of the bodhisattva for the purification essential for the future transformation of society:

If Christianity was to be requickened in agnostic Western Souls through a winnowing of the chaff out of the wheat, this palingenesis could be achieved only through suffering; and suffering is an experience that takes Time—and takes it at a length which is proportionate to the measure of chastening that is required for the sufferer's salvation. If this is the truth, then what was required, above all things, of homeward facing agnostic Western souls in the twentieth century of the Christian Era was the creative endurance exemplified in the age-long ministries of the bodhisattvas. Resisting the temptation to hide themselves in the rock, and facing the blast of the rushing night wind that bloweth where it listeth, these pilgrims through the valley of the Shadow of Death must let suffering do its unhurried work within them till, in the fullness of times and seasons which it is not for them to know, they should receive power through the anguish of being Born of the Spirit.[103]

Leaving aside his *Reconsiderations*, Toynbee closed his *Study* of history with a further account of seven mystical experiences he had had and a prayer. His mystical experiences had culminated in a vision shortly after the First World War: while walking through a London street in 1919 he suddenly felt possessed by a direct experience of the entire past of the race. He felt "the passage of History gently flowing through him in a mighty current and his own life welling like a wave in the flow of that vast tide."[104] Toynbee's closing prayer in *A Study of History* was an invocation to the saving incarnations of the past and the gods of the future religious synthesis; "Christ Tammuz, Christ Adonis, Christ Orisis, Christ Baldur, hear us, by whatever name we bless thee for suffering death for our salvation . . . to Him return ye every one."[105]

• • •

In the years following the final publication of the *Study*, Toynbee continued in the face of both public adulation and scholarly condemnation to prophesy and to equivocate over the fate of the modern West. It was, at least theoretically, an open question to him; past cycles were not determinative of the future, laws were really more tendency than destiny, and at any rate, historical ends were the result of willed human action, which is unpredictable. Even so, Toynbee tentatively tied the beginning of the breakdown of Western civilization to the disintegration of the core institutions of Christendom in the late Renaissance where the rise of vernacular languages, the wars of religion, and the compromise of *cuius regio eius religio* provided the impetus for the growth of national versus ecumenical organizations.[106] In this shift, the notion of a Chosen People was recreated at the national level. This closure of identity remained up to the present in Toynbee's eyes as a legacy of original sin and set the stage for the next imperative in the cycle of the West. In a letter of June 1940 Toynbee claimed that the West was contemporary with the Hellenic world of 40 B.C., having gone deeply into its time of troubles and approaching a universal state hegemony; already one could look for signs of the renaissance of a transfigured religiosity.[107] As we have seen, Toynbee had claimed earlier that World War I was contemporary to the Greek crisis of 431 B.C. in its experience of the violent divisions that preceded the establishment of a universal state.[108] Aside from his ambiguous historical parallels here, Toynbee came to see cumulative processes of *secular* history that demanded the coming unification occur expeditiously. Like H. G. Wells, Toynbee became an evangelist heralding the arrival of the World State, as the only hope of human survival in the modern age of technology.

To Toynbee, the World State became an ecological imperative; for one thing, the atomic age necessitated the immediate abolition of war; for another, population demographics demanded a world authority to supervise world food production and distribution.[109] The declining cycle of Western civilization boded poorly for the resolution of these twin crises; united willed action was required to prevent a disastrous outcome. In 1966 Toynbee posited three steps that were vital to the retention of Western civilization: first, a constitutional federation of the world into a cooperative government; second, a working compromise between socialist and capitalist economic systems, and finally, a shift to put the secular superstructure of society on a religious foundation.[110]

Toynbee did not take a naively utopian view of the nature of the World State but saw any form of world order as inherently repressive, at least in the short run. In the first place, nationalism remained ascendant in the present, like a "death wish" that had to be overcome by "world mindedness" even against the will of the majority of people who, left to themselves, were recalcitrant toward unification and would commit suicide by their inaction. Modern large-scale institutions, even without the world state, dwarf the individual; there is a "trend toward regimentation in all fields." In a world state, these institutions would become even more powerful and oppressive, but again: they may be essential for human survival. Toynbee retained from the 1930s a sense that the world state, when it came, would probably not be voted into being; more likely it would require a Lenin, Napoleon, or even a Hitler, and be "imposed upon the majority by a ruthless, efficient and fanatical minority inspired by some ideology or religion." To Toynbee it seemed probable that the world state would bear a price; survival might demand a loss of liberty or a new deification of the state or of a great leader.[111] Though Toynbee felt the loss of freedom might be essential in the short term, he advocated a worldwide leadership by creative minorities to take the initiative and avoid the use of dictatorship.[112]

Toynbee's solution for the stress in the potential need for an oppressive order in the short run is predictable. In religion people find compensating and true freedom; a spiritually open society with a plurality of religious frameworks, led by a Christian vision of an eternal and personal God and united in Mahayana toleration, would allow psychological release, especially in arts turned toward the sacred, and in contemplation devoted to God.[113] If the religious infusion of the megalopolis to come does not occur then our "spiritual vacuum" will remain in place and we should expect a compensating reversion (akin to those of totalitarian communism or fascism) to the perennial worship of collective human power in a "relapse to sub-human animality" that would, perhaps, rob humanity of its higher spiritual destiny.[114]

As Toynbee aged he came to see modern technology as a new and potentially devastating force in history. He believed that the "progress and acceleration" of technological change prompted a "psychic catastrophe" in individuals, where a fissure widened between the conscious and unconscious elements in the mind.[115] At the same time we have become prisoners of technology; massive starvation would result if we retreated from it.[116] In his last major effort, *Mankind and Mother Earth*, a narrative world history on the relations between men and the biosphere, Toynbee addressed the issue of human greed as the engine of material and technological progress and argued that humankind must embrace a contrary ideal—like that exemplified by Saint Francis. Again he asked for a transfiguration, even as he felt that the ecological climax was upon us, to "redeem" Mother Earth by "overcoming the suicidal, aggressive greed" that threatened to make the biosphere uninhabitable. In his opinion, "the only way we can prevent catastrophe is austerity."[117] At times Toynbee took his environmentalism, which was always permeated like much of his thought by apocalyptic antimodernism, to primitivistic extremes. In 1956 he speculated that in the "Westernizing world of the later twentieth century there might be a revulsion against Science and Technology like the revulsion against Religion in the later decades of the seventeenth century," as it was discovered that these material obsessions were but new vents for the "original sins" of human pride and greed.[118] By the 1960s and early 1970s, Toynbee became a leading voice in the nascent environmental movement. Here again his arguments were coached in apocalyptic rhetoric as when he claimed that human ecology demanded a religious revulsion against modernity and that perhaps only a catastrophe could stir men to the necessary change of heart.[119] In his last years Toynbee worked with Constantine Doxiadis, the Greek leader of the new community planning Ekistics organization; along with this group Toynbee sought a political and civic devolution to a scale small enough that community members could know one another—this was essential for any "victory of personality over technology."[120]

• • •

Perhaps a good measure of Toynbee's importance lies in the massive critical response he provoked. Toynbee was easily the most criticized historian of the twentieth century to date and perhaps of all time. One must admit that the process of the study of world history is by its nature more synthetic than archival and recognize that W. H. Walsh's critique of Toynbee as an "interpreter of History" rather than as a historian per se is clearly true.[121] Bearing in mind that in history as a discipline interpretation is inextricable from history in itself, one must agree that the problem of interpretation is multiplied for the world historian who attempts a coordinative function in bringing together the end products of historical specialists. The world historian inevitably adds a level of interpretive relativism to what the specialists have already injected through their perceptions of the crucial events and personalities of their respective areas. Toynbee takes the interpretive aspect of his task to the extreme by centering on an ambitious analysis of historical meaning as opposed to attempting a narrative history of civilization. Pieter Geyl, one of Toynbee's most consistent critics, expressed what has become something of a consensus among professional historians, that what Toynbee accomplished "C'est magnifique, mais ce n'est pas l'histoire." Crane Brinton labeled it instead a "Theodicy," and Rudolf Bultmann examined how the eschatological projections of Toynbee's *Study* asked questions of "being in itself" for which history can have no answer.[122] A brief review of the now standard criticisms of Toynbee will help to set his *Study* in perspective.

First, Toynbee's claims to scientific empiricism have been rejected by a wide range of scholarly reviewers; there is a general sense, again articulated by Geyl, that Toynbee employed a priori conclusions confabulated with "erudite decoration."[123] Toynbee then mixed metaphors by retaining an underlying macrohistorical leviathan subject to laws even as he posited human freedom for individuals; he retained Spencerian and Spenglerian biologism in his challenge and response paradigm.[124] Third, Toynbee's golden mean of challenge and response is tautological; according to Toynbee, if a civilization exists then it must, by definition, have met its challenge. Toynbee reifies categories, concludes from analogies, and acts as though "mental reconstructions" are self-evident truths that do not require concrete definition.[125] Critics argue that civilizations are conceptually indistinct and awkwardly employed as objects of study. Geyl asserted that national histories are as valid as objects of history. Kedourie rejected civilizations as meaningfully discrete units; to him they were extracted arbitrarily out of the "seamless web of history." Niebuhr agreed that civilizations were not independent and rejected Toynbee's notion of the sharp break between civilization and primitive societies. Christopher Dawson denied the philosophical equivalence of civilizations while Ortega y Gasset stressed their unique paths of development.[126]

Toynbee has also been chastised for errors of fact and proportion: Geyl noted that many civilizations *have* died from violent external influences, and Borkenau and Niebuhr have noted that only four or five of Toynbee's enumerated list of civilizations ever produced religions in their breakdowns or dissolutions.[127] Many have ridiculed Toynbee's claim that Egyptiac civilization broke down a full two thousand years before its disintegration and that the Hellenic civilization began its breakdown in 431 B.C., before Alexander, Plato, or Aristotle.[128] Bruce Mazlish has pointed out that many of Toynbee's errors resulted from his transposition of what he perceived as the cycle of Hellenic society into a universal paradigm.[129] A host of critics have taken Toynbee to task for his treatment of the modern Jews as but a fossilized remnant of a dead Syriac civilization rather than as a people within a still-living stream of history.[130]

Perhaps some of the most trenchant critiques are those that attack Toynbee for his transposition of his personal prejudices and religious quest into metahistorical laws. Trevor-Roper condemned what he saw as Toynbee's perverted egoism in expressing his own personality as the law of history.[131] At the foundation of Toynbee's version of the present crisis of the West was a profound antimodernism—a rejection of the contemporary secular decadence and a call for a neomedieval flight from this world.[132] There is a consensus among his critics that Toynbee did not appreciate what was new and good in the modern West, from material and security gains and technological progress to intellectual freedom and democracy.[133] Here the attacks on Toynbee climaxed; his cosmic pessimism, or as Trevor-Roper put it, his "Messianic Defeatism," demanded an "escape into religious mysticism" in the wake of the downfall of all that we most value in modern culture; only conversion could save us; all the political arts, the laws and social gains that have been made are only ephemeral coatings on our failure as a civilization.[134] Karl Popper spoke for many critics when he disparaged this view as "apocalyptic irrationalism."[135] Isaiah Berlin and others have rejected the "colossalism" of Toynbee's "irresistible rhythms" as tending to undermine the sense of responsibility citizens of the West must take to resolve real world dilemmas.[136]

Finally, few of Toynbee's critics shared his faith in the conclusive achievement of a religious syncretism. Niebuhr predictably rejected "history as a redeemer"; Dawson was offended by Toynbee's "reduction of history to theology" and joined protesters who claimed that religions had qualitative differences, which made real syncretism unlikely if not impossible.[137] Worst of all the criticisms were personal attacks on Toynbee aimed at his hints as to his own role in suffering his critics for the sake of the new era; his religion was ridiculed as "Toynbeeism" in which Toynbee presented himself in monstrous egoism as the savior of the West.[138]

In the wide barrage of criticism that Toynbee received, both the succinct and documentable, and the critiques of Toynbee's personal psychological impositions in his history, there is a wide latitude of truth. Clearly Toynbee's *Study* is not strictly historical but contains a metaphysical framework colored by post-facto fact selection. Despite his claims to empiricism, Toynbee never really denied this. He claimed that such relativism is utterly inescapable in any study of history; in *Reconsiderations* he emphasized that his use of analogies was a heuristic device for grasping an ultimately unknowable reality.[139] Moreover, Toynbee insisted that "every student of human affairs does have a theology," an underlying belief system that conditions his judgments. Toynbee complained that he was attacked for putting his cards openly on the table, an essential practice in a relativistic age.[140] To a great extent Toynbee's later evangelism confirmed the judgments of the critics of *A Study of History*. He referred to his own sufferings as providing his vision, he asserted that historians like himself have the clearest vision and importance in "Times of Troubles" like his own. He expounded mythical views of the meaning of his *Study*. His views on the relativism essential to his work made his earlier claims to science and empiricism meaningless; he admitted that his "chart" of the "Mysterious universe" was in large part a response to his fear of death; he castigated modern decadence and dreamed of himself in a medieval monastery.[141]

Despite all of the attacks on Toynbee's history, however, only the most cynical of reviewers could deny the dignity of the ambitions of *A Study of History*, which will contribute to its survival as a work of art long after most of its attackers have been forgotten. It is unlikely that Toynbee's *Study* will be judged seriously as an empirical history in the future any more than Augustine's *The City of God* is today, but the *Study* will remain an intellectual monument and an unsurpassed challenge to a holistic world history. If one follows William McNeill's lead in choosing a poetic criterion for the judgment of the art of writing history then one must rank the incredible compendium of world mythology and exotic fact in the *Study* as a work of genius. Like any great work of art it must be adjudged less on the definitive answers it provides than by the reflective perceptions that it stirs within.

The extent of Arnold J. Toynbee's general historical knowledge of the world may have been unparalleled in his day, yet his paradigm of world history is already hermeneutically useless. Within the framework of history, it raises existential and other-worldly questions that history cannot answer and no amount of documentation can reasonably prove. Toynbee, however, approached other questions essential to modern civilization that the profession as a whole has renounced as outside its area of specialization, especially the questions of individual moral responsibility in the face of world divisions, international tensions, nuclear standoff, and continuing environmental destruction. In the long run Toynbee may be perceived to have been quite correct in his perception of the imperative of overcoming national and local parochialism and individual narcissism and greed (which are at the base of misguided militarism and ecological devastation). He may have been right that the modern Western secular ideology cannot stimulate individuals to look beyond their ever-increasing personal needs to make the sacrifices necessary for global survival. Many of Toynbee's conclusions can be discounted as the irrational by-products of his search for religious truth: the ultimate problems with which he grappled, however, still confront the modern West and the world as a whole, and scientific history has too often overlooked their origins and implications as areas of scholarly concern.

The Imperatives
of Supersystem Transitions
Pitirim Sorokin's Metahistory

With material comfort vanished, liberties gone, sufferings increasing at the cost of pleasures; Sensate security, safety, happiness turned into a myth; man's dignity and value trampled upon pitilessly; the creativeness of Sensate culture waned; the previously built magnificent Sensate house crumbling; destruction rampant everywhere; cities and kingdoms erased; human blood saturating the good earth; all Sensate values blown to pieces and all Sensate dreams vanished; in these conditions the Western population will not be able to help opening its eyes to the hollowness of the declining Sensate culture and being disillusioned by it. . . . By tragedy, suffering, and crucifixion it will be purified and brought back to reason, and to eternal, lasting, universal and absolute values.

—Pitirim A. Sorokin[1]

PITIRIM SOROKIN employed sociological technique to elaborate the most systematically integrated cultural history of Western civilization written in the twentieth century. While his metahistory concentrated on the West over a three-thousand-year period, he also considered Indian, Islamic, and Chinese civilizations, and the dynamics of cultural phases in general terms that could be applied universally. The scope of his research was monumental, his manipulation of data staggering, as he analyzed the breadth of cultural mentality and all its subsystem components and traced their fluctuations from Minoan to modern culture. In achieving this task Sorokin created a new model of sociological epistemology, a paradigm of metahistory, and a series of sociocultural moral imperatives toward the salvation of the modern West. While maintaining a leadership role in the field of positivistic sociology, Sorokin founded a theory of social and cultural change that incorporated intuition, validated faith, and served as an oracle for the prediction of cultural fluctuations in the long duration of history, especially apocalyptic prophesies of catastrophe, and the spiritual reunion of Western culture in a new age of faith.

Don Martindale has divided Sorokin's intellectual development into three major phases that correspond closely with Sorokin's view of his

evolving succession of world views.[2] The first period, from his childhood up to the age of sixteen, can be seen as dominated by the
religious climate of his environment. At age sixteen Sorokin converted
to a "semi-atheism" and an organicist-positivistic *Weltanschauung*,
which he retained through his schooling, his activism as an "itinerant
missionary of the revolution," his imprisonments, and up to the
debacle of the Russian Revolution and his eventual banishment in
1922.[3] In his third stage, Sorokin developed a new and "integral"
world view that served as the basis for his sociological system most
thoroughly expressed in his four-volume *Social and Cultural Dynamics*,
which he conceived in 1929 and completed in 1941. To these stages
should be added a fourth, which followed without a break in his
schematic world view but that is primarily represented by evangelical
expositions of his view of the crisis of the modern West and exhortations toward moral and spiritual regeneration in an Ideational or
Idealistic cultural revolution.

• • •

Pitirim Alexandrovich Sorokin was born in 1899 to a Great Russian
father and an Ugro-Finnish mother in Touria, surrounded by the
endless primeval forests of northern Russia. Throughout his life he
retained a strong affection for the purity of his origins in the wilderness
and for the simplicity of rural life in general along with an antipathy
for modern urban living. As he put it: "I feel lucky to have had an
opportunity to live and grow in the elemental realm of nature before it
was blighted by industrialism and urbanization."[4]

There is a saying attributed to the Catholic church: "Give us the
child for the first six years of his life and he will die a Catholic." While
there may not be a strictly determinative line here, few would doubt
the essential power of religious and moral imprint on subsequent
character development. Sorokin's early world was suffused with piety;
the simple faith in a Russian Orthodox God and His innumerable
retinue of saints and heavenly hosts blended with the belief in the
animated spirits of the natural world as well as in the demons of the
underworld and the brooding shadows of the dead.[5] Sorokin grew up
among the Komi people of northern Russia, whom he remembered as
living their lives according to the Golden Rule and the Ten Command-
ments,[6] ideals that Sorokin retained and by which he judged and
condemned modern, materialistic, "Sensate" culture. Sorokin retained
a love of Komi folklore and music throughout his life. He identified
with their "spirit of egalitarian independence, self reliance and mutual
aid," and he idealized their life as one without class struggle, parties,
or vested interests, where periodic land redistributions by village

councils ensured that no one became substantially more wealthy than anyone else. In the world of the Komi, Sorokin says, "I was a member of a peasant community at peace with the world, fellow men and myself."[7]

Sorokin's first memories were of the death of his mother when he was three, of being fed by strangers and attending her funeral services where he watched a priest throw a handful of soil on the coffin while he intoned the words "dust to dust."[8] Sorokin's father was an itinerant icon painter, a gilder of steeples, and a handyman about the paraphernalia of Orthodox worship. He remained celibate after the loss of his wife and took to drink in his grief. Early on, Sorokin and his older brother, Vasily, went into business with their father while their younger brother lived on a farm with an aunt and uncle. The brothers had a nomadic youth; they endured terrible hardships on the road, both from exposure and from hunger to the point of near starvation. Pitirim had a problem of "rickety legs" from periods of chronic malnutrition. Compounding physical tribulations was the psychological trauma of leaving villages just as they came to know them and venturing on to cold receptions in unknown and often distant settlements.[9] When Pitirim was ten and Vasily fourteen, their father attacked them with a hammer in a drunken rage, badly injuring Vasily's arm and hitting Pitirim in the face, giving him a scar he would bear the rest of his life. The two fled from their father to go into business for themselves; their father continued to work in a circuit that paralleled the boys' movements but they were never to see him again. He died the same year.[10]

A religious aura pervaded Sorokin's life on the road. He moved from place to place in the center of a religious culture, often staying with and spending his evenings in discourse with local Orthodox clergy. From these clergymen, Sorokin picked up the rudiments of an education; he learned to read and was able to borrow books, especially inspirational literature such as a series on the lives on the saints, which he read avidly. He lived in a "religious climate"; he "tried to become an ascetic-hermit and many times retired for fasting and praying into the solitude of the nearby forest."[11] He acted as an acolyte in ceremonies where he acquired an "intimate knowledge of religious texts and rituals." As a traveler he learned the music and rituals of the church as well as intervillage news; he carried this information to isolated communities where he acted as a choir leader and as a "teacher-preacher" of the peasantry. Sorokin understood clearly in his later years the importance of the socialization that he underwent in this period and its role in the development of his later theories. He recognized that the mysticism integrated into his theoretical scheme was a residue of the "tragic mysteries of the mass" and his early religious experience of life.

"The moral precepts of Christianity, especially the Sermon on the Mount and the Beatitudes, conditioned my moral values not only in youth but for the rest of my life. The roots of the Harvard Research Center in Creative Altruism, established by me in 1949, go all the way back to the precepts of Jesus learned in my boyhood."[12]

While working in a village, Sorokin happened to hear of a local school entrance examination—he took the test on a lark and was offered a scholarship of two-and-a-half rubles to attend. This was money enough to support him at school for a year and he accepted the award, leaving Vasily to ply his trade alone. At the Gam village school in the Russian far north, Sorokin tied together the various strains of his beliefs into an integrated *Weltanschauung*. "It was an idealistic world view in which God and Nature, truth, goodness and beauty, religion and science, art and ethics were all somehow united in harmonious relationship with each other."[13] It was not to last but it marked an early anticipation of his later all-encompassing world view.

In 1903 at age fourteen Sorokin graduated from the Gam school and entered the Khrenvo Teacher's Seminary in Kostroma Province, an institution directed by the Russian Orthodox church. Here his exposure to the larger world of modernizing Russia and the impact of current political events conspired to produce Sorokin's "first Crisis," which tested his former values, especially the teachings and rituals of Russian Orthodoxy, and found them wanting. The harmonious world view of his childhood was shattered by his "contact with urbanized 'civilization' and the explosion of the Russo-Japanese War and the Revolution of 1905."[14] Sorokin joined the Social Revolutionary party (the S.R.'s), a largely peasant party whose populistic socialism demanded the overthrow of the czar but included an idealistic ideology rather than the economic determinism of Bolshevism. Suffused with "revolutionary zeal" and expelled from school, Sorokin became a "missionary" of the revolution and was soon arrested for the first time. He spent five months in jail in this first of six imprisonments (three under the czar, three under the Soviets). In prison Sorokin studied radical literature and became, on his release, a professional itinerant revolutionary, traveling in the underground from factory to factory starting up revolutionary cells. After a few months of this peripatetic activism, Sorokin evaded growing pressure for his arrest by fleeing to St. Petersburg, where he signed on to study at the Psycho-Neurological Institute and, later, at the University of St. Petersburg.[15] In this period he produced his first sociological treatise, *Crime and Punishment* (1913).

Sorokin's new world view embraced the contemporary current of neopositivism, an empirical, optimistic view that held to a close behavioral methodology and a faith in the progress of the human race as a whole. The spread of reason and the progressive application of rational social management could eliminate the current social evils inherent in czarist autocracy. In this period Sorokin adopted a Comtean perspective on the perfectibility of humankind and received training in behavioral psychology from Ivan Pavlov, who later became his close friend. Elements of his behavioral training are evident throughout his work but especially in his early studies on *The Sociology of Revolution* (1925) and *Social Mobility* (1927), where he retained conditioned and unconditioned reflexes to explain behavior. An objective, behavioristic, and quantitative methodology was preserved in his system throughout his years of research, in conjunction with a Comtean view of sociology as the generalizing science and culmination of the social sciences. As Jacques Maquet has pointed out in his study of Sorokin's sociology of knowledge, despite the changes in Sorokin's view of the inclusiveness of positivistic empiricism, he always held to a perspective of sociology as a hard science and never deliberately wrote an "as if" or analogous theory of culture.[16]

In St. Petersburg, Sorokin rose rapidly in the turbulent prerevolution society. He received his magister degree in 1916 and began teaching at The University of St. Petersburg. He became an important S.R. leader and in 1917, with the February Revolution, a cofounder of the Russian Peasant Soviet, a member of the Council of the Russian Republic, and the editor of *The Will of the People* and later of *Regeneration*. Sorokin was important in the development of the Constituent Assembly and acted as Kerensky's secretary before the "holocaust" of the October Revolution. In the wake of the Bolshevik takeover, Sorokin was again imprisoned, just before the dissolution of the Constituent Assembly on January 5, 1918. After a fifty-seven day stay in the Peter and Paul fortress, he was released. Sorokin continued S.R. agitation, now against the Bolsheviks, in Moscow. He was subsequently sent to Archangel to help lead in the "Regeneration" counter-revolutionary movement there. After the failure of his attempt to travel into the White area, Sorokin was sheltered by peasants as the Red Army sought him; he later hid in the forest for five weeks before being forced to turn himself in to avoid starvation or the condemnation of those who would shelter him. Imprisoned under a death sentence, Sorokin awaited a final word from the central Checka for six weeks while his cellmates were intermittently led out to be shot.[17]

In his autobiography, *A Long Journey* (1963), Sorokin dramatized the spirit of his prison experience with a powerful vignette: one evening guards entered his cell with a list of six prisoners to be shot that day, one of whom was a student of Sorokin. The student bravely admonished his guards with a rousing patriotic speech—upon which a guard leveled a gun at his head and ordered him out of his cell. The student instead challenged his executioner to kill him then and there. Sorokin watched as the youth received three shots and died.[18]

In the end, through the influence of two old friends in Lenin's cabinet, Piatakov and Karakhan, Lenin himself gave the order that led to Sorokin's "resurrection" from the "kingdom of death."[19] Sorokin's death sentence and subsequent release roughly parallel Dostoyevsky's death sentence and its suspension almost seventy years earlier. Dostoyevsky's turn away from social radicalism toward a spirit-infused perspective on Russia's destiny resembles Sorokin's call for an "Ideational" shift away from a dying phase of Western materialistic culture and his repudiation of his earlier revolutionary world view.

Upon his release, Sorokin lived a "death in life" in a devastated Petersburg.[20] He was confronted by starvation and the madness, executions, and suicides of his colleagues and friends. A young woman who, with her mother, shared a flat with Sorokin and his wife threw herself out of their window to her death. Both of his brothers died in the White cause during the Civil War, and his peasant aunt and uncle, who had been an oasis of love and security in his youth, also died during this time. In 1920–21 Sorokin moved to the country to avoid the authorities and to observe the effects of the current famine on social organization. In a systematic study of Saratov Province, Sorokin saw hunger in all its stages and to its most horrifying ends: starvation on such a scale that there was no strength left to bury the dead, and cannibalism.[21]

The Great War, the Revolution, and the Civil War acted together as a massively traumatic experience of death and dread that shattered Sorokin's optimistic world view and served as a dialectical fulcrum for the reintegration of his perspective. The war disproved any naive theory of progress.

> The Revolution of 1917 . . . shattered this world-outlook with its positivistic philosophy and sociology; its utilitarian system of values, and its conception of historical process as a progressive evolution toward an ever better man, society and culture. . . . This unexpected world-wide explosion of the forces of death, bestiality, and ignorance in the supposedly civilized humanity of the twentieth century categorically contradicted all 'sweet' theories of progressive evolution of man from ignorance to science and wisdom, from bestiality to noble morality, from barbarism to civilization, from the 'theological' to the 'positive' stage [of Comtean progressivism], from tyranny to freedom, from poverty and disease to unlimited prosperity and health, from ugliness to ever finer beauty, from the man-beast to the superman-god.[22]

After the breakdown of his second world view, Sorokin reformu-
lated his perspective in such a way as to resurrect the sense of harmony
and the idealistic and spiritual elements of his youthful belief system.
This reintegration of a personal idealistic outlook was, perhaps, an
imperative psychological adaptation in response to personal and sociocultural catastrophe. It was an answer he subsequently projected as
the "creative mission of humanity." In the Revolution, he encountered
an extreme personal experience of the "mental, moral and social
anarchy of our disintegrating Sensate order."[23] Sorokin came to see
the war and revolution as the first signal of the decay of Sensate
culture; they prompted a "personal quest" into the deeper patterns of
the history that allowed their occurrence—thus the crisis dialectically
provoked his researches leading to the *Social and Cultural Dynamics*.[24]
With this break from the contemporary world view held by his colleagues in the field of sociology, Sorokin became a self-conscious
outsider and a moral judge of society; in his words, "I deliberately
became a 'stranger' to its glittering vacuities . . . hypocrisy . . . and
civilized bestiality."[25] In response to this dislocation, Sorokin projected
his life's work: the development of an integrative epistemology incorporating both empiricism and intuition, even revelation, a sociology of
knowledge, a cyclical conception of cultural phases in replacement of
linear progress, a massive digestion and quantification of Western
history in demonstration of these cycles and in confirmation that the
present spiritual and moral collapse was not a historical end product of
linear accumulation but a phase preceding a new Ideational era.
Through these tasks, Sorokin found a mission as the prophet and
spokesman for a new epoch, a leader who offered models of altruistic
personal transformation toward transcending the declining course of
Western culture.

A Freudian psychohistorian would find evidence of a grand return
of the repressed in Sorokin, a reversion to a neurotic dwelling in the
"oceanic feeling" of infancy in response to adult psychological
trauma.[26] This trauma and its response could then be seen to form the
basis for a projection of his personal psychological disposition upon
the world as a whole. While recognizing the real reversion to meaningful symbols and the idealistic conception of reality from his youth,
speculation on the psychological mechanism involved in the restoration
of his earlier world view is unnecessary. It is better to see Sorokin's
reconversion as he did, as a reintegration that did not bypass but
retained, in large measure, basic elements of his positivistic and scientific world view. He reinterpreted the role of positivistic methodology
as a process that could contribute one facet of the truth. He came to
believe that the quantitative measurement of worldly "becoming" made

accessible, through reflection and confirmation, a deeper manifold truth, that of "being in itself."

Before turning to a more systematic examination of Sorokin's new outlook and exploring the foundations of his sociological and historical paradigm in his major opus, *Social and Cultural Dynamics*, and other works, it is necessary briefly to detail Sorokin's subsequent career. Sorokin was banished in 1922 because of his book on the sociology of hunger. In exile, Sorokin and his wife traveled to Prague where they were the guests of President Masaryk, who helped Sorokin get on his feet with a scholarship. Sorokin soon traveled to the United States on a lecture tour, the success of which prompted a job offer from the University of Minnesota, where he held a chair until 1929. The success of his publications led to a Harvard appointment, where he founded the Department of Sociology in 1929 and, eventually, the Harvard Research Center for Creative Altruism in 1949. From the completion of his *Dynamics* volumes in 1941, Sorokin increasingly directed his activities toward what he saw as resistance to the progressive decadence of Western culture. "The pressure of the crises grew so strong that it prompted me to the investigation of the means of preventing the imminent annihilation of the human race and of ways out of the deadly crisis."[27] This shift toward activism and moral invocation marked a return to his "teacher-preacher" role, no longer in an isolated peasant community but in a postwar world whose apocalyptic direction, now magnified by its nuclear potentialities, increased the urgency of his prescriptions. These apocalyptic themes will be examined in more detail later; it is sufficient here to point out that Sorokin's assertions of moral imperatives toward the deterrence of catastrophe and the regeneration of humanity follow from his image of himself as having grasped the true key to historical progression, and hence a clear view of Western cultural destiny. It is no accident that this prescriptive perception corresponded so closely with his own psychological pattern of progression; he built a world to replace one that had died.

• • •

Sorokin's method of sociological analysis was closely founded upon his "integrated *Weltanschauung*." He attempted to unite all historical forms of knowledge into a working epistemology, as a system for the examination of the historically specific, for general historical overview, and as a guide into the next phase of the evolution of the Western mentality, that of Idealistic or Ideational integralism. Sorokin proposed a "logico-meaningful" addition to the current sociological mode of "causal-functional" or empirical-inductive examination. His idea was to use creative reason for analysis and generalization and then to test propositions thus conceived both deductively and inductively.[28] In this way he felt he could avoid the empty and sterile results of the "strainers at the gnats" and the "Lilliputian fact-finders,"[29] whose insignificant examinations of "surface and trifles" had left the fundamental realities of cultural dynamics outside of their sociological scope. "Pure fact-finding is thoughtless [for] without logical thought there can be no relevant 'fact.' "[30]

Essential to Sorokin's way of approaching truth is a convergence of empirical verifications with "logico-meaningful" connections and evaluations. The "logical" side of this postulation and evaluation process is simply a rigorous attention to the rules of rational discourse to avoid logical incongruities and in the assertion of theoretical interconnections. The "meaningful" aspect is the most critical element in his evaluation. An example will best illustrate this point. At one level Chartres Cathedral can be seen and "known" empirically as a conglomerate of measurable elements. It can also be considered as a building that is functionally integrated both physically, as a self-contained and schematically designed architectural structure, and culturally, as a place that serves a particular sociocultural purpose. There is also a sense in which, when Chartres is observed by the viewer, it is perceptually unified; there is an "all-embracing meaning" to it as a cultural entity. This intuited experience of Chartres has epistemological validity as an integral element in it as a cultural representation. This truth-value is not found in atomistic examination of its discrete physical elements. Sorokin's "logico-meaningful method of cognition" aims at the "central principle (the 'reason') which permeates all the components, gives sense and significance to each of them, and in this way makes cosmos of a chaos of unintegrated fragments." One may find a similarity here with Spengler's epistemology in defining the prime symbol of a culture; like Spengler, Sorokin locates this unity outside of causal formula and includes a prominent role for "intuition."[31] This intuitive element acts, in theory, by providing rationally and empirically testable hypotheses; Sorokin claimed that the use of intuition is critical in any creative science. The better part of his *Dynamics* volumes are compilations of empirical data in demonstration of intuited cultural unities.

Sorokin's epistemological emphasis was directed against the progressive view of social development of Marx and Spencer. Both Marx and Sorokin developed a sociology of knowledge, a *Wissenssoziologie*, that emphasized the existential determination of knowledge as conditioned by social factors; Sorokin considered cultural dynamics as more important than the process of social change itself, as culture is more determinative than the social system (of which class structure is but a subsystem).[32] In his view, both Marx and Spencer mistakenly employ a monocausal system of "functional integration" in culture: Marx through his attribution of determinative primacy to the mode of production over the mentality of classes in history and Spencer with his view of evolution to the complex stressing the progress of man to perfection. According to Sorokin, no such "attempt to apply the main factor has succeeded."[33] In fact, such linear views, based as they were on a single functional line of development, were symptomatic of the current reductionistic epistemological system of Sensate culture, and, even so, were scarcely supported by empirical demonstration.

Sorokin's own study of the sociology of knowledge attempted to explore the various forms of epistemological premises that have been employed in different historical periods, each of which is presumed to have a relative truth-value, and, when combined in an integral approach, a complete one. Each major form of truth that has existed in the past—rationalism, empiricism, a truth judged by faith, or intuition—is seen under Sorokin's system as partly true and partly false; each is ultimately inadequate. The major addition that Sorokin wanted to make to modern epistemology was that of faith, revelation, or intuition, as a valid component of a complete truth. He argued that some type of gnosis was active in the verification of any system, even of those that find truth in reason or in the senses—ultimately one must have faith that what one thinks or perceives to be true actually corresponds to reality. Sorokin also argued that intuition had been one of the most fruitful origins of scientific, mathematical, and philosophic inventions as well as of great artistic, moral, and religious systems. To Sorokin, intuition was the basis of creativity, an essential factor in cognition and the "ultimate foundation of the beautiful, and of the ethical or moral. . . . There is hardly any doubt that intuition is the real source of real knowledge, different from the role of the senses and reason. If so, then the truth of faith, derived from and based upon intuition, is the genuine truth as much as the truth of the senses and of reason."[34]

• • •

From Sorokin's perspective, a culture is premised in part on its epistemological system, which is an integral part of its unifying mentality. A culture "can be viewed internally as having an overarching 'culture mentality' " or "externally in terms of objects, events, processes . . . these external phenomena belong to a system of culture only as they are the manifestation of its internal aspect," which is "paramount" over the external.[35] To understand what Sorokin means, one must grasp his conception of culture as a logico-meaningful construction. There can be four basic types of cultural integration: that of pure spacial/temporal contiguity, which produces "congeries"; that of association due to an external factor, a "relation"; a causal or functional integration, as in economic determinism; or an all-inclusive "Internal or Logico-Meaningful Unity."[36] The highest integration of culture is obviously at this last level; in fact, a series of cultural subsystems in hierarchy is subsumed under a meaningful unity that integrates the subsystems into a cultural "supersystem." This cultural gestalt provides a mentality including a world view and a basic personality type. This omnipresent aspect of the culture as a whole integrates its various elemental systems and material expressions.[37] "We see that the systems are living unities animated by their sense of meanings articulating itself through the vehicles and human agents."[38] It is this logical integration, this interdependence of systems and subsystems in a culture, that differentiates a culture from mere congeries of dis-integrated or nonintegrated material vehicles and cultural subsystems. Seen as hegemonic gestalts embracing subsystems into unities, the supersystems function as wholes. The evolution of their phases and the process of their passage form the single-most meaningful dynamic of history.

These definitions gain clarity in Sorokin's exposition of historical phases and his coordination of empirical studies into a supersystem rubric. It is important to emphasize, however, before any examination of Sorokin's historical phases, that his integral epistemological system posits change in the common mentality as the highest level of sociocultural development. "The Word (meaning) is the first component of any cultural phenomenon; when it is made flesh (acquires vehicles and aspects) it becomes a system of this empirical, socio-cultural reality."[39] In Sorokin's system, and at the cornerstone of his development of a philosophy of history, reason and intuition *precede* the enumeration of historical facts; empirical compilation and correlation are post-facto tests of intuitively conceived patterns.[40] Sorokin's intention in his epistemological schema is to unite all the forms of truth-value or epistemology that have been employed under the various supersystem cultural unities in Western history. Each historical form of truth, "separated from the rest, becomes less valid or more fallacious, even within the specific field of its own competence."[41] As when all the hues of color are combined, integral truth is "white"; there is a "whole truth" that is the union of its partial forms.[42] Although complete truth may be accessible "only to the Divine Mind," Sorokin did his best to grasp it.[43] This unity of truth will be examined later in review of Sorokin's view of the crisis of the West (which includes an epistemological crisis) and his postulation of a cure.

Sorokin contrasted his unit of study, the cultural supersystem, sharply with the civilizations observed by Danilevsky, Spengler, and Toynbee, which in his view may be ethnic entities, religious orders, social organizations, or territorial states. To Sorokin, these civilizations are really only social systems and as such are not the essential level of study but contain a central system alongside a multitude of differing and perhaps contradictory subsystems or congeries.[44] He ridiculed Toynbee's division of twenty-one civilizations carved out of a cultural field. He also rejected the organicism of the earlier systems. Cultural systems and subsystems are not born and do not die but may become more or less integrated under a supersystem and hence have more or less cohesion with the larger field and its current phase. Civilizations are not organisms with a life cycle; they exist only as an arbitrary and unsystematic way of perceiving the cultural field, as an error of taking the part for the whole, a subsystem for the determinative and overarching gestalt.[45]

When he came to examine cultures in history, Sorokin conceived three possible forms of cultural mentality or supersystem. An Ideational culture is one in which reality is perceived as having a nonmaterial and spiritual base, where human needs are primarily seen as spiritual and where the physical world is denigrated to a relatively low value. "Ideational truth is the truth revealed by the grace of God . . . the truth of faith."[46] Ideational culture may be dominated by one of two subforms. In an Ascetic Ideational Culture, individuals seek to deny self, to undermine physical needs, and to vanquish the sensuous world of the flesh. Active Ideationalism is dominated by the impulse to transform the sensual world in accord with a spiritual vision.[47] Ideational culture centers on absolute, eternal, and transcendent moral values, on being as opposed to becoming, on an introverted control of oneself; it employs heroic models of great moral leaders, gods, and saints. Sensate culture, on the other hand, perceives as "reality only that which is presented to the sense organs." Physical needs and material/sensual values predominate in an extroverted mentality that aims at the maximal exploitation of the material world. There are subdivisions here also; the Active Sensate mentality works toward the efficient and rational use of material resources to maximize satisfactions, to provide the greatest pleasure to the largest number of people. The Passive Sensate culture languidly exploits the world to fill its immediate sensual wants, and the Cynical Sensate employs "ideational masks" to cover its hedonistic sensuality.[48] To the Sensate mentality, all is in flux, existence precedes essence, the world is in process; nothing is immutable, everything is becoming. Truth is empirically based and relative to one's experience: it is pragmatic, and it responds to one's wishes. "Material wealth is the criteria of comfort" and the "money-makers are the leaders."[49]

Idealistic culture in the West has historically followed Ideational periods. It is an infrequently occurring mentality that combines Sensate elements with an Ideational predominance. Idealism is the logical union of the two; as such it is a mixed mentality.[50] It is from the Idealistic standpoint that Sorokin attempted to conduct his sociology of knowledge and his examination of the history of the West.

When he turned to the study of Western history as a whole, Sorokin found that the three cultural mentalities acted in phase. Basically, Western history, including that of Greece and Rome as early parts of the Western cultural continuum, has gone through two complete cycles of cultural phase since 500 B.C. The dominant value system in each measurable subsystem has altered in congruence with the other systems under the general cultural mentality; each integrated system reflects the change of phase of the cultural supersystem. The overall plan of Sorokin's masterwork, *Social and Cultural Dynamics*, was to track the changes of phase in subsystems through the three possible forms—the Ideational, Idealistic, and Sensate—and to reveal the chronological concurrence of various phases in diverse cultural vehicles, to demonstrate the encompassing dynamic of the cultural form that unifies them. In volume 1 Sorokin charts "Fluctuations in Forms of Art"; volume 2 examines "Systems of Truth, Ethics and Law"; volume 3 evaluates fluctuations in social relationships and the Western experience of war and internal disturbances or revolts and revolutions. In each of these cultural areas, Sorokin found intermittently recurrent fluctuations in both the style and substance of these cultural manifestations rather than an accumulative movement from primitivism to increasingly high levels of accomplishment and integration. A brief demonstration of Sorokin's analysis of phase in these subsystems will serve as a further point of departure for an examination of the supersystem phases and as a basis for his rejection of the ideology of progress and his assertion of the modern cultural crisis.

In an integrated culture, art as a system manifests the mentality of the supersystem form; the style of art directly reflects the cultural *Weltanschauung*.[51] "Pure art," for its own sake and for pleasure, fluctuates historically with "purposeful art," that which presents a message or inspiration, just as the Sensate fluctuates with the Ideational form of supersystem.[52] Ideational art seeks to portray the supersensory, the "unchangeable ultimate reality" of being. The Ideational artist sees surface impression as mere becoming, he attempts to present transcendental apperceptions and to symbolize invisible realities. The artist often remains anonymous; his art is toward a higher cause than art for its own sake, self-expression, remuneration, or glory. His canvas aims at moral or spiritual inspiration and has the collectivity as its highest social value. Sorokin asserted that an error is often made by considering primitive and medieval art as immature and lacking in technical skill. Actually, much of this art is Ideational; it emphasizes a non-Sensate view of reality that includes sacred and magical perspectives rather than those of strict visual representation.[53] Sensate or "Visual" art has an opposite style and interest; its subject is the world as it strikes the senses, the beautiful, the pretty, the aesthetically pleasurable or sensual image. It is dynamic; it captures a moment. Visual art emphasizes the portrait, the landscape, the nude, the fashionable: its culmination is Impressionism, an attempt to capture light as it strikes the senses. While Visual art claims the value of "art for art's sake," its affirmation of freedom seems a fabrication to Sorokin; Sensate art serves the artist, who is often highly remunerated (and anything but anonymous), and the current Sensate version of pecuniary worship or sex appeal.[54]

The Idealistic artist employs material from the senses to present an Ideational message. His or her art aims at the eternal and static but may employ the drama of the Sensate in order to inspire. Idealistic art is generally traditional, employing recognized symbols in a realistic manner to display an underlying reality or mood.[55]

In his examination of these styles in history, Sorokin employed recognized art experts to judge in twenty-year intervals all the known works of art of Western culture and set them into his three categories. These researchers were "blind" to his design; they had no briefing on his thesis.[56] Among the variables empirically tested were nudity, sexuality and love scenes, religiosity, emotionality, and genre style. These, when taken together, served to document the cultural phase of an artistic period.

Turning to Greek and Roman art, Sorokin found a pattern of long waves of the dominance of a particular form. Creto-Mycenaean art (before the ninth century B.C.) exhibited a strictly Visual/Sensate content. From the ninth to the sixth centuries B.C. Greek art was dominated by an Ideational mode. This was followed by a decline in the Ideational and the gradual rise of Sensate art, which produced an Idealistic age between the sixth century B.C. and the fourth century B.C. After this period, Visual art became increasingly pervasive. This Sensate dominance was gradually infused with Idealistic elements in the Rome of Augustus but the period remained one of "pseudo-idealism," actually dominated by Sensate forms into the fourth century A.D.[57]

Here Sorokin insisted that Roman Visual art did not decay, as most critics have assumed. The decline in techniques necessary to paint or sculpt realistically was not the critical factor in the shift from Roman to the early Christian art of the medieval period. Rather, a new wave of Christian Ideationalism "engulfs" pagan art; its subjects were limited to the sacred and were depicted in the abstract as symbolic images of God.[58] These symbols dominated the Ideational period, which succeeded the dissolution of the Roman Senate, from the sixth to the twelfth centuries A.D.

The medieval Ideational stage gave way in the thirteenth century to the rapid development of "perfect visual technique" where the Ideational artist turned to the material world for the images to clothe his inspiration. In the resulting Idealistic period, anonymous artists presented harmonious and serene models *ad gloriam Dei* that reflected a perfection similar to that which the Greeks produced in their classical Idealistic period.[59]

From the fourteenth to the late nineteenth centuries, Sorokin saw the long, gradual encroachment, and then dominance, of Sensate art in which all the traits found in the Roman Sensate period again became pervasive. Art evinced a loss of faith, a rise in eroticism, secularization, and an ever-increasing sensuality. By the end of the sixteenth century, Western art embraced "compulsive becoming," ostentation, and theatricality; a Sensate series of fashionable art styles was scarcely interrupted by the neoclassicism of the late Enlightenment (best represented by the work of David), which was purely imitative of the Idealistic spirit and portrayed only empirical subjects.[60] To Sorokin, the accelerated change in artistic style into the late nineteenth century highlighted the incoherence and bankruptcy of the Visual form in a period of declining Sensate culture. Writing in the 1930s, Sorokin felt that Sensate art was in complete collapse after its most extreme expression in Impressionism.

According to Sorokin's theory, Sensate art in decadence presents increasingly superficial and morbid psychological types. There are no positive heroes; nothing is sacred. Instead, artists concentrate on criminality, they evince sexual imbalance by their concern for prostitutes and the deranged, and they lower any subject to depravity through satire and caricature.[61] Late Sensate art is reaching for its materials to the bottom of the "socio-cultural sewers" and hence must eventually change its direction.[62] From Sorokin's perspective, twentieth-century experiments in art showed a tendency to reject Visual representation in pursuit of some underlying reality; although these were currently unsacralized, Sorokin saw them as tentative expressions of a new shift in art style back toward Ideational representations.[63]

Such an "anti-Visual reaction" would be strong evidence presaging a shift in the all-encompassing cultural form of the West.

Looking at the long waves in the evolution of artistic mentality, Sorokin discerned extended cycles of movement from Sensate forms to Ideational to Idealist and back again to Sensate. He documented the validity of these artistic cycles in massive columns of data, categorized by twenty-year periods, for the thirty-one centuries under study.[64] His next step was to demonstrate, in contradiction with several earlier theorists of artistic cycles,[65] that, while music, architecture, and literature evolve at varying rates and may lag or precede developments in art to a small degree, they follow the same general lines found in the artistic phases.[66] Sorokin described the same general process everywhere in modern history: the Ideational Age of Faith gave way to Idealism in the thirteenth century, which was followed by a gradual desacralization into the Sensate which, as one approached the present, began to degenerate as it moved toward its final disintegration. His evocation of this pattern in discussing the evolution of modern literature is representative of his views of art, architecture, and music:

> From God and His Kingdom and His Saints, the heroes of literature become the semi-deified knights of the Idealistic Period; from these they turned into more and more human beings, until everything heroic disappeared almost entirely in the realistic literature and the scene was entirely occupied by ordinary mortals with their ordinary life events, which in turn began to be replaced more and more by the subnormal and negative types and events of human society.[67]

Having established a chronological architectonic of the arts, Sorokin outlined in his second *Dynamics* volume the complete exposition of his sociology of knowledge applied to the same periods. Each type of cultural mentality embraced a particular form of truth; each epistemological mode could be tracked historically as a cultural subsystem. Having done this, Sorokin found, not surprisingly, that Ideational truth existed in close correlation with Ideational art forms, and Sensate epistemology with Sensate art. Greece before the fifth century B.C. had a primarily Ideational view of knowledge. The fourth and fifth centuries were Idealistic, finding their truth in reason and accepting empiricism alongside faith. With the third century, Sensate forms of truth achieved a general hegemony and rationalism declined.[68] Then, in the third and fourth centuries A.D., the Age of Faith began to emerge, culminating with the "monolithic unanimity" of the Middle Ages (sixth to twelfth centuries) where "the wisdom of the world is foolishness with God."[69] In the eleventh century there was a gradual rise in

Idealism, which reached its high point in the thirteenth century before its gradual decline in the fourteenth and fifteenth centuries, when a parallel rise in Sensate forms of knowledge took its place. Sensate truth then came to hold a near absolute sway up to the present "age of incertitude."[70] To Sorokin, the empirical offensive was so strong that all other systems of truth or individuals with idealistic or ideational world views were forced to "imitate . . . the weapons, the tactics and the strategy of the triumphant scientific truth of the senses."[71] Clearly, Sorokin is guilty of this himself to some extent in his use of a post-facto testing methodology.

Sorokin used his research to show the historical error of the pro-gressive view, which asserts the linear rise of the "scientific truth of the senses" as the culmination of the history of epistemology. Sorokin situated this view, held by Turgot, Condorcet, and Comte, at the height of Sensate development in the currently dominant cultural phase, but denied this as an ultimate goal that has finally been achieved in the maturation of humanity's reasoning abilities. Instead of linear progress in epistemology, Sorokin found "trendless fluctuations" in systems of truth, thus invalidating any one form as a final theory of knowledge. He postulated an overall pattern where the final inadequacy of any one form stirred the development of an oppositional system of truth.[72] This motor of progression will be examined in more detail further on.

Having found a direct correlation of epistemological systems and systems of art, Sorokin turned to an empirical evaluation of discoveries and scientific advances and found that discovery had a positive corre-lation with eras dominated by the Sensate form of truth and a negative one with Ideational periods. He observed no linear line in the incidence of discovery and invention: instead he found that they peaked with Sensate hegemony and declined with Ideational epochs in an erratically parabolic pattern. Science and invention, like the arts and forms of truth, did not show linear progress. Indeed, Sorokin recorded an "unmistakable retardation in the *rate* of increase in the last years of the nineteenth century and the first eight years of the twentieth." The number of new discoveries was actually decreasing. This general "fa-tigue" was even apparent in World War I, where the *rate* of inventions declined.[73]

To systematically examine philosophical first principles in history, Sorokin again employed "blind" research assistants to compile lists of all recorded philosophers for each twenty-year period in the thirty-one-hundred-year era he took as his unit of study. These philosophers were set into one of three categories: those whose theories were based upon idealism and claimed a spiritual base to reality, those who maintained materialistic theories, and those who embraced a mixed category of systems. Not surprisingly, Sorokin's figures documented that philosophical idealism corresponded historically with systems of truth in faith and Ideationalism in art; likewise, materialism fit with empiricism and Sensate art, while mixed systems tied in with Idealistic art and epistemology. Philosophic first principles, then, corresponded directly with the long-fluctuating waves of cultural phases.[74]

Views of time and morality as cultural subsystems also evinced a direct correlation with other cultural form fluctuations. From the fourth to the fourteenth century A.D., for example, temporalism disappeared from philosophical discourse and the concern for eternal being was ascendant. In the modern Sensate period, Sorokin asserted that truth excluded eternal concepts; the world is of "fleeting conventional, relative shadows" leaving the modern mentality "an eerie and phantasmagoric complex," void of any "fixed point of reference."

What happened to truth, to the arts, and to views of time has also suffused modern ethics. Relativistic perception has evaporated the distance "between right and wrong, beautiful and ugly, noble and ignoble, sacred and profane."[75] Ethical phases have fluctuated in history from those of Ideational periods to the Sensate. Ideational moral systems claim to have received their moral norms from God; ethical values are then eternal and changeless absolutes. In Sensate periods, morality is hedonistic and utilitarian; the Sensate ethos aims at maximal enjoyment and can degenerate into "moral atomism, relativism [and] nihilism," where every man is "his own moral legislator."[76] To Sorokin, our modern decadence rests on this relativistic and pragmatic hedonism, which is devoid of moral absolutes and eternal values. In tune with the decaying Sensate phase, modern people perceive all theories under a schema of process; both philosophy and life-style are dominated by the clock, which imprisons all with the "curse of temporalism."[77]

In examination of the fluctuations between philosophical Nominalism, Conceptualism, and Realism (in his meaning, where objects and their mental representations are considered real and not simply mental figments, as in Nominalism), Sorokin found direct historical connection with periods of Sensate, Idealistic, and Ideational culture.[78] In social first principles, Social Nominalism sets the tone in Sensate periods where society is seen as a fiction, and Singularism, a view of the individual as an existential first principle, dominates. In the West, the Singularism of Rome in Sensate decline gave way, with the rise of Christianity, to a "mystical integration" or Universalism where society was seen as of the highest truth-value (Sociological Realism) for the duration of the Medieval Ideational period. In the present Nominalism, individuals cease to recognize society as a real entity outside the narcissistic ego.[79]

In other philosophical areas, determinism correlates with Sensate periods, indeterminism with Ideational; linear views of cosmic, biological, and social processes correspond to Sensate periods and cyclical ones to Ideational.[80] Scientific theories evolve from Sensate atomism to Ideational immaterialism, and from Idealistic vitalism to Sensate mechanism.[81] Views of space shift concurrently from an idea of sacred centers and super-sensual levels of space to strictly empirical measures of distance and height.[82]

Sorokin's analysis also found overarching types of social relationships that oscillate along with the historical supersystem phase. Familialistic relations subsume the "I" to the "we" as in true communism, church societies, guilds, and feudal corporate organization. Familialistic bonds combine with some compulsory relations during Ideational periods. Sensate periods, on the other hand, dominated by utilitarian self-interest, are organized on contractual lines.[83] These patterns are closely identified with evolving views of liberty and the role of the state.[84] Thus, cultural supersystems closely intertwine with the dominant political and social organization of a period.

Sorokin's rather questionable measurements of the incidence of war and internal disturbances in history do not show a direct correlation with Sensate, Ideational, or Idealistic periods. What is significant to him is that these disturbances so often correspond statistically to periods of transition; they occur at interstitial points where a cultural mentality is in breakdown and another in formulation.[85] In line with the rest of his data, Sorokin found no linear progress in history toward increased pacifism; in fact, when he analyzed the first twenty years of the twentieth century he found them among the bloodiest in all history.[86] As such they presaged a transition that was universally implied by the rest of his data and the metahistorical pattern he found in the whole. The unity of cultural systems that Sorokin demonstrated pointed conclusively at the overwhelming crisis of the twentieth century, a crisis inherent in a Sensate period in utter decadence. It also presented the absolute necessity (and inevitability) of an Idealistic or Ideational transformation of the contemporary mentality as the superstructure guiding the transformation of all subsystems.

Theoretically, the cause of supersystem phase transition lies in the limitations of each of its integrating forms and the limit to the number of possible forms of human cultural organization. Change in cultural systems is an immanent principle: a culture develops to a Sensate level beyond which it cannot go, producing contradictions inherent in a single conceptual and organizational pattern that inevitably demand resolution in an oppositional formulation. Sorokin's immanent dialectic parallels those of Vico and Hegel as well as Aristotle's "Doctrine of the Mean," fixing a "Principle of Limits" that stirs the proposition of antithetical principles and values.[87] Like Spengler, Sorokin held that each cultural whole, or supersystem, bore an internal unity and a destiny. "From the moment of its emergence, any empirical sociocultural system is a self-changing and self-directing unity that bears in itself the reason for its change . . . and the essentials of its destiny . . . from an acorn . . . only an oak develops, and nothing else."[88] The development of any cultural system reaches a point of fulfillment where all its possibilities are exhausted; after this point of limitation the supersystem begins to break down. For example, the end of the Middle Ages was precipitated by squabbles over various revelations, with disputants citing various biblical references and relying increasingly upon logic and empirical evidence to resolve their arguments, thus giving rise to reflective skepticism and eventually to an empirical/ Sensate criteria of truth. Likewise, in the present Sensate decline, Sorokin held that empirical truth is driven to its limitation point by its extreme relativism, which becomes increasingly useless in any sort of meaningful explanation of otherwise disjointed, dis-integrated data.[89]

• • •

The encompassing pattern of the *Dynamics* allowed Sorokin to believe that he could diagnose the present and future of Western Sensate culture; to him its decadent decline was apparent and its catastrophic and inevitable overturn was imminent. He held that the West would undergo cataclysmic upheavals in its nascent "time of troubles," that is, in the transitional period between the dying Sensate culture and the rise of a new Ideational or Idealistic synthesis. Following up his predictions of wars and further upheavals in his first three volumes, he was able to assert in 1941 that "history, so far, has been proceeding along the schedule of Dynamics."[90] In his view, the crisis that had begun was one that would include all facets of sociocultural existence. There was an epistemological crisis as "Sensate values . . . become still more relative and atomistic until they are ground into the dust devoid of any universal recognitions and binding power."[91] Since there are no eternal verities in Sensate epistemology there can be none in ethics; there will be a continual decline to moral "bankruptcy and self-destruction." In response to moral and social collapse, Sorokin systematically formulated the next stage in the development of Western culture, and in doing so set a historical and moral imperative for contemporary society. The Sensate decline of the West would, through "tragedy, suffering, and crucifixion . . . be brought back to reason, and to eternal, lasting, universal and absolute values."[92]

In Sorokin's emotional rejection of Sensate culture, his predictions followed closely from his hopes. Sorokin yearned nostalgically for a lost Age of Faith such as he had experienced as a child. In the Sensate world of his adulthood in exile, and with the destruction in his time of "holy Russia," "man as a bearer of the divine ray in the sensory world, as an incarnation of the Charismatic grace, was declared a superstitious illusion."[93] Sorokin's epistemological integralism affirmed that this transition was an error; only the "white" truth of idealism could encapsulate meaningful reality. Sensate society, to Sorokin, is a Fall from Grace, a loss of God that, if one is to have any hopes, must be in a cyclical historical pattern, rather than a progressive one from the dawn of culture. In this way Sorokin could reinfuse the divine in history; he could include Providence and revelation (as valid forms of intuitive apperception) by affirming the soundness of the medieval world view and the inevitable rise of a new consciousness, a new integral society, and a new sense of place for individuals in a corporative harmony with a new moral consensus. Like his compatriot and fellow exile, Nikolai Berdyaev, Sorokin felt that there was to be a new land and covenant after the Sensate wanderings in the desert, a land molded on the unity and harmony that Sorokin remembered from his youth and projected upon a mythical Middle Ages of the past Ideational stage and another still to come, where he romantically located his utopian social, political, and, most important, religious ideals.

With the completion of his *Dynamics* volumes, Sorokin took on the role of prophet of an Ideational transformation. His 1941 publication of *The Crisis of Our Age* was billed on its cover as a "prophetic view of the future by one of the masterminds of this generation." In it Sorokin predicted an apocalypse that most people and some social subsystems would survive but that would utterly convert the integral principles of the dominant cultural systems. The egocentric contractual social and political relations of the Sensate period would lose their coercive hold on popular consciousness. In their place, familialistic relations would be extended "potentially over all of humanity" to form a "collective we." Likewise, marriage would shift from the current "sensate selfishness" and the "traffic in sex partners" of the divorce courts, to a firm and sacred bonding in "godly familialistic relationships."[94] Moral and legal relativism would be replaced by absolute ethical norms, Sensate degeneracy by new heroes and by saints and ascetics in "new monasteries and new deserts."[95] The overthrow of modernity would take place as such processes always had: "Crisis" would give way to "Catharsis," a period of dynamic upheaval and polarization that would be succeeded by "Charisma" where new leaders would lead a cultural "Resurrection."[96]

In his investigations of the phases of past societies, Sorokin had found a "law of polarization" that described the reactions of individuals to famine, war, and social catastrophes like those facing the modern West. In periods of such upheaval, some people turn toward earthly utopias seeking material comforts; for others, calamity stirs an "apocalyptic mentality" that provokes "penitence and asceticism," religious revivals, and a disposition to give away one's earthly possessions.[97] In wars and revolutions two oppositional groups emerge: a materialistic, sensual, and greedy division of society and a mystical, stoic, messianic one dominated by a view of the "Transcendental Kingdom of God."[98] For this latter group, war can be the most potent force producing altruism in society. Since the present crisis is one of the greatest of all history, according to Sorokin, we can anticipate extreme polarization; there will be a rise in mental disturbances and death rates, a disorganization of institutions, a continued emergence of calamity-minded arts, and a rapid growth of a variety of forms of apocalyptic mentality among various segments in the population.[99] Society will split into two hostile camps, one of sinners, criminals, and lowlifes and another of saints, altruists, and stoics. "Militant atheism will be countered by religiosity of the greatest intensity, and utter moral depravity by sublime moral heroism. . . . Opposite the materialistic and utopian city of man will be built the city of God. . . . Earthly utopians will contend with God's Messiahs."[100] Catastrophe, then, acts dialectically through polarization to stir responses that can resolve the fundamental imbalance inherent in its etiology: the breakdown of an integrated cultural system. The latest crisis will stir a cultural "revolution" in the "hearts and minds of individuals and groups."[101] So it has been and so it will be.

Like Toynbee and most other twentieth-century metahistorians, Sorokin included a central role for challenge and response in historical evolution. From Sorokin's perspective almost every personal religious conversion in history, from those of Augustine and St. Paul to Luther's, followed from the impact of catastrophe on a personality. In the same way a numerical preponderance of geniuses in the arts and sciences was stimulated by contact with crisis. Culture itself achieves religious and moral progress at its highest pitch during and just after crises.[102] While crises affect all individuals in a society, they are intellectually grasped and articulated by elites. The present cataclysm will serve to focus the "best minds of Western Society [its] Saint Pauls, Saint Augustines" and others toward its resolution.[103] One can imagine on which side of this conflict Sorokin places himself and his view of his own role in the coming transformation. As Augustine looked to a City of God with the Fall of Rome, so Sorokin prepared for a new City of God in the wake of the forthcoming "fiery ordeal." Purified in catastrophe, the new leadership would exert a "charisma" that would act as a key in the regeneration of creativity into the new age. Sorokin clearly sees himself as having foreseen the crisis and its only possible resolution, and of having provided a new *Weltanschauung* for what Berdyaev had termed a "New Middle Ages." After the 1940s Sorokin spent his life promoting his vision of personal transformation and the "reconstruction of humanity."[104]

Sorokin's numerous books and articles after *Social and Cultural Dynamics* can best be seen perhaps as "guides to the perplexed": attempts to lead to a positive adaptation to a historical inevitability as well as, ironically, to lead to its fulfillment. He posited five steps for his readers to take in making the transition to the Ideational (or Idealistic) as painless as possible. His adherents should recognize the crisis, recognize that the Sensate was but one form of culture, recognize the necessity of an Ideational shift through a profound reexamination of Sensate premises, and reject Sensate "pseudo-values." Finally one must realize that beyond the Sensate there is a "supersensory aspect of which we get a glimpse through our reason and through charismatic grace or intuition in its sublime forms, that this supersensory side is the supreme aspect of the value-reality and as such it is absolute. . . . Man is not only an organism but is also a bearer of absolute value . . . he is sacred."[105] Sorokin as a teacher-preacher has been resurrected, an evangelist proclaiming the word, and here again, his primary modus is epistemological.

Sorokin asserted that humankind must believe that the word became flesh and dwelt among us when he claimed the union of faith and empiricism. He presented a psychological system in direct contrast to the "morally . . . degrading and socially . . . disastrous" Freudian analytic model dominated by animalistic id impulses. Beyond the Freudian libido and ego complexes there was a "superconscious," a set of energies that acts as the "divine in man," a fount of creativity where the ego dissolves into the "Infinite Manifold of Godhead, transcending the limits of human personality and individuality."[106] This connection with ultimate transpersonal realities at the superconscious level allows intuitive knowledge. It is also this experience of Samadhi, or in Berdyaev's words, "God-Manhood," that is Sorokin's main hope for the possible resurrection of a renewed Western culture. The similarity of Sorokin's psychological system to an Eastern view of self and Atman is no accident but reflects Sorokin's religious syncretism and his later personal and academic affiliations. While his articulation of the union of self and the means to knowledge in this form of Platonic participation is a later evolution of his thought, the predilection to faith in an "Infinite Manifold" is apparent in the basic epistemological premises at the foundation of his study.

In 1946 Eli Lilly sent Sorokin $20,000 to finance research on mental and moral cultural regeneration. After Sorokin's *The Reconstruction of Humanity* appeared in 1948, Lilly was so impressed that he sent an additional $100,000 as seed money to the Harvard Center for Creative Altruism.[107] In the manner of Saint Simon, Comte, Fourier, and (Bruce Mazlish would argue) even Karl Marx, Sorokin's later researches were dominated almost exclusively by his eschatological predictions and millenarian projects.[108] Through the center, Sorokin produced his study of *Russia and the U.S.* (1950), in which he promoted the application of the Golden Rule to international relations to bring about a "temple of Lasting Peace" between the superpowers, who in their mutual Sensate decay must avoid war and so progress to his envisaged Ideational union.[109]

In this later period Sorokin rejected the Sensate study of the pathological (as in psychoanalysis) for the study and promotion of the ideal. His analysis of forty-five hundred "Good Neighbors and Christian Saints" in *Altruistic Love* is a sociological 'lives of the saints,' designed to guide individuals in self-sacrifice and self-transformation toward including all of humanity in their sense of in-group or family. This is the "agenda of history." "If we fail, hate with its satellites—death, destruction, misery and anarchy—will continue to blot human history and perhaps end in its mad destruction."[110] The goals that Sorokin promoted were increasingly beyond the mere survival of apocalypse. He foresaw a union of his saintly followers into a "free World Federation" that could circumvent established political structures to develop a reign of "Truth, Goodness and Beauty"—the old Platonic universals—under the leadership of "scientists and experts" and "sages and saints," reminiscent of Comte's synthesis of order in society under his version of the religion of humanity.[111] Part of the role of the Harvard Center for Altruism was to provide such leaders, to investigate scientifically the "ways and powers of love" as the foundation of a new positive science of man: "Amitology . . . the science of moral and spiritual education, and of friendly relationships between persons and groups."[112] World government alone could save mankind from imminent self-annihilation in the nuclear age; Sorokin's theory predicts cataclysmic war at this juncture until a new supersystem mentality is in place. Sorokin's goal was to bridge the two eras and to help to usher in the new Age of Faith with the education of the West in altruism and his own integrated world view.

Sorokin's activism toward this end was exemplified in his 1954 symposium sponsored by the center. It included a group psychological study by Gordon Allport, an anthropological presentation by F. S. C. Northrup, works on Zen Buddhism, Sufism, Hutterite, and Mennonite practices, and seventeen expositions of yoga and other Eastern "ego transcending" techniques.[113] To Sorokin, it was the mastery of the subconscious by the superconscious that was the personal basis of self-sacrificing altruism; this could be pursued through "spiritual exercises" that could be seen as repressive from a psychoanalytic point of view. Sorokin recognized this possibility but noted the successful sublimations of the great religious traditions as positive ego subordinations to absolute superconscious values.[114]

Looking at Sorokin's work as a whole one can recognize that Sorokin's call for moral and spiritual rebirth followed logically, in his own mind, from the scientific test of logico-meaningful postulation through the empirical measurement of wars, philosophies, and world views in history. Sorokin's activism, founded as it was on a postulation of cultural collapse and dissolution, was never, on the whole, defeatist as some of his critics have maintained. Alex Simirenko chastised Sorokin for his rejection of modern civilization, his assumptions that humanity was inherently evil and that technology had no positive value. Crane Brinton considered the *Dynamics* a "Social Astrology" in which Sorokin gloated over the difficulties and potential decline of the West. Elton P. Guthrie rejected Sorokin's seeming claim that everyone except himself was deluded by the Sensate mentality and his call to "embrace the 'inevitable' return to a medieval mentality." To Guthrie this invocation was a call to a despair and fatalism akin to that of fascism. Lewis Mumford condemned the system's justification of irrationalism in the face of a crisis that demanded rational ameliorative action.[115] Sorokin's defeatism is ultimately more utopian than pessimistic; his thought is dominated by the utopian resolution of the ambiguities of modernism along with a messianic sense of his role in this process.

To say that Sorokin's view of a dynamic dialectic between the three forms is but a figment of his psychologically disposed imagination is to make too reductive a case. It is difficult, however, to accept the scientific objectivity of his system as a whole; despite the admirable complexity of the interconnection of cultural systems and forms, it evinces a certain convenience of correlation that can only be the result of the careful coordination of variables and data toward a foreseen end. Sorokin's use of Sensate documentation follows his initial intuitions; as in any Idealistic system, the Ideational truth or message is ascendant.

In his vociferous replies to his critics, Sorokin is devastatingly incisive in cogent point-by-point rebuttal.[116] There is a sense, however, that he is battling his critics with logical and empirical tools to defend premises that his epistemological system recognizes as faith. This is more than obvious, for example, in his selection of the *rate* of new invention as his unit of study rather than a measure of production, such as tons of steel produced, or a graph of the use of power resources. Other variables have been used in the modern period to assess progress or development, such as life span, per capita consumption, infant mortality, education and literacy, and so forth. The accumulation of technologies and inventions, the long perspectives that moderns can take of the history of thought because of the assembled cultural vehicles available to them such as libraries, educational institutions, and museums, demonstrate processes of compilation arguably more important than the phases that Sorokin attempted to prove. He systematically ignored these processes in the interests of a more powerful presentation of his apocalyptic case.[117] It has been argued that Sorokin's data could be manipulated to show the increase in actual numbers of thinkers in all of the categories and a rise in their ability to communicate with one another over time.[118] This would support a progressive view of culture regardless of Sorokin's phases. Sorokin never used his data to assert that there was a lack of Sensate thought during Ideational periods; his phases always exist on a continuum and are not mutually exclusive. The overall progressive growth of culture could be seen as skewed by the interruptions of social and political catastrophes rather than from the immanent dialectic of phase transitions. The bias of his data is also magnified by the time period he chose to evaluate; the accumulative aspect of cultural history becomes less avoidable when development is examined in a longer duration, or is looked at in a cross-cultural context. Sorokin ignored the accumulative aspects partly because he so strongly disapproved of them. To him material success in the modern West was a negative phenomenon, the result of and a contributor to the maintenance of a corrupt Sensate mentality. Sorokin's choice of empirical fact evidenced a profound antimodernism.

There are logical contradictions in Sorokin's exposition. Except for his rather shrill predictions of doom in his later crisis volumes, the reified supersystem forms seem to go their own way regardless of the psychological participation of individuals. Sorokin's metahistorical fluctuations are so glacially massive and inevitable that his own efforts, like those of Marx under his system, are made to seem predictable and inconsequential. The dialectic follows its own immanent logic, it neither heeds nor requires prophets to alert and arm the people but will roll over them in any case. As Toynbee put it in reviewing Sorokin's ideas, "a cultural rhythm cannot be self-regulating literally," it has no "self to do the job."[119] Without a view of psychological participation, a self-regulating cultural rhythm that produces change is tautological.

Sorokin systematically ignored the individual psychological integrations that are at the root of mentality change except to posit his law of polarization that acts in *response* to imminent supersystem collapse. Here an inevitable cultural catastrophe drives some to God and others to the devil in a mindless Manichaean behavioral reaction to discordant stimuli. Individuals do not wander forward in conscious struggle with existential realities toward a blind future but unknowingly follow the deterministic imperatives of their times—some to Sensate damnation and others toward the white light of truth and sanctity. Even as he ascribes a mechanically reactive psychology to society as a whole, Sorokin reserved for himself and other elites active ego battles to creatively formulate new *Weltanschauungen* in conjunction with divine eternal forms superconsciously perceived. His own experience in developing a world view can in no way demonstrate that change is immanent rather than existential and volitional; in ignoring these elements he makes culture a massive mechanism and refutes his own efforts to inspire conscious cultural change.

A further contradiction inheres in Sorokin's use of altruism itself. He foresaw an age suffused with altruism that would effectively prevent what would be a globally suicidal war.[120] Since, as we have seen in volume 3 of the *Dynamics*, there is no correlation between the form of the supersystem and the incidence of wars and internal disturbances, this is surely a fatuous notion or else is premised upon a new form of supersystem phase.

• • •

There is an underlying sense of finalism in Sorokin's work of which he may not have been conscious. Since he has integrated all forms of truth into a white manifold, there should not be a limitation that would spur a dialectical shift in epistemology in the future as there would be in the incomplete forms of truth of each independent subsystem of epistemology. If there *are* eternal verities, and if Sorokin has grasped them and incorporated their various forms and cultural vehicles, then he has achieved a final form of knowledge, a blueprint for a stable cultural order and, as Don Martindale has suggested, he has found a "final deliverance" from cultural cycles and the crises and wars of their transitions.[121]

Sorokin's projection of a future Age of Faith mirrored his deep-seated psychological need for a cohesive belief system to replace the harmony he knew in his youth among the Komi. Sorokin's friend and intellectual biographer Carle C. Zimmerman has described him as a "conservative Christian anarchist" (using Henry Adams's words), and this label fits him well.[122] Sorokin's vision is of a society with a consensual sense of place where each individual agrees on eternal verities, moral norms, and familialistic social responsibilities so that the state can "wither away." In his *Power and Morality* (1959), Sorokin presented a program for the dismantlement of "nuclear" government and the institution of pacifistic society (despite his earlier findings on war and internal disturbances). In his idealized anarchical social order, the leadership of a Comtean elite would not rest on its power (which is ultimately corrupting) but on its articulation of the united consensus of the new medieval unanimity.

Sorokin's union of truth in his white manifold is clearly dominated by a single theological perspective. The whiteness is not a union of colors but a coat of enameled unity concealing a multihued reality. Jacques Maquet has argued that for Sorokin his Sensate empirical validation "decides in the last resort" and that Sorokin did maintain a creditable empiricism.[123] Others have argued that his manipulation of facts is merely "staticism" used to support a system of faith.[124] Clearly, regardless of the accuracy in his quantifications themselves, faith does precede reason and empirical validation, both temporally and in importance, in Sorokin's postulatory epistemology, in his world view, and in his system of metahistory.

• • •

Through much of his career there was little affection between Sorokin and his sociological colleagues. Sorokin offended his peers by his lack of modesty and as an antiestablishment figure who predicted the collapse of the West and the "military-industrial complex." In the sixties, however, Sorokin came to be lionized as the prophet of a cultural revolution, particularly by countercultural sociologists in the "Sociological Liberation Movement" who wore "Sorokin Lives" buttons to the 1969 American Sociological Association Meeting in San Francisco after his death in 1968.[125] It is easy to see how Sorokin's metahistorical vision could have been incorporated into the countercultural ethos, but more difficult to imagine Sorokin accepting other subsystems in this culture such as the ethos of drug use and sexual liberation.

Depending on the critic's own epistemological premises, Sorokin's work can be viewed as a bastardized quantification to support ideological vacuities or as a magnificent and epic achievement of history as art. To reduce the *Dynamics* to Sorokin's psyche alone is to invert his immanentist exclusivism; his creative formulation and systematization of his psychological experience did not occur in a historical void but in dialogue with major events of the twentieth century and deeply explored trends of the West. While his moralizations and spiritualizations of history can be judged by a variety of standards, Sorokin undoubtedly produced a perspective of culture that will be recognized in the future as a powerful though one-sided exposition of the cultural mentality of the twentieth century, if not as a complete assessment of historical progression.

Christopher Dawson

The Tension between History and Its Ends

We attain to heaven by using this world well, though it is to pass away;
we perfect our nature, not by undoing it, but by adding to it what is
more than nature, and directing it towards aims higher than its own.
—John Henry Newman[1]

God not only rules history, he intervenes as an actor in history.
—Christopher Dawson[2]

CHRISTOPHER DAWSON may have been the most important
Catholic historian of the twentieth century. As a Christian metahistorian he took up his role of defender of the faith in a lifelong study of
culture from its origins to what he saw as the contemporary crisis of
the West. As much as any of the historians reviewed in this volume,
Dawson combined the skills and scholarship of the critical historian
with the world vision of a philosopher or theologian. Dawson charted
a cyclical cultural path in the 1920s that both anticipated Spengler and
corrected his most obvious errors of closed cycles in a way that allowed
progress to civilization in general even as its adherent peoples fell into
decline. As a social critic, Dawson delivered trenchant attacks on what
he saw as the faithlessness of modern individualism and the apocalyptic
dehumanization that follows from it. In the last analysis, the crisis of
the twentieth century was part of a sacred drama to Dawson; heaven
and hell, apocalypse and damnation, judgment and salvation were
invisible realities behind historical phenomenon. The struggles of
Western culture to resolve its divisions and its soullessness were tied to
a shrouded interaction between individual wills and the ineluctable
mystery of divine providence.

To Christopher Dawson, as to Lord Acton, "Religion is the key to
history." Any viable civilization is grounded in a common consciousness including a common view of nature, the cosmos, and the ultimate
setting of human life in a transcendent or divine order. "Behind the
cultural unity of every great civilization there lies a spiritual unity, due
to some synthesis which harmonizes the inner world of spiritual

aspiration with the outer world of social activity."[3] When the unity of this binding vision is lost or broken, a culture will decline and ultimately be superseded by a new synthesis, generally one at a more inclusive or catholic level. Alongside the technical progress of the world there is a religious progress that has culminated with the rise of the West and the cultural hegemony of its intellectual and sociopolitical heritage worldwide. This cultural expansion, however, has occurred even as the West has desacralized its own tradition so that, while its by-products have been exported, its spiritual core has been considerably constricted, leaving the culture of the West in a state of perilous imbalance. In their transplantation, the liberal, communist, and even fascistic products of the Western tradition have undermined the spiritual bases of religious cultures worldwide but have provided only shadowy secular substitutes for organic spiritual unity and so leave in their wake ecumenical disorganization, psychological dislocation, class conflict, and division that, in an age of progress in technology and the mechanization of society, make for a crisis of apocalyptic dimensions. According to Dawson, the solution, a cohesive social order, cannot come in a syncretistic mishmash (like that proposed by Toynbee) or a Comtean ahistorical fabrication but must bear the weight of an organic and historical spiritual tradition. The common root of the modern secularized world cultural synthesis, the Catholic religious tradition, must take its place in reconsecrating the skeleton of modernism and providing a humanizing direction in pursuit of the transcendental City of God. Only in this way can the mythic foundations of modernism, progress and humanism, be rescued from the mechanized Antichrist of political totalitarianism, psychic depersonalization, and spiritual enslavement.

Having conceived the goal of resacralization through the extension of the study of Christian culture, Dawson dedicated his life to this task. He believed that if modern Western society could agree on the meaning of its history it would take a great step toward the reestablishment of its roots and the healing of its political, social, religious, and psychological divisions. His writings center upon this theme of lost unity and seek to provide an intellectual foundation for its renaissance. His work as an editor, leader of "The Sword of the Spirit," lecturer, professor, and critic of education all aim toward the same goal: the establishment of an education in our Christian culture in history that demonstrates its continuity up to the present, along with what he believed to be its logically inherent moral and spiritual imperatives. Dawson declaimed a desire to return to the Middle Ages but sought an evaluation of their historical implications as a foundation for a progressive step toward a new cultural synthesis, one that would retain the progressive inheritance of the modern period if it could regrasp a consciousness of past historical fulfillment and a sense, from the perspective it supplied, of spiritual direction.

To some, Dawson's argument for Catholicism and the dominance of the Catholic center to Western history and its role in world progress could be dismissed as a shallow Eurocentric and papist apologetic that ignores political and social realities and denigrates the viability of other cultural and religious traditions. Dawson was not, however, a mono-causalist who blindly subsumed economic, geographic, or sociological factors to the hegemony of his church. He set religious heritage and aspiration as one sociological factor among others that is conditioned by and in turn conditions other aspects of culture. In the manner of William James, Jung, and Eliade, Dawson made a profound study of religious parallels in varying cultural traditions and claimed that the very universality of the phenomenon, from a sociological standpoint, demonstrated that a religious point of view, of one sort or another was essential to human nature. From a theological point of view, he held that this provided evidence for a "natural theology" that evolves progressively in culture and, seen historically, is transmitted by diffusion in time as an increasingly universal cultural inheritance. While this position is similar to that of modern syncretists like Toynbee, Dawson's argument reasserts a European cultural ethnocentrism in his claim of the lead that the Catholic religion must take as the most advanced world religion. The Church has been the origin of the dynamic world view that has propelled the West into scientific, technological, and hence military and political world dominance, and has, in its secularized version, been the foundation of modernism elsewhere.

Much of Dawson's view of the crisis of the West, which with Western cultural expansion has become a world crisis, is conditioned by his reading of Nietzsche. Nietzsche demonstrated that since God is dead all the fundamental bases of Western cultural purpose along with the Western framework of time and the place of humanity in the cosmos are suspended. Dawson recognized the nihilistic individualism of his time as a result accurately analyzed by Nietzsche. His solution, however, was not an ahistorical revaluation to invent new gods or to deify humanity in the superman, but centered on a profound examination of the roots of Christian culture to demonstrate the continuity of Christian history into the modern era and to reassert the activating ideals that have been the unifying principles throughout Western history. His program for the renewal and salvation of the West (and thereby the world) was one of education in the Christian tradition; it relied on the questionable assumption that a recognition of the roots of secular culture in a sacred tradition would make manifest the imperative for regrasping the entirety of the Western cultural inheritance, including its sacred vision and moral order. Even further, Dawson felt that the objective facts of historical progress revealed a two-way process—one of aspiration toward a Christian millennial ideal, and one of God's progressive revelations to his people in time. The progressive unfolding of God's plan in history first grasped by the Jewish people and then universalized by Christianity is the root and justification of all the various progressive views of society; if God is dead then these ideological faiths will soon follow, leaving only a nihilistic materialistic degeneration and the increasing dominance of the mechanical order of secularized government and corporate social control. Dawson's work as a historian then is that of a conservative Christian activist: in demonstrating the error of the division of Christendom through an analysis of its political and sociological roots, his history aims at reconciliation; in describing the process of progressive world unification under Western spiritual ideals, he attempts to further it; in analyzing the historical response to crisis by the Catholic Church in reforms, in the revitalization that follows a renewed divine dispensation, and in universalization, he provides a model for resolving the crisis and escaping mechanized dehumanization and Armageddon.

• • •

Christopher Henry Dawson was born in 1889 at his mother's ancestral estate at Hay Castle, Wales, the son of Henry Philip Dawson, an explorer and adventurer with the Royal Artillery, and May (Bevan) Dawson, whose father had been archdeacon of Brecon and a prominent Welsh church historian.[4] Hay Castle was a twelfth-century medieval relic with haunted rooms, secret passageways, and an empty ruined tower, all suffused with an atmosphere of immense antiquity. The home symbolized to Dawson an earlier era and a tradition of the union of social, religious, and political authority and influence.[5] In 1896, Henry Dawson retired from the service and removed his family to his inherited estates in Yorkshire where he built Hartlington Hall.

To an early friend of Christopher's, Hartlington Hall provided a home where "every detail [was] steeped in spirit." The Dawsons prayed together each morning and evening and Christopher received a half hour of religious instruction every day from his mother.[6] Christopher was a precocious child; he learned poetry and the lives of the Welsh saints from his conservative Anglican mother and received an early grounding in philosophy, the classics, and writers of the Christian mystical tradition through his Anglican Catholic father.[7] At six he wrote a story of "The Golden City and the Coal City," of an epic battle between Christians and heathens. He had a rich imaginary world where religion was associated with the drama of art and poetry, as in his father's beloved edition of Dante with Botticelli's illustrations, and with a God immanent in the forces of nature, especially in the river at Hay, and, through the "enchanted world of myth and legend," in history itself.[8]

In his autobiographical sketch, "Tradition and Inheritance" (1949), Dawson claimed that his childhood was dominated by a deep sense of stability and tradition in the Yorkshire community around Hartlington; this sense of cohesion was inextricably bound to the "undisputed social and cultural leadership" that the Anglican Church still exercised in this pastoral holdover where yeomen farmers still worked their own land and the pall of the industrial revolution was only a smudge on the southern horizon. At an even deeper level, from Dawson's perspective, was the impression of a sacred past that was witnessed by the ruins of abandoned Catholic monasteries, like that of the Bolton Priory a few miles from Hartlington, which symbolized to Dawson "the perfect embodiment of this lost element in Northern culture—a spiritual grace which had once been part of our social tradition and which still survived as a ghostly power brooding over the river and the hills."[9]

At ten, Christopher was finally sent off to school at Bilton Grange near Rugby. After his happy early childhood immersed in the religious myths and bucolic settings of his family life, Christopher was predictably out of place. To his mind the school seemed a profanation: it was hostile to culture and religion. He failed at school sports, his eyes were poor, his health suffered, and he developed chronic bronchitis; he hated school. In 1903 he moved on to Winchester, which of all the English schools embraced tradition and religion, and where Arnold Toynbee attended at the same time, though the two never met. At Winchester Dawson spent hours in the cathedral and joined in the activities of the Archeological Society, but again he could not meet the physical exactions of school sports and activities because of his bronchitis and he left the school in 1904. Dawson next found instruction with a tutor, Mr. Moss, in Bedfordshire, where several boys, including his lifelong friend E. I. Watkins, were left largely to their own devices to read in pursuit of their own interests.[10] According to Watkins, during this time Dawson read Catholic mystics and saints, who made an "indelible impression" on him; even so, Watkins, a sensitive Catholic, hit him over the head with his chair back for the agnostic pronunciations Dawson made soon after he joined the tutor. According to his daughter, Christina Scott, Dawson had lost his faith for a time but regained it in 1908 when he entered Oxford on a Trinity College scholarship.[11]

Watkins and a circle of Catholic friends became central to Dawson's social and intellectual life at Oxford: throughout his tenure he studied the works of the Christian mystics; he wrote about St. John of the Cross and on the unity of the mystical experience. In 1909 he went to Rome for the first time and on Easter Sunday he sat on the Capitol steps, where Gibbon had been inspired to write *The Decline and Fall of the Roman Empire*. As he sat, he felt an inspiration to his vocation and made a vow to write his own history of culture; "I believe that it is God's will I should attempt it."[12] In the same year Dawson fell in love at first sight with an eighteen-year-old Catholic, Valery Mills, whose photograph, in the guise of the Maid of Orleans, he obtained and carried about even before he knew her. In 1911 Dawson traveled to Sweden to study economics under Gustav Cassel and then returned to Oxford to do postgraduate studies in history and sociology.

Soon after his engagement to Valery in 1913, Dawson underwent a conversion to Catholicism, which he saw as a culmination of a gradual intellectual and spiritual progress much like the one that John Henry Newman, in many ways Dawson's spiritual model, had undergone at Oxford in the mid-1840s. For Dawson, however, taking the vows at St. Aloysius's in 1914 was deeply disturbing both in the break with the religious tradition of his father and of his emotional relationship with his mother; his daughter testifies that the tensions of his conversion nearly led him to a nervous breakdown. Dawson was later to give expression to his identification with Newman's fundamentalist anti-modernism in his 1933 apology for the "spirit of the Oxford Movement" that vindicated Newman. Dawson shared Newman's view of modern secular liberalism and even embraced his solution to the crisis of faith that was apparent even in Newman's day but which, in Dawson's opinion, had reached unparalleled proportions in the twentieth century.[13]

After Dawson had received degrees, his father set him toward a career in church or politics. He initially took a position in the London office of Sir Arthur Steel Maitland for which he found himself unsuited, preferring to put his energies into a thorough study of Huysman's mysticism. His father next sent him into a postgraduate course in agricultural economics at Oxford; that was also unsuitable. During World War I Dawson worked for a time in War Trade Intelligence and Admiralty Research. Though he was a patriot, he was incapacitated by his health for more active service. By 1916 Dawson's father thought of him as a near invalid who could not work at a steady position, and so gave him a modest income that allowed him to marry and to pursue his research and a career as a free-lance writer.[14]

After the war Dawson began his writing career with an essay on "The Nature and Destiny of Man," for Father Cuthbert's volume on *God and the Supernatural*. Over the next few years he articulated the major themes of his world view in *The Sociological Review* and, after 1927, in *The Dublin Review*. During these years Dawson integrated into his writings the two most important influences on his sociology: Le Play's concept of culture, acquired in part through Patrick Geddes at *The Sociological Review*, and Ernst Troeltsch's sense of the essentially religious nature of human culture, the organic root to modern culture in Christianity, and its consequent imprint on the very sense of being of the modern Western mentality. Meanwhile, his planned history of culture coalesced into a five-volume outline of world history that included volumes on the "Age of the Gods," or the archaic religions that preceded and provided a base for the first civilizations, "The Rise of the World Religions," "The Making of Europe," "The Breakdown of European Unity," and "The Modern World."[15] Dawson only completed two volumes of this outline: *The Age of the Gods*, a product of ten years of study, came out in 1928 and related the history of primitive culture and religion from the animistic worship of the *mysterium tremendum* up to the monotheistic synthesis of Iknaton and the emergent religious cultures of Assyria, Greece, the Persian Empire, and the Etruscans.

Dawson's best-known work, *The Making of Europe* (1948), demonstrated the rise and triumph of the medieval synthesis as the cultural cornerstone and essential underpinning of modern culture, where the Christian religion, classical culture, and the vitalizing energy of new people worked together to produce the most continuously progressive culture that the world has ever seen. In 1929 Dawson published an introductory summary of his world view in *Progress and Religion*, where he set forth his principle that material progress was not progress at all but a secularized ghost of true progress, along with his career-long thesis, which bound his history to his apocalyptic prophesies and transformative goals: when the religious vision of a culture fades, the culture declines toward its disintegration. Although he never finished his history of culture as planned, Dawson's numerous books and articles over a fifty-year period fill the gaps in his outline and provide as a body the functional equivalent of his planned magnum opus.

With his success as a free-lance cultural historian and sociologist of religion, Dawson earned a position as a lecturer in the history of culture at University College, Exeter, where he taught from 1930 to 1936. In 1934 he also lectured at Liverpool University and was asked to address the British Academy on Edward Gibbon.

By 1935 Dawson had turned to a study of totalitarianism, which he saw as a result of the decline of the Western religious culture. As the war approached he became the staunch foe of fascist and communist tyranny and the elements of totalitarianism he perceived in the mass machine of the liberal democratic allies. Dawson's 1935 work on *Religion and the Modern State* was criticized as a pro-fascist treatise, however, for its empathetic account of the psychological and spiritual roots of the fascist sense of family, community or people, and nation.[16] This criticism was valid in that Dawson shared the fascist desire for an organic community and did not condemn authoritarianism out of hand (as he demonstrated by his support of Franco in Spain). Dawson wrote that the chief evils of nazism were in its means, which were antithetical to the Christian principle of treating each personality as an end in itself, not in the ideals themselves.[17] In Dawson's view the Catholic Church shared an antiliberal and corporative vision of the state as essential to a viable social order: "There is nothing else but the Corporative State and there seems no doubt that the Catholic social ideals set forth in the encyclicals of Leo XIII and Pius XI have far more affinity with those of fascism than with those of either liberalism or socialism."[18] Dawson's vision of social harmony, however, was based upon the irreducible free moral personality; he condemned fascism as a false and depersonalizing religion and had no sympathy for racist historicism or ideology. In 1932 Dawson had taken part in an intellectual congress in Mussolini's Rome on "Europe" that included Alfred Rosenberg and Hermann Goering as German representatives. He rather courageously flouted the spirit of the times and spoke on "Interracial Cooperation as a Factor in European Culture," emphasizing the vitalizing contributions that new peoples of several racial stocks had provided to the classical (humanist) and Christian cultural strains that made up Europe.[19] By 1940 Dawson led in what he saw as a Catholic crusade against fascism, both through his books and through his writings in *The Dublin Review*, which he edited until 1943, and as vice president of Cardinal Hinsley's "Sword of the Spirit" anti-fascist organization.[20]

Dawson was an influential member of the Catholic literary revival of the early twentieth century, which had its lead in the French movement of Catholic intellectual resurgence under Jacques Maritain, Charles Péguy, and Etienne Gilson, among others, and which in England included Hilaire Belloc, G. K. Chesterton, and T. S. Eliot. Dawson had no close affiliation with these men, however; he did not consider Belloc a serious historian but a poet. Though he agreed with Belloc's *Europe and the Faith* (1920) view of the centrality of the Church in

Western culture, he rejected the monistic view of culture inherent in such statements as "The Church is Europe: and Europe is the Church," which lost sight of the dualistic origins and nature of Western culture that provided its essential dynamism.[21] The same holds for T. S. Eliot's analysis of culture as in his 1948 "Notes toward a Definition of Culture." By assuming an identity between religion and culture and calling for a new Christian culture on this basis, Eliot would eliminate both freedom and progress by building a monolithic social order that, like any organization of this world, would be subject to the legacy of the Original Sin, the corruptions of power, and the inherent sinfulness of human nature. Religion, to Dawson, while a dynamic force in cultural creativity, must maintain an "otherness" in the transcendence of its manifested cultural forms.[22]

After the war, Dawson had the singular honor of being asked to give the Gifford lectures at Edinburgh for both 1947–48 and 1948–49, where he spoke on the relation between religion and culture. He continued to publish numerous books and articles through the 1950s and in 1957 a retrospective selection of his world historical work was compiled by John J. Mulloy. In 1958 Dawson achieved what was perhaps the climax of his career when he was asked to accept the newly created Stillman Professorship of Roman Catholic Studies at Harvard. The five-year offer was an answer to his dreams. By this stage Dawson had come to see the spread of education in Christian culture as the one long-term key to the resolution of the contemporary world dilemma; the spotlight this position afforded would be an ideal platform for the spread of his ideas in America, where his audience was already larger than at home. Dawson felt that the offer was "a call" and that his tenure at Harvard was meant to be.[23] At Harvard Dawson was seen as an eccentric scholar in "quiet isolation"; he spoke so softly that only those students sitting in the front of the class were sure to hear him. He was painfully shy, physically frail, and heedless of course structures to the point that in his first year he neglected to assign papers, exams, or grades to his students and thereafter relied on his teaching assistants for nearly all the structural administration of his courses. His classes dwindled to a dedicated core of advanced students.[24] His last lecture in the first series was devoted to the idea of a universal spiritual society as the goal of history, not one of Toynbee-style syncretism but one led within the organic tradition of the Catholic Church.

Dawson's Harvard tenure was cut short in 1962. He had a stroke in December of 1959; a second in the winter of 1962 made both speaking and writing awkward and difficult but did not affect his lucidity. He was forced to give up his teaching in June of that year and returned to Budleigh Salterton to continue his writing in retirement. A further series of strokes incapacitated him more extensively. In May 1970, Dawson suffered a heart attack, followed by pneumonia and eventually a coma, from which he emerged only once before his death on the twenty-fifth of May. According to his daughter, on Trinity Sunday Dawson awoke and startled those at his bedside, who had made no mention of the day, with a big smile and the words, "This is Trinity Sunday. I see it all and it is beautiful," before falling into his last sleep before death.[25]

• • •

To Christopher Dawson, the basic unit for historical study was not the nation-state or the civilization but the culture. A civilization is a supercultural conglomeration; it may be composed of several constituent cultures or peoples, which are its dynamic elements. A culture, as the "intelligible field of study," is "an organized way of life which is based on a common tradition and conditioned by a common environment." It entails a "common way of life, involves a common view of life, common standards of behavior and common standards of value and consequently a culture is a spiritual community which owes its unity to common belief and common ways of thought far more than any uniformity of physical type."[26] In essence a culture finds its unity in a religious vision that manifests for a people the end and purpose of life and so unites individuals psychologically in pursuit of shared goals.[27] While peoples may have their cycles of birth and death, cultures do not; they acquire the means, through education, to disseminate their achievements, in the case of the downfall of a constituent population or set of social structures, to a new ground, thereby preserving their legacy in a new population.[28] Dawson argued, like Ibn Khaldun of Tunis, that there was a dual dynamism in historical movement, that of the tribe or people and that of religion. In Dawson's view, there are organic movements in the life cycle of a people and so the idea of historical cycles has some validity. At the same time he asserted that religion carried forward through these cyclical phases as a world-transforming progressive force.[29]

Dawson saw culture as a function of four interdependent factors. From Geddes and Branford he adopted Le Play's three conditions affecting cultural development: first, a "community of place" or a geographic environment with its particular ecological imperatives on cultural development; second, a "community of blood" or a people who can be described in racial or genetic terms, and third, a "community of work" or the economic functions and occupations of a particular society. To these elements Dawson added a fourth, a "community of thought" or the psychological factor, which allows a progressive "inheritance of acquired characteristics" and manifests itself in the religious outlook of a people but that, in itself, could never dominate a culture unilaterally in independence of other conditions.[30] Indeed, the most common error in cultural interpretation and in social organization in line with an interpretation was, in Dawson's view, the extraction and elevation of one set of conditions above the others, sometimes even to the level of a misconceived "spiritual truth." Taken in isolation and made the principle of social order, the "community of place" led to the secularized religion of nationalism; the "community of blood" lent itself to fascistic and racist world views, and the "community of work" supported the unidimensional order of communism. Each error reduced reality to a constituent element and elevated it into a false god that, by its lack of integration with transcendental religious aspiration, sought a worldly millennium. In fact, the four elements are interdependent and any one of them is largely conditioned by the others. Dawson agreed with Spengler, for example, that race itself was a function of culture as a whole, the beliefs, practices, and ecological relations of a particular people to a particular environment; all left their marks on a genotypic racial community; thus, "race is a product of culture," not its cause.[31]

The continuity over time in Dawson's history of culture is remarkable. Long before he read Spengler, as far back as 1922 in an article for *The Sociological Review* entitled "The Life of Civilizations," Dawson had conceived a cyclical pattern of cultural progression that included a period of growth, or cultural synthesis, as a new cultural unity emerged from a degenerating cultural constellation; a period of progress, when the old synthesis from the last cycle disintegrated and a new identity fully coalesced; and a period of maturity, when the new synthesis maintained a hegemony and a new cultural cycle began to form. Dawson's three-beat cycle closely resembled Vico's presentation in *The New Science* of his three phases in a cultural cycle: the Age of Gods, the Age of Heroes, and the Age of Men. In the Hellenistic world, for example, Dawson charted a period of growth from 1100 to 500 B.C. when a cultural configuration developed, even as its predecessor cultures of Egypt and Mesopotamia went into decline, and came under the dominance of a "civic-religious culture" like unto an Age of the Gods. In the period of progress, the time between Pericles and Augustus, there was an age of heroic political, scientific, and philosophical achievement. This epoch was followed by an Age of Men from Augustus to the time of Justinian, when the old civic-religious culture slowly disintegrated to give way to a new cultural synthesis that was connected to a nascent undercurrent of religiosity in Christianity, the classical legacy, and the élan provided by the new blood of the barbarian *Volkwanderung*.[32] Despite his use of a three-stage cycle, Dawson, like

Troeltsch, rejected the Hegelian notion that the idea in history evolves in dialectic and each successive spirit of the age is the realization of that spirit in the world. For one thing, Dawson believed that beyond Hegelian becoming there is an eternally antithetical being outside of the world who leads humanity in history but remains ever separate; the idea is never manifested but only approximated.[33] Furthermore, Dawson held that the thesis that emerges in history is a progressive realization that meets no antithesis, except that of worldly conditions; Catholicism, for example, can be furthered, expanded, and progressively realized but never negated in history.

Dawson found that the cultural cycles he described had been repeated worldwide in four successive ages of culture. In the first age, from 4500 to 2700 B.C., the first valley civilizations had emerged in geographic isolation from one another. These societies grew as cultures in an interactive ecological, religious, and economic movement where external changes conditioned internal psychological states, which in turn stimulated efforts at environmental transformation. In *The Age of the Gods*, Dawson traced the origins of the archaic civilizations in a progressive religious and organizational pattern through Paleolithic pantheism and totemism, into the period of the earth-mother goddesses and the development of female-dominated agriculture. This movement was followed by a shift to the worship of the goddess's son or lover with the domestication of the ox and male-dominated agriculture, until, with the prototypical rise of Ishtar and Tammuz, there was a seasonal birth and death of the son/consort god in Mesopotamia. This religious evolution was accompanied by the rise of a temple economy and a state socialism under a theocratic god-king. Cities emerged around the sacred sites, the person of the king, and the increasingly centralized economy. This growth provided for an educated leisure class, writing, calendars, and the first inklings of a scientific view of a fixed cosmic order that could be grasped and predicted.[34] Each of the archaic civilizations was a ritual culture that, through its economic arrangements and intellectual accomplishments, laid foundations for subsequent civilizations.[35]

In the second world age, from 2700 to 1100 B.C., the isolation of these cultural centers ended and intercultural diffusion flourished, spurring the development of collateral civilizations such as the Minoan and Mycenaean civilizations, while parallel developments occurred in India and China. The new cultures of Assyria, the Persian Empire, the Etruscans, Romans, Greeks, and so forth, did not last long in comparison with the archaic civilizations but acted as an "intermediate and transitional stage between two or more permanent forms of religion-culture"—between the archaic god-kings and the almost completely otherworldly religious conceptions of life and the theocratic states of

Sassanian Persia, the Byzantine Empire, Islam, and medieval Christianity.[36] The third world age saw the development of the great classical
world cultures culminating with the inception of the higher religions,
which would coalesce into religion-cultures in the fourth age. We have
seen the phases of this development for Greek culture; it is critical in
understanding Dawson to see that these phases occur on a worldwide
level in the parallel world ages. The period of progress in this third age
took place as a universal intellectual and religious awakening that
Dawson views in much the same way as does Karl Jaspers in his
description of the Axial Age. This was the era of the Hebrew prophets'
articulation of their sacred linear history, the time of the flowering of
Greek philosophy, the writing of the Upanishads, the meditations of
the Buddha and Lao Tzu, and the articulation of the Confucian world
view. To Dawson, "the individual mind outgrew the traditional social
and religious forms."[37] A worldwide cultural shift occurred with a
change in humanity's view of reality; from the Mediterranean to India
and China there was a realization of a "universal cosmic law," an order
that acted as an underlying unity behind the perceived forms of
things.[38] With the ascendance of this view of a transcorporal reality, a
dualism of intellectual and religious culture arose that led to criticism
and reflection and a nascent sense of moral idealism, a sense that there
was a difference between the ways of the gods and the ways of men, a
discrepancy between what was and what ought to be.[39]

The third age ended in the mature flowering of these new spiritual
visions and their institutionalization in the cultural forms of the great
world religions and philosophical systems; this marked both the end
of an era and the foundation of a new world age. The nascent sense of
an eternal order led to manifestations of law, as in Judaism, the Way of
Confucianism and Taoism, the eternal forms of Plato, and the numer-
ology of Pythagoras, and served as a metaphysical basis for Aristotelian
science. At the same time the trend toward a transcendental reality was
taken to its final point by the oriental religions as they rejected the
world and declined into a retrograde and stationary fatalism. The
Greeks, in falling to a similar sense of recurrence, lost the world-
transformative élan of their earlier culture and turned to a resigned
stoicism. In Dawson's view, of all the religious traditions only the
Hebrew religion did not simply transcend the social and temporal
order but imposed an uncompromising and intolerant morality on its
people, a morality conceived not in terms of an impersonal cosmic
order but as the will and expressed word of a personal deity. For the
Jews, God manifested a moral purpose in history through his covenant
and its unique prophetic and apocalyptic tradition.[40]

The fourth age of the world, the modern period, had its period of
growth in the West in the medieval era. The rise of the fourth age

began in the final collapse and breakdown of the old material culture of the Roman Empire; in its place and upon its legacy rose a new Christian culture that preserved the classical tradition, now infused with the Judaic sense of dualism and linear time, and that digested the vitalizing new blood of the barbarian invaders.[41] What is most significant in Dawson's view of the fall of the Roman Empire, as opposed to Spengler's and that in Toynbee's early writings, is that the "synthesis of religion and culture which it had achieved did not die with it."[42] Cultural centers rise and extend themselves with the infusion of new peoples into a cultural field and the growth of unifying religious cultures; they decline with the passing of tradition. In Greece, the degeneration of the city-state culture that occurred with the rise of a cosmopolitan civilization sapped the internal moral and social life of its citizenry, based as it was on a faded vision of the ideal polis. Dawson held that consequent population degeneration through homosexuality, infanticide, and abortion led to the steady disintegration of the Greek body social.[43] Dawson's view of the fall of a civilization has much in common with Lewis Mumford's; he emphasized in the Fall of Rome that the city had become a vast megapolitan parasite, which like modern civilization had a "false relation to its environment." Dawson, however, never viewed a culture as a sealed whole but rather as an organic syncretism in constant process. In analyzing the fall of the classical synthesis of Greco-Roman civilization he therefore considered its significance not in terms of the decay of the civilizational structures of the Roman Empire but in its merger of oriental and Western streams of culture tied together by a new people who, by their very barbarism, had escaped the degenerating megapolitan effects of civilizational decay—they remained a rural people tied to the family and soil.[44]

Instead of emphasizing the decline and fall of a civilization, Dawson tried to demonstrate how the transformation at the Fall of Rome led into the fourth age and the flowering, from the ninth to the twelfth centuries, of Gothic medievalism in the West, the Byzantine efflorescence in the Christian East, and parallel cultural achievements in India and Islam. In this period there was a worldwide attempt by philosophers to digest the ancient wisdom of the last world age and to reconcile it with the new religious bases of society. In the later part of this period of growth, the ancient parental cultures of the world showed a marked decline; China, Persia, India, the Levant, and Mesopotamia were all devastated by invasions from the thirteenth to the fifteenth centuries, leaving the West in a position of relative strength going into the progressive phase of the modern period.[45]

The central dynamic element in the fourth age in the West was, of course, the Christian Church. Dawson distinguished six ages of the

Church, each of which had its origin in a crisis, was founded in a new and intense spirituality, and had brought forth a new apostolate. In a second phase of each age the Church was renewed by a fresh wave of Christian culture; a new way of life and thought was inspired. In the third phase of each age, however, the Church retreated into complacency and new tensions between the Church and the world stirred a new attack from without. The first age of the Church, the Apostolic Age, was marked by the three centuries of struggle with Rome; the victory of the Church and the nascent ideal of the Christian empire was its product and led into the second age, which extended from the conversion of Constantine to the fall of Jerusalem to Islam. This was the Age of the Fathers, of St. Basil, St. Gregory of Nyssa, St. John Chrysostom, Augustine, and Jerome. In the third age, from the seventh to the tenth centuries, the demographic center of the Church shifted to the rural north as Christendom was pressed between the barbarian invaders and Islamic expansion. This was the period of missionary work par excellence, led by Boniface and the Benedictines. In this time the Church became, in Dawson's view, the "schoolmaster of Europe" and all subsequent achievements of the West rested on her work. The fourth age was sparked by monastic reformers and antisecularists whose program to free the Church from the feudal state reached Rome in the mid-eleventh century. The ideals of St. Francis—the renunciation of private property and the acceptance of the poverty of Christ, the spiritual product of this reform cycle—prefigured the Reformation, which in practice, however, was dominated by sociological and nationalistic tensions rather than by any truly spiritual division. The fifth age opened with the challenges of Renaissance culture, the discovery of new worlds, and the Protestant revolutions that sparked the union of humanism and reformed Catholicism in Baroque culture and a new world missionary effort of the Church. The sixth age began in the defeat and disaster of the French Revolution from which the Church had recovered by 1850.[46] Central to Dawson's perspective on the progressive ages of the Church is the notion that Christianity is not a closed doctrine but an organic way of life conditioned by and conditioning history; it is a society that responds to stagnation with a continuous tradition of spiritual growth, actualization of principle, and reversion to unity.[47] Only Europe, in his view, has seen such a recurrent succession of spiritual movements; this is the reason for both its uniqueness and its power.

Looking at Western history in terms of Dawson's four world ages, one can see that the progressive phase of the fourth age began between the fourteenth and sixteenth centuries, when a working synthesis of ancient and modern knowledge was achieved. This synthesis, combined with the dynamic tension of the Christian tradition, fed Western cultural and technological expansion and the subsequent discovery and conquest of other lands. Concurrently, however, the disastrous divisions of the Reformation undermined Christian unity and gave birth to a bourgeois secular culture opposed to traditional Christian principles. To Dawson, Luther retarded the Renaissance in the North; he slowed the humanist's revival of learning and the reformation of religion. Luther's instinctive distrust of reason, his sense of sin as universal, as an element of libido rather than a choice made in the conscious will, and his sense that redemption is unearned and never merited divorced the individual's actions from the willful pursuit of a sacred ideal and so desacralized the world.[48] To Dawson, the Reformation was no reform at all but a sociological, political, and nationalistic revolution that used perceived discrepancies between the Christian vision and the external and historically ephemeral forms and practices of the Church as excuses for a break.

In conjunction with the rapid secularization the Reformation set in process, a new creed of worldly progress was articulated by Locke, Pope, and the philosophes in the mature culture of the seventeenth and eighteenth centuries. In Dawson's view the new doctrine acquired all of its positive aspects from Christianity but set a revolutionary model for breaking the connection between the two worlds embraced in its traditional millennial form. The idea of remodeling society in line with an ideal was peculiarly powerful in Western culture; when this guiding ideal was broken from a religious and organic grounding in the Christian tradition it became the "Revolutionary attitude" that has progressively disrupted the cohesive bonds of Western society.[49] In place of a Christian progressivism, the Enlightenment provided a science devoid of spiritual content that gave the West the material resources to unite the world but also provided a faith in abstract reason in isolation that met its test and failed in the French Revolution. Dawson took an essentially Burkean view of the Revolution's attempt to build a new culture a priori; he follows in the conservative tradition of De Bonald and Le Play in his perspective that the subordination of social and personal relations to economic relations led inevitably to social disorganization and dehumanization.

Dawson held that Western cultural expansion has provided for an unparalleled world revolution; a practical economic world unity has come into being so that world culture as a whole is dominated by a Western-imposed synthesis that has undermined the viability of indigenous cultures.[50] "These external conditions of world unity are, however, but the necessary preparation for a new world synthesis, which shall bring to an end the spiritual disorder and social anarchy which has been growing in the midst of all the achievements of knowledge and material power of the period of progress."[51] In the Western scientific, political, and economic expansion, the religious synthesis of the period of growth has been distorted or set aside and its material products taken for its spiritual foundations, leaving a secular shell of "material unity and control over external nature," which, unless it is reconnected to its roots, may become "merely the organs of a world tyranny of a complication of machinery crushing out true life."[52]

The bourgeois spirit that was the product of the Enlightenment divorced the soul from the world and made economics the center and measure of life. This spirit has remained common to the bastard offspring of Christian secularization, capitalism and communism, between which modern Christianity stands isolated.[53] The bourgeois spirit is the mentality of what Dawson echoed Geddes in calling the "Necropolis," as in Rome before the Fall and in the modern West, where the destruction of the natural world, as in the "devastated areas of industrial England and the cancerous growth of the suburbs" is symptomatic "of social disease and spiritual failure."[54] To Dawson, Christianity was antithetical to the idolization of self-interest in capitalism, and to the materialism and repression of free will in communism; he held that it must withdraw from the inevitable collapse of modernism as the seed to a new cultural synthesis.

Dawson was not denying progress in Western history or even in the modern period. He felt, however, that "True Progress" was not a "quantitative advance in wealth and numbers, nor even a qualitative advance in technology and the control of matter, though all these play their subsidiary parts in the movement. The essential fact of progress is a process of integration." This movement of the consolidation of "group consciousness" is "real and incontestible"; Dawson's task as a historian was to draw out its progress. Since all the lines of history seem to head in the direction of a "common consciousness," it did not seem utopian to Dawson to look toward world unification, a "synthesis in which every region can bring its contribution to the whole." Dawson agreed with Comte and Wells that progress was the successive realization of unity: he concurred on the dual nature of the optimally progressive society, which would unite science and technology and religious cohesion with a leading elite of engineers and technologists and a complement of priests. He argued, however, that the synthesis of the future would find its root in its spiritual inheritance and the continuity of tradition rather than in a revolution into an order designed by scientific abstraction.[55]

Dawson's position on the coming unification was close to that of Charles Ellwood, who held that "there is every reason to believe that when the true Christian spirit once fully dominates the Christian

Church, it will gradually permeate and transform the non-Christian religions so far as they are capable of surviving under conditions of true civilization."[56] Yet, again, Dawson differed from Ellwood in rejecting the view that Christianity can be arbitrarily rebuilt to meet modern needs for unity by rational means. In the end Dawson felt that "we must accept the existence of this independent order of spiritual truths and values" whose manifestations may be examined but whose formulation and evaluation must be left to theologians.[57] Religious inspiration and the otherness of inscrutable divine ends made history, in the last analysis, unpredictable. Rationalism could not penetrate its mystery. Dawson held to a Christian theology of history that sought the historical expression of "divine purpose and election" and that denied the ultimate power of discernment of any philosophy of history. From Dawson's perspective the Apocalypse was the Christian substitute for secular philosophies of history.[58]

Dawson sought to subsume cultural relativism to his view of the historical primacy of Catholicism through his perspective of a "Natural Theology." The universality of religious aspirations in history and the religious basis of every culture are evidence of the existence of a human need for religion, an "innate tendency toward God." Any way of life, then, acts as a "service of God" or else it is a depersonalized "way of death" that has lost its basis in human nature and is in the process of disintegration. All cultures produce a class of spiritual leaders, all perceive some elements of spiritual reality, all are historically conditioned paths to God. All cultures, in the development of taboos and laws, establish a divine sanction, a "Natural Law" or a sacred law. Prayer and mysticism are universal in the higher religions. In history the evolution of higher religious consciousness has proceeded as the spiritual realizations of a cultural era are passed on successively in each new age. There is a movement to more universal forms of religious institutionalization—those that are open to all peoples, that emphasize the unique personality, the irreducibility of the self from an end to a means, and the unity of the Godhead.[59] This process of evolution has reached its climax with the consecutive waves of Catholic reform and the extension of its secularized legacy worldwide.

The Catholic religion has acted as the dynamic foundation of progress because of its dual nature both in the world as an institution and in society, and by its aspiration to manifest the transcendental order. Dawson saw Eastern religious experience as the functional equivalent of the Western mystical tradition but considered it an imbalanced and partial form of religious experience. To him, the totalistic introversion and concentration in soul-searching and self-perfection in the loss of self into an absolute transcendental reality was a *via negativa* as in Indian Buddhist meditation and Hindu asceticism.

The Eastern "religions of negation" provide a bridge between religion and culture that provides passage in only one direction—through an escape into the spirit that allows culture to weaken and stagnate. When religion is totally married to culture it leads to stasis and the eventual loss of both spiritual and cultural vitality; this was the fate of the archaic religious cultures, where images of and by men were substituted for gods with a loss of the sense of transcendental reality. Modern world religions, on the other hand, have sometimes erred in going too far in the rejection of the world, leaving culture with no essential concern for freedom, social justice, or the willful improvement of material conditions in general. The central problem of religion on the world level, according to Dawson, has been to separate the intuition of the dependence of human life on a divine law that is eternal and transcendental from the sociological and historical imperatives of a particular culture at a particular point in time.[60]

Of all the religions, in Dawson's opinion, Christianity is most clearly founded on the dualism between the aspiration to manifest the City of God in this world and the recognition of the historically binding City of Babylon.[61] This deep sense of dualism, incarnate at the origins of Christianity in the dual nature of Christ, inspired and nourished the unparalleled moral, political, and scientific creative genius of the West by providing the aspirational dynamism at the root of the Western mentality.[62] H. G. Wells's and Lewis Mumford's views on utopias are secular parallels to Dawson's view that the dynamics of historical progress are motivated by the tension between ideal and temporal reality. Dawson takes this a step further in a profound analysis of the Western view of time itself as a movement, whatever its secular disguises, in the direction of Jerusalem, so that the future, like the past, is always sacralized. The Apocalypse, as the first Christian history, is the model for subsequent views of history and sets itself always between first and last things, the alpha and the omega. Though he categorically rejected deistic and utopian evolutionary perspectives, like the one of Teilhard de Chardin, Dawson recognized them as products of the Christian sense of time.[63] His own view is more closely modeled on that of Augustine; it is essentially tragic in that the two cities will continue in their tension, and evil will remain until the end of the world. Humankind must always live in the face of the Apocalypse.

In this tragic view, however, there is a surface inconsistency between Dawson's sense of a millennial progress toward a world civilization integrated on Christian principles and his view of the apocalyptic tendencies of the modern era and the unpredictability of the future. He states, for instance, in 1942, "I believe that the age of schism is passing and that the time has come when the divine principle of the Church's life will assert its attractive power, drawing all the living elements of Christian life and thought into organic unity."[64] Elsewhere he claims that "the Christian Church is the organ of the Spirit, the predestined channel through which the salvific energy of divine love flows out and transforms humanity."[65] An internal consistency underlies Dawson's view here; any millennial solution to the present world crisis is but temporary; there can and will be no worldly utopia. While a progress in realization of God and in world unity does occur, it underlies a continual failure and suffering in the world. According to Dawson, the Catholic Church does not preach optimism or social progress but constantly reminds people that when things are bad one must look to the end of things.[66] In the last analysis Dawson, like Augustine, subsumes the millennial tradition to a purely spiritual eschatology based on divine ends actualized historically that cannot be fully realized until the end of time.[67]

Christian dualism makes life an epic struggle against evil; Dawson adopted Pareto's view that the secular forms this has taken in the modern period—the liberal virtues of freedom, equality, and social justice, and those of communism, cooperation, economic justice, and brotherhood—have a like root in this Christian dynamic tension.[68] The modern scientific view is also founded in this tension and in the conception, as articulated by Aquinas, of a divine order underlying worldly phenomenon; to Dawson, the scientific world view remains entirely reconcilable with the Christian concept of divine reason.[69]

The breakdown of the barriers between the five or six major world religions has come about through the impetus of the West. In the process the viability of non-Christian religious cultures has been deeply undermined, but Dawson claims, the resultant material world cultural synthesis has provided an opening for world unification through the extension of the spiritual principle, which preceded and gave impetus to political, socioeconomic, and technological integration. The present spiritual vacuum in the East is partially filled by communism, which bears the secular legacy of the dynamic tension of Christianity.[70] Going back to Dawson's natural theology, one can see that the present secular transformation is ephemeral; it cannot last without a corresponding principle that unifies the culture spiritually; the "new scientific culture is devoid of all spiritual content" and hence is "no culture at all in the traditional sense." Alone it is but the victory of technology over culture. Human nature itself inevitably calls for an integrating principle. In the absence of one, the failure of the current secular models of liberal mass democracy, communism, and fascism will become increasingly apparent.[71]

Dawson sees civilization as a unitary process. In this he reverts to a nineteenth-century view of civilization led by Europe. At the same time his theory of world ages recognizes the universality of world historical processes. The foundation of his progressive view lies on the movement of peoples into new areas where they vitalize an established tradition, or on the extension and diffusion of that culture through a process of bilateral dispersion that feeds mutual growth and allows cultures to come under the widening umbrellas of the higher religious traditions. He defines civilization as the "cooperation of regional societies under a common spiritual influence" and he looks toward world unification on the basis of this universal religious inheritance.[72]

At the same time, this diffusion is not equilateral; Europe has played the central role in the breakdown of what had been a state of relative world isolation. Dawson saw the expansion of European hegemony in the modern period, in the Europeanization of Russia, the autonomous growth center in North America, the English conquest of India, and worldwide economic penetration, as a positive growth that was "cosmopolitan rather than imperialist in spirit." He justified the expansion of the British Empire as part of the civilizing process: "The process which is now regarded as the exploitation of the weaker peoples and classes by Western capitalism, was seen by contemporaries as the great means of world progress and international peace." The interchange benefited both parties as Western engineers and civil servants "performed the essential task of breaking through the inherited tyranny of prejudice and custom and thrusting the new scientific and technological order on a hundred unwilling peoples" who would not have adapted without Western control. He asserted that only Japan had overcome her reactionary tendencies to modernize voluntarily. He further claimed that all the modern triumphs of oriental nationalism and modernization, even in reaction to colonialism, were due to education in the ideas, knowledge, and ideals of the West.[73]

Dawson rejected Toynbee's postulation of the philosophical equivalence of civilizations (which Toynbee himself applied inconsistently) out of hand. He agreed with Toynbee's later position that the higher religions have been the goal of history and that the central dynamic has passed from civilizations to modern higher religions, but believed that Toynbee was in error to think that civilizations could simply wither away or that in a new religious synthesis the religions could disinterest themselves in the fate of civilizations. Central to Dawson's perspective of the Christian legacy is the notion of the transformative action of religion in the world, its attempt to mold civilization in line with spiritual values and ends. This is the foundation, as we have seen, of Western cultural dynamism, the theory of progress and Western scientific and technological success. In contradistinction to Toynbee and Spengler, who noted cultural extension through imperialism in the period of breakdown and decline, Dawson located it in periods of health and cultural vitality. To Dawson, the progressive historical sense of the West and the constant tension that it provides between cultural reality and spiritual aspiration is the unifying and essential element in any modern world synthesis. He consequently denigrated Toynbee's syncretistic union of world religious traditions as one where the ahistorical and polytheistic patterns of the Mahayana and Hindu religions would absorb the creative Christian tradition and so lose the activating sense of time and duality so critical for world development and unity. At the same time he claimed that the overall historical trend was toward monotheism.[74]

Only Christianity was in a position to bridge the chasm between the mystical East and the secular West.[75] And only in this bridge, which allows the inscrutable waters of the divine will to separate the two aspects of culture, can freedom be retained. Catholicism cannot degenerate, as secular religions are sure to do, into totalitarianism because it divides church and state and makes the individual will the locus of decisions of good and evil; the individual is responsible for his works in a way not included in the Eastern tradition or indeed in the elective theologies of Protestantism.[76]

Dawson put the blame for the degeneration of the West squarely on the shoulders of elites. The betrayal of the modern intellectual class manifests itself in its failure to take the place of the sacerdotal class that it overturned and to provide instead only the "devitalized intellectualism" of negative criticism and the disintegrative analysis of disconnected specialties without supplying any new principle of unity. The intellectual elites have "proved unable to resist the non-moral, inhuman and irrational forces which are destroying the humanist no less than the Christian traditions of Western Culture."[77] As a result, the principle of authority is undermined, culture is left guided by mass appetites, and social responsibility disappears; the human personality is diminished, the will enervated, as worldly institutions take decisive control in all spheres of social and personal life.

By 1936 Dawson foresaw the universal rise of an omnicompetent state that would "mould the mind and guide the life of its citizens from the cradle to the grave"; he seemed to consider this process as inevitable then and was more concerned with the spiritual conversion of this state than with its economic and political arrangements. He asserted that the dynamic tension between the two orders of church and state must be revived to preserve spiritual freedom under the present centralizing order.[78] His only answer to totalitarianism was a parallel and independent order based upon the "politics of the World to Come."[79]

At the height of World War II Dawson warned that even without an Axis victory modern technology and war organization produced an unprecedented and unconscious centralization that threatened freedom by forcing individuals to "bring themselves into line with the mechanized efficiency of a totalitarian mass state." In a mechanized order, even a democratic one, central organs acquire the means to direct public opinion. He opposed this to an ideal of the "free personal community" as a goal for the postwar world.[80] He argued in 1944 that "we are faced with a choice between social regimentation and social regeneration."[81] By 1960 Dawson had adopted a view of the military-industrial complex much like that of Lewis Mumford; he held that "education and science and technology; industry and business and government, all are coordinated with one another in a closed organization from which there is no escape." Like Mumford he came to see the power complex as following imperatives increasingly beyond human control, to increasingly view technical development as bearing its own momentum, and to describe the movement in the personality that corresponded to technological progression as an automation of the individual and the transformation of society into an "ant heap."[82] The great danger is brought to the individual level as mechanized production supplied goods that became the *raison d'être* of modern people; this is accompanied by a hedonistic degeneration where family and nation devolve into a herd without personality, faith, tradition, or any end beyond sensual gratification.[83] This renunciation of will that Dawson sees in modernism, the collapse of the duty to transform society in line with faith, can only have been a most grievous sin in his eyes, one that certainly included the violation of the first commandment.

These trends in modern life are deeply disturbing to Dawson. One occasionally finds in his apocalyptic rhetoric that he is not speaking in figurative but in literal terms of the reign of the Antichrist who will precede a final judgment. During World War II he claimed that "if our civilization denies its Christian tradition and inheritance it still bears the burden of them in an inverted form. It becomes not a humanist or a secular or even a pagan civilization, it is an apostate civilization—an anti-Christian order."[84] Like the majority of cyclicist metahistorians of our century, Dawson saw the modern age as equivalent to that of the Fall of Rome and he felt that a tremendous trial was imminent "in which the mystery of iniquity that was already at work in the world would come out in the open and claim to stand in the place of God Himself."[85] In *The Judgement of Nations* (1942), he claimed that "no human power can stop this progress to the abyss"; the enemy of the Sword of the Spirit was the authoritarian organization of society on anti-Christian lines, the "totalitarian Antichrist."[86] He believed that the

modern break between morality and politics was rooted in a secularization that depersonalized evil and made the modern period more like
the Apocalypse predicted by John than the times of Augustine.[87]

• • •

Next to the stridency of his social criticism and his apocalyptic sensitivity, Dawson's remedy for the crisis of the West was relatively mild and
slow paced. He advocated an education in the sociology, history, and
theology of Christian society to regain the lost roots of modern
culture. His life's work must be seen as an effort to implement this
program, to heal Christian divisions, to show the sacred roots of
modernism, and, in presenting his perspective on the crisis of the West,
to demonstrate the way back to God that would fulfill the Western
tradition and the movement of world history toward unity. His call for
education is for a reapplication of Christian culture to a fertile new
ground—modern secularized barbarism; it is more than an academic
exercise as it aims at a transformation of man. As such it betrays an
ambiguous Christian utopianism. Can a revival of Catholic education
have the world-transformative impact necessary to produce the changes
Dawson sought?

Dawson called for a new age of the Church in line with the pattern
of reform, which he described in *The Historic Reality of Christian
Culture* (1960), and in response to the present threat to Western
Christian civilization. In this work he demonstrated that a living
religion is a product of inheritance revitalized by historical movements
that attempt to regrasp its historical roots. The six past cycles in the
Church's history demonstrate that a time of renewal always follows
crises and so leads to an expectation of a resurgence in the present.[88]
"What the world needs now is not a new religion but an application of
religion to life," a "new asceticism," "an heroic effort like that which
converted the Roman Empire."[89] The success of this movement "involves not only the fate of our own people and our own civilization
but the fate of humanity and the future of the world."[90] He believed,
rather optimistically given his view of the modern order, that education
was the last and most powerful mode of influence left to Christianity
and that the modern leviathan was vulnerable to an orchestrated
movement from the inside to revive the cohesive world view of the
traditional West.[91]

Dawson saw the need to restrict the use of some technology but
held that a strong social order and planned economy were necessary
and probably inevitable developments that would require a corresponding planning in culture. If this were so, then planning must be

in a "really religious spirit" rather than toward a devitalized mechanism. "The only way to desecularize culture is by giving a spiritual aim
to the whole system of organization, so that the machine becomes the
servant of the spirit and not its enemy or its master."[92] Even so,
Dawson never called for a monolithic order dominated by the Catholic
church but for a renewal of cultural balance in the binary organization
of secular and sacred orders; the Church must never fuse with the
secular community of its organization.[93] Instead, desecularization
would work at a personal level to instill a "new ethics of vocation," a
sense of place, and an altruistic aspiration for the good of the organic
whole of the society, which, having their origin in the individual will,
would preserve freedom, even under the exigencies of a planned social
order. Dawson's vision of a hierarchical organic religion-culture depended on the subservience of each person to an accepted vocation; a
state he modeled on that of the Middle Ages and supported with Paul's
notion that "to each is given the manifestation of the Spirit for the
common good," and the vision of the participation of individuals as
members of the mystical body of Christ.[94]

• • •

There are major ambiguities in Dawson's ultimate solutions and goals.
When he writes of the machine or large-scale social planning he
sometimes asserts its inevitability and the need only to infuse this order
with the Christian spirit to preserve freedom. His assertions elsewhere
on the imperatives of technology make his spiritual freedom rather
ambiguous and put it clearly at odds with the ideal of freedom in a
liberal democracy; his freedom is etherealized to such a point that
there may be no outlet for it in the world. This ambiguity sometimes
gives way in his work to suggestions of antimodernist and primitivist
solutions. He longs for the pastoral peace and social unity he felt in his
own childhood and described as the legacy of the Middle Ages, but
can provide little vision of how these ideals could be achieved in the
twentieth century. His work contains a contradiction between his
tragic sense of the historical condition, with its division of the City of
Man from that of God, and his rather utopian view of the new age of
unity that may arise in the face of modern apocalyptic possibilities, a
unity now worldwide but molded on the "oasis of peace" of the Middle
Ages.[95]

Dawson's fundamental antimodernism and antiliberalism and his
hostility to the mass culture of democratic society rest on his desired
reversion to a cultural system founded on authority, tradition, and
supernaturalism. It is easy to argue that Dawson errs in the foundation
of his work by holding so strongly to the continuity of Western culture.

Arguably the modern scientific view is not reconcilable to his faith; only when secularization, the *breakdown* and destruction of medieval faith, occurred, could rationalism and the modern scientific view emerge. The two may be antithetical.

Though he strongly attacked the union of secular and sacred realms in his critiques of modern bourgeois democracy, communism and fascism, his own return to tradition could only be manifested in an equally totalitarian, and for most individuals in Western society, a priori, imposition. Dawson demanded the separation of church and state and the independence of politics, yet he also idealized the union of life and faith in the saints, especially in his highest model, St. Francis, and in the Middle Ages where a theocratic church and a theocratic empire were both inspired by an "all-embracing Christian Society—The City of God on Earth."[96] Though he postulated a progressive view of history, Dawson's own goals and desires are regressive, even reactionary; despite his contrary assertions, his calls were for a quixotic return to a past synthesis, which, because it is now antithetical to the spirit of the times, would require and manifest in many ways the revolutionary attitude he so condemned. Perhaps, as other metahistorians have suggested, the new religious synthesis for the fifth age of civilization will be an evolutionary deism or even some form of world religious syncretism. Though these alternatives to a Catholic world revival and hegemony horrified Dawson, they would seem more likely to follow from his initial macrohistorical theories of cycles and synthesis than a reversion to a single religious tradition of a past synthesis. His history of world religions, especially in *The Age of the Gods*, is one of the progress of a natural theology that digests and includes earlier dialectical stages of religious development as well as the products of the bilateral diffusion of varying strains of religious aspiration.

Dawson claimed that cultures are syncretistic, he championed a diffusionist perspective on world history as a product of the mutual contributions of all associated peoples, yet he denigrated the results of this process in the East by his rejection of a Toynbeean continuity of world religious syncretism and his claim for a unique dispensation. Dawson asserted that a historian could only view the past through the eyes of his own culture. His aversion to any modern relativism leaves him with a rather arrogant justification for his Eurocentrism, and his admission of cultural bias undermines the validity of the universalist premises and implications of his work.[97] The claim of a unique dispensation in a past cycle is inconsistent with his early presentation of a cyclical view of world history and his four world ages. Under this paradigm, the syncretistic product of one period provides the base for the growth and progress of another age but, in the end, is included in a larger synthesis at a more universal level. Dawson wants this to occur in the territorial extension of a revitalized Catholic tradition alone as the key to world history; consequently he rejects the likelihood of the inclusive religious movement that his theory of world ages would seem to predict.

Behind Christopher Dawson's rational prospectus on the coming age is a guiding faith that in the end history is a cultural movement of aspiration by humanity, in line with its progressive religious vision, toward God, that is mirrored by the active interventions of God in history through His revelatory inspiration of saints, mystics, and spiritual leaders who articulate successive approximations of the divine order. Seen in this light, the progressive reformations of Catholicism and its inspiration of European cultural and socioeconomic expansion have been Providential. The survival of Christianity after the French Revolution has been "miraculous."[98] In our modern "apocalyptic age" or "time of judgement," the "obscurity of history is suddenly illuminated by some sign of divine purpose"; there is a modern Revelation obvious to Dawson in the movement toward world unity: salvation will come in the spiritual unity that can fulfill it.[99] This is the new dispensation that Dawson offers in his Christian education; its alternative is a spiritual death and cultural disintegration.

Does the predominance of Dawson's faith reduce the historical significance and interest of his work? Is it possible to make any historical statement without faith in some first principle that establishes a context and meaning, that provides an epistemological and philosophical setting? Dawson, whatever his errors, made his premises explicit. At the same time his studies of the mentality of the Middle Ages and of primitive religions have intrinsic interest as well as value to the scholar; Dawson's empathetic rendering of these historical periods is of exceptional literary quality. His stress on the role of Christianity as the root of our civilization, and on other religions in their own settings, is an incisive antidote to the dominance in modern historiography of studies of the politics and economics of earlier periods, even of the structures of everyday life, that sometimes lose a sense of the psychological reality that can be observed only in recognizing the central role of a people's system of shared significant symbols— in the case of the West, those of the Christian faith throughout its historical evolution. His evaluation of the deep roots of the Christian tradition in the West and the legacy of that tradition in the modern mentality is a brilliant attempt to turn Nietzsche on his head; by demonstrating the penetrative power, endurance, and modern extension of these roots Dawson sought to demonstrate that Christianity still supplies the implicit order of our culture.

Dawson's historical works, from his study of archaic civilizations to the making of Europe, demonstrate solid scholarship and extensive erudition. As a metahistorical theoretician his work holds up better than most in its historical explanation of particular periods. His macrohistorical theories anticipated Spengler's and Sorokin's cyclicism and Toynbee's final mixture of cycles with a progressive religious movement. After 1954 Dawson felt that Toynbee's final progressive view of four world historical stages of civilization and religious cycles was essentially the same as the one he had outlined back in 1922, with the major difference being in their forecasts and the locus of historical dynamics rather than in their architectonic frameworks.[100] As a Christian exponent of a metahistorical paradigm developed through specific historical studies, Dawson must stand in the first rank among those in the twentieth century who have written metahistory in response to the perceived crisis of the West.

CHAPTER SEVEN

Lewis Mumford

The Generalist as Metahistorian

There are parts of Asia Minor, of Northern Africa, of Greece and even of Alpine Europe, where the operation of causes set in action by man has brought the face of the earth to a desolation almost as complete as that of the moon; and though, within that brief space of time which we call the 'historical period,' they are known to have been covered by luxuriant woods, verdant pastures, and fertile meadows, they are now too far deteriorated to be reclaimable by man. . . . The earth is fast becoming an unfit home for its noblest inhabitant, and another era of equal human crime and human improvidence, would reduce it to such a condition of impoverished productiveness, of shattered surface, of climatic excess, as to threaten the depravation, barbarism, and perhaps even extinction of the species.

—George Perkins Marsh[1]

Man has become a slave to his own marvelous invention, the machine.

—Nikolai Berdyaev[2]

As FAR BACK AS THE MID-1920S Lewis Mumford conceived a vocation for himself of realigning the self-perception of Western civilization in the decay of prewar progressive ideology toward a renewal of life. He sought to provide a new conception of the basic nature of man and a redefinition of the relationship between man and the machine. Mumford directed his works to shift the contemporary perspective of "the entire history of Homo Sapiens" toward this end. In 1925 he wrote to a friend, saying:

If we are to have a vision to live by again it will have to be different from all the past efforts of religion and philosophy; and yet it will have to draw from them and contain them . . . a synthesis of, not of knowledge, for that is impossible except in abstract forms, but of attitudes and experiences which will lead out into the life through which even the darkest parts will become assimilable and humanly self sustaining. To tell the truth, I am a little frightened when I contemplate the size of my task.[3]

Mumford modeled his life on that of the mythical universal man of the Renaissance; a professional generalist, he wrote a history of utopian projections and seminal works of literary criticism of nineteenth-century American literature and philosophy. He was among the leading architectural reviewers of the twentieth century, rivaling Ruskin in the nineteenth century in the influence of his criticism. A leading internationalist of the Old Left before World War II, Mumford was a persistent foe of fascism and helped to sway the isolationist and pacifistic Left in the late thirties toward recognition of the practical and moral necessity of confronting the Nazi menace and succoring England. Mumford led in the movement within the United States for urban surveys, regional planning, and urban/rural revitalization from the 1920s up into the 1970s. As a philosopher and a man of letters he has been compared to Emerson. In a psychological vein, Mumford presented a model of the natural personality in opposition to Carlyle's perspective of man as a "tool-using animal" and Bergson's view of man as "Homo-Faber"; Mumford's idea of man as a "self-fabricating animal" emphasized the primacy of man's symbolizing functions as the element that most makes him human.[4] His review of world history concentrated on the evolution of man in symbolic relation to his technics, where the technical constellation is an expression of human nature, a materially grounded set of abstract symbolizations that, at any particular historical point, provide a dialectical baseline for the subsequent formulation of symbols by individuals, including those of their own self-perception.

Mumford lived his monistic philosophy and articulated its implications as one of America's most persistent, staunch, and philosophically consistent ecohumanists of the twentieth century. As a cultural critic in the Cold War era, Mumford was perhaps unsurpassed in his trenchant attacks on the psychologically debilitating and morally sapping effects of nuclear technics, the perverse dehumanization of modern capitalism with its pattern of cancerous growth fed by the lowest common denominators of greed and the blind desire for power, and most important perhaps, on the modern, now worldwide, dominance of the all-devouring Moloch of the military-industrial complex: the megamachine, for which we have recreated ourselves in the image of automation. As a world historian, Mumford sought to present a cohesive view of the development of the modern megatechnical complex and to demonstrate that this process has gone forward in pursuit of human ideals and symbolic ends. In his holistic view of humanity as the procreator of symbols and directing ideals, Mumford showed that human beings could seize upon that creative power and thus envision a guiding view of the future where the free personality could regain its place as humanity's end and being rather than the suborned means of mechanical accretion and agglomeration.

Like the other metahistorians discussed herein, Mumford was driven by a utopian vision of a desired future that was confronted by a potential cataclysm, either by the material destruction of the biosphere through war or the decimation of the natural environment, or from the process of dehumanization, which accompanies environmental degeneration. To Mumford, a "collective compulsive neurosis" afflicts modern society through a Faustian bargain for material power and goods for which it has left its soul hostage.[5] The material destruction of the environment, the lack of nonmaterial values in modern urban life, and the mechanical imperatives of contemporary patterns of production and consumption progress of a piece; the personal and material aspects of life are intrinsically bound into a single development. For Mumford, like Emerson, "the world is emblematic"; macrocosmic development reflected that in the myriad mirrors of the microcosm and was there reflected in its turn.[6]

Mumford, the generalist as metahistorian, is a moralist and seer who takes up where the specialist leaves off, often at a point where he believes that humane judgment of the implications of historical findings is required. As he puts it: "My specialty is that of bringing the scattered specialisms together, to form an overall pattern that the expert, precisely because of his overconcentration on one small section of existence, fatally overlooks or deliberately ignores."[7] Modern specialization is the result of the "automation of knowledge," its compartmentalization into arbitrary and deactivating intellectual categories where it may conveniently be stored to prevent the association of meaningful truth. In an age when the utility of knowledge is defined by the interests of the cash nexus, in a machine economy, "we find that the very words, *human, history, value, purpose,* and *end,* were excluded as extraneous and undesirable for any method of quantitative measurement and statistical prediction." Mumford could not accept the separate hegemonies of C. P. Snow's 'two cultures' in the modern age; the scientific model had come to dominate in all areas, even those for which it was inapplicable.[8] Mumford instead held to a Jungian conception of the balanced unity of opposites in society as in the fully expressed personality. He held to a philosophical holism where distinctions between body and mind, spirit and matter, self and society, man and nature, and science and humanism were extrinsic and arbitrary categorizations masking an underlying unity.[9]

• • •

Lewis Mumford was born "out of his time" in Flushing, New York, in 1895.[10] Elvira Conradina (Baron) Mumford was a widow before Lewis was born; her husband had left her years earlier to go to Canada, and the marriage was annulled before his death. Elvira worked as a house-keeper at the home of a wealthy older bachelor with whom she shared a platonic love. Lewis was conceived when a nephew of her employer took a lengthy stay with his uncle and became Elvira's lover; the relationship was broken with the pregnancy, and Mrs. Mumford left her position with a pension rather than give up the child for adoption. Lewis was born to an unhappy, even bitter woman who ran a boarding-house and was a chronic and perhaps hypochondriacal invalid for more than thirty years. He never asked about his father until 1942 when his own boy, Geddes, approached his manhood.[11]

Despite the poverty of his early surroundings, his lack of a father, his mother's incessant and compulsive gambling, and the closed social world of an extended family given to perpetual feuds over petty trifles and insipid poker games, Mumford grew up with a strong sense of inner confidence.[12] In his early youth Lewis and his mother moved to Manhattan, across from where the Lincoln Center is now. He then found three routes of escape from his oppressive home: his grand-father, a retired headwaiter from Delmonico's, took him for extended daily walks throughout the city; from 1903 to 1908 he received his first formative exposures to rural life as he and his mother traveled to a Bethel, Vermont, farm to spend each summer. His third mode of flight consisted of an involved inner world of daydreams.[13] Although Lewis maintained a high level of self-esteem, he also manifested an early insecurity that was evidenced by his ever-present fear of death; until he was ten years old he could not go to sleep unless an adult lay beside him.[14] Lewis was an excellent student in grade school; he received the prize as best student and was named valedictorian before going to Stuyvesant High School, where his academic record was not nearly as good but where he became a cheerleader and was voted the most popular boy in his class.[15] At age sixteen Lewis's interest in classical literature was sparked, not by his school, but through his attraction to an older girl whose wider knowledge and literary interests demanded a corresponding fluency.[16]

According to a 1930 memoir, Mumford at age fourteen had faith in a personal God, one who helped him to get high marks in school. Aside from the influence of his fervently pious Catholic nanny, the religion of his home was superficially expressed within the frame of the Episcopal Church of America without any serious sense of commit-ment. When Lewis was sixteen he left the church in favor of the God he read of in Spinoza; subsequently, "God was in me and I was in God, but the sky from that time was empty."[17] He was later to have two mystical experiences that stayed with him throughout his life, one on the Brooklyn Bridge and the other in Newport in his Navy days, when he experienced a feeling remarkably like that which Toynbee reported, a sense of the entire past and future sweeping through him.[18] Though they were both agnostic to one extent or another when they first had these experiences, neither Toynbee nor Mumford described them as imaginative or emotional but rather as mystical, with all the connotations and implications of a transcendental state.

In the days of his youth Mumford held to the somewhat utopian optimism of the progressives, that the errors and imbalances of industrialism and urban poverty were about to be overcome: "We all had a sense that we were on the verge of a transition into a new world, a quite magical translation, in which the hopes of the American Revolution, the French Revolution and the Industrial Revolution would all be simultaneously fulfilled."[19] This utopianism, though shattered by World War I, remained as a current throughout his life's work, most clearly in the Renewal of Life series beginning in the thirties, and, after the capping blow of World War II, with diminished hope but no less fervor, in his last works on the development of the megamachine and the required transformation of man.

On graduating from high school, Mumford attended the City College of New York during the evening and worked as a copyist for the *Evening Telegraph* during the day to help support himself and his mother. He also began to write essays, articles, and plays, which he hoped to publish. After earning two years of credits as a night student Lewis applied for day registration and was accepted—as a freshman! The insult was all the more galling since he was already being published in *The Forum*; his subsequent collegiate career was marked by a lack of concentration in his coursework, deliberate nonconformity, poor marks, and extracurricular writing—both at school and for independent publications.[20]

In 1914 Mumford entered a contest in *Metropolitan* magazine to answer a challenging article by George Bernard Shaw on "The Case for Equality." Though he lost the contest to Lincoln Steffens, Mumford's article was also printed. Mumford was strongly influenced by Shaw in his youth; he retained Shavian perspectives throughout his life on the impossibility of a return to nature as unnatural, and he agreed with Shaw on the need for Supermen to lead in the salvaging of Western civilization.[21] In 1915, tuberculosis and a month's recuperation at Ogunquit interrupted his college attendance. After convalescence he resumed his studies at New York University, Columbia, and

City College without ever taking a degree, although he had plenty of credits.[22] In 1917 he sought to avoid the army draft by obtaining employment in a scientific laboratory and, later, by enlisting in the navy, where he served for ten months. In this last year of the war Mumford served as a radio technician. He was stationed comfortably in Cambridge, Massachusetts, where he had the leisure to study architecture, write in the Harvard Library, and survey the city and its museums. During the war Mumford hopefully anticipated "the Revolution . . . an uprising on the part of the downtrodden that would overthrow the master class and bring about a regime of equality and brotherhood."[23]

On his discharge from the navy in 1919, Mumford returned to his studies, now at the New School for Social Research, with classes by Graham Wallas and Thorstein Veblen.[24] Veblen served as a model for Mumford in this period; traces of his theories, like the evils of pecuniary society and the impact of the machine divorced from the instinct for workmanship, are retained throughout Mumford's writings. Veblen also worked with Mumford. In 1920 Mumford had obtained a position as an associate editor on *The Dial*, where Veblen held a seat on the editorial board. *The Dial* was a radical publication of the "Younger Generation," a group of disillusioned rebels in postwar Greenwich Village who sought "reconstruction," the rehumanization of all institutions, as an antidote to what they perceived as a coming dark age.[25] Though he was only with *The Dial* for seven months, his tenure there reinforced Mumford's direction in the future as a literary and social critic and as a defender of the sexual liberation of the twenties; it also introduced him to Sophia Wittenberg, who would become his wife and amanuensis.[26] As a member of *The Dial* staff, Mumford spoke out against the injustice of the Peace of Versailles and regretfully opposed the League of Nations. At around this time his disillusionment with U.S. politics, imperialism, and isolationism led him to conceive of the need for a "wholesale rethinking of the basis of modern life and thought."[27] Mumford's biographer, Donald Miller, describes him as a "communist" of sorts during this period; one who, in the tradition of Kropotkin, Ebenezer Howard, and Geddes, sought a "Green Republic" and rejected the Marxist view of a proletarian revolution in which progress and industrial growth would be united.[28]

In the early twenties Mumford began to make a name for himself as a writer and critic; over the years he contributed actively to the *New Republic, Harper's, The American Mercury, The American Caravan*, and other magazines. He published his first work of architectural criticism, with the characteristic title, "Machinery and the Modern Style," in *The New Republic* in 1921. By 1924 he had produced enough articles of architectural review to bring them together in his first book on the subject, *Sticks and Stones*, which made him a name in the field. Early in his career Mumford favored the clean lines of functionalist architecture in a reaction to the Victorian clutter of his childhood home; he celebrated the works of Richardson, Sullivan, and Wright as providing a new basis for the urban landscape. Later, from 1931 until his retirement, Mumford made his bread and butter by writing his *New Yorker* column, "The Sky Line," on architecture in the city. From 1932 to 1937 he doubled as the art critic on the magazine.[29] Even as he established a reputation in the twenties as a new and powerful voice in architectural criticism, Mumford was doing important work in another field, that of literary criticism and cultural history, through his books on *The Story of Utopias* (1922) and *The Golden Day* (1926).

Mumford's first book-length work of literary criticism, *The Story of Utopias*, established him solidly within the idealist tradition. He divided works in the utopian tradition between "escapist" fantasies and "utopias of reconstruction," which guide progressive activists toward the resolution of historical dilemmas. While rejecting the reductive utopias of nationalists and the tired radicalism of populist and progressive dogmatists who sought to remake the world by realigning the economic bases of society, Mumford praised those works that sought to regenerate the ideational superstructure of society. In this period he held that the utopian tradition and the "will to utopia" could act as a remedy to what Spengler had just defined as the decline of the West.[30] The saving revolution must be one of artists, like Thoreau, Emerson, and Whitman. Mumford rejected the utopias of the past, like Bellamy's *News from Nowhere* and Bacon's *New Atlantis*, which were dominated by technocratic elites. According to Mumford, the utopian tradition contained three key ideas that could be salvaged: land should be owned communally, work should be a "common function," and men should aim at genetic improvement.[31] In line with his later work, Mumford believed that these three elements should be cultivated at the regional level by local inhabitants as a means of social progress. Utopia must evolve from the grass roots as the result of the collective will of particular communities and not be imposed from above by external specialists.[32] Mumford criticized the utopian tradition as backward on this point. Though he rejected these historical visions from the past because of their top-down formats he insisted on the validity of the utopian inspiration as a means of guiding action toward future goals: "Desire is real."[33] As he later expressed it, "life is by nature directional and goal seeking."[34] Utopia by any earlier definition was the perfected society. In Mumford's view, especially later in his career, this was impossible and unnatural; he projected Eutopia—the "best possible place"—instead as a process, an ideal that guides action but never arrives at a final steady state. "Damn utopias! Life is better than utopia."[35]

The most formative influence on Mumford's early career and world view was the work and personality of Patrick Geddes, in Mumford's words, "the authentic father of city planning."[36] One hates to take the sexualized and almost universally maldescriptive Oedipal complex too seriously but in Mumford's case Geddes clearly became a moral and intellectual authority who stood in the place of the father that he had never had. Before he came under Geddes's influence Mumford had planned to attain a Ph.D. in philosophy; at another time he set himself the goal of becoming a successful playwright. From his first readings of Geddes when he was eighteen, however, Mumford gradually made Geddes the model of his own adult psychological and vocational development. Geddes's influence kept Mumford from specialization and justified his role of generalist; Geddes's work in biology and town planning "exemplified the basically ecological doctrine of organic unity" that was to become Mumford's philosophic goal.[37] The surrogate relation was a mutual one; on the first meeting of the two in 1923, Geddes claimed that Mumford was the very image of his son who had died in the war: "You must be another son to me Lewis, and we will get on with our work together." Mumford stated that "this almost unmanned me."[38] He felt a "complete paralysis" in the presence of Geddes, whose mumbled stream-of-consciousness soliloquies on architecture, biology, town planning, history, and the future were impossible for Mumford to follow and nearly drove him to tears.[39]

Geddes was a man of wide-ranging but unframed ideas and unwritten theses who saw Mumford as the man to act as his secretary and collaborator and to write up his legacy. While Mumford did adopt and extend Geddes's ideas, he also rebelled against the unequal relationship; he felt Geddes "wants all or nothing, and without seeking to get more deeply into one's own life, he sets before one the thwarted ambitions and ideas of his own."[40] After their initial meeting in 1923, when Geddes was on a U.S. tour that Mumford had arranged for him, the two nursed disappointed hopes over the lack of depth of their personal relationship. Though they corresponded regularly, they met only once again, in 1925, before Geddes died in 1932. Writing about Geddes later, Mumford recalled his own need to assert his identity to escape a symbiotic absorption in the work of his intellectual father and end as a mere popularizer of the Geddesian system: "The tragedy of the relationship between teacher and pupil is that every disciple who is worth his salt betrays his master."[41] Even so, he named his firstborn son Geddes Mumford.

Mumford never really betrayed Geddes's ideals, despite his refusal to become a secretary to his mentor and his rejection of Geddes's charts, graphs, and optimistic reliance on Comte. Mumford remained true to Geddes's view of history, the present problems of modern urban civilization, and the regionalist movement. In 1923 he joined and later became the executive secretary for the Regional Planning Association of America, led by Clarence Stein and Henry Wright, which was instrumental in the planning of Sunnyside Gardens in Long Island City and later in the New Town of Redburn, New Jersey, and in planning for the New Deal Greenbelt Program from 1938 to 1940. In 1925 Mumford, along with Benton MacKay (the founder of the Appalachian Trail), edited the Regional Planning Edition of the *Survey Graphic*; they presented a systematic ideal of regional surveys and planning as solutions to urban congestion and sprawl.[42] After the Second World War and up into the seventies, Mumford was the most visible advocate of the New Towns movement and the ideal of regional planning to integrate rural and urban culture and land use and to act as an antidote for centralized state power. Mumford consistently championed Geddes's program for "cities cut to the human measure": "We must drain away its population steadily into smaller centers until the metropolitan areas themselves can be reconstructed into a constellation of relatively self-contained communities, built on a more open pattern and separated from one another by parks and green belts."[43]

In the early thirties Mumford's career and politics began to crystallize. During that time he taught a course on "The Machine Age in America" at Columbia. Over the years he was to become a popular lecturer: he received visiting professorships at Dartmouth, Alabama College, Harvard, North Carolina State, Stanford, Berkeley, the University of Pennsylvania, and M.I.T. In 1930 Lewis and Sophy purchased an old farmhouse in Amenia, New York, and in 1936 they moved there permanently; Mumford would travel two days a week to New York and do his writing at home. The decade was dominated for the Mumfords by a growing uneasiness and then vehement opposition to the rise and spread of fascism. In 1935 Mumford supported the United Front against fascism and was the only leftist intellectual interviewed by *Calverton's Modern Monthly* who thought that the United States should go to war to defend Europe against Hitler.[44] In 1938 he made a "Call to Arms" in *The New Republic* and then wrote the rousing *Men Must Act* in 1939 and *Faith for Living* in 1940. In "The Corruption of Liberalism" in *The New Republic* (April 1940) he condemned the appeasing and isolationist liberals as "passive barbarians" who let the fascist religion spread. In his view, fascism had "the capacity . . . to integrate action, to create a spirit of willing sacrifice, to conjure up in the community that possesses it a sense of collective destiny which makes the individual life significant, even at the moment of death"; such a faith can only be countered by another that is equal to it.[45] Liberals, in their suspension of judgment, "castrate the emotions" and fail to see evil as evil: "Good and evil are real, as virtue and sin are real."[46] Mumford held at this time that active resistance to evil was essential even if it tainted virtue—as it presumably would through his own prescriptions for censorship, the jailing of all U.S. fascists, and the organization of the country for total war.[47]

In his argument against isolationist and pacifistic liberals Mumford made a distinction between "Pragmatic Liberalism," founded on the traditional liberal ideal of the unrestrained individual motivated by self-interest, where interests are subject to utilitarian measurement of solely material ends, and "Ideal Liberalism," which took as its paramount value the ideals of justice, order, and culture, and founded itself on the good of the social whole. He had faith that this latter constellation of ideals and community was what made people human and was worth fighting for. The united Left should rise as one and embrace these ideals of liberalism as the hammer of fascism; as he put it in *The Culture of Cities* (1938), "Instead of accepting the state cult of death that the fascists have erected as the proper crown for the servility and brutality that are the pillars of their states, we must erect a cult of life: life in action."[48]

As the war approached, Mumford attempted to rouse his personal associates to the coming watershed; he set out a series of articles calling for action, he debated isolationists like Hamilton Fish, whom he called a Nazi accomplice, and he even bought himself a thirty-gauge rifle, for, "with a Nazi victory in prospect, . . . we who believed in democracy might presently be fighting, perhaps underground, for our lives."[49] In 1940 he resigned from *The New Republic* because of its unwillingness to support war preparation, and after the war he resigned in protest when the American Academy of Arts and Sciences, of which he had been president, elected to give Charles Beard, a prominent prewar isolationist, an award.[50] When the war finally came, Mumford was an unflagging supporter of the Allied cause. After young Geddes died in France in 1944, his father wrote a heartrending biography of his son's short life as an act of catharsis for himself and for all the parents who had also made the supreme sacrifice.[51]

Before the war Mumford had hoped that it would be the crucible for a renewal of human values and an overturning of the power-mad order of capitalism, fascism, and misdirected Soviet communism. Like Wells before World War I, he felt that this was to be the "last great crisis of this megapolitan power civilization" that would "displace the power personality." A Nietzschean transvaluation of values would produce a new man and ground decentralized social power in regional variations of the triad of family, land, and the internal self.[52] This historically necessary "large-scale conversion" would be "deep-seated, organic, and religious in essence."[53] In fact, to a critical reviewer, the transformation that Mumford sought and his "ideal liberalism" with its subordination of self-interest to community and order had much in common with the spirit of self-sacrifice and the desire for an organic social unity on which fascism itself was modeled. From Mumford's perspective, the essential difference would be in the rejection of the megatechnic power structure for the organic local community. The irony of this commonality between his "ideal liberalism" and some fascist ideas was compounded as he also saw the necessity for the technical and organizational means of total war to defeat fascism. At war's end he was left with a deep sense of tragedy over the retention of these means in the Allied victory. He came to see Hitler as an "agent in the modernization of the megamachine"; "In the very act of dying the Nazis transmitted the germs of their disease to their American opponents."[54]

In the wake of the war Mumford was one of the first to call for the public control of worldwide nuclear technology. He repudiated the wartime error of indiscriminate bombing of civilian targets as a fascist technique that culminated in the use of the atomic bomb. In 1946 he condemned the Bikini Island tests and called for a national moral examination over Hiroshima and Nagasaki. To Mumford, the retention and stockpiling of nuclear weapons in peacetime must be averted at the start and he denounced nuclear strategy in no uncertain terms; it was as if "the secretary of Agriculture had licensed sale of human flesh as a wartime emergency measure and people had taken to cannibalism when the war was over as a clever dodge for lowering the cost of living." He also claimed that "madmen govern our affairs in the name of order and security."[55] Throughout the 1950s Mumford was one of the nation's most strident foes of nuclear weapons; in his view the planning for genocidal obliteration bombing marked a moral reversal in the West; the new conditioned acceptance of the American people to the modern goal of war, mutual extermination, evinced an overturning of liberal virtues and democratic control.[56]

By the 1960s, both reflecting and contributing to the countercultural and New Left critiques of modern America, Mumford condemned what Eisenhower had called the "military-scientific-industrial elite," and the "military-industrial complex" with its "permanent state of war."[57] He was one of the first and most vociferous opponents of U.S. involvement in Vietnam. He condemned the power machine's actions against the Vietnamese people: they were "terrorized, poisoned and roasted alive in a futile attempt to make the power fantasies of the military-industrial-scientific elite seem 'creditable.' "[58] The U.S. space program was also high on his list of errors—it was but Keynesian 'pyramid building' to put a man on the moon, just another manifestation of the machine's conspicuous waste.[59] In the sixties Mumford explored the rise of the "megamachine" historically in three works that in his opinion marked the "climax of his thinking": *The City in History* won a National Book Award in 1962, and the two-volume *Myth of the Machine* came out in 1967 and 1970. In 1972 Mumford received a National Medal for Literature. He continued his critique in journal articles into the seventies, his central arguments now permanently set in their direction and tone. In the late seventies and early eighties, the now elderly Mumford produced several revealing autobiographical works.[60] Lewis Mumford died in January 1990.

• • •

Mumford went through two major phases in his conception of the historical progression of man in evolution with his technics. The early half of his life's work, roughly until the end of World War II, coalesced into the Renewal of Life series, an initially optimistic historical survey of man and technology from A.D. 1000 to the present that anticipated the emergence of a "Biotechnic" power and industry that would circumvent the worst abuses of "Paleotechnic" industry and social organization. The second half to Mumford's major metahistorical work was a parallel sequence of books that centered on *The Myth of the Machine* and dealt with its themes from the dawn of civilization.

The goal of the Renewal of Life series is foreshadowed in Mumford's seminal work on U.S. philosophy and literature from 1830 to 1860, *The Golden Day* (1926). Through this work Mumford was influential in resuscitating the reputations of the writers of the period who had been scorned in the Gilded Age. From his perspective, the writings of Emerson, Thoreau, Whitman, and Melville were in response to the breakdown of the medieval synthesis, the last period in which man and the world could be viewed as a whole. "During the Middle Ages the visible world was definite and secure."[61] The breakdown of the unified symbol system of the medieval order through the disintegrative movements of the Renaissance and Reformation was accomplished in the rise of abstractions that disconnected the intellectual and spiritual man from his natural environment. In the new financial order of money and credit a man's work was disconnected from his goods. In science, a breakdown of the human-centered universe and the rise of mathematical quantification of distance and movement depopulated the heavens and pictured the body as a machine. In political thought, the individual was extracted from his society.[62]

To Mumford, Emerson typified an authentic and original American response to this dislocation through his assertion that matter and spirit were but "phases of Man's experience" and were not in conflict; matter passed through man's spirit to be formulated into symbol and meaning, and spirit passed into matter and gave it form; in this juncture between symbols and forms man found his essence.[63] Emerson, in Mumford's view, called for a revitalization of philosophy by turning to a nakedness, to the freshness of one's own consciousness and the independent world of ideas in order to bypass the dead forms of the European past; "Life only avails, not the having lived."[64] This renewal of philosophy and at the same time "life style," as Nietzsche was to call it, anticipated Nietzsche's transvaluation of values. In Mumford's opinion, "there is little that is healthy in Nietzsche that was not first expressed in Emerson."[65] To Mumford, Emerson's neo-Kantianism was richer than any contemporary philosophy in Europe; the transcendental response to the downfall of the medieval synthesis and the rise of the mechanical world view was perhaps the most potently conceived answer to the machine yet invented.

Along with Emerson's transcendentalism, Mumford found in the 'golden day' warnings of the dominance of urban decadence and the new industrial age by critics from Thoreau to Melville. In 1929 Mumford wrote his study on the thought of *Herman Melville*, which did a great deal to revive Melville's reputation. Mumford used the metaphor of the Pequod as the West driven by a power-intoxicated Ahab in pursuit of a nature that, out of blind resistance to madness, might destroy its antagonist.[66] The golden day ended tragically with the Civil War, a battle between two forms of slavery: the system of black subjugation, and in the North what George Fitzhughs had condemned as slavery to the machine. In the victory of the machine "the guts of idealism were gone" and the ideal of the organic relationship of man and technics in the pastoral garden was dismissed as romantic sentimentality. In the wake of this disillusionment, American intellectuals turned again to Europe for inspiration or, like Henry Adams, bemoaned their psychological displacement in an era dominated by "men on the make."[67]

Mumford's early study of utopias and his analysis of the golden day clearly foreshadowed the main themes of his Renewal of Life series. In writing these four volumes Mumford set out to build a "reconstructive utopia," a base plan for the transformation of society toward a "biotechnic," human-centered culture and economy. The path to this utopian ideal involved the resolution of the very difficulty with which

Emerson and his generation had grappled: supplying a psychological, philosophical, and practical foundation for an indigenous community that could fill the void left in the disintegration of medievalism. The renewal of life would occur as humanity grounded itself in a new humanistic synthesis where its best interests and purposes would guide in the formation of its technics rather than be ignored and bypassed by the automatic movement of technical agglomeration.

Mumford formulated his historical works in part as an answer to Spengler's thesis on the downfall of Western civilization. Spengler's timetables for the stages of civilization concurred with Patrick Geddes's characterization of the cultural-phase progression in the evolution of cities from polis to metropolis to megalopolis to parasitopolis to pathopolis to necropolis. In 1926 Mumford felt that Spengler's "feeling for history" was "magnificent," "sound," and "brilliant." He agreed with Spengler's positioning of the West: "I am quite ready, for one, to grant that we have reached the final stage." But Mumford argued that this intellectual realization itself changed the fate of the West. Possessing an understanding of this degenerative cycle, we could, perhaps, prevent and reverse the decline of the West or, at any event, the West need not be succeeded by barbarians. "May we not, perhaps for the first time, make the transposition consciously, from a finished civilization to a new and budding culture?"[68] Mumford later disavowed Spengler's "disembodied Platonism," especially his artificial separation of a spiritual culture and a materialist civilization, both of which exist as elements in a dialectical balance in any society.[69] His later criticisms of Spengler as the prophet of Nazi barbarism cannot gloss over the certain sympathy that Mumford felt for Spengler's view of the fall of the West and to which he connected his own version of a sort of conscious barbarism, one that required a clean slate for an Emersonian renewal or Nietzschean revaluation, but that would be established from the start on humanistic principles. While he condemned Spengler's imposition of his martial values in history as pasting his own photo on the lens of history, he applied his own humanism in its place in his call for renewal.

The four volumes of the Renewal of Life series were published over a seventeen year period: *Technics and Civilization* came out in 1934, *The Culture of Cities* in 1938, *The Condition of Man* in 1944, and *The Conduct of Life* in 1951. With the first volume, Mumford established his reputation as an advanced pioneer in the history of technology. In this work Mumford was at his most optimistic. Surveying the interaction between Western society and its technics, he found that "the machine is ambivalent"; the "purposeless materialism" of the present is not a result of any imperative found in the machine itself but is a product of our lack of values in its application. With the imposition of new values the machine could be an instrument of liberation, and technological growth could be a step toward the biotechnical economy. When Mumford employed Spengler's word *technics*, he referred to the "entire technological complex," which included the symbols of aspiration manifested in technical solutions, the corresponding structure of society, and the personality associated with its stage of development.[70] Thus, in describing technics and its history Mumford portrayed the evolution of mentality in the West, including an idolum or symbolic field, which preceded and justified technological progress.

Technics and Civilization, to Mumford's later chagrin, held to the progressive era's optimism that rationalization of production, efficiency and uplift, would produce a plenty that would do for all: reason merely demanded a victory of "sound machine esthetics" over what Veblen had called "the requirements of pecuniary reputability." As a supporter of functionalist architecture, an enthusiastic proponent of hydropower and rural electrification, and an optimist over the possibilities for the widespread distribution of goods in the emerging new economy, Mumford held that "we cannot intelligently accept the practical benefits of the machine without accepting its moral imperatives and esthetics forms," and further, "the economic: the objective: the collective: and finally, the integration of these principles in a new conception of the organic—these are the marks, already discernable, of our assimilation of the machine not merely as an instrument of practical action but as a valuable mode of life."[71] At this point he felt that standardization and Taylorism were good things and looked forward to the growth of a rationalized, large-scale agriculture in place of the outmoded private ownership of land.[72] To be fair, Mumford's optimism (which he later rued) was conditioned here by his long-term perspective on the imminent emergence of a biotechnic, human-centered economy. In his mind, the mechanical world picture was now breaking down, capitalism, the "economy of acquisition," was a spent force, and technics would henceforth serve a post-Marxist basic communism with socialized distribution at a "vital standard" that would end the progressive pattern of increased consumption.[73]

Mumford inherited and extended the historical categorizations of Patrick Geddes, who had divided the history of technics into Paleotechnic and Neotechnic periods.[74] He employed three overlapping historical periods in his early works starting with the Eotechnic, which began around A.D. 1000. The Eotechnic period was the dawn of modern technics, "one of the most brilliant periods in history," in which the West, through a syncretism of inventive technological contributions, synthesized an order based upon the new power sources of wind, water, and wood (replacing man and horsepower). There was a balance of agriculture and small-scale, community-based, guild-regulated industry that employed canals for transportation and contributed glass for lighting and the printing press for the dissemination of knowledge.[75] Mumford argued, against Weber's thesis of the conjunctive origins of capitalism and the Calvinist mind-set and work ethic, that the capitalistic order had its origin in the disciplines of work and prayer established in the early Eotechnic Benedictine monasteries: the clock, and thereby an incrementally atomized and symbolically mechanized time, regulated canonical hours and instituted an internalized relation between segments of time and tasks to be performed. Simultaneously, mining and spinning industries began to advance faster than other economic areas; the production of textiles began to shift from the individual home to the factory. Concurrently, the technics of the mine, like the standardization and mass technics required by the army, developed a breakdown of process steps and specialization, the pattern of continuous shifts and new tools like pumps, bellows, and engines, all of which required extensive capitalization. The nascent technics of the Eotechnic mine and factory would become the dominant technics of the Paleotechnic period.[76] The other half of the emergent vanguard was war, "the chief propagator of the machine." Warfare was the main agent in promoting the growth of the mining industry, especially with the large-scale use of cannon; the cannon led to the consequent intensive fortification of moats, canals, bridges, and outworks, which required the services of military engineers. To Mumford the military machine was an ideal form toward which technics tend when not directed toward human ends.[77] The Eotechnic order lasted until 1750 in Britain and later elsewhere, but by the end of the Renaissance it was already in twilight. Industry grew more backward from a human standpoint even as it advanced as a mechanical system.

The shift from the Eotechnic to the Paleotechnic era was preceded by a corresponding shift in the symbolic abstraction of value, noted earlier in both science and capitalism, which gave birth to the mechanistic world picture. The division between primary and secondary qualities by Galileo, and the corresponding reduction of reality to the measurable, the dualistic Cartesian view of the body as a machine, the division of knowledge and the limitation of field symbolized by the expulsion of the humanities as objects of study by the Royal Society, the concentration on the external world and rejection of the internal one: all evidenced to Mumford a turn away from an organic approach.[78] Mumford characterized the Baroque Age as an "age of abstractions" when the transformation to the Paleotechnic was accomplished by isolating the part and classifying away any unifying wholes.[79] By the end of the Eotechnic period, material goods had replaced a communal sense of place or a religious aspiration as the measure of wealth and goal of life, making the "greatest good for the greatest number" a mechanistic justification for an ever-increasing production of goods without a standard of human need or any intrinsic sense of human happiness. Mumford's view of the new era of technics was basically an idealist one: the change in world picture in part preceded change in technology just as dreams, visions, and aspirations, like Leonardo's dream of flight, provided a model later materialized by invention.[80]

The Paleotechnic era started around 1760 without a sharp break with the past; as we have seen, the idolum was in place and the technical model of the army and the mine had established a pattern for its implementation. The Paleotechnic complex came together with the use of coal and, later, oil as an energy source, iron as a building material, and the steam engine as a motive power. To Mumford's mind the railroad and mine system led to a widespread perversion and destruction of the environment, partly through their collateral conurbation (a Geddes neologism), or unrestrained urban growth and sprawl at railroad junctures, mining centers, and centers of industrial production.[81] The Paleotechnic period was a "disastrous interlude"; it destroyed living standards, undermined the health of cities, and demanded imperialistic adventures to provide forced outlets for manufacturers and the control of raw materials. Accompanying these physical processes was the ideology of progress, which measured value by time calculation and overturned Kant's dictum that man must be an end and not merely a means. The factory system came increasingly to dominate all aspects of life, turning skilled craftsmen into machine tenders, and extending its discipline into the school and bedroom so that "life was judged by the extent to which it ministered to progress, progress was not judged by the extent to which it ministered to life," and "survival of the fittest" served as the post-facto justification of an idolum, not as a true measure of man's nature.[82] With the rise of "individualism," the decline of "personality" sparked the compensatory Romantic movement and, in the twentieth century, the irrationalism and sexualization of art, both of which can be seen as stopgap efforts to protest the hegemony of the machine.[83]

Following the Paleotechnic abuses and resolving many of them was the current rise of the Neotechnic order. Hydropower electricity would allow regional decentralization and local market economies; automation would save laborers from drudge work; new alloys, technologies of instantaneous communication, new technologies of light such as telescopes and microscopes, the industrialization of agriculture, conservation practices, birth control, collectivization, all would serve to humanize the machine, to integrate its positive benefits with human needs. The very inventiveness of the Neotechnical order will provide technics that will resolve the human problems of the Paleotechnic. And this is not all.[84] Once the Neotechnic age frees itself from the fossilized remnants of the Paleotechnic configuration, a cooperative, liberating paradise might be forthcoming in a culminating Biotechnic order. Mumford's ideal of the Biotechnic partly anticipates Herbert Marcuse's New Left analysis of the potential for the elimination of the "surplus repressions" of the past that would allow a return to a polymorphous sexualization and turn work into play in a garden of technologically produced abundance. "When automation becomes general and the benefits of mechanization are socialized, men will be back once more in the Edenlike state in which they have existed in regions of natural increment, like the South Seas: the ritual of leisure will replace the ritual of work, and work itself will become a kind of game."[85] An "organic ideology" replacing that of the machine will emerge in the Neotechnic period as we absorb the lessons of machine production, of objectivity, the concept of a neutral world and the quantitative and rational side of existence—while these are not complete, they are necessary to future growth and, first of all, for the rejection of the religion of the machine, the Paleotechnic doctrine of progress.[86]

The locus of the change in the symbols of any society is with those individuals who foresee the imperatives of their age and are able to present symbolic resolutions that can be materialized by the society in its art, institutions, and life-style. According to Mumford, the Biotechnic order has already been foreshadowed by a wave of creative leaders, men like Robert Owen, Geddes, Ebenezer Howard, the father of the New Towns movement, William Morris, Kropotkin, Frederick Law Olmstead, George Perkins Marsh, and Alfred North Whitehead.[87] Mumford conceptualized the individual role in creation much as Toynbee did with his withdrawal and return paradigm and perspective on the spread of cultural creations by mimesis through society at large. Like Toynbee he owed debts to Bergson and Nietzsche. He held that "only a handful of people in any age are its true contemporaries. Only sluggishly do the mass of the people respond to the events that are sweeping through the ruling classes or the intellectual elite."[88] The "creator or transvaluator" is an artist with symbols "who brings forth out of his own depths new forms and values that amount to new destinations," who must work to "overcome or transform the demonic and to release the more human and divine elements in his own soul."[89] The first step in social transformation then, history tells us, is to "find yourself" and there "establish a fresh starting point."[90]

Such is the metahistorical platform that underlies the Renewal of Life series and serves as a baseline for the later *Myth of the Machine*

volumes. In *The Culture of Cities* (1938), Mumford charted the unhappy movement of conurbation from the ecological balance of the
human-scale medieval walled town to the Paleotechnic megalopolis;
the loss of scale at the end of the medieval period was "symptomatic of
social pathology." *The Culture of Cities* is a landmark in the writing of
the history of the city, especially of urban growth or, as Mumford
called it, "unbuilding," which is the destruction of ecological balance.[91]
He traced the effects of capitalist value on land use, the impact of
increased bureaucratic centralism and military imperatives on urban
grid patterns, and architectural disharmony through the Paleotechnic
phase. But then Mumford turned the second half of his massive tome
to the prospective Neotechnic urban emergence by tracing the movement of urban reform through the nineteenth century. The book
reached a climax with evangelical exhortations for the New Towns
movement and bioregionalism. He also speculated ahead to the Biotechnic, where decentralized "Garden Cities" would be limited in size
to where each member of the community could know the others,
where in the breakdown of the factory system people would revert to
the full expression of what Veblen called the "instinct of workmanship"
through a revival of the arts and crafts, and finally, where the world
economy would be diminished in scale to a simple "reserve for surpluses and specialties."[92]

Mumford's view of the city is like that which we will see in the
review of William McNeill's work in chapter 8; it is "the point of
maximum concentration for the culture of a community," holding the
sum of a cultural heritage.[93] As such it materially reflects the idolum of
its time and society. Mumford's holistic philosophy attempted to unite
the study of urban development and town planning with an analysis of
the pattern of symbol integration in the collective psychology of a
people. When he turned to *The Condition of Man* (1944), he was able
to trace the history of ideas and mentality in the West alongside the
patterns he had elaborated in his books on technics and cities. "Every
practical manifestation of a culture tends to leave a shadow self in the
mind"; the obverse is also true.[94] Throughout the series, Mumford was
able to pull together historical strands of evidence and unite them
under his monistic system to produce a coherently unified perspective
on culture as a whole.

Mumford was profoundly influenced in his analysis of the increasing
speed of technical change by Henry Adams's "Rule of Phase Law" of
the progressive movement of sources of power and their symbols, a
progress that would result in man's annihilation. He rejected the
pseudoscientific elements in Adams's view that found the catalytic
degeneration of the will to reason in history in its successive conversion

in line with the second law of thermodynamics (entropy), but after his early period of optimism he was wholly in sympathy with Adams's view of the timetable of the disintegration of Western civilization.[95] According to Mumford, "Events have magnificently vindicated Adams' interpretations." In Adams's scheme, the religious phase (symbolized for him by the Virgin) lasted ninety thousand years of human history. It was followed, around A.D. 1600, by a mechanical phase, similar to Mumford's paleotechnic. This was succeeded by an electrical phase of only seventeen-and-a-half years and an etherial phase of about four, leaving humankind in 1921 with an ultimate source of power but degenerated in will and humanity to such a point that it would use this new energy to its own destruction.[96]

World War II and the atom bomb symbolically if not chronologically vindicated Adams's timetable of inverse squares by giving humanity a power source of cosmic violence that had the potential of fulfilling his dire prediction of extinction. Mumford believed that Adams, alone in his day, appreciated the technics surrounding radium; he alone understood the potentially devastating effects of an ultimate power in a world without a sense of purpose. Geddes had made similar warnings on the acceleration of history, and we have seen in 1945 Wells's 1914 anticipation (in *The World Set Free*) of a single bomb destroying a city. Mumford felt that our sight had been disastrously foreshortened when we failed to heed these prophetic voices. At the same time he put himself in the position of these other prophets, as in 1954 when he warned of the tremendous environmental hazard of even the peacetime use of atomic energy when there was no systematic provision for long-term waste disposal.[97] Mumford admitted his own error in discounting Adams's predictions of catastrophe and his undue optimism in *Technics and Civilization*; he recognized that he had repressed his fears of nuclear technology, and he "only awoke after Hiroshima."[98]

Adams's dilemma coalesced with Mumford's larger metahistorical point of view and the arrival of the nuclear age to stir Mumford to the revision of his history and technics series and set three problems that would be central to the *Myth* volumes. For one, Adams saw the progress of power transfers as outside of human control. Second, Adams, confronted by the inadequacy of reason, cast it away from himself in the end and instead embraced feeling at the feet of the Virgin, much as Mumford felt that Toynbee leapt into the spiritual to escape real-world contingencies.[99] Third, Adams's despair in his sense of lost purposiveness, in a world where God was dead and evolution was an accident, must be resolved with a new biological synthesis that reasserted an Aristotelian purposiveness to nature and to the emergence of humanity.[100]

Mumford's resolution of these difficulties was a core concern of his later work. He had already demonstrated his idealistic perspective on guiding symbols to which the technological complex contributes and on which it is built, and his postulate that inspired individuals can transform the idolum: the human will and artistic vision, when activated, can be determinative of the pattern of technics. Second, Mumford's analysis of the inadequacy of reason was not nearly as absolute as Adams's. Mumford held with Sorokin a sense that reason alone, isolated by specialization, compartmentalization, and the consequent "straining at gnats," is inadequate and "existentially . . . underdimensional"; but reason, supplied with vision, in service of ideal and bolstered by faith, is an important component in humanity's search for truth and self-improvement toward a better future.[101] The third element in Adams's dilemma was also partly resolved through Mumford's view of the importance of guiding purposes or symbolic ideals in history. In *The Conduct of Life* (1951), the closing volume of the Renewal of Life series, Mumford confronted Adams's pessimistic forecasts in the wake of their partial realization in World War II and its aftermath. Here he formulated an evolutionary perspective of humanity's symbol-making ability and the accumulation of culture that guides in new ideal formation. There is a human purpose to this evolution that allows it to transcend cycles like his own cycles of civic degeneration or Adams's entropic movement of will. In rejecting Toynbee's mystical flight from the world and the inevitabilities of Spengler and Sorokin, Mumford asserted that "man has repeatedly altered his archetypal biological plan of life by creating, through culture, a social function and drama, formed by his own needs and conforming to his own emerging purposes."[102] Evolution is goal directed because man himself, through his symbol-making ability, supplies a guiding purpose to it. To go even further: the nature of *all* organisms is "teleological, goal-seeking, self actualizing"; our biology, not to mention our culture, is an accumulative coalescence of goals.[103] There is then no real cycle to history as a whole even if there are cyclical processes in the rise and fall of particular communities.

Seen in this light, Mumford's metahistory is at least existentially progressive; like Toynbee and Dawson he rescues a progressive sector from the process of cyclical decline. The great negation of modern history, however, has been the failure of transvaluation, the resignation of moderns to mechanical imperatives rather than to active creation. To Mumford, Nietzsche's death of God was but a step in humanity's self-fashioning. Seen historically, God in all His local forms is a means to account for existence and so to complete the meaning of human life. To Mumford, God is unfinished, an evolving entity, actively created by humanity, one who, to use William James's metaphor, needs our help.[104] The religious realm is a "fourth dimension" to every structure humans build; it is the highest realm of idealism and acts as a socialized public superego that rightly distributes guilt to those who fail to achieve their potential under that particular idolum.[105] The task of renewal is a religious transvaluation and a completion of Nietzsche. What is required is an "Axial change," a "conversion," like those that have followed earlier periods of dislocation, as in the downfall of the Roman Empire. A new axial change would transcend the life-denying elements in the religious dispensation of the past and embrace the "new universalism" that comes from our modern Neotechnical complex with its cultural relativity, ease of communication, and one-world economy. The goal and ideal of this transformation must be a new "Universal Man" or "One World Man" who will devote himself to the newly conceived organic whole. Mumford waxes mystical over this new god of universalism; this God, like those before, "symbolizes the utmost conceivable potentiality: power transformed to omnipotence, time extended into eternity, life transposed into immortality, love overcoming all antagonism and separation." Humanity must reestablish the transcendental, if only on a symbolic level, as a ground for a new superego and the only way to a real transformation of society.[106] Clearly, though Mumford talks in terms of symbols and remains tied to his monism, he has his own brand of millenarianism like that for which he criticizes Toynbee. One of his central criticisms of the hope for a palingenesis of Christianity is that Toynbee is here guilty of archaism; one must look to the religion of the future![107]

Mumford's climactic metahistorical synthesis appeared from the late 1950s to 1970 in his works on *The Transformation of Man* (1956), *The City in History* (1962), and the two-volume *The Myth of the Machine*: *Technics and Human Development* (1967) and *The Pentagon of Power* (1970). These volumes superseded his earlier work without overturning the paradigmatic formulations; Mumford retained his view of the pattern of urban development and unbuilding as the basic rhythm of civilization alongside a de-emphasized perspective on the modern periods of technics. Mumford's postwar pessimism, however, increased the urgency of his call for transformation, and his study of history led him into the more distant past. In fact Mumford's antimodernism solidified as he conceived a startling prospect of a mechanical revolution, heretofore invisible to the archeologist, at the dawn of history and at the foundation of civilization. Mumford discovered that the first machine was composed of men.

Looking back speculatively toward the dawn of human history, Mumford came to idealize the ecological, pacific, and feminine order of the Neolithic village.[108] It was an age of "idyllic calm." There *was* a Golden Age. At the end of the last ice age there was yet no exploitative class, no compulsion to work for a surplus, no conspicuous luxury, "no jealous claim to private property" or unrestrained power, and no war.[109] Mumford's antimodernism here turned toward a romantic primitivism as he looked back to the "amicable, non-predatory practices of the Neolithic village, where forbearance and mutual aid prevailed, as they do generally within pre-civilized communities."[110] According to Mumford, women were the first domesticators of nature; in the shift from gathering to horticulture and food and seed storage, the feminine container symbolized the settlement of people from Paleolithic nomadic hunting to the matriarchal Neolithic village. With this shift went an increase in sexuality, which exalted women and formed the basis for sublimation and the formation of religion. In an essentially Freudian view, Mumford held that consciousness of sexuality, an "essentially religious consciousness," in the Neolithic era was the "dominating motive power" for the domestication of the Paleolithic hunter and for subsequent religious extrapolations like the myth of the Great Mother.[111]

To Mumford, history can be read as the evolution of a "human vocabulary of symbols" and their materialization.[112] His concept of city formation predictably stresses its symbolic role in advance of its practical function as a granary, trade center, and citadel.[113] In contrast to Toynbee's view of "etherealization" or dematerialization as the mode of progression, and in a sense his justification for his flight to the City of God, Mumford asserted that this process is balanced by a materialization as symbols are implemented in concrete.[114] The sublimated sexual symbols of the nascent religious traditions of the Neolithic villagers materialized in sacred centers, collective burial grounds and places of sacrifice and thus provided a fundamental base for the development of the city. Mumford speculated that war also had its origin in the symbolic, as a ritual sacrifice, a mode of gathering individuals for sacrifice to local deities—particularly as oblations to the fertility of the Earth Mother. War, in turn, resuscitated Paleolithic, male-dominated tribalism with the new leadership of successful warriors and chiefs alongside intercessory priests to the gods. Ultimately this development resulted in early forms of kingship as war leaders became managers and distributors of the communal grain supply, which had also to be protected and so became a secondary cause for the growth of the citadel village center.[115] The evolution of kingship in conjunction with the city is reflected in the rise of a class of propitiative priests, royal retainers, and slaves, the institution of private property, as the king owns the grain and allots incremental amounts in distribution, a division of labor and specialization, and the rise of a justificatory and explanatory idolum of divine kingship.[116] Cities are not the result of environmental imperatives as in Wittfogel's hypothetical collective management of water; they are born as religious and temporal power centers and, through their power to transform people, were *consequently* able to conquer their physical environment.

This is where the "invisible" machine comes in. Mumford first conceived of his extended historical view of the machine while contemplating the pyramids at Giza and the mystery of their being built without mechanical devices, without even the wheel. He realized that "the mechanization of men had long preceded the mechanization of their working instruments."[117] He saw civilization as the organization of men, in hierarchical order, divided by function, to produce a mechanized leviathan, a "labor machine." From its onset, this mechanization acquired its greatest impact in warfare. In war, the machine grew internally within a society and simultaneously forced its opponents to adopt its technics or perish; thus the machine reproduced itself.[118] The "Myth of the Machine" is the idolum of the mechanical man, a set of symbols that was developed under divine kingship and that has continued to dominate civilization, with some interruptions, to the present. Civilization, then, can be seen to be based on five institutions: the centralization of power; the mechanization of production, be it human or automated; militarism; economic exploitation; and one or another form of slavery for industry and the military.[119] The skeleton of the structure is a bureaucratic power monopoly whose drive for increased power becomes an end in itself. The city, with its opportunities for communication, cultural accumulation, and creative syncretism, is the machine's finest flower. Along with the positive effect of the growth of civilized centers, however, came regimentation, division of labor, and class differentiation, all contributing to a "dismemberment of man" and a remolding of human beings in the service and image of the hegemonic machine.[120]

As a guiding and justifying image of evolution, the contemporary myth of the machine reaches its most heinous level in projections like Buckminster Fuller's idea of a technically produced millennia or in the eschatological propositions of Teilhard de Chardin. Mumford was appalled by Teilhard's call for the control of heredity and directed evolution toward the growth of a "noosphere" of mind. To Mumford, Teilhard's vision was an "etherealization of the megamachine" that would make human beings cells in a posthuman "ectoplasmic superbrain" for which they would have to uncreate nature and destroy the highest manifestations of their personalities.[121]

The machine has never gone entirely unquestioned. The influence of Morris, Veblen, and Kropotkin even in the dark days of the Paleotechnic is evident in Mumford's idea that there has always been an

irrepressible "Democratic Technics" of small-scale handicraft manufacturers that parallels "Totalitarian Technics" and in some eras actually
dominated the machine.[122] Aside from the day-to-day resistance of
individual craftsmen, history has been marked by wide-scale revolutions against the machine, none entirely successful—but perhaps one
can recognize in them Mumford's proposed transformation. Mumford
held that the axial religions and philosophies from the ninth to the
sixth centuries before Christ were revolts against the dominance of the
personality by the machine. "Whatever their individual accents, these
axial ideologies revealed a profound disillusionment with the fundamental premises of civilization; its overemphasis on power and material
goods; its acceptance of grade and rank and vocational division as
eternal categories; and . . . the injustice, the hatred, the hostility and
perpetual violence and destructiveness of its dominant class-structured
institutions."[123] The prophets and philosophers, from Jesus, Plato,
Solon, and Confucius to Isaiah and the Buddha, represent the aspiring,
ideal-making element in human nature; in articulating a new internal
self-consciousness, they attempted to humanize the machine, with
some success. Christianity in particular overgrew the machine after the
Fall of Rome, though, tragically, the Church gradually became a
worldly bureaucracy in the model of the state it superseded. Ultimately
the Church gave way before a resuscitated machine with the renaissance
of the myth of the machine in the seventeenth-century "world revolution," the rise of a new mechanistic *Weltanschauung*.[124]

In the final volumes of his series on megatechnics, Mumford came
up against Jacques Ellul's disturbing book on *The Technological Society*
(1964). Ellul expressed a view of the imperatives inherent in technological development much like that held by Henry Adams. In a long
argument against Mumford's *Technics and Civilization* he derided the
optimistic forecast of a Biotechnic age as a "pious hope" without any
foundation. Technics, in his opinion, contained their own inexorable
direction. Reason has sought in the past, and will always seek in the
future, the most efficient technical channel, and in doing so, it progressively transforms society in its own image; it encapsulates incrementally
all aspects of life and is, essentially, inescapable. He opined that "it is
infantile to wish to submit the machine to the criterion of the ideal,"
as the law of our age contends that "everything which is technique is
necessarily used as soon as it is available." Just as Mumford held that
the axial religions were absorbed in the end by the machine, Ellul
analyzed the sociological functions of all movements against technics
and found them to be diversions of an aggressive instinct into channels
that could be deactivated and encompassed. To Ellul, Mumford's own
proposals to release humanity from the clutches of rationalized

technology were escapist utopian fantasy; any concrete implementation of Mumford's regionalist solution would have to be based on exceedingly intensive and rigid planning of production, distribution, and land use—"or, in other words, further applications of technique."[125]

Both Ellul and Mumford had similar views of the end order from the continued application of mechanization. A world state of totalitarian efficiency and "chromium gleam" may be established, where the media message will be a desensitizing monologue, where life would be dominated by mind-numbing therapies of adjustment and the individual would become a genetically engineered "organization man," a "depersonalized servo-mechanism in the megamachine."[126] Mumford, foreshadowing Christopher Lasch's description of *The Culture of Narcissism*, believed that unless the current process of mechanization were averted all that would be left of humanity would be automation and the infantile id.[127] Still, Mumford desperately called for an alternative; he retained an idealist perspective that a change in mentality could precede and determine the evolution of the technical complex, and he called for a new model of man as the basis for an ecology. In 1970, even as the communal movement in the U.S. reached its peak and the environmental movement took on a new momentum, Mumford's vision reached the zenith of its popularity and influence. He claimed that "we must reject the Faustian pact with technology, control and limit its application; withdraw from the citadel of power . . . and quietly paralyze it," in order to restore personality and community as a basis for regeneration.[128] Unlike Ellul, Mumford felt that modern man could disconnect the machine and restore his freedom.

• • •

Mumford has been criticized for the use of undue speculation, which occasionally took rhetoric for reality; this is especially obvious to his critics in his constructive mythmaking about the Neolithic period and the rise of the city.[129] William Kuhns has argued that his "scholarship edges on an almost desperate apologetic" and that his pessimistic view of history does not really take into account the dramatic discontinuities in technics in the modern era.[130] He is attacked for his "Ahab-like hubris" against the city, for his "old testament" doomsday prophesies, and for his major postulate that any transformation must be total and of a piece.[131] Mumford's position against incremental reforms led him to oppose busing in the cities, to reject the Model Cities program and small-scale self-help programs for blacks, and consequently drew charges of racism against him.[132] To some critics the lack of empirical grounding to his plans for transformation, along with his totalistic holism, left Mumford with no practical reforms to propose; this was compounded in the eyes of some as he rejected science as the means of resolving present social ills.[133] His utopianism, in Roger Starr's opinion, led to a "fatal confusion between the needs of the world and the illusory possibilities of reapplying or bringing to birth a Golden Age."[134] Other critics have seconded this view of Mumford as being caught up in metaphysical subtleties and utopian absurdities at the expense of real-world dilemmas; they claim that his "self righteous" denial of scientific solutions, coupled by his demand for wholesale conversion and his Cassandra warnings, make him difficult to take seriously.[135] To many progressives, Mumford is seen as an "organic reactionary" like Eliot, Pound, and Adams, whose analysis is at best useless, and at worst paralyzing. Finally, Peter Shaw's criticism of Mumford encapsulates some of the most trenchant attacks when he claims that in Mumford's a priori approach to culture he is not really producing an analysis of culture but is merely "expressing an attitude toward it."[136]

There is no doubt that Mumford's message does, in part, come before his history and that it is difficult to verify empirically. How does one measure the invisible machine? By what standard are we to weigh our dehumanization? Is there a proportional relation between passive hours before the television or our per capita consumption of useless, trivial, and ecologically destructive material wants and needs and our loss of soul? As a prophet Mumford was a voice threatening what he saw as our deserved damnation, if not in an otherworldly eternity, at least symbolically, through our extinction. Like most world historical writing, Mumford's history is selective and in service to his ideals and goals, to his humanism, environmentalism, and his version of the ecumenical ideal. This is not to say that there is no truth to his diagnosis but only that history cannot provide its own framework and that the questions which Mumford raised may have no determinative answers. To a large extent Mumford accepted this: his history is an impressionistic pastiche—a pointillist portrait of the machine, which artistically invoked transvaluation as its paramount aspect and provided a running commentary on history by means of argument. As a metahistory of values, Mumford's work strains as often to impose his own values on his age as to investigate those of the past. As a generalist, his generalizations sometimes precede his facts.

Lewis Mumford's originality is not primarily in novel ideas. His debts to Emerson and Thoreau, Nietzsche, Geddes, Spengler and Toynbee, Henry and Brooks Adams, Smuts, Bergson, Whitehead and Berdyaev, Freud and Jung, Owen, Olmstead, Marsh, Kropotkin, and Howard are transparent and acknowledged. Mumford's genius lay more in his ability to digest, absorb, and fuse ideas, if not into a system (a word he abhorred as mechanistic) then into an organic synthesis. Mumford's history is two sided; it contains an idolum, a collection of meaningful symbols as a means to examine the process of evolving mentality, alongside a perspective of the materialistic effects of this mentality in history. His analysis is founded on a world view that posits a modern loss of soul and an apocalyptic potential for dehumanization and destruction in the Faustian pact with technology. To Mumford we are at the stage where the modern God of progress and plenty has died, leaving only a life-devouring soulless mechanism, and so dialectically stirs a needed transvaluation.

Mumford's world history cannot be placed in the class with those of Toynbee or McNeill; it is not universal, and Mumford's historical skills are those of the now out-of-fashion man of letters rather than the trained rigorous researcher. He did no serious study of any culture other than that of the West. His later research, going back to Sumeria and Egypt, traced a preconceived process rather than interpreting these cultures as having any essentially distinguishing unity and validity in themselves. His sidestepping of other civilizations except for references to their contributions to Western technics was based on the assumption that the Western megatechnical complex was *the* critical determinant in world history and that a change in *Western* hearts and minds was the probable locus for any future transformation—this is a closure that Toynbee, for one, never committed and would have condemned. As a metahistorical Daniel, however, Mumford's apocalyptic vision of the crisis of the West echoes and amplifies his predecessors' and focuses the sense of crisis in areas that they had not attended as closely: postmodern urban degeneration and the corresponding loss of will and soul to automatism, the destruction of the natural world, and the place of nuclearism in the contemporary dilemma. More than any other world historian Mumford brilliantly highlighted the ecological relationship of historic human mentality and its contemporary technology. He is unsurpassed in his evaluation of the world historical roots and implications of the modern megatechnical complex.

Mumford, like the other world historians reviewed in this volume, used history to invoke a required transformation. The necessity for a cultural revolution reflects a profound personal discomfort with a postmodern lack of identity and a desire for a symbiotic sense of community, which he felt existed in the Neolithic village and in the organic medieval town. A Freudian psychohistorian would undoubtedly find Mumford's works, with their sexual longings and abhorrence of male-oriented megatechnics, a projective transposition of the Oedipal complex to world history, and his desire for an organic community as a symbolic retreat to the womb of the all-embracing mother, a desire he shared sympathetically with Henry Adams, whose call to the Virgin as an escape from the new age of "men on the make" echoed in all of Mumford's writings.[137] It is perhaps symbolic that Mumford's sympathy with Freud was tempered by his criticism of the Oedipal complex; Freud was interested in only half of the equation, that of the repressive father and filial rebellion; he neglected the aspirative element, or the ideal of the female principle within.[138]

But perhaps this oversimplified Freudian review simply reduces life to metaphor, an error Mumford himself, for all his contrary exhortations, committed repeatedly. Clearly Mumford was as dissatisfied emotionally as he was intellectually with the idolum of modern capitalism. His faith in the symbols of progressivism and "the revolution" was overturned by the aftermath of the First World War; his hope of a Biotechnic society was undermined by the rise of fascism, the Second World War, the Cold War, Vietnam, and the continued progress of the military-industrial complex. Mumford was left in a desperate state of dislocation. With the old symbols—God, progress, science, and democracy—shattered or devoured, he spent his career working toward the revitalization of personality that would stir resymbolization and so provide a meaningful and life-giving alternative to the dehumanizing myth of the machine. It remains to be seen whether the West can activate itself to avert wholesale environmental destruction and perhaps extinction; whether there are ideals for which modern Westerners will sacrifice unrestrained material consumption. Whatever his faults, Mumford was a brilliant diagnostician and critic, and he may have been right that human survival will require sacrifices that only a new superego, a new ego ideal, can instill. Perhaps ultimately the validity of Mumford's work is in the artistic impact it has in articulating some of the dominant undercurrent questions about the modern experiment in industrial civilization. Mumford the world historian, who provided an unparalleled insight into the interaction of the material aspects and myths of technical change in history, was always balanced by Mumford the artistic revolutionary, who contributed a vision of a renewed culture. As a generalist Mumford wrote works of world history whose provocative interpretations of technics and mentality provide a deep perspective on the modern "environmental crisis" and its world historical setting—one that may yet prove useful in its eventual resolution.

CHAPTER EIGHT

William H. McNeill's
Ecological Mythistory
Toward an Ambiguous Future

Instead of enhancing conflicts, as parochial historiography inevitably does, an intelligible world history might be expected to diminish the lethality of group encounters by cultivating a sense of individual identification with the triumphs and tribulations of humanity as a whole.
—William H. McNeill[1]

Like all other forms of life, humankind remains inextricably entangled in flows of matter and energy that result from eating and being eaten.
—William H. McNeill[2]

IN 1954 WHEN TOYNBEE PUBLISHED the last volumes of *A Study of History*, William H. McNeill began work on his self-appointed task of writing a narrative history of the complex web of interactions between civilizations—in less than a thousand pages. In *The Rise of the West* (1963) and subsequent works, McNeill has done much to overturn some of the major formulations of his mentor, Toynbee, even as he has assumed a metahistorical mantle as a recognized leader in the world historical genre. McNeill's works have been, on the whole, gratefully received by his professional colleagues who have respected his erudition and are, above all, relieved by the restriction of the range of his discourse to "this worldly" movements of power and peoples. Since 1963 McNeill has been perhaps the most powerful voice in the promotion of the idea of world history as a means to a global consciousness and as an antidote to the catastrophic potentials inherent in current historical trends of militarism, the increasing closure of a united disease pool, and xenophobic nationalism. McNeill has produced a new macrohistorical model of ecological history that may act as a fulcrum for a new generation of world historians.

McNeill's works in the field of world history have acted to clear the air of metaphysical obscurantism, cyclical determinism, and the organicism of self-contained civilizations that pursued predictable life courses. He has repudiated the millenarianism of his predecessors, sometimes in characteristically restrained critical evaluations of them, but more profoundly in the example of his own work, which follows in the affirmative secularism of an early mentor, Carl Becker. He has rejected the utopian aspirations of his precursors who formulated speculative ideal futures or anachronistic returns to a mythical cohesion in the past in response to their sense of the tragedy of modernism. McNeill has dismissed naively tragic and transcendentally expectant views of history and maintained a qualified optimism. He asserts that with creative growth in technology and social management there were increases in human choice, material well being, artistic range, and the richness and variety of communications between individuals. While recognizing the multivalent ambiguity of modernism, especially in the tension between individual freedom and the hierarchical managerial order, McNeill has emphasized a cumulative pattern of interaction in world history that encompasses the complex and pluralistic strains of technological and ecological evolution and posits a fulfillment of the growth of humanity as a whole in our increasingly unified modern world order.

Under McNeill's criteria, the culmination of progressive world development in the historical acquisition of power in areas as diverse as demographics, technology, the arts, and intellectual life, has produced a world bureaucratic order whose justification is its success in past adaptation and its necessity in resolving current dilemmas in world development. McNeill argues that the arms race, the environmental emergency, burgeoning world population growth, and potential epidemiological crises in a united disease pool all require concerted management on a global level to avert catastrophes that are made more potentially devastating with each increment of growth, technological dependency, and ecumenical closure.

McNeill's *The Rise of the West*, though profoundly influenced by Toynbee's and other world historical systems, made a clean sweep of utopian faith and Augustinian parallels. Instead of cyclical patterns of Spenglerian rise and fall, which in Toynbee and Sorokin correspond to periods of creative mysticism and sinful degeneracy, McNeill has traced a unified and continuous pattern of communication, technological transfer, and social, political, and religious growth broken intermittently by ecological catastrophes and man-made disasters. Despite these interruptions, an accumulative pattern of historical growth predominates and survives the passage of peoples and empires; it has increased the complexity and breadth of human life even with the psychological dislocations and apocalyptic potential it bears. McNeill's repudiation of Spengler is evident in the title, yet *The Rise of the West* is a peculiar heading for a history of the world as a whole. It situates McNeill in the Western world historical tradition and marks the very cover of his work with a commanding ambition: to overturn the most predominant world historical perspective of the twentieth century, to demonstrate the continuity of world history as a total process that has produced modern Western dominance as a world historical rather than a national or even civilizational dynamic and thus to open historical discourse upon a view of world unity as a living reality from the rise of civilization. *The Rise of the West*, then, is not a stage in a closed Western cycle that will give way to its inevitable dissolution. It is a world historical fulfillment, a union of the contributions of past ages and peoples of the ecumene. At the same time the title underlines McNeill's sense that modern civilization is a Western synthesis in its most current manifestation. McNeill hopes that Western liberal ideals of freedom, equality, self-determination of peoples, and so forth as embodied in the charter of the United Nations will moderate the blind movements to world integration in the technical and economic fields. In a self-critical review of *The Rise of the West* twenty-five years after its publication, McNeill points out that his 'great book' could be seen as a history from the point of view of the winners. Seen in the context of U.S. leadership of the West at the height of the Cold War, McNeill recognized that *The Rise* could be perceived as "a rationalization of American hegemony, retrojecting the situation of post–World War II decades upon the whole of the world's past by claiming that analogous patterns of cultural dominance and diffusion had existed always." Even if there is a partial truth in this McNeill can defend himself by pointing out the deeper historical currents reflected in his own time.[3]

Of all the macrohistorians considered in this study, McNeill is clearly the most tough-minded in William James's sense, the most scientific in his use of models, the most detached, clinical, and dispassionate. Yet McNeill claims that modern epistemology has made any postulation of absolute historical truth impossible in either microhistorical analysis or in definition of global patterns of development. He opts instead for a view of "mythistory" where historians accept their role of providing a sense of the past, a broad meaningful interpretation as a ground for action. Any significant study of history requires "intuitive leaps" into generalization, which can then be evaluated by their usefulness in dealing with additional information.[4]

McNeill's relativism is moderated by a view of emergent truth in the open marketplace of ideas. He is a pragmatist of liberal faith. Taken as a whole the study of world history is itself progressive as models evolve to include broader categories of material and a more inclusive perspective. The measure of truth in any area of study must then be its historical success, its evolutionary adaptability, and its usefulness; the truth will come out in time, and evaluation of interpretations by historical evidence can further the process. McNeill claims that generalization is inevitable even in the most specific study and that the historian bears a duty to coordinate a useful past in the face of present world contingencies. Historians, whether they like it or not, are mythistorians who provide ideational grounding through generalization for a climate of opinion; in McNeill's work this task has the weight of a moral imperative: to ignore current macrohistorical dilemmas in fragmentary analysis of discrete shards of a past is a *trahison des clercs*.

McNeill's own mythistory is not without its contradictions. His clinical perspective on historical patterns of epidemiology, technology transfer, the history of ideas, and religious development emphasizes a basic Darwinian analysis of the survival value or use value aspects of these patterns. In the struggle for existence, "microparasitical" relations of endemism, which allow maximal survival of pest and host, and rationalized "macroparasitical" arrangements between elites and conquered populations provide prosperity to host and parasites, and so provide adaptive success. In intergroup relations, success requires the immediate and perpetual adoption of increasingly lethal forms of killing technology, along with a world view that justifies and perpetuates these arrangements and a religion that adjusts individuals to their most painful effects. The major historical patterns McNeill reveals are end products of human adaptation in line with Spencer's dictum of "the survival of the fittest." In the end McNeill charts the blindly devastating influence of microparasitism and the passage of the technological and organizational imperatives of macroparasitism, as well as the conditioning effects of evolving climates of opinion that often seem to do little but reflect these underlying and compelling forces. The liberal postulates inherent in McNeill's goals in writing are occasionally undermined by his sweeping generalizations about the climates of opinion that often leave the question of leadership, creativity, and inspiration aside. In his paradigmatic formulations, diffusion sometimes assumes the weight of a near-universal explanation so that individual creativity is de-emphasized or glossed over. McNeill's ambiguous conclusions on the future, his projection of an equilibrium in the realm of micro- and macroparasitism, and his expectation of a world union under a government of potentially self-interested social managers seem to deny his liberal hopes. Yet McNeill evinces a sense of optimism that is central to his personal climate of opinion but that does not follow logically from the patterns of history he charts. In the end McNeill's work begs the question: Can an ecological view in world history preserve a central role for the free will and action of the individual? Viewed from the outside, can the history of humanity at the species level be more than contests in power machination that end with the hegemony of the strongest?

• • •

William Hardy McNeill was born in Vancouver, British Columbia, in 1917, the son of John Thomas and Netta (Hardy) McNeill. The McNeills moved to the United States when William was ten. John McNeill, a leading expert in the history of Calvinism, was a professor at the Chicago Divinity School for seventeen years and then taught church history at Union Theological Seminary until his retirement in 1953. By the time he was ten McNeill had already decided to "do history" in his father's footsteps. From his father McNeill received his most important early influence in his orientation to broad-based historical patterns and the focus on points of interconnection between individuals and groups. John McNeill's work ran across denominations and through centuries of Christian history. McNeill admits that "my sort of history is indeed a secularization and geographical expansion of his."[5]

McNeill attended the University of Chicago, receiving his B.A. in history in 1938 and his Master's degree a year later. After starting his Ph.D. work at Cornell, his education was interrupted by World War II, during which he served in the U.S. Army (1941–46), from 1944 to 1946 as an assistant military attaché in Greece with the rank of captain, "a graduate student of history in uniform."[6] His war experience led him to write three books on Greece, which contributed to the dialogue surrounding the Marshall Plan.[7] During the war McNeill met Elizabeth Darbishire, the daughter of Robert Shelby Darbishire, Toynbee's traveling companion in Greece, and married her in 1943.[8] At the war's end McNeill wrote a doctoral dissertation at Cornell on the influence of the potato upon Ireland, which foreshadowed his later ecological interests.[9]

At Cornell McNeill took a seminar with Carl Becker and acted as his teaching assistant. He had read Becker's *Modern History* textbook as a junior in high school in 1932 and believed that "everything I have since thought or written about modern European history is no more than embroidery upon and modification of what I then absorbed."[10] Following the influence of McNeill's father and a high school teacher, Becker further opened up the "magic" of history to McNeill and presented him with a modern moral dilemma that is one root of McNeill's macrohistorical synthesis. Becker charted three elements in modern history: a history of past politics, a history of the progress of the idea of liberty, and a history of changing means of production. In

Becker's view, changes in contemporary mentality, or as he called it, "climate of opinion," acted in relation to ecomonic and political interests to precede accomplishments in history. With World War I, the three lines of historical progression he charted intersected, leaving an incoherence he sought to alleviate in part by his text, by revising and adapting a climate of opinion that would make sense of these developments and lead to action to resolve current contradictions. McNeill's goals in writing history are clearly foreshadowed here; his own attempt to educate and inculcate a new climate of opinion in the world as a whole is in response to the same dilemma. He saw this as the contemporary task of uniting the heritages of the past to make civilization worth preserving.[11]

Three other elements of Becker's historical analysis influenced McNeill. Becker repudiated F. J. Turner's thesis on the unique dispensation that frontier conquest provided for the development of the distinctively American character, and thus positioned U.S. history as a part of a wider Western historical tradition; in this instance among others McNeill believed that Becker anticipated his own global perspective.[12] McNeill also retained Becker's skepticism, his sense that eternal truth is impossible to attain, so that 'everyman is his own historian' who brings himself into his history, and makes the writing of history a continuous, even a progressive process, building upon the perspectives of those who came earlier. Finally, Becker epitomized for McNeill his own "conundrum of detachment." To the historian, a reflective distance before historical evidence must remain a guiding ideal even though one cannot achieve it and is, like Becker, committed to liberal principles.[13]

A second central influence in McNeill's education was from the field of American cultural anthropology, especially the work of Robert Redfield. As an undergraduate McNeill studied under Redfield at Chicago, where Redfield taught his interpretation of the "transformation of man," the revolutionary shift from primitive to civilized society that occurred with the convergent processes of urbanization and the development of agriculture. Redfield's idea of civilization as the "antithesis of folk society" may have conditioned McNeill to accept (at least in the short term) Toynbee's more case-oriented approach to the independent "outbreaks" of the first wave of civilizations.[14] Redfield emphasized the unraveling of the cohesive order of primitive society, a breakdown of rules and beliefs that countered the advantages of civilization. With this unraveling came new psychological burdens of "dreadful freedom," when decisions formerly prescribed by an established custom had to be made through isolated personal judgments. McNeill has retained throughout his work a sensitivity to the ambiguity of progressive advancement that, in its inception, is both creative and painfully disruptive of an established "cake of custom."[15] In his later studies he refers to civilization as a "kind of cancerous growth" that is resisted to some extent by the "overwhelming majority of mankind [who are] always trying [to] regain this lost ancestral Eden."[16] McNeill has maintained that the shift to civilization was a destabilization from a Neolithic equilibrium that was not replaced until a civilized ecumenical balance was obtained just before the coming of Christ.[17] This problem will be examined in further detail in review of McNeill's perspective on current ecumenical problems; it is sufficient here to note the ambiguity of progress for McNeill as each advance entails a dislocation.

When McNeill came upon Toynbee's first three volumes of *A Study of History* in the Cornell Library in 1939 he was fully prepared to adopt their metahistorical orientation. He had read Spengler in 1936 but was left unmoved by Spengler's abstractness. As Toynbee had read Thucydides before World War I and had been inspired by the parallel between the two ages, McNeill read Thucydides in his first graduate year at Chicago, wrote a master's thesis on Herodotus and Thucydides, and felt the "remarkable echo between the ancient Greek political patterns and those of my own day." Like Toynbee, McNeill was sufficiently moved by this sense of recurrence to project the task for himself of writing a book that would explore the cyclical parallels between ancient Greek and modern European history.[18] Only upon reading Toynbee did McNeill extend his scope; his ambition grew to embrace the history of all civilizations.[19]

On reading Toynbee McNeill was "transported" with "rapture"; "for awhile his thoughts were my thoughts." Toynbee had done all that McNeill had conceived in tracing the parallels and more with "dazzling virtuosity"; he was "an authentic hero of the lamp." In his recent book on mythistory, McNeill forthrightly admits that he was moved to the point of making a "leap of faith" in accepting Toynbee's world view— "even though I half recognized its kinship to the other leap toward Christian faith which I boggled at making."[20] McNeill also acknowledged that he had a deep-seated affinity from his Calvinist background for the idea of predestination, for a sense of destiny that transcended human consciousness and free will, where freedom would exist in submission to world historical processes.[21] Clearly Toynbee's paradigm resonated early on with this affinity in McNeill, and McNeill's leap of faith into a macrohistorical framework was in some ways a secular functional equivalent and substitute for accepting the Christian world view. This faith, however, did not survive Toynbee's own increasingly blatant Augustinian imperatives and his invocations of a mystical syncretism. The incipient Christian teleology inherent even in

Toynbee's earliest formulations, like those of his calls to the elected historical supermen and saints who create and transform civilizations, may, however, have echoed McNeill's early Calvinist conditioning and his youthful struggles for identity and a cohesive world view.

McNeill met Toynbee in 1947 when Toynbee was at the height of his fame in the United States, just a few weeks after Henry Luce's *Time* cover story. The two met at McNeill's father-in-law's house in Kentucky where they hiked, got lost together, and apparently became friends. In 1950, after publishing books on Greece, finishing his Cornell doctorate, and teaching in Chicago, McNeill moved to London on an invitation to work at Chatham House on Toynbee's *Survey of International Affairs*. The two met daily and talked over Toynbee's work on the final volumes of the *Study*. McNeill would express his reservations about Toynbee's scheme and present his own ideas on technology, the importance of current anthropological perspectives, and contacts between civilizations, but Toynbee seemed set in his path and unable to make any serious reexamination of his ideas. When McNeill examined volume 8 and gave Toynbee some specific written criticisms of problems he found with basic issues in the text, Toynbee simply included McNeill's comments in direct transcription as footnotes. While both historians came to drop the cyclical conception of history at around the same time, McNeill boggled as Toynbee turned his sights toward the divine, and McNeill instead reaffirmed his agnosticism and reached to the "dusty earth," "to understand how flows of matter and energy sustain human lives."[22]

During his time at Chatham House McNeill wrote *America, Britain and Russia* (1953) for the *Survey*. This work on the diplomacy between the three Allied superpowers from 1941 to 1946 foreshadowed many of the central concerns of his future macrohistorical work. McNeill charted a parallel development among all of the participants in the Second World War, especially the Big Three, of progress in administrative technique and technological development coupled with an erosion of social tradition. War organization marked a "social revolution," a "tremendous victory for instrumental rationality," and left as an ambiguous legacy the "myth of peace through human planning."[23] While giving prominence to Roosevelt's myths of international order, the idea of the Grand Alliance and the importance of the individual leaders of the alliance, McNeill also noted that personalities are most often unimportant in the final decisions, that demographics, military imperatives, resource management, and so forth are the determinative factors.[24]

In 1954 McNeill set about the task of writing his own world history even as Toynbee completed the culminating volumes of his *Study* of world history and religious syncretism. As he put it: "I proposed to turn Spengler and Toynbee on their heads, as Marx claimed to have done with Hegel." He believed that Toynbee and Spengler both erred in asserting the independence of civilizations and emphasizing the internal rhythms of particular civilizations, which made external influences seem relatively incidental. McNeill's approach, "influenced by anthropologists, assumed that borrowing was the normal human reaction to an encounter with strangers possessing superior skills." Diffusion, the adoption by societies of technologies, skills, customs, and social arrangements that they perceive to be finer or more empowering than their own, has been the critical dynamic in world historical change. McNeill's world history focused from the start on points of contact between civilizational centers and the resultant stimuli produced by cultural diffusions.[25] Looking at Toynbee's work some thirty-five years later, McNeill retained a great deal of respect for Toynbee's achievement, especially in the discourse he opened,[26] but McNeill's own paradigm makes a sharp break with cyclical metahistory. In its place he has formulated an internally consistent perspective of challenge and response that emphasizes the accumulative nature of trans-civilizational diffusions and the culmination of this process in evolving ecumenical hegemonies.

Part of McNeill's originality lies in his introduction of the insights of modern cultural anthropology into the discipline of world historical writing. He is perhaps the foremost world historian promoting a diffusionist view of culture. Cultural interaction in his paradigm, rather than any internal cyclical dynamism, is the "major motive power" for historical change. Diffusion occurs under these circumstances: "When a group of men encounter a commodity, technique or idea that seems superior to what they had previously known, they will try to acquire and make their own whatever they perceive to be superior, but only as long as this does not seem to endanger the values they hold dear."[27] Diffusion does not always occur under conditions of free choice, however, where the superior adoption is sought for its positive value in promoting cultural progress; in many cases McNeill presents cultural borrowing as an urgent requirement, as in the adaptability of a conquered population or in the case of adoptions accepted to ward off external threats.

McNeill has found that the contribution of diffusion to a society is subject to a "Rule of Compound Interest" wherein "societies that have already accepted important changes within living memory are likely to provoke invention" among their members. He agrees with Sorokin and with Alfred Kroeber's idea of "constellations" of invention that cluster historically in time and space. With the rise of civilizations, emergent metropolitan centers shift from being the open receptors of cultural influences from equally semibarbarous neighbors or from other nascent external civilizational centers. They become radiant foci, which diffuse their own borrowings and the innovations these borrowings have stimulated, to their peripheries. Centers in time form "cultural slopes" through their barbaric fringes and toward primitive frontiers beyond. With the rise of multiple centers diffusion acquires a complex topography as peaks and slopes intersect in a mutually stimulating confluence of cultural growth.[28] The success of diffusion outward from a center is critical for that center's viability as each center must sustain its growth, and, for epidemiological and demographic reasons, its very existence, by drawing on its external rural population and converting them into its citizens.[29] Thus McNeill's perspective on diffusion leads into his view of a punctuated equilibrium between civilization and its peripheral hinterlands; he has explored this dynamic most extensively in the relations between steppe-dwelling nomads and civilized agricultural peoples who must periodically convert the conquering barbarians or invent and adopt technologies that can hold them off.

McNeill's world history has acted to synthesize two major strands of macrohistorical theory, the Spenglerian and Toynbeean study of the rise and fall of civilizations and current theories of cultural development held by leading anthropologists. Aside from Redfield's influence, McNeill read Ruth Benedict, V. Gordon Childe, Margaret Mead, and Ralph Linton.[30] Linton held that the "so-called rise and fall of civilizations . . . is marginal in certain respects [and] actually only affected the surface of culture." These superficial changes overlay a cumulative cultural matrix that is inherited in time and in its displacement to new peoples on the periphery. In *The Tree of Culture* (1955) Linton analyzed this matrix as a worldwide process of cultural diffusion that served as an underlying unity (like the trunk of a tree) supporting peripheral differentiation. Linton anticipated McNeill's outlook on the accumulative pattern of growth and even in his forecasts for the future; he warned of a trend toward the end of free competition worldwide as massive corporations, bureaucratically integrated under a web of governmental controls, absorbed smaller businesses and promoted an increasingly sharp system of class divisions.[31]

Alfred Kroeber, the dean of American cultural anthropology, also conceived patterns of cultural growth that parallel McNeill's macrohistorical perspective. His *Configurations of Cultural Growth* (1944) broke with Spenglerian and Toynbeean systems in three major areas: Kroeber denied, first of all, that there was a "master pattern" to which all cultural development in distinct civilizations must respond; second, that all civilizations followed through essentially parallel stages; and third, that civilizations die of themselves.[32] Although Kroeber in his *Configurations* attempted to sort out patterns of cultural constellations, to analyze the valleys and peaks of their incidence in a somewhat naive recapitulation of Sorokin's study of cycles, his more enduring contribution may be the finding that "cultures merge into one another and so cannot have the individual entity of higher organisms."[33] Along with this postulate he presented the baffling problem of the role of the individual within the cultural matrix; to Kroeber, and this is sometimes implied in McNeill as well, personality can be seen more clearly as a vehicle than as an agent in cultural development.[34] Finally, again like McNeill, Kroeber attempted to examine cultural patterns while maintaining a clinical distance to avoid apocalyptic pronunciations on destiny or millennial exhortations to utopia; he held that "the study of civilization can hardly become truly scientific or scholarly until it divests itself of emotional concern about crisis, decay, collapse, extinction, and doom."[35]

What unites the cyclical theorists and the cultural anthropologists as their fundamental common root is the culturally Darwinian perspective that Toynbee's challenge and response paradigm most directly epitomizes. As Carroll Quigley points out in his *The Evolution of Civilizations* (1961), Petrie, Toynbee, and Spengler held to the view that environmental conditions or contacts with other peoples are primary among the challenges that produce cultural growth.[36] In addition, Spengler exemplifies most obviously, but the others share the perspective, that with the comforts of civilization may come a relative stasis in the lack of challenge, as in Spengler's "civilization" stage, which acts as a functional equivalent to degeneration as other cultures are able to surpass the stagnating civilization due to the élan they acquire in continuous struggle. Quigley aptly describes this process in his seven-stage system of the movement of social organization in response to challenges: "The civilization rises while this organization is an instrument [of adaptation in the face of challenge] and declines when this organization becomes an institution."[37]

McNeill applies the challenge and response paradigm with more consistency and balance than any other modern world historian. His ecological analysis allows him to examine an exceedingly complex variety of man-made and ecological crises as cultural stimuli.[38] Where Toynbee found these stimuli most often in the origin and growth stages of civilization, as in his recurrent use of Wittfogel's hydraulic hypothesis and the "taming" of the original homes of his distinct civilizations, McNeill employs an overarching perspective on perpetual stimulus-response relations of human beings with disease fluctuations, agricultural technology, zootechnical advances, and resultant changes in food supplies, human habitat, and environmental control. Moreover, Mc-Neill brings this process to the present in his evaluations of the continuous line of growth and integration, which he charts as the central dynamic of history.

McNeill's macrohistory is, then, a study of the challenges of survival presented by humanity's evolving relationship to its environment and in the punctuated equilibrium of the struggle between groups. Mc-Neill's entire overview of the process of diffusion centers on two aspects, the individual's aspiration for superior goods and a more satisfying material, social, and even spiritual life, and perhaps even more critically, the competitive race of contiguous societies for technology and social order to maintain their independence or extend their power over their neighbors. The stimulus of political/military competition is perhaps the dominant ecohistorical pattern in McNeill's history. This is clearly the case in his view of the rise of the West after A.D. 1000 where variety, instability, and the lack of a hegemonic economic power promoted European economic growth, and chronic warfare—endemic to nascent European multinationalism—proved to be one of the "powerful mainsprings of the West's vitality."[39] McNeill's position on the stimulating effects of competition leads him to his conclusions on the ambiguous future in a world increasingly unified by technology, transnational economics, communications, and intersecting bureaucratic institutions. Will the future united ecumene suppress disruptive stimuli to the point where human creativity is fatally undermined?

In 1954 McNeill addressed these issues in *Past and Future*, a work that in many ways schematically anticipated *The Rise of the West. Past and Future* included a brief outline of world history, a perspective on what McNeill took to be the central dilemmas of the present and an evocative exposition of future contradictions, and the prospect of their ambiguous adjustment. McNeill claimed, in contradistinction to Toynbee's view of the independent paths of the first civilizations, that "the history of civilized mankind can be considered as a product of the progressive breakdown of . . . isolation," through four epochs in the development of human mobility and contacts.[40] Each point of transition, from pedestrian to equestrian movement (2000 B.C.), from land transport dominated by the steppe frontiers to the central role of oceanic travel (A.D. 1400s), and to the rise of mechanical transportation with the Industrial Revolution, occurred as a point of crisis on a progressive continuum that required resolution and a new ecumenical equilibrium.[41]

McNeill's view of the present in 1954 emphasized the modern period as a horizon point, an era of crisis where the older equilibrium had broken down and rapid innovation had made society "everywhere uncertain, unstable, and uncomfortable," where nationalism, the foundation of secular psychological cohesion in the downfall of sacred world views, had fallen into eclipse, leaving a "pervasive unease" and a "haunting sense of the futility of human life."[42] Along with this view of psychological dislocation McNeill held a perspective on the mechanization of the human social order much like Lewis Mumford's. The professional specialization of invention, which McNeill later documents in *The Pursuit of Power* (1982), and the reemergence of command economies and social management bureaucracies in the modern era after the dominance of market economies, threaten the foundation of liberal society. McNeill echoed Weber and Mumford in his view that as people transform "themselves, their fellows and the physical environment in conformity to rational calculation," the free citizen becomes "no more than a replaceable part in a great machine."[43]

In turning to the future McNeill described ecological imperatives for the renewal of an equilibrium upon which the preservation of the species depended. First, reason demanded an armed world authority to eliminate international war. A monopoly of power by a governing body of technicians and administrators obeying a central authority that united the world militarily and bureaucratically was essential and indeed "the only rational way" to avert catastrophe. In 1954 McNeill expected a third world war, even a nuclear war, with world hegemony going to the victor in a world dominance by a single state, Comintern, or the United Nations.[44] He foresaw this imminent world union on the model of Toynbee's "Universal State" and felt that in the absence of war the West would be the leader in the integration process. Indeed, Americans should set the World State as their guiding vision, a heroic task that required heroic effort and sacrifice.[45] McNeill elaborated these themes over the next nine years as he wrote *The Rise of the West*.

The product of twenty-five years of conception, ten years of writing, incorporating the input of four research assistants and the review of twenty-eight historical specialists, *The Rise of the West*, judged by the standards of current professional historians, may be the foremost single volume of world history written in the twentieth century.[46]

To McNeill, the world was one from day one. Civilizations are not anthropomorphic beings willfully following their destinies and then dying of old age but are representatives of a single, and from the first, relatively unified process of growth, spread, and integration that has culminated with the dynamic disequilibrium of the present. In his study of civilization and diffusion McNeill set out to identify in any given age where the center of highest skill was located as the focal point of ecumenical development.[47] *The Rise* charts the breakthrough to civilization in Mesopotamia with the invention and diffusion of agriculture, the development of the traction plow and irrigation, and from these techniques, male-dominated farming and husbandry, the rise of urban centers, and the "social engine" of concentrated surplus food supplies controlled by managerial leadership under nascent kingships. He documented the leapfrogging diffusion of the Mesopotamian adaptations to like environments on the Karun (Elamite civilization), the Jordan (Jericho), the Indus, and the Nile and the adoption of digestible techniques by peripheral areas of "high barbarism," some of whom adapted civilization to rain-watered lands (around 2000 B.C.) in Minoan Crete and Asia Minor. A "double pulse beat" of ancient civilization was dominated in its initial phase by the growth and expansion of Mesopotamian and Egyptian civilizations from 2700 to 1700 B.C. This development was interrupted around 1700 B.C. by a barbarian *Volkwanderung* through the entire Middle East region, which by 1500 B.C. had harnessed the horse to the chariot to give attackers an overwhelming technological superiority over indigenous agricultural peoples and swept the length of the Eurasian ecumene to reach the Yellow River by 1300 B.C. The barbarian wave of new peoples and the diffusion of skills from Mesopotamia gave birth to a second wave of civilizations, which in turn produced gradients of influence into the barbaric periphery.[48]

By 500 B.C. a balanced equilibrium came into being with the end of Middle Eastern cultural leadership. Across Eurasia, four civilizational centers emerged in tension with their barbarian fringes; this marked the end of a world historical era. For the next two thousand years each civilization existed in a land-centered balance with its peers, which was threatened in turn by Greek expansion under Alexander, Indic growth, the Islamic movement, and finally Chinese hegemony over their landed periphery and movement into the Indian Ocean.[49] From 500 B.C. until A.D. 1500 this Eurasian balance allowed contacts and borrowings among "roughly equivalent" centers—after 1500, these borrowings would be dominated by the West and were necessary for survival in the rest of the ecumene as Europe forced modernization in its image on the non-West.[50]

The continuum of civilization achieved by 500 B.C. inaugurated a period that McNeill refers to as "the closure of the Eurasian Ecumene." From 500 B.C. to A.D. 200 the relative isolation of the four centers of Eurasian civilization was broken down through trade, communications, and military extensions from one end of the ecumene to the other. This brief flowering of closer interconnection and transfusion affected the arts most and first but may also have diffused the common soteriological strand of Buddhism and Christianity from a Greek center.[51] The disastrous epidemiological effects of the newly opened Eurasian continuum on relatively immune-deficient peoples on the extreme ends of the continuum, in China and the Roman Empire, will be discussed in the context of McNeill's later work; it is sufficient here to state that *The Rise of the West* noted the epidemiological contribution to the Falls of Rome and the Han Empire and the subsequent demographic vacuum that was filled in the East and West by a new wave of steppe barbarians.[52]

While China survived its epidemiological catastrophe and civilized the influx of barbarians, and India (A.D. 200–600) went through its golden age in intellectual and religious development, Western civilization was nearly overcome. In contrast to other world historians, most notably Christopher Dawson, McNeill held that "Christian culture was at low ebb between 600 and 1000 A.D."[53] Only with the belated adoption of the Iranian armed cavalry cataphract and its accompanying feudal social organization could the West resist epidemics of barbarian incursion and achieve a relative stability. Meanwhile China achieved a new unity under the Sung (960–1279) and by A.D. 1000 had obtained an ecumenical leadership in the development of technology that was only offset by its Confucian hierarchical denigration of the warrior and especially the merchant classes. This led to a decapitation of merchant groups as successful businessmen withdrew from the unseemly marketplace to take up more prestigious roles as conservative rural landlords.[54]

Between A.D. 1000 and A.D. 1500 McNeill noted two major disruptions of ecumenical balance: the steppe incursions of the mongols, which in the end may have been most important in extending Chinese technology into the Islamic world and to the West, and second, the consequent Western expansion stimulated by the acquisition of gunpowder, printing, the compass, and improved naval technology.[55] From 1500 on, the "Era of Western Dominance" proceeded as a "vast explosion" incomparable in range and scale to any other place or period. Western expansion was fed by international military and economic rivalries that promoted a competitive borrowing of techniques and ideas from rival nations and Islam. Concurrently, the old domination of landed empires and the perpetual threat from the semibarbarous steppe were lessened with the demographic changes and technological transfers that gave massed infantry and cannon a firepower advantage over marauding horsemen, and the European ships an edge over any they met on their worldwide expansion. By 1700 an unprecedented level of diffusion was reached, a leavening "cross stimulation" of the reunited world ecumene; attempts to withdraw from the upheaval into a tradition-retaining isolation were doomed to failure and participation became an urgent necessity. "World history since

1500 may be thought of as a race between the West's growing power to molest the rest of the world and the increasingly desperate efforts of other peoples to stave Westerners off, either by clinging more strenuously than before to their peculiar cultural inheritance, or, when that failed, by appropriating aspects of Western civilization."[56] Elsewhere McNeill claims that "power, in short, ingests weaker centers of power or stimulates rival centers to strengthen themselves. This fact . . . has dominated the whole history of mankind," as civilized history is a "series of breakthroughs toward the realization of greater and greater power."[57] When he came to outline this period of history (1500 to 1917) in *The Rise of the West*, McNeill chronologically offset by fifty years his analysis of the advances of the West and historical sections dealing with the impact of rising Western power upon developments in other areas of the world.

It is not surprising that McNeill's perception of the Renaissance and Enlightenment differs sharply from those of cyclical theorists like Sorokin who see in the Renaissance a rising sensate society that has undermined and disrupted the organic cohesive unity of the Middle Ages. For one thing, McNeill traces his own intellectual roots to the secularizing rationalism of Galileo, Descartes, and Newton and up to Adam Smith, Malthus, and Marx.[58] Paralleling the rise of military and economic power of the West, McNeill describes a growth of intellectual power. He perceived the breakdown of dogma in a different and more positive light than had the cyclical theories of his predecessors; with the disintegration of the medieval framework, people were presented with a new stimulus, a choice of belief systems, and a freedom of thought that was both unsettling psychologically and stimulating of new techniques and ideas. In line with these developments McNeill isolated two central features of modernism: the growth of human control over inanimate matter and energy, and an activist readiness to tinker with social institutions and customs. Taken together the two are equivalent to "the progress of human reason applied to man."[59]

Along with this progress went increasingly conscious management of industry, technology, finance, and society punctuated by the French Revolution's impetus toward centralization and consolidation of power, Bismarck's managerial machine, and the culminating war "machines" of the world wars of the twentieth century, motored by "the invention of deliberate invention."[60] McNeill's speculations on the ambiguous resolution of these patterns in the future dominate the last sections of *The Rise of the West*. He noted that the pattern of the extension of sovereignties achieved in the contemporary situation of world duality dominated by superpower spheres led to the logical expectation of a "single world sovereignty" in the future, either through war or by the convergence of American and Soviet societies.[61] McNeill examined the ominous process by which wartime coordination of production and social order continued into peacetime as "human engineering [of] 'machined' individuals . . . into interchangeable parts" in managerial economies. He warned that the elites of this order may in the future be swayed by a "bureaucratic self interest" that would put into place "elaborate rules and precedents" that might in time make claim to "the semi-sacredness of holy ritual" in an attempt to throttle back disruptive scientific initiatives and social change to produce a conservative bureaucratic world hegemony.[62]

Since 1963 McNeill admits to two major changes in his perspective: he is no longer satisfied with the concept of distinct civilizations that he employed in *The Rise* but emphasizes even further the web of communications between cultures as more critical than their relative independence. At the same time, McNeill has increasingly focused on the ecological context of the movement of world history.[63] McNeill's incipient ecological approach pervaded his earlier work from his interest in the fixed ecological niches of civilized planting peoples and the nomads of the grasslands on the Eurasian steppe in *Past and Future*, to his doctoral dissertation on the potato in Ireland and the confluence of overgrazing, the loss of forests, and the plague that contributed to the seventeenth-century decline of Venice.[64]

In 1976 McNeill produced his first major work in world epidemiological history, *Plagues and Peoples*, in which he approached the study of "microparasitism," the reciprocal relations between human beings and parasites in human history. Humankind is here observed in a petri dish as "an acute epidemic disease"[65] in relation to other animals. McNeill takes this approach further in his later work on "macroparasitism," the interrelationships between human parasites and their host societies. What concerns McNeill in *Plagues and Peoples* is the history of human relations with infection and the ramifications of these associations on demographic patterns, the rise and fall of states and empires, and the intellectual and religious aspirations of societies.

In 1972 Alfred Crosby explored the complex exchange of disease patterns with the European discovery of America, a mutual transfer that led to the greatest epidemic of all time in the New World with the plague of European smallpox, measles, and other Old World infections and included the movement of food crops to Europe, which helped to support the population explosion that coincided with the growth of European hegemony and the subsequent Industrial Revolution.[66] McNeill applied this approach to the world as a whole and postulated what Crosby later called "McNeill's Law," that disease works with conquest, that microparasitism allies itself in history with the expansion of civilized centers whose endemism provides them with a devastating invisible weapon in its contacts with peripheral peoples. The decimations in the Americas, when the complex endemism of a united Eurasian disease pool was brought to bear on a population lacking immunities to the most common Eurasian "childhood diseases," were but an extremely devastating instance of a process begun in the first civilized centers.[67]

In *Plagues and Peoples* McNeill tentatively charts a world history of epidemiology to open what he sees as a neglected area of concern in history. He describes the "gradient of infection" from south to north that benefited those primitive groups who undertook migration from tropical to temperate zones. With the coming of civilization he marks the shortened food chains, the reduction of biological variety, the importance of the struggle with weeds, and the political imperatives inherent in plowing, irrigation systems, and protection from rival groups. He records the passage of an epidemiological horizon point with the concentration of people that cultivation allowed, the new disease contacts domesticated herds provided, and the emergent new pattern of disease with the rise of cities. New "diseases of civilization" emerged in the nascent urban centers where population densities allowed an uninterrupted infectious chain.[68] Civilized societies "learned to live with" these diseases, which struck "replaceable youth" as childhood diseases, often providing an immunity to those who survived. The endemic diseases and immunities of a civilized center acted as a weapon in new contacts with rural and isolated populations where the childhood diseases of civilization killed young and old alike, contributing to processes of demoralization, economic breakdown, and loss of faith in protective gods and totems—all of which aided the political and cultural expansion of the civilized center. Civilizations in history have "digested" their primitive peripheries, having "masticated" them with war and disease.[69]

From an epidemiological standpoint history is the story of the mutual adaptation of disease and a host population. By 500 B.C. four relatively independent disease pools had coalesced in Eurasia; China, India, Persia, and the Mediterranean world each had endemic diseases that facilitated its expansion.[70] In *The Rise of the West* McNeill had pointed out the interconnection of these centers in the period between 500 B.C. and A.D. 200, a period of the "closure of the Eurasian ecumene." By 128 B.C. Chinese diplomatic contacts were extended as far as the Oxus and Jaxartes; by 101 B.C. Chinese armies had followed these contacts from oasis to oasis to open the Silk Road across the southern Eurasian steppe, which extended from China through the Kushan Empire and the Parthian Empire as far as the Levant and the Roman Empire. In addition, Roman maritime expansion from the West reached Indian ports even as China linked itself to the subcontinent by sea.[71] The closure of the ecumene through this transportation and commercial transmutation led to a continentwide infectious chain as the Old World disease pools came into mutual contact and disease transfers swept through these united populations, leading to disastrous die-offs on the relatively isolated ends of the infectious chain—Han China and the Roman Empire.[72] Thus McNeill applies a natural history perspective to the Fall of Han and of Rome in place of a biological metaphor of life cycles and inferences of moral decay and degeneracy resulting from the loss of spiritual cohesion.

The opening of contacts through Eurasia led to the Roman plagues of what were probably smallpox and measles of A.D. 165–180, and their recurrence in 251–256. This began the population decay of the urban Mediterranean, led to breakdowns in literacy, culture, and central authority, and gave demographic advantage to the northern rural barbarian peoples who were invited into the empire to fill the population vacuum. In 542 bubonic plague reached the West, triggering a new wave of devolution and dooming to failure Justinian's attempt to reunite the Mediterranean. In the resultant dark age, the Church provided a positive model of adaptation as it looked for succor in the next world in the face of the suffering in this one and emphasized charity, including the tending of the sick. A final result of the disease ravages was the power vacuum in the West, which facilitated the Moslem expansions beginning in 634.[73] China suffered from major epidemics that paralleled those of Rome (A.D. 161–162 and A.D. 310–312), contributed to the Fall of Han (A.D. 221), and left demographic openings for steppe incursions. China, however, was able to convert the barbarians and so evaded a similar break in its cultural continuity.

The downfall of empires on the ends of the Eurasian continuum interrupted that continuum. When a new line of communication and trade was opened to the north across the Eurasian steppe by the Mongols, a new wave of infection was precipitated. The bubonic plague, carried by black rats to China and Europe, again led to large-scale die-offs; in this round, however, the peoples of the steppe were decimated in turn, leaving the ultimate demographic balance in favor of the agricultural civilizations.[74] In Europe the Black Death led to an interruption of medieval faith, to phenomena as diverse as the flagellant sects, the Dance of Death, and an anticlericalism that contributed to the Renaissance and Reformation as civic authorities, especially in Italy, responded positively to the challenge while priests were shown to be impotent in the face of the pest.[75]

The Eurasian disease pool was extended by the European voyages of discovery, conquest, and trade to the American continent and worldwide, precipitating massive die-offs as peripheral peoples were digested in the closure of a world disease pool.[76] With this convergence came a relative decline in epidemics in Europe that, from McNeill's perspective, allowed a deistic view of God to emerge. Without epidemiological crises, and in the context of a new scientific dialogue, Divine Providence was no longer a necessary adaptive belief.[77]

As a parallel to microparasitism McNeill applied epidemiological terminology analogously to the relations between peoples in macroparasitism. Just as the total destruction of a human host population is an inefficient mode of adaptation for bacteria, McNeill asserted that human macroparasites early found that genocidal conquest and seizure of the entire food supply was an inefficient mode of exploitation and consequently adopted modes that allowed endemic relations such as imperial conquest with tribute or taxation; this allowed continuous health for the host population while maximizing the durability and spread of macroparasitical infection. Under such a system surpluses grown to satisfy conquerors and to prevent their rapacity act as antibodies, and the successful government of a conqueror would immunize, through the collection of taxes and rents to build a military defense, against further short-term epidemics of conquest, plunder, and rapine.[78] Macroparasitism is an ambiguous balance—since social diversity was founded at the dawn of civilization by those specialized elites who did not cultivate grain but were able to extract grain from others, macroparasitism could be called the "hallmark of civilization."[79] Just as populations needed to reach a threshold to maintain microparasitic endemism, so a critical size allowed a large enough support for a conquering population; a civilization dominated by a warrior caste then became "lethally formidable" to other peoples, especially to peripheral groups who had not come under a cohesive macroparasitic hegemony. Depending on external threats to a social order, macroparasitical scale could shift in adaptation. According to McNeill, "most of European political history, in fact, can be viewed as an unending fluctuation between imperial consolidation and feudal devolution, punctuated from time to time by epidemics of nomad invasions whenever the defenses of settled agricultural communities became insufficient to hold back armed raiders from the steppe."[80]

In his stimulating study of The Pursuit of Power (1982), McNeill outlined a world history of the increasingly adaptive efficiency of macroparasites in competition, in a Darwinian struggle in which the incrementally refined technologies and psychological instruments of power prove victorious over ever larger hegemonies up to the present era of Western dominance.[81] As the twin to *Plagues and Peoples* it is another *tour de force*, a brilliant analysis and historical exposition of the ecological relations of organized human groups in competition for the resources and techniques of power. At the same time it is a disturbing book; McNeill charts a modern shift away from the Western "aberration" or "eccentric period" of a free-market economy that rose in the fifteenth century, to the reemergence of "bureaucratic command structures" in the reversion to the historical norm of the "command economy" since the 1880s.[82] This shift received its most powerful impetus by the continual arms race in the West, where the bureaucracy became a dynamic force in pursuing invention and promoting "command technology."[83]

Political history, like that of human adaptation to disease, in McNeill's view, can be examined with the use of ecological principles, especially the concept of evolving equilibria. In opening new historical boundaries McNeill sets his ecohistorical framework outside the moral judgment of systems of exploitation, such as that which one may infer behind the arguments of the dependency theorists. In noting the universal and mutually adaptive role of macroparasitism in the history of the species, McNeill analyzes exploitation and dependency as natural relations between groups that follow natural paths of efficiency analogous to those of disease.

McNeill's analysis contains problems that are perhaps inevitable and inherent in broad generalization and the pursuit of historical detachment. His model is applied to some extent metaphorically, and he never wants to make the reductive claim that world historical processes are nothing but the interactions of microparasitism, environmental challenges, and a macroparasitism made increasingly formidable by the invention and diffusion of technology and modes of social control. McNeill's metaphor, his emphasis on adaptive evolution on the epidemiological model, often suggests a blind process of the organic growth of power hegemonies in area, sophistication, and even depth of psychological management, which can scarcely be balanced much less directed by the wills of the individual bacterium or the cells of the social body.

McNeill recognized the incipient elements of determinism in his work as at least in part a legacy of "the Calvinist World View," which holds that "massive largely unconscious processes . . . operated at a level below deliberate political-military planning and action." He believes that this underlying "order means limits, and such a vision of historical processes ought also to remind us that we are never wholly sovereign, whether as individuals or citizens of even the greatest of states."[84] McNeill's sense of the ecological roots of necessity in history is very similar to Fernand Braudel's analysis of the underlying economic and ecological processes active in the long duration, which provide the deep structures upon which the epiphenomenon of battles and kings takes place. McNeill sees Braudel as a "kindred spirit"; Braudel's *The Mediterranean and the Mediterranean World in the Age of Philip II* was the most powerful book McNeill read during the ten years that he wrote *The Rise of the West*. The two historians share a common root in the study of Marc Bloch and the *Annales* school, but McNeill resists what he sees as Braudel's tendency to reduce all history to economic and market relations.[85] With his own holistic ecological approach he attempts to avoid a structural determinism by claiming that the underlying patterns he describes are challenges that condition but do not define the free responses of individuals. The problem is magnified here, however, as these responses occur within a social psychological framework or, from a history of mentalities perspective, in conjunction with a delimited set of mental equipment that further conditions the range of free expression. An analysis of McNeill's view of religion in history can perhaps illustrate this problem further.

McNeill analyzes religious phenomena in history as movements of belief systems or "climates of opinion" that allow positive adaptation to material and social conditions. He takes an "ecological view of religion," examining it "from the outside" for its contribution to human adaptability and survival.[86] The axial religions in the period of the first Eurasian ecumenical union, for example, originated among marginal "excluded elites" and swept through civilized areas because these faiths "fitted the needs, the feelings and the life position of the majority of civilized humankind."[87] In doing so they contributed to human survival. The axial religions were universalist, open to all ethnic groups, and inculcated generous rules and prescriptions for dealing with strangers at a time when a uniting ecumene made for increasing contacts with diverse peoples. In addition these religions contained ideals of heavenly compensation for troubles in the world, from plagues to invasions, and thus promoted an adaptive forbearance in the face of adversity. According to McNeill these religious traditions smoothed contacts between people, fostered coexistence, and thus supplied the foundations of the "commercial transformation of human society."[88] The axial "half sisters" of Christianity, Mahayana Buddhism, and Hinduism provided "the first really satisfactory adjustment of human life to the impersonality and human indifference that prevails in large urban agglomerates."[89] Religion has thus played an ecological role in history by adapting to given social and material conditions and in turn conditioning societies toward future adaptations; religion under this paradigm is more a conditioned response to ecological imperatives with a social and psychological use-value than it is a free aspiration, much less a providential contact.

On the analysis of inner religious experience, McNeill is silent. He believes that religion in the present is in a "transitional phase" and that this may be the "most agitated and critical growth point of our time." Yet he cannot personally bridge the gap between the "incandescent" faith of true believers and the rational analysis of religion from the outside, and is unable to "converse with true believers, whether secular true believers, or transcendental, traditional true believers." Ironically, given the distance in his work from any sort of religiosity, McNeill maintains that modern society may require religious grounding as an adaptation to rapid social change. He seems to take a Voltairean perspective: exhibiting no religion himself he calls for a plurality of vibrant faiths as "requisite for the maintenance of the stability of civilized society."[90]

In *Past and Future* McNeill analyzed the gap in belief systems with the integration of the military-industrial complex and in the light of a future world union. Here again, a religious or spiritual adaptation is presented as a necessary requirement under the new order: "Without religious renewal [in a postmodern united world] on a grand scale, I should think it likely that moral lassitude, and perhaps a supine fatalism would increasingly gain hold of men's minds; and, having nothing much worth while to live for or strive for, they might even cease to propagate their kind."[91] The ideal goal of the West in these troubled times should be a "liberal cooperative, civilized world order in which all mankind could find a spiritual as well as a physical home."[92] The influence of Toynbee on this early formulation is patent and needs no further analysis; what is perhaps more pertinent to McNeill's later view of religion is the usefulness of religiosity, if only as an adaptive delusion in Freud's sense in *Civilization and Its Discontents*, one that accommodates individuals to society and particularly to the repressive features of any civilized social order.

William McNeill, despite his mission as a world historian, is clearly no utopian. One gets a sense that the "spiritual" world order that he invoked in 1954 is only on the "outside," an adjustment to the mechanization of man that McNeill outlined just as clearly as Lewis Mumford had but for which he could not develop any kind of explicit faith in an ameliorative "transformation of man" or true spiritual revitalization. Instead McNeill recognizes the continuity of repressions, even their growth, with the inevitable and even necessary rise of bureaucratic organization and social control in an increasingly complex and unified world. Despite his progressivism McNeill has no illusions on the perfectibility of man or the end of human history in an earthly sacralized paradise. "Human affairs always exhibit . . . an alloy of gain and loss, good and evil, advance and retrogression."[93] Any world bureaucratic order would likely resist change, preferring a conservatism that would slow social change and promote a new balance as the moral and religious sphere caught up with the social changes that have occurred.

In a 1980 reply to Alexander Solzhenitsyn's oratorical attack on Western decadence at the 1978 Harvard commencement, McNeill analyzed the modern vacuum of belief and the lack of courage he located in a lack of a self-defining and encompassing sense of group identity. "The critical deficiency of our secularized vision of the 'true end of man' as inherited from the eighteenth century, seems to me to rest in its individualism. Human beings are social creatures, and happiness depends mainly on effective participation in groups, where shared values and goals, cooperative behavior, and mutual aide can flourish."[94] McNeill asserted that with the decline of traditional religious values in the West, nationalism has substituted as a primary mode of identification, a functional equivalent for the lost faith. Now, with the breakdown of the credibility of national states after the First and Second World Wars and the increasingly international scales of organization, a lack of grounding has resulted. In answering Solzhenitsyn McNeill asserted that he would not follow him down "new and unspecified pathways to salvation" in hopes of reviving the West but felt that, in crisis, the secular ideals of the West would prevail in the end. "I prefer to believe that in time of need sufficient unanimity can be achieved within the pluralistic framework of Western society to keep us strong enough to survive."[95] In the setting of this dialogue McNeill's work can be seen as a program of moral education. In making a deliberate shift in historical orientation from a national to an ecumenical level, McNeill sets up his mythistorical system as a secular substitute for the Augustinian Christian and syncretistic epos that Toynbee reverted to in the end. Rather than follow Toynbee, McNeill's version of world history emphasizes the unity of humankind in this world and the potential for good or evil action in the future; it is then, like our other world visions, at once a grounding toward a postnational sense of identity, a warning, and a call to action. In the preface to *The Rise of the West* McNeill implied his sense of purpose in writing his world history. He believed that "a single book such as this one may become a real force in the cultural history of mankind."[96] In revealing the interconnections of the past and shedding light on the contributions and distinctive pathways of non-Western cultural traditions McNeill educates his readers to think in terms of ecumenical unity. In 1986 he asserted that "ecumenical history" was the "moral duty of the historical profession in our time," a means to redefine the in group, to overcome the divisive nationalism that national history consciously or not tends to promote.[97] Ecumenical history, seen from this perspective, has been a secular mission to McNeill, a conscious means of "preparing readers for more successful membership in a world system."[98]

McNeill's work is a demonstration that we have wider loyalties to humanity as a whole. He typifies this orientation throughout his writing, a characteristic instance being his seemingly dispassionate approach to polyethnicity. In demonstrating that polyethnic empires of one sort or another have been the historical norm of civilized human organization, he attempts to provide a grounding for modern movements to increased polyethnicity with the opening of national frontiers and in anticipation of what he foresees as an upcoming age of *Volkwanderungen*.[99] His selection of critical patterns in the field of world history is in line with his view of the central dynamics of the present and the moral choices that are presented by historical conditions and that will guide future adaptations.

• • •

The ambiguity in McNeill's presentation of history is revealed rather dramatically in his sympathetic identification with Lord Acton's struggle and failure to write his great book, *The History of Liberty*. Predictably McNeill rejected Acton's scientific view of empirical epistemology, the idea that one can allow massively accumulated facts to speak for themselves without architectonic intervention by the historian; in his view, facts only acquire meaning as part of an interpretive scheme.[100] McNeill's work, however, places him in the same dilemma that he ascribes to Acton of reconciling the Whig interpretation of history, "the notion that all mankind has been toiling upward toward the pinnacle of English (and/or American) constitutional liberty," and the march of increasingly concentrated power that, by its tendency to corruption, denies this advance. According to McNeill, Acton wanted to write a history of the rise of liberty and virtue but was derailed by his confrontation with the evidence of the concerted emergence of centralized power; this left the father of Whig history unable to complete his self-appointed task of applying it to the world scale.[101] In this context McNeill views the work of Spengler and Toynbee as attempts to present an inclusive historical perspective in response to the dethronement of Whig history by World War I. On the whole such attempts must be seen as relative failures in his eyes, for most modern historians, including McNeill, retain an ambiguous sense of the meaning and direction of history. In his words, they "remain at least as unsure as Acton ever was of whether history is a record of the advance of human freedom, of human power, of both freedom and power, or of power at the expense of freedom."[102] Yet McNeill has retained as his own the task of salvaging what can be rescued from Whig progressivism in an age whose central metaphor is ecological and whose social order is increasingly centralized and bureaucratic.

In a lively review article Walter A. McDougall has characterized McNeill's stand as one of "uncomfortable liberalism"; he quotes a letter from McNeill that admits a technocratic world order is the likely outcome of historical patterns but that optimistically affirms "what really matters is relations with other human beings on a face to face basis."[103] According to McNeill it has made no sense since World War I to speak of European history as the rise of liberty, and we must therefore create a new mythistory, a new ecological and global vision, to make the world intelligible.[104] When McNeill charts the progress of the mechanization of man, enforced diffusion, micro- and macroparasitism, he often presents these historical patterns as if they were underlying determinative structures that belied liberal assertions of free will. He claims that "the ideal of freedom, according to which individuals cooperate in public matters of their own volition because of common recognition of dangers from without and costs of civil strife within, stands and has always stood in persistent conflict with experience."[105] A Calvinist sort of freedom pervades McNeill's work like the one that Redfield posits in the Neolithic community, a freedom to act in terms of a faith or a prescribed pattern of life. Civilization breaks this cohesion and sharpens choices but also imposes certain behaviors in line with particular social and historical conditions. Freedom then is always relative and in a context. "Indeed the price of complete personal freedom is to consume only what one can produce for oneself in a place where risk of armed attack by outsiders has somehow been effectively exorcised. Such places are few and far in our world," and the costs of such freedom from mutual dependence outweigh the benefits for most of us. Seen in the light of Redfield's view of primitive cohesion and its breakdown with the onset of civilization, one can view the elaboration of rules and social order in civilization as "a real liberation."[106]

In 1955 McNeill wrote an evaluation of A. J. P. Taylor's study of European diplomacy between 1848 and 1918 that criticized Taylor for ignoring ideology and belittling the importance of individual statesmen as nothing but "calculating machines, registering tremors in the balance of power with seismographic accuracy." He called

Taylor a "Cartesian Historian" for "abstracting from history all that made it human in order to achieve a clear and definite idea."[107] Following the publication of *The Pursuit of Power*, the same type of criticism has been applied to McNeill's work. Alvin Bernstein found that McNeill, like Braudel, studied underlying patterns in history to the point of excluding individuals, as though personalities and politics had nothing to do with the progress of power. He called *The Pursuit of Power* a "mechanical, deterministic view of the historical processes" that ignored conscious decision, distorted the innovative process by overemphasizing the stimulus-response necessity of technological adaptation, and posited wars as the inevitable results of technological advances and demographic pressures.[108] A Cartesian duality is apparent in McNeill's work; he emphasizes the systematic forces propelling human history in each of his works even as he continually affirms the importance of the individual and the role of belief in the outcome of events. The conundrum of determinism is particularly evident in his sweeping employment of challenge and response as a macrohistorical process: individual creativity is scarcely ever examined in detail in his work and, at any rate, seems to fulfill a sort of historical necessity in resolving macrodilemmas rather than personal aspirations.[109]

McNeill does not try, however, to overcome through a simplistic formula the complex duality of freedom versus determinism in history or to draw a firm line between ecological imperatives and individual free choice. Rather than choosing a single and reductive pattern of explanation McNeill has attempted the more difficult task of demonstrating the various ecological patterns in history, including that of individual choice and action, as interacting balances in history that act as a hierarchy of equilibria in response to one another and to environmental changes. In correspondence with the author McNeill argues that

> individual acts and refusals to act do add up to make a difference in ecological and statistical terms. . . . The most changeable and therefore the most disturbing element in any ecological situation is human purposes: for as they alter and direct human action, sometimes mass action, the differences wrought in ecological systems becomes [*sic*] enormous. . . . We are surely free to do things differently; and in so doing change patterns and deflect processes into new paths, but we never entirely prevail, nor is there a perfect fit between words and things, hopes and realities, ideas, ideals and behavior.[110]

Human beings can direct their own destiny although not within conditions of their own choosing. Elsewhere McNeill asserts that "in human society . . . belief matters most" and the myths that we employ to make sense of life and to guide our action are "often self-validating."[111]

• • •

According to McNeill, only a world government can match modern commercial exchanges; on the analogy of macroparasitical exchanges this would act as an adaptive "climax equilibrium." While seeing the necessity of a World State and sometimes optimistically calling for one, McNeill holds to a Weberian view of the rise of the "iron cage" of bureaucracy and rationalized social order. A World State, dominated by elites and interlocking bureaucratic managerial patterns, may leave no room for questions of direction or meaning. As he puts it in his concluding remarks in *The Rise of the West*, "administrative routine may make rational definition of the goals of human striving entirely super-fluous."[112] He also stated his hope that people might yet prove refractory to the machinations, of the bureaucracy, in particular to its potential, through bioengineering, to produce a managed posthuman population of subhuman toilers and superhuman elite leaders, each as "specialized in function and various in type as the social insects are now."[113]

One can argue that his characteristic predisposition to end his works on a positive note is belied by his perspective on the progressive nature of the acquisitive movement of human power. Alongside his invocation to individuals to resist such machinations he claims that scruples over the use of human power have never permanently turned the flow of this movement aside; if an empowering technique is rejected out of fear of social or cultural consequences, adventurers in other areas will seize upon it, thus forcing opponents and neighbors to copy them or succumb to their improved efficiency.[114] This is as true in the area of social management as it is in the area of mechanical technology: "Once having deliberately set hand upon the levers that effect human behavior, it is hard to stop short of a far more complete mastery of the art of manipulating others than men have anywhere yet achieved." This art may in the future come to include control of irrational social forces and psychologies of the unconscious developed in the twentieth century but still not fully plumbed for use in social control.[115] The imperatives contained in technology and social management as adaptive strategies that empower elites in a struggle for survival seem to act almost lawfully in McNeill's paradigm and to support conclusions at odds with his optimistic forecasts.[116]

In a recent article on "Control and Catastrophe in Human Affairs" (1989), McNeill reverts to a Wellsian theme of our "race between intelligence and catastrophe."[117] He claims that there is a law of the "Conservation of Catastrophe"; that with each civilized adaptation we move away from individual ecological self-sufficiency and we up the ante of the potential for interhuman catastrophes, through our abilities to destroy one another or from other ecological disasters. In the modern period two major changes have occurred that bring the present disequilibrium into high relief. McNeill assumes a neo-Malthusian view of worldwide population growth as threatening the long-term stability of the species. On the positive side global communications and transportation allow action on a global level in response to catastrophes from drought in Africa to earthquakes in Mexico.[118] Even this opening and uniting of the ecumene is not without its downside, however, as McNeill had earlier noted the dissolution of the 'cakes of custom' with the rise of communications and the proportionate decline of traditional agricultural life-styles; the present transition point has left individuals without moral and religious convictions, not yet adapted to postagricultural conditions.[119] Furthermore, the open communication of disease between vast modern populations makes the modern disease pool one that invites disasters and demands early and systematic response to new infectious adaptations on a global level.[120] From an ecological/ epidemiological perspective humankind has reached a state of perilous imbalance through overpopulation. McNeill can be far from sanguine in his appraisal of our modern victory over death. He holds that the successes that humanity has achieved have upped the stakes but that "a series of sharp alterations and abrupt oscillations in existing balances will occur in the future just as they have in the past."[121]

William McNeill believes that so far in history human intelligence has responded successfully to the challenges natural and man-made disasters have presented. More than any other historian reviewed in this volume, McNeill emphasizes these break points in history, catastrophic interruptions through microparasitic or macroparasitic epidemics or environmental changes. And yet, of all the metahistorians he is perhaps the least eschatological and the most optimistic over the ability of civilization to adjust to the future. "We ought not to despair," he says, "but rather rejoice in how much we human beings can do in the way of capturing energy from the world around us and bending it to our purposes and wants, intensifying the risk of catastrophe with each new success."[122] McNeill holds that despite the apocalyptic possibilities in the competitive pursuit of power and the Ellul-like imperatives that he records in technological development, our era is an unprecedented golden age that gives us ground for optimism. He has frankly admitted, however, that "I tend to discount . . . eschatological views, probably more for temperamental than for intellectual reasons."[123]

In the end McNeill leaves the future open. He recognizes that, on the surface, his work could lead to a gloomy prognosis for the West and the world as a whole but, despite the ecological processes that provide the boundaries of human life and from that which humanity will never extricate itself, he is optimistic that human intelligence can transform the conditions of life, can adapt in the face of the worst, and can guide the species forward. "I attest my lively faith in the power of words to alter the way human beings think and act," he says, and he affirms this faith in his view of the validity of macrohistory as a means of guiding human beings toward future successful adaptations, especially in the present shift necessary for world citizenship.[124]

William H. McNeill has investigated patterns in world history that have set the discourse into the future. In line with his perspective, and of course no less influenced by the dramatic requirements of our times, the ecological study of history seems likely to reign paramount in the efforts of world historical scholars into the new century. World studies of progressive patterns of environmental management, disease control, racial and ethnic integration, and the process of the growth of sovereignties in history will continue to serve as ground for understanding as these processes are furthered, perhaps toward some of their logical conclusions. Gaps in McNeill's ecological paradigm, particularly in the systematic evaluation of land and water use, species loss, pollution, and consumptive waste, will presumably spark further world historical work in line with these areas as vital concerns for survival into the future.

In McNeill's paradigm of world history, human intelligence has thus far prevailed in a great and ennobling adventure, and a blind one, into a future at once unknown, dark, and forbidding, and full of challenges that may lead humanity to new heights of power and self-discovery.[125] His work is itself an articulation of these challenges.

CHAPTER NINE

World History and Eschatology
The Goals of the Metahistorians

The pursuing the inquiry under the light of an end or final cause gives
wonderful animation, a sort of personality to the whole writing.
—Ralph Waldo Emerson[1]

NIKOLAI BERDYAEV claimed half a century ago that "the philosophy of history is always prophetic and cannot be otherwise. . . . History has meaning only if it is going to come to an end."[2] History, particularly world history, is founded on a sense of meaning in the present that is conditioned by our anticipations of the future. It might be said that our future determines our past; in many cases prophesy precedes and justifies, as well as completes our histories. World historians do not write outside of time but compose a unity that is made up of future vision and present imperatives applied to the chaos of historical data and conditioned by the perspectives applied by their predecessors. To confront world history is to confront the ultimate questions of human destiny.

This is not to say that the world historian is nothing but the proponent of myth; clearly there are varying levels of historical accuracy and comprehensiveness in the work of twentieth-century metahistorians, and not all interpretations are equal. Individual historians do take positions of relative distance from the ideologies of their times and attempt relative levels of objectivity in viewing the past as a whole. Even so, if they are judged pragmatically as hermeneutical tools, world historical theories by definition are to be seen in terms of their use-value to explain and ascertain the meaning of history as an entirety and to correctly locate the discrete evidence of the past in a plausible framework, one that can be reconciled with our prospectus on the future. The data itself is secondary to this. The epistemological standpoint of the modern West does not allow us to step beyond the sense of useful construct to assert the truth of a world historical system; claims to the absolute or finished truth of any world historical model are dismissed by most scholars as delusions of grandeur or unprovable expressions of faith.

A consensus emerges among the authors studied in this work that modern epistemology is flawed by its reduction of reality to discrete atoms of data that in themselves can bear no meaning. Each of these authors proposes a supersensory way of knowing that is antithetical to this modern reductionism and that serves as a basis for their own macroscopic perspective; they also posit this way of knowing as a means to creativity in culture and so a root to the births and growths of civilizations. Spengler evokes the integrative ability of the imagination, which in the modern West acts as the Faustian lens that allows one to discern the soul of a culture. Sorokin claims an Ideational form of perception that goes beyond the dissecting epistemene of the Sensate period; Mumford's work occasionally falls back upon a similar sense of transcendentalism. Toynbee relies on a Bergsonian sense of inspiration that has a holistic mysticism, a subtle revelation, as its foundation; Dawson goes but a step further to place this providential source in a Catholic framework. William McNeill utilizes a pragmatic sanction declaring "mythistory" to be an essential task of the historian, the presentation of a useful, if not absolute, framework for understanding processes of the whole. In the last analysis historical knowledge becomes existential knowledge;[3] it provides a setting useful in the psychological adjustment of individuals and the social cohesion of groups. This is not to say that there is no historical reality independent of the individual's point of view, only that the subject of this study is the perspectives of twentieth-century world historians and not world history in itself. Because the focus of the discourse is thus aligned, no attempt is made to judge the use of evidence but only the intent of the writers selected. The danger of reducing world history to individual psychology is a real one, but the emphasis of this argument is not on how closely these metahistorians have mirrored historical realities but on the use and meaning they have applied to their work.

In highlighting the religious and psychological elements in the writing of modern world history, it is not my intention to claim a monocausal determinism of the world historians' religious outlook, independent of cultural and historical exigencies and the documentary material available to them, but to uncover one aspect of their work—a common search for meaning in the movement of the whole. At bottom, world history has been written to provide a useful model—which in some cases may require faith for its usefulness to be realized—from the needs of the present and particularly as a means to promote a desired future. This is probably inevitable given the dialectical nature of human thought and the mental conditioning inherent in our ability to anticipate and plan for the future, along with the near-universal prospective of moderns who, even in their intellectual rejection of progress, retain (if unconsciously) an ameliorative attitude toward the future. One

must look at history, particularly world history, as the reflection of a
desired future.

In the twentieth century, world historical writing has been in pursuit
of a unitary perspective in confrontation with the crisis in confidence
in the meaning and direction of world history prepared by Nietzsche
and expressed most fully by Spengler in his *The Decline of the West*.
Spengler typifies the modernist loss of faith in progress, continuity,
and a historical goal or end point that provides a unifying ground to
action. His nihilism, the product of his disturbed inner psychological
antiworld and German cultural despair, was expressed in a corresponding forecast of collapse, destruction, and cultural dissolution enlightened only by the glories of victory for those barbarian overmen who
could grasp power in tune with the times. Yet even his tragic vision, as
has been seen, is a call to action; it presents a world with moral
imperatives, a lawful cosmos in which one acts according to one's time
and destiny. Spengler's hard morality postulated regional ends to
history. There could be no movement of the whole, only a series of
almost unrelated, closed civilizational cycles.

Twentieth-century world history since Spengler has been dominated
by what could be called the ecumenical impulse, the desire to reinvest
the past with a functional unity and an aspiration to revivify a progressive movement to the ecumene, even one subject to cyclically recurrent
movements within culture or in series among civilizations or empires.
Central to this impetus is the attempt to rescue a continuity that
extends through the cycles of the birth and death of civilizations.
Under the ecumenical impulse, the controlling element in each major
world historical system since Spengler, world history is guided by
varying perspectives on a single goal for the future. World history has
become a pursuit of world unity. While this goal has been inherent in
the millennial anticipations of a unified Christendom and continued
into the Enlightenment designs of Condorcet and Kant, the ecumenical impulse has been fueled in our century by the sense of progress
threatened presented by the real apocalyptic potential of the modern
era.

So much has been written on the subject of progress that it could
almost be *the* major problem in the intellectual history of our century.
Where the nineteenth century has been somewhat naively typified as
dominated by the ideology of progress in its myriad forms despite the
dissonant voices raised against it, the twentieth century is seen as one
where the very foundations of progress are problematic. There are
those who, like Pitirim Sorokin or Dawson, charge all of modern
history for the desperate groundlessness of the present. Like Rudolf

Bultmann they see the Renaissance and Reformation, the Enlightenment and the French Revolution, as progressive steps in the breakdown of a sense of divine authority that certified man's existence and gave order and an eschaton to human life.[4] Robert Nisbet closes his *tour de force* on progress with the assertion that "only . . . in the context of a true culture in which the core is a deep and wide sense of the sacred are we likely to regain the vital condition of progress itself and of faith in progress—past, present, and future."[5] Christopher Dawson, the only world historian studied in this volume who actively allied himself to a particular historical religion, agreed with Nietzsche that the reverberations from the death of God must topple all the progressive perspectives underlying modern social and political institutions and individual psychology. His solution was not to attempt to disprove Nietzsche's world historical insight but to call for a renewed Christian education to combat the atheism and consequent groundlessness that made those insights so psychologically cogent. Twentieth-century world historians have confronted the secularization of the progressive perspective and found it on the whole inadequate. For most of the world historians studied here, the progressive view of becoming rather than being leaves modern man only as a process—constantly "making himself" without ever realizing his essence. In the pursuit of becoming, man has lost his being. The antimodernism of the world historians is toward recapturing the solidity of an "eternal" referent through their perspectives on the ecological balance of the Neolithic village, the unity of the Middle Ages, or by means of a sense of eternity or supersensual reality outside temporal cycles, outside the tragedies of history, outside of the subjectivity and relativism of the modern mentality. In the absence of the sacred, progress is reduced to increased material consumption or, as in McNeill's work, a Weberian rationalization of society and its technics that is ambiguous at best and at worst threatens the viability of creativity in the human spirit.

In contrast to Enlightenment progressives from Condorcet and Kant to Comte, twentieth-century world historians have, like Nietzsche and Spengler, viewed the movement from the origins of culture in the sacred dramas of myth to the skeptical perspective of rational urban individualism in a negative light. Even H. G. Wells, who in his rather naive sense of continuing enlightenment had no sense of just how far the whole Western perspective of progress was being undermined, wrote of progress threatened, idealized a new community, and founded a set of myths to guide in its formation. William McNeill, the only figure examined in detail who retains a secular progressivism, qualifies his statement of progress by extending Robert Redfield's sense of the breakdown of social cohesion and the unity founded on common myths at the dawn of civilization to the pattern of growth in civilization as a whole. The ecumenical impulse that dominates the twentieth-century writing of world history is a sometimes desperate attempt to establish progress on a new footing, one that transcends the limited perspectives of regions and the ideologies of nation-states, toward a world unity or a world state as a logical and even a spiritual culmination of world development. World historians have attempted to reanimate a sense of sacred time in order to reinvest meaning in history.

Along with the teleological sense of the ecumenical impulse in the writing of twentieth-century world history is an attempt to incorporate Nietzsche's resurrection of what Mircea Eliade has called the "myth of the eternal return," the archaic historical sense of perpetual reoccurrence and participation in the primal myth of the beginnings of a people and a culture. Where the Judeo-Christian tradition emphasizes becoming and historical irreversibility (allowing for ritual participation through reenactment), in Eliade's view of the "archaic ontology" the emphasis is on the return to mythical being. Eliade holds that modern metahistorians attempt to defend against the "terror of history" outside a teleological framework by reverting to a sense of eternal return.[6] This is most obvious in Sorokin's paradigm, which presents the inevitable evolutionary return to an Ideational age, but it is inherent as an undercurrent in all the cyclical theories we have examined. Spengler sought a return to his culture's supposed source in a Germanic barbarian virility; Wells, a community of saints in a rationalized post-Christian religion; Dawson, a resurrection and spread of the Christianity of the early disciples. Toynbee looked toward a transformative, transcendental unifying religion based on his perception of the unity of the Western mystical tradition within Christianity and the tolerant universalism of the Mahayana. Lewis Mumford looked back to the harmonious balance of the human community with its myths and technics in the Neolithic village and the medieval independent town.

The post-Spenglerian cyclical theorists examined in this volume, including Sorokin, Toynbee, Dawson, and Mumford, agree that a new religious age is in the offing.[7] The consensus is even more widespread in twentieth-century world history that the West is in a perilous position, one functionally equivalent to that of Rome before the Fall. Even William McNeill, from his clearheaded agnosticism, has claimed that a new religious revitalization may be an essential adaptation for racial progress and survival. Spengler predicted the return of a second religiosity, though for him it is only toward a fellaheen stasis. Surely it is no accident that Spengler, Sorokin, Dawson, Toynbee, Quigley, and Kroeber all conceived cultural or civilizational cycles within a generation. This is not to say that these authors have experienced Jungian archetypes somewhere in the nether regions of their collective psyches. It seems more pertinent to locate the antimodernism implicit in their historical cycles in a common uneasiness with the breakdown of the collective myths and symbols of Western society, and a common experience of the psychohistorical dislocation of modernism and the cataclysm of the First World War. Pitirim Sorokin expressed what is probably a typical view of modernism among these authors when he claimed that "we are in the midst of an enormous conflagration burning everything into ashes."[8] Sorokin believed that linear and apocalyptic views dominant in the late Sensate period of a culture give way before cyclical perspectives in the Ideational[9]; all the other authors studied herein have agreed in their analysis of the present century as an axial age.

There *is* a crisis in the twentieth century, one of historical confidence, that acts as a psychological impetus in the projection of world historical theories.[10] This desire for a return to the sacred roots of culture, alongside the aspiration for a purpose to history as a whole, makes twentieth-century metahistory a curious blending of ahistorical cultural cycles with a direction that transcends their declines. The pervasiveness of the cyclical perspective is due, at least in part, to a common recognition that Western civilization is threatened with collapse. The death of God, the world wars, the breakdown of progressive faith, urbanization and conurbation, the consumer society, the mechanization of man, and the fragmentation of traditional forms of social cohesion: all symbolize to twentieth-century world historians a break in the cultural continuity of Western civilization. A cyclical view in a twilight period of civilization provides faith that a renewed civilization will rise from the ashes. A cyclical view in the last resort can provide a progressive setting that transcends the short-term collapse of civilization. Cycles can thus act in a manner equivalent to Teilhard de Chardin's apotheosis of evolution. To Teilhard de Chardin, evolution countered the second law of thermodynamics (which was also Henry Adams's nemesis); it was an "anti-entropic" teleological movement that promoted the progress of the whole in the face of physical laws of decline.[11]

This rescue of progress by the metahistorians is, however, closely bound to what could be called their "deep conservatism," a conservative stance connected to their sense of return to the formative point of civilizational development and cultural creativity. This conservatism, reactionary as it may seem on occasion, is not founded within the contemporary political boundaries of right and left, but like Henry Adams's conservative Christian anarchism it reverts to a mythical period of cultural origins to establish at a fundamental level a sacred point of departure that provides goals for the future and an ethical ground toward their realization. The fundamentalism of the world historians' attempt to isolate an architectonic of the long duration has contained implications for the organization of a new order that parallels the twentieth-century orders of Soviet communism and European fascism. Both these systems were grounded in deep readings of world history; their proponents justified the new order by reference to deep and determinative patterns of economy and race charted in world history by their ideological predecessors. While of the metahistorians we have studied only Spengler can be sincerely considered a proponent of fascism, each of the other authors examined, excluding McNeill, expressed aspirations for an antimodern world order—often one based on a transcendent faith—that would establish a new sense of place beyond what they saw as disintegrative individualism, and a new sense of social cohesion under a moral and spiritual authority. The desire to reinvigorate or reproduce societal myths as the foundation for a new civilizational order, and the sense in Spengler, Sorokin, Toynbee, Mumford, and Dawson of the disintegrative tendency of the rationalism of the last men of culture, often led them to antirationalism and anti-intellectualism. With the twentieth-century new orders of the Left and the Right, the metahistorians shared a fundamental aversion to modernist anomie and nihilism and looked to a new community based on a shared faith and unified social purpose. Spengler, Mumford, Sorokin, Dawson, Toynbee, and Wells shared a yearning for a corporative organic social order in their writings in the 1930s. However, with the exception of Spengler's culpability in preparing the ground, Toynbee's doubts and equivocations, and Wells's increasing pessimism, all fought actively against the fascist response to modernism.

John T. Marcus has written in his *Heaven, Hell and History* a survey of "redemptive historicity . . . the use of historical consciousness as a redemptive faith."[12] Marcus echoes numerous critics who have noted that the faith in history climaxed in nineteenth-century rationalism, positivism, and socialism and that in the twentieth century there has been a "collapse of historical consciousness." Like Robert J. Lifton, Marcus sees faith in history as a form of "symbolic immortality" that has for many individuals taken the place of immortality symbolizations from traditional religious and mythical systems. Marcus claims that "particular historical ideals merely serve as the means through which the individual seeks a self-transcending identification with the encompassing unity that gives purpose to human existence and a vicarious release from death." The breakdown of earlier formulations of meaning in history, the loss of a historical ground and setting for individual life, and the accompanying sense of immortal participation in a pattern that transcends individual existence leaves moderns in a "profound moral and psychological void."[13] As sober an analyst as Fernand Braudel testifies to the breakdown of symbols of connection and grounding in modern society: "All society's dearest symbols, or nearly all—including some for which we would have sacrificed our lives yesterday with hardly a second thought—have been emptied of meaning."[14] Robert J. Lifton has systematically analyzed the breakdown of the sense of connection that immortality symbolism provides in a series of psychohistorical works that attempt to locate the collective symbols of a people and the predominant "mode of immortality" that prevails within particular historical societies.[15] From such a perspective the writing of history becomes meaningful in formulating boundaries for individual experience and a setting of cosmic scope, be it cyclical or progressive, that allows a sense of psychological continuity beyond the inevitability of biological death. With the breakdown of a progressive, historical symbolic consensus in the modern period, the foundations of the psychological setting for a sense of symbolic immortality are undermined. This dialectically stirs an investigation by intellectuals designed to fill this psychological gap in terms of the collective symbols (or even mental equipment) of a society. Seen in this light the writing of world history is an integrative process where individual psychological aspirations connect with shifts in the collective symbol system of a society. In the writing of twentieth-century world history one can distinguish a response to the disintegration of progressive symbols in modernism and an attempt to regain an immortal setting for human action in an age of weightlessness and existential dread.

• • •

One can argue that this analysis of world historical thought in the twentieth century is biased from its outset toward visionary and even religious philosophers and selectively ignores the works of those who are not encapsulated by its central themes. From the start this study has chosen to present a short list of metahistorical paradigms or models rather than to attempt a sweeping but more shallow survey of the host of writers of world history in this century. Certain authors are obvious; no one could write a history of this subject and ignore Spengler, Toynbee, and McNeill. Wells wrote the most popular work of history of all time and typifies, for our purposes, prewar progressivism and the tremendous impact of the war on the Western prospect on the future of civilization. After Spengler and Toynbee, Sorokin arrived at a perspective on cultural cycles that is highly original and contains an immense erudition in the quantification of cultural history. In Dawson there is a judicious summation of Christian metahistory in the twentieth century. Finally Mumford's profound examination of the problem of the relation of humanity to its technics in world history is a crucial expression of a perpetually central issue in the historiography of the twentieth century.

Any selection contains elements of subjectivity; the criteria for the definition of one's subject must be specified as clearly as possible. First, world historians, as defined for the purposes of this study, are those who have attempted to grasp the whole of history with a theoretical construct or ideal type and have tested their theory by writing a concrete work of comprehensive world historical scope, one that embraces the known ecumene from the dawn of historical time. These individuals are not simply abstract philosophers of history; they must claim the title of historian and apply their philosophy in historical analysis. A second major criterion, and perhaps a rather debatable one from the standpoint of intellectual history as a discipline, was the popularity of a particular model. One does not read H. G. Wells to find an accurate or even an especially penetrating analysis of the dynamics of civilizations, but in part for his ability to express as well as to capture and mold the contemporary climate of opinion; his popular success testifies to this. Originality and influence were also taken into account in selection but scholastic credentials per se have not been of primary concern. Evidence suggests that outsiders avoid the stigma attached to metahistorical speculation by the academic disciplines and so evade the narrowed focus within a particular genre that academia promotes.[16] Finally, one could argue that this work centers on a particular tradition in the writing of world history, albeit a central and diffuse one, initiated in our century by Spengler and brought to at least a partial conclusion with William H. McNeill.

Since McNeill there has not been a full-blown world historical paradigm that has taken the cycles of civilization as its starting point. The movement from the writing of the history of civilizations to world ecumenical history that has occurred from Spengler to McNeill reflects the closure of a nascent worldwide civilization. It may also be that in *The Rise of the West* we see the end of a chapter in world historical discourse and to some extent a limitation of that discourse in the immediate future (at least academically) to the comparative study of historical and political organizations without a framework for their ultimate goals and ends. Postmodern history is open-ended. In the face of this trend there is also, however, a continued sense of the apocalyptic potential of our time, now largely shifting from the fear of nuclear annihilation of the Cold War to one rooted in the present consciousness of environmental crisis. New world historical perspectives will probably emerge in line with the modern environmental discourse, and one might also expect that issues of world unity and structural reorganization will be addressed with the end of the Cold War.

Whether these issues will coalesce around renewed attempts to resurrect religious ends to history is a question one must leave to the future.

The definition of the world historian presented here is anything but airtight. Spengler can hardly be said to have written a concrete and comprehensive world history. H. G. Wells falls to a large extent outside the tradition specified above; he really represents a popularization of nineteenth-century positivistic progressivism and, though he writes in response to his fears of the decline of the West, he does so without having been exposed to Spengler or modern cyclical metahistory. Sorokin, Mumford, and Dawson are decidedly Eurocentric in their emphasis and prospectus. Toynbee, Spengler, and McNeill to a lesser extent, centered on patterns presented by an education in Greco-Roman antiquity. Finally, William McNeill, far from attempting to redeem history from materialism, has been motivated by the conscious intention to detach world history from the metaphysical and theological speculations of his predecessors to establish its solid credibility in academic discipline. Even so, McNeill never makes dogmatic claims to having found hard and fast empirical answers to the problems of world history but recognizes the usefulness of metahistory in providing a mythic background for the study of the humanities. As he puts it, "unalterable and eternal Truth remains like the Kingdom of Heaven, an eschatological hope. Mythistory is what we actually have—a useful instrument for piloting human groups in their encounter with one another and with the natural environment."[17]

• • •

Important works that occasionally border on the defined field of discourse have been omitted, particularly those of dialectical materialism in its various forms. Immanuel Wallerstein's paradigmatic formulations of world history may prove to be the most influential of these. If he has not merited a chapter in this work it is not because he escapes the teleological orientation of the included world historians. Like them his work contains a conscious mission, expresses the ecumenical impulse, and is prophetic and end oriented. Wallerstein rejects the progressive ideology of the nineteenth century, especially that of Marxian inevitability, to affirm morality as the determinative element in the progress of civilization into the future.

Wallerstein has likened the modern world capitalist system to Rome before the Fall; it is a decadent order of exploitation whose contradictions are economic but perhaps even more essentially moral, demanding correct choices for progress to occur.[18] He has scarcely hesitated to prophesy the fall of the modern world order through the structural crisis of capitalism that is now occurring and will end in the next century. He holds at a fundamental level a perspective of the relativism and pragmatic usefulness of his own work and a moral imperative fueled by his sense that exploitation in the capitalist world economy is unequivocally "unjust." The resolution of world injustice is in no way guaranteed by history; it "will be the outcome of our collective human intervention and is not ordained."[19] Wallerstein defines socialism, the moral goal of the positive and antisystemic movements in the modern world system, in opposition to capitalism. If in capitalism economic decisions are made in terms of optimum profitability, in socialism they are based on social utility. If capitalism contains a progressive inequality in the distribution of its products, socialism diminishes these inequalities. If capitalism permits only those liberties that do not threaten the political structures upholding world economic injustice, then socialism will root liberty at a depth in the social fabric where it cannot be subject to political machination. To Wallerstein, there is no socialist state in existence and there can be none while the capitalist world system maintains its hegemony.[20] While he holds that "communism" is a utopian ideal, "the avatar of all our religious eschatologies," he argues that his socialist future is by contrast a "realizable social system."[21] Wallerstein is unable to fully escape the utopian proclivity of Marx, however, and the eschatological religious undercurrent in Marxism has been belabored enough to require no further elucidation here. Wallerstein has made the anachronistic claim that the entire history of the world since the Neolithic era has been a series of revolts against inequality, and that "in the long run the inequalities will disappear as the result of a fundamental transformation of the world system."[22] The first half of this polemic is clearly at odds with the ideas of Wallerstein's mentor, Fernand Braudel, and the *Annales* School in general, whose analysis of the structures of everyday life focuses on the immersion of the individual in an ecological material life and mentality that underpins and conjoins with events (like those of revolts) of wider historical dimensions. The second half of this contention is clearly a statement of faith, even if one based on economic analysis of contemporary historical trends. Suffice it to say that central elements of Wallerstein's application of dependency theory do fit well with the theses of this volume.

Wallerstein, however, like Braudel, is primarily a student of capitalism and the "modern world system" and not of world history as a whole.[23] In extending Andre Gunder Frank's idea of the "development of underdevelopment" historically, Wallerstein has begun by analyzing what Marx called the "original sin" of capital accumulation at the foundation of the modern world economic order.[24] Obviously, structural relations of unequal exchange and dependency between core and peripheral areas have existed throughout human history, at one scale or another and through the evolutionary movement of economic centers. But neither Wallerstein nor anyone else in the dependency school has yet completed a full world history of dependency relations and their connection to the rise and decline of known historical civilizations. Instead, for the most part they confine their analysis to the history and prospects of the modern capitalist world system. One could speculate that the fundamental tenet behind Wallerstein's moral condemnation of the capitalist world system, that of the *absolute* increased immiserization of the proletariat (when viewed on a world scale),[25] becomes problematic before the fifteenth century and in particular it supplies no place to the infrastructural progress that Marx claimed as essential to the development of successive stages of production. By subsuming all productive arrangements of the present under the determinative world capitalist gridiron, Wallerstein sometimes glosses over variations in dependence that exist concurrently and that precede capitalism even as he reduces class struggle to that between economic powers (nations) and favors an emphasis on exchange and distributive relations over those of production. Even more seriously, perhaps, he de-emphasizes the mutualism inherent in historical exchange relations, like those explored by Eric Wolf in his *Europe and the People without History*.[26] Using an anthropological perspective, Wolf investigated the mutuality of relations involved in exchange and in particular the classes and individuals within so-called dependent societies that freely enter into relations that benefit them economically and in terms of their power within the existing social system. He rejected the view of the periphery as a passive agent, and he demonstrates effectively that core exploitation is in turn dependent upon its ability to gain alliances within the indigenous class structure and to interface with the cultural system; dependency is a two-sided interaction.

One could also argue from a Marxian point of view that dependency relations have historically fulfilled a progressive function and, judged in terms of intrinsic merits in particular historical settings, dependency, or mutual dependency, has fulfilled a socially useful and even creative function. But clearly this is outside of Wallerstein's definition of dependency as a modern exploitative phenomenon in a particular "world system." Wallerstein's and other dependency theorists' contributions to the dialogue in world history are immensely important; dependency theory in general is one of the most useful hermeneutical tools in analysis of contemporary history and international politics. For the purposes of this study, however, the work is of secondary significance as it has demonstrated its usefulness explaining only the modern period and has not approached the problem of our selected authors; that is, the rise and fall of civilizations.[27]

• • •

The writing of world history has until recently been a Western phenomenon. This reflects the combined influence of Judeo-Christian linear
time and Enlightenment relativism, along with the progress in empirical techniques of historical research through the nineteenth and twentieth centuries. No universal and comprehensive world histories (in the
modern sense of the term) have been written from a traditionally
Chinese, African, or Indian perspective. Although Jawaharlal Nehru
wrote a world history during his stay in a British jail in the 1930s
aimed at demonstrating in part the bases for Indian independence, his
education and sources were Western and his inspiration was *The
Outline of History* by H. G. Wells.[28] K. M. Panikkar's contribution to
world historical research marks the progressive extension of world
historical technique and foreshadows a true universalization in the
writing of metahistory, one that will in the future increasingly incorporate the insights and historical experience of diverse cultural traditions worldwide.[29] It is interesting if predictable that the former Soviet
Union produced little in the world historical genre. Berdyaev and
Sorokin were exiled in the same expulsion in 1922.[30] Official post-
Stalinist world history until recently provided one volume before and
another after the world-transforming October Revolution[31]; the standard interpretation allowed little room for metahistorical speculation.

Among the authors studied here in depth, an intriguing pattern of
national origins emerges. Spengler conceived his first volume before
World War I and completed it before Germany's defeat in expectation
of an emergent Germanic imperium. His subsequent works stressed
Germany's dominant position as the hinge of Europe in the period of
contending states and the nascent era of conquest and world hegemony. H. G. Wells wrote in a time when the British colonial system and
world trade hegemony were under increasing strain and after a world
war whose outcome defied his hopes for world union. Toynbee and
Dawson began their major works when Britain was clearly in decline as
a power and their later works when the empire was in a shambles.
Mumford and Sorokin wrote in the period of growing economic and
military power of the United States and achieved their highest popularity at the height of American hegemony in the 1960s, when the fate of
American civilization came under increasingly critical scrutiny. Mc-
Neill's *The Rise of the West* was completed during the optimism of the
Kennedy presidency when an ideology of moral courage and determination anchored a faith in the progressive spread of European civilization and the American Way. His later work, on the pursuit of power
and epidemiology, traces ambiguous elements in *The Rise* and earlier
works. The question of the destiny of civilizations has been integrally

bound to the perceived position of the writer's historical setting. Perhaps at the height of hegemony and in the initial phases of decline of a nation's power the concern for the patterns of civilization becomes most acute; then one is tempted to look, as Spengler and Toynbee did, to the fate of preceding civilizations as a model for the prediction of the future.

World historians have confronted the macrohistorical dilemmas of the twentiehth century with attempts at producing a common ground or a common memory that might serve in uniting individuals toward their resolution. From the standpoint of the environmental movement of the 1990s their view of the problems of an industrial society and the consequent mechanization of man provides an enduring pattern of reaction to the machine. There is continuity from Adams and Spengler, who were impressed with the near-Satanic force that humanity had acquired through machine technics and that threatened its extinction, to Sorokin's belief that Ideational technics would soon replace the Sensate, and on to Mumford's Cassandra-like warnings about technocratic dominance and the sinister pervasiveness of the mechanical myth and Toynbee's uneasiness with the Faustian bargain of man with his tools. Even William McNeill, who alone of our subjects has maintained a liberal perspective on world history, has anticipated a new era dominated by a technocratic and bureaucratic elite and sees the realm of real freedom shrinking to the dimensions of our personal relations. These issues along with the sense of crisis now surrounding environmental issues on a world scale and the need for global environmental education make world ecohistory an imperative for the profession.

In his recent biography of Toynbee, William H. McNeill claimed that Toynbee had led the way in outlining the central question before the historical profession of the present age, that of finding an "accurate and adequate framework for all human history."[32] From a strictly methodological point of view enormous progress has been made in the research and writing of world history in the twentieth century. It is a far step in the empirical use and documentation of historical evidence from Spengler and Wells to Sorokin and Toynbee, and probably as great a step again to the restraint of Christopher Dawson and William McNeill. There is a seemingly continuous progress in extension of historical knowledge horizontally into the cultural history of non-Western civilizations and vertically with the steady increase in information on the earliest civilizations and protocivilizations. A progress of sorts may be observed historically in these paradigms; they become more inclusive as the ecumene is extended, and nationalistic and Eurocentric elements are progressively minimalized. This progress in the technical application of historical method can never fully resolve the great unknowns in the question of the meaning of world history. Ranke put this well when reviewing his own efforts at world historical research: "I have often raised the question, whether it would be at all possible to compose a universal history in this sense [that of truth based on critically documented research]. The conclusion was that it was not possible to satisfy these most stringent standards, but it is necessary to try."[33] Instead of empirically provable world history we are left with models approximating critical accuracy with relative degrees of success, which act as artistic attempts to shift the chaos of data into a meaningful historical landscape. The use of ideal types is essential despite their subjective elements; any world history is bound to accentuate certain features of ground and diminish others to provide a sensible image. Historical models work like scientific tools (or Kuhnian paradigms), as lenses that allow observation of secondary qualities and not the thing in itself. Despite the relativism and indeterminism of the modern Western mentality, world history fulfills an essential if often unrecognized function. The absence of critical world historical research and the avoidance of broad historical questions of historical meaning and direction would be a repudiation of an essential function of the historical profession, a *trahison des clercs*. The historical field would be left to those who abstract the minutia from the setting that provides it meaning, who denigrate and disintegrate myth and meaning in their impossible attempt to divest the writing of history of any imposed values, or to those whom McNeill has called "ignorant and agitated extremists" who take up the occupation of mythistory when critical professionals despair of it.[34] Peter Gay has argued, in defense of the use of psychological interpretation in the study of history, that "whether he knows it or not, [the historian] operates with a theory of human nature."[35] In a similar sense a world historical framework is implicit in any work of history; the study of the particular in history relies, consciously or not, on a frame of reference, be it of patterns of exploitation and dominance, of the progress through ancient, medieval, and modern periods, or a standpoint of the independent movement of particular civilizations. The direction and goals of world history are inextricably tied into the ground of any historical study; when these issues are ignored the historian relies on an implicit framework of development, if only one of blindly accumulative causation, that is assumed as a process operative on a global and deep historical scale. When one approaches the study of world history as a whole these questions become unavoidable; indeed they become the most obvious and critical questions for history, as the study of human nature revealed in time, to examine. It is no accident then that the works of many of the authors presented in this volume straddle the fences between the historical profession and anthropology, sociology, moral philosophy, and religion.

• • •

The twentieth century has seen a progressive movement in the writing of world history from the linear dead ends of the Nietzschean experience of the superhistorical and Henry Adams's theory of entropy to Spengler's closed entropic cultural cycles; and from Toynbee's hope of a transcendental gain in each cycle and Sorokin's scheme of how one cycle gives way to the next to Dawson's faith in this progress and McNeill's postulation of progress in the diffusion of culture through the whole. There is, to some extent, a completed cycle here: from a nineteenth-century progressive teleology, to entropy, to a cyclical theory, first of closed cycles and then gradually with the rescue of residues, to a renewed progressivism. Our cycle in the writing of world history is by no means a closed circular one, however, as McNeill's idea of progress is not that of Wells or of the Enlightenment. It is a tentative progress that questions teleology and lacks eschatological faith. Far from the Enlightenment prospect on the end of history in the perfectibility of man, McNeill and other contemporary world historians, while having overcome to a large extent the theories of entropy and closed cycles, have left us with an open future. It is a future that must be made, as far as one can see into the discernible future, among continuing apocalyptical possibilities that are the legacy of the success of the species.

NOTES

PREFACE

1. See entries in the bibliography for each of these authors.

CHAPTER 1: WORLD HISTORY IN THE WEST

1. Sir Walter Raleigh, *The History of the World* (1614; reprint, London: Thomas Basset et al., 1687), face page.

2. G. Buchanan, from "De Sphera," quoted by Peter Heylyn, *Cosmographie in Four Books; Containing the Chorographie and Historie of the Whole World* (London: Philip Chetwind, 1666), 1095.

3. Henry Adams, *The Education of Henry Adams* (1918; reprint, Boston: Houghton Mifflin, 1961), 398.

4. Christopher Dawson, "The Problem of Metahistory," *History Today* 1 (1951): 9.

5. Pieter Geyl, *Debates with Historians* (New York: Meridian, 1958), 113. For a more detailed discussion of the divisions between world historians and specialists, see Walter A. McDougall, " 'Mais ce n'est pas l'histoire!' Some Thoughts on Toynbee, McNeill and the Rest of Us," *Journal of Modern History* 58, no. 1 (1986): 19–42.

6. Sigmund Freud, *New Introductory Lectures on Psychoanalysis*, standard ed., edited by James Strachey (1933; reprint, New York: Norton, 1965) 22: 95.

7. Robert Nisbet, *History of the Idea of Progress* (New York: Basic Books, 1980), 264.

8. John B. Bury, *The Idea of Progress* (1932; reprint, New York: Dover, 1955).

9. Nisbet, 30.

10. Rev. 22:12. "I am the Alpha and the Omega, the first and the last, the beginning and the end." See also Rudolf Bultmann, *History and Eschatology* (Edinburgh: Edinburgh University Press, 1957), 23–37.

11. Augustine, *The City of God* (London and Toronto: T. M. Dent and Sons, 1931). Frank E. Manuel, *Shapes of Philosophical History* (Stanford: Stanford University Press, 1965), 4–33.

12. Bultmann, 56.

13. Norman Cohn argues that Joachim de Fiore was the most influential prophet before Marx and that his faith was a central antecedent of the works of Lessing, Schelling, Fitch, Hegel, Comte, and Marx. Norman Cohn, *Pursuit of the Millennium; Revolutionary Millenarians and Mystical Anarchists of the Middle Ages* (New York: Oxford University Press, 1970), 108. See also Karl Löwith, *Meaning in History: The Theological Implications of the Philosophy of History* (Chicago: Univ. of Chicago, 1949), 150–59.

14. Nisbet, 66, 81.

15. Niccolo di Bernando Machiavelli, *The Discourses, The Portable Machiavelli*, ed. Peter Bondanella and Mark Musa (New York: Penguin, 1979), 177–79.

16. Raleigh, passim.

17. John of Sleidan (Johanne Sleidannus or Johann Philippson of Sleidan), *The Key to History, or A Most Methodicall Abridgement of the Four Cheife Monarchies* (1558; reprint, London: University Microfilms/Nathaniel Rolls, 1695 ed.).

18. Jean Bodin, *Method for the Easy Comprehension of History* (1583, 1595; reprint, New York: Columbia University Press, 1945), 11.

19. Bodin, 54, 92. See his evolutionary speculations on p. 144.

20. Ibid., 236. On p. 235 Bodin critiqued Aristotle's argument in *Politics* where he claimed that numbers had no significance. To us Bodin's argument by examples is no longer convincing: "Why then does the seventh male heal scrofula? Why does the child born in the seventh and ninth month live, that born in the eighth never? Why seven planets, nine spheres? Why has the abdomen the ratio of seven to the length of men? . . . Why is the seventh day of starvation fatal?"

21. Ibid., 336, 362–4.

22. Jacques Benigne Bossuet, *Discourse on Universal History* (1681; reprint, Chicago: Univ. of Chicago, 1976), 20, 183.

23. Ibid., 289, 278.

24. Ibid., 294.

25. Ibid., 360–74.

26. Giambattista Vico, *The New Science* (1744; reprint, Garden City: Doubleday, 1961), 20, 22. "Our new science must therefore be a demonstration, so to speak, of what providence has wrought in history, for it must be a history of the institutions by which, without human discernment or counsel, and often against the designs of men, providence ordered this great city of the human race" (p. 60). See also Max Horkheimer, "Vico and Mythology," *New Vico Studies* 5 (1988): 66 passim.

27. Vico, 284. "This is the unity of the religion of a providential divinity, which is the unity of spirit that informs and gives life to the world of nations."

28. Ibid., 3, 30, 76. On p. 56 Vico asserted that man became human only through "some divinity, the form of whom is the only powerful means of reducing to duty a liberty gone wild." He later made the creditable claim (p. 134) that "no nation in the world was ever founded on atheism."

29. Ibid., 286.

30. Bury, 69. Nisbet, passim, held that progress existed as the dominant myth of the West for twenty-five hundred years; the Enlightenment marked only a particular manifestation of this faith and not its birth.

31. François Marie Arouet de Voltaire, *Essai sur les moeurs et l'espirit des nations*, 2 vols. (Paris: Garnier Frères, 1963). Cf. also John Barker, *The Superhistorians: Makers of Our Past* (New York: Scribners, 1982), 108.

32. Anne-Robert-Jacques Turgot, "On Universal History," in *Turgot on Progress, Sociology and Economics*, ed. Ronald L. Meek (Cambridge: Cambridge University Press, 1973), 69.

33. Adam Ferguson, *The History of Civil Society* (1767; reprint, Edinburgh, Edinburgh University Press, 1966), 53.

34. Ibid., on challenges, 210. On Rome and Greece, 209, 223, 240, 279, 60.

35. Ibid., 105, 208.

36. Jean-Antoine-Nicholas de Caritat Condorcet, *Sketch for a Historical Picture of the Progress of the Human Mind* (London: Weidenfeld and Nicholson, 1955), 199, 189.

37. Ibid., 200–201. On 202, Condorcet again notes this consolation: "He is filled with true delight of virtue and pleasure at having done some lasting good which fate can never destroy by a single stroke of revenge." For Condorcet's place in the history of progress, see Löwith, 96.

38. Gotthold Ephraim Lessing, "Education of the Human Race," in *Literary and Philosophical Essays* (New York: Collier, 1961), 203. Education has as its goal a "time of perfecting."

39. Ibid., 193, 185. Aside from his progressivism Lessing anticipated Nietzsche's sense of historical recurrence. "Why should not every individual man have existed more than once upon this world? . . . Is not a whole eternity mine?" (205–6).

40. John Godfrey Herder, *Outlines of a Philosophy of the History of Man*, 2d Ed. (London: J. Johnson, 1803), 1:xiv, 225, 416.

41. Immanuel Kant, "Ideas towards a Universal History from a Cosmopolitan Point of View," in *On History*, ed. Lewis White Beck (Indianapolis: Bobbs-Merrill, 1963), 23.

42. Gertrude Lenzer, ed., *Auguste Comte and Positivism* (Chicago: Univ. of Chicago, 1975).

43. G. W. F. Hegel, *Reason in History; A General Introduction to the Philosophy of History* (New York: Liberal Arts Press, 1953), 44, 95.

44. Marx tacitly agreed with Hegel that "the individual does not invent his content; he is what he is by acting out the universal as his own content." Hegel, 38.

45. Marx and Engels anchored the Communist struggle of 1847 to a world historical foundation with their challenging first statement in *The Communist Manifesto*: "The history of all hitherto existing society is the history of class struggles." Karl Marx and Friedrich Engels, *The Communist Manifesto* (New York: Washington Square, 1964), 57.

46. George Perkins Marsh, *Man and Nature, or, Physical Geography as Modified by Human Action* (1864; reprint, New York: Scribners, 1874), 10, 24, 35, 134.

47. Arthur comte de Gobineau, *The Inequality of Human Races* (New York: Fertig, 1967), 210.

48. Ibid., 171, 211.

49. Houston Stewart Chamberlain, *Foundations of the Nineteenth Century* (New York: Fertig, 1968), 1: xxiv.

50. George L. Mosse, Introduction to Chamberlain, 1:xiv.

51. Chamberlain, 2:223, 258.

52. Jakob Burckhardt, *Judgements on History and Historians* (Boston: Beacon, 1958), 32.

53. Leopold Von Ranke, *The Secret of World History: Selected Writings on the Art and Science of History*, ed. Roger Wines (New York: Fordham University Press, 1981), 160.

54. Ibid., 159.

55. William H. McNeill, Editor's Introduction to *The Liberal Interpretation of History*, by Lord Acton (Chicago: Univ. of Chicago, 1967), vi–xvii.

56. Nicholai Danilevsky, "The Slav Role in World Civilization," last chapter of *Russia and Europe* in *The Mind of Modern Russia*, ed. Hans Kohn (New York: Harper and Row, 1955), 195. "Only a false concept of the general development of the relationship of the natural to the pan-human, a concept incompatible with the real principles of the systematization of scientific-natural phenomena, as well as a so-called progress, could lead to the confusion of European or Germano-Roman civilization with universal civilization."

57. Ibid., 200, 201, 210. "From an objective factual viewpoint, the Russian and the majority of the Slavic peoples become, with the Greeks, the chief guardians of the living tradition of religious truth." For an excellent detailed summation of Danilevsky's theories, see Pitirim A. Sorokin, *Social Philosophies of an Age of Crisis* (Boston: Beacon, 1950), 49–71.

58. Friedrich Nietzsche, *The Birth of Tragedy* and *The Genealogy of Morals* (Garden City: Doubleday, 1956), 136–37.

59. Friedrich Nietzsche, *The Use and Abuse of History* (New York: Macmillan, 1957), 10–11.

60. Nietzsche, *The Birth of Tragedy*, 102, 138.

CHAPTER 2: EVOLUTIONARY ETHICS
AND THE RISE OF THE WORLD STATE

1. H. G. Wells, "My Auto-Obituary," in *Interviews and Recollections*, ed. J. R. Hammond (Totowa: Barnes and Noble, 1980), 118.

2. George Bernard Shaw, "Back to Methuselah," in *Complete Plays* (London: Odham, 1937), 888.

3. Jean-Antoine Condorcet, *Sketch for a Historical Picture of the Progress of the Human Mind* (London: Weidenfeld and Nicholson, 1955), 192.

4. Ibid., 127.

5. H. G. Wells, *World Brain* (Garden City: Doubleday, Doran, 1938), 20. Wells claimed that he sought to reproduce "Diderot's heroic efforts."

6. Christopher Dawson has called Wells the "last of the Encyclopedists," *The Dynamics of World History*, ed. John J. Mulloy (New York: Sheed and Ward, 1957), 359.

7. Anne-Robert-Jacques Turgot, "On Universal History," in *Turgot on Progress, Sociology and Economics*, ed. Ronald L. Meek (Cambridge: Cambridge University Press, 1973), 68; and "Progress of the Human Mind," same volume, 88.

8. H. G. Wells, *The Outline of History* (Garden City: Garden City Publishing, 1920), 855.

9. Thomas Henry Huxley, *Evolution and Ethics and Other Essays* (New York: Appleton, 1905), 83. See also John Robert Reed, *The Natural History of H. G. Wells* (Athens: Ohio University Press, 1982), 31–34.

10. Ibid., 32.

11. Ibid., 45. See also the "Law of Civilization and Decay" employed in Henry Adams, "The Degeneration of Democratic Dogma," *The Tendency of History* (New York: Book League of America, 1929), passim.

12. Shaw, 888.

13. H. G. Wells, *The Definitive Time Machine*, ed. Harry M. Gedulds (Bloomington: Indiana University Press, 1987). The Eloi and the Morlocks are degenerate men of the future, the results of a class and functional specialization of an effete aristocracy and a brutalized and mechanized caste of machine tenders. Other examples of science mismanaged by human greed include *The Island of Dr. Moreau* and *The Invisible Man*. In *The War of the Worlds*, Wells demonstrates what inhuman intelligence allied with advanced technology is capable of while he warns that no species can escape its place in natural cycles and that cosmic accidents are always possible. This fundamental theme enters into several of his romantic novels and acts as a saving grace in another scientific romance, *In the Days of the Comet*. In *When the Sleeper Wakes*, Wells portrayed an Orwellian future where a misdirected social order evolved into a totalitarian nightmare. For more complete discussions of Wells's distopian fiction and the problem of science divorced from humanity, see Mark Robert Hillegas, *The Future as Nightmare:H. G. Wells and the Anti-Utopians* (New York: Oxford University Press, 1967), 4–56. Jack Williamson, *H. G. Wells: Critic of Progress* (Baltimore: Mirage, 1973), 47–81.

14. H. G. Wells, *Experiment in Autobiography* (1934; reprint, Boston: Little, Brown, 1984), 25, 42–45.

15. H. G. Wells, "A Complete Exposé of this Notorious Literary Humbug," in *Interviews and Recollections*, 110–11. See also Wells, *Experiment*, 104, where Wells considers his mother as a symbol of blind enslavement.

16. Wells, *Experiment*, 56. Anthony West, *H. G. Wells: Aspects of a Life* (New York: Random House, 1984), 180.

17. Wells, "A Complete Exposé," 112.

18. Steven J. Ingle, "The Political Writing of H. G. Wells," *Queen's Quarterly* 81, no. 3 (1974): 396. Wells, *Experiment*, 34.

19. Wells, *Experiment*, 53. Ingle, 397. West, 180.

20. Alfred Borrello, *H. G. Wells: Author in Agony* (Carbondale: Southern Illinois University Press, 1972), 8. Ingle, 397.

21. Wells, *Experiment*, 45.

22. Wells, *The Outline*, 72.

23. Anthony West, "H. G. Wells," *Encounter* 7 (Feb. 1957): 58. Wells later rejected the concept of independent or pure races as a "phantom of the imagination." H. G. Wells, *The Open Conspiracy* (Garden City: Doubleday, 1928), 110.

24. Wells, *Experiment*, 88–96.

25. These writings were the bedrock for his later use of the fantastic in his science fiction, his utopias, and his anti-Marxian socialism. *The Republic* was his "first encounter with the Communist idea." He noted the influence of the Platonic utopia on his view of morality, the social contract, and social order as a means to progress: "So by way of Plato, I got my vision of the Age of Reason that was just about to begin." Wells, *Experiment*, 142, 143.

26. Ibid., 118, 106–18. Montgomery Belgion, *H. G. Wells* (1953; reprint, London: Longmans, Green, 1964), 15. West, *H. G. Wells*, 18–190.

27. Wells, *Experiment*, 159.

28. West, *H. G. Wells*, 277.

29. Ingle, 398. Wells, *Experiment*, 239–45.

30. Wells, *Experiment*, 246.

31. Ibid., 255–308. Ingle, 398.

32. Borrello, 2.

33. Wells, *Experiment*, 532, 420. Wells, "My Auto-Obituary," 117.

34. Wells, *Experiment*, 414. Williamson, 36.

35. Wells, *Experiment*, 529.

36. See, for example, H. L. Mencken, "The Late Mr. Wells," *Prejudices, First Series* (New York: Knopf, 1919), 22–35. Mencken held that by 1912, Wells had sacrificed his art. By then he was in "obvious decay . . . his days as a serious artist are ended."

37. Warren W. Wagar, *The City of Man: Prophesies of a World Civilization in Twentieth Century Thought* (Boston: Houghton Mifflin, 1963), 66–72. Warren W. Wagar, *H. G. Wells and the World State* (Freeport: Yale University Press, 1961), 272.

38. Williamson, 124.

39. Wagar, *H. G. Wells*, 6.

40. Wells, *Experiment*, 425.

41. Ibid., 552. Pierre Teilhard de Chardin, *The Phenomenon of Man* (New York: Harper, 1959), 29.

42. Wells, *Experiment*, 558. Hillegas, 57–58.

43. Wells, *Experiment*, 562.

44. Edwin Emery Slosson, "H. G. Wells," in *Six Major Prophets* (Boston: Little, Brown, 1917), 84. West, *H. G. Wells*, 255. H. G. Wells, *Anticipations* (London: Chapman and Hall, 1902), passim.

45. Wells, *Experiment*. See p. 562 on his classification scheme for a hierarchy of meritorious citizen types, and p. 568 for conditions in the new society.

46. H. G. Wells, *The Shape of Things to Come* (New York: Macmillan, 1934), 431. H. G. Wells, *A Modern Utopia* (London: Chapman and Hall, 1905), passim.

47. Wells, *Experiment*, 400. On the Fabian period see also Arthur Salter, "Apostle of a World Society," in Wells, *Interviews and Recollections*, 71–73. On the Co-efficients Club see Bertrand Russell, "H. G. Wells," in Wells, *Interviews and Recollections*, 53–54; and David C. Smith, *H. G. Wells: Desperately Mortal* (New Haven: Yale University Press, 1986), 106; and William J. Hyde, "The Socialism of H. G. Wells in the Early Twentieth Century," *Journal of the History of Ideas* 17, no. 2 (1956): 218.

48. Wells, *Experiment*, 397–400.

49. Ibid., 397–410. West, *H. G. Wells*, 289.

50. H. G. Wells, *Men like Gods* (New York: Grossett and Dunlop, 1922), 87.

51. West, *H. G. Wells*, 325, 332, 11.

52. Wells, *Experiment*, 565. West, *H. G. Wells*, 140.

53. Wells, *Experiment*, 570.

54. Ibid.

55. West, *H. G. Wells*, 62. Smith, 238.

56. Wells, *Experiment*, 573–75. Wells evinces an awareness of Freud's view of the origin of God the Father in the feeling of "infantile helplessness." Sigmund Freud, *Civilization and Its Discontents* (New York: Norton, 1961), 19.

57. Wells, *Experiment*, 573–75. H. G. Wells, *God the Invisible King* (New York: Macmillan, 1917), 22, 25, 69, 98–99.

58. Wells, *God*, 85, 107, 99.

59. Ibid., 108.

60. Wells, *Experiment*, 643.

61. H. G. Wells, *The Way the World is Going* (London: Ernest Benn, 1928), 322.

62. Wells, *The Open Conspiracy*, 143.

63. Wells, *The Shape*, 428–30.

64. Wells, *Men like Gods*, 106.

65. Patrick Parrinder, "H. G. Wells and the Fiction of Catastrophe," *Renaissance and Modern Studies* 28 (1984): 53.

66. Borrello, 66.

67. Wells, *Experiment*, 623. Malcolm Cowley gives evidence of Wells's postwar eclipse; he criticized Wells as a naive, prewar, optimistic utopian whose faith had outlived itself. See his "Outline of Wells' History," *New Republic*, Nov. 14, 1934, 23.

68. H. G. Wells, *The Salvaging of Civilization* (New York: Macmillan, 1922), 103–4.

69. Wells, *The Salvaging*, 104–5, 107, 113, 138, 196. Wells, *The Way*, 5.

70. Immanuel Kant, "Ideas towards a Universal History from a Cosmopolitan Point of View," in *On History*, ed. Lewis White Beck (Indianapolis: Bobbs-Merrill, 1963), 23.

71. Ibid., 24.

72. *Plato's Republic*, trans. G. M. A. Grube (Indianapolis: Hackett, 1974), 24.

73. Wells, *The Outline*, 94. H. G. Wells, *A Short History of the World*, rev. ed., edited by Raymond Postgate and G. P. Wells (New York: Penguin, 1965), 37. Freud's *Totem and Taboo* preceded *The Outline* by seven years. Wells's views on the evolution of consciousness also parallel the mature perspective of Carl Jung on the importance of the collective unconscious—see Wells, *The Outline*, 304.

74. Wells, *The Outline*, 104.

75. Ibid., 843.

76. Ibid., 204, 300.

77. Ibid., 304.

78. Ibid., 305.

79. Ibid., 305–8.

80. Ibid., 361–62.

81. Ibid., 375–76.

82. Ibid., 378, 362.

83. Ibid., 1094–98.

84. Ibid., 507.

85. Ibid., 654, 812.

86. Ibid., 499–522.

87. Ibid., 492.

88. Ibid., 466–67.

89. Ibid., 552.

90. Ibid., 817–25.

91. Wells, *The Open Conspiracy*, viii, 196.

92. Wells, *World Brain*, 20.

93. Wells, *The Open Conspiracy*, 117.

94. Wells, *The Way the World Is Going*, 3, 43, 63, 66.

95. H. G. Wells, *The World Set Free* (New York: Dutton, 1914), 178. Wells, *The Salvaging*, 14.

96. Wells, *Experiment*, 142. Wells, *The Way the World Is Going*, 110.

97. Wells, *The Way the World Is Going*, 49. "We may be only in the opening phase of this sort of political religiosity." In his autobiography Wells discussed his distaste for Marx; he rejected class war, "the simple panacea of that stuffy, ego-centered and malicious theorist." Wells, *Experiment*, 143. In H. G. Wells, *The New World Order* (New York: Knopf, 1940), 35, Wells argued that the idea of class war was a "perversion of the world drive toward collectivism."

98. Wells, *The Salvaging*, 24–25, 37.

99. Wells, *The Shape*, 428. Education would seek to "establish a new complete ideology and a new spirit which would induce the individual to devote himself and to shape all his activities to one definite purpose, to the attainment and maintenance of a progressive world socialism." Wells, *The Shape*, 398.

100. Wells, *Men like Gods*, 80.

101. Wells, *The New World Order*, 19–23. Wells closed *The Outline*, 1098, with a plea to save other species from extinction.

102. H. G. Wells, *The Fate of Homo Sapiens* (London: Secker and Warburg, 1939), 308–12.

103. Wells, *The Fate*, 280–81.

104. Wells, *The New World Order*, 105. Smith, xii.

105. Warren Wagar presents an evocative picture of Wells's despair: Wagar, *H. G. Wells*, 21. H. G. Wells, *Mind at the End of Its Tether* (London: William Heinemann, 1945), passim.

106. Smith, 457.

107. Mencken, 28.

108. Williamson, 6.

109. George Orwell, "Wells, Hitler and the World State," in *Collected Essays, Journalism and Letters of George Orwell*, eds. Sonia Orwell and Ian Angus (London: Secker and Warburg, 1968), 2:143.

110. Hillegas, 56–57 passim.

111. Cowley, 22. Orwell, 143. Orwell asserted that "I doubt whether anyone who was writing books between 1900 and 1920, at any rate in the English language, influenced the young so much. . . . The mind of all of us . . . would be perceptibly different if Wells had never existed." Bertrand Russell claimed that Wells did more than any other figure to popularize British socialism. Russell, 55. David Smith concurs in this assessment. Smith, 311.

112. West, *H. G. Wells*, 133–34. For Wells's account of the meetings, see *Experiment*, 665–67.

113. William H. McNeill, "Some Assumptions of Toynbee's Study of History," in *The Intent of Toynbee's History*, ed. Edward T. Gargan (Chicago: Loyola University Press, 1961), 32.

114. Wells, *Experiment*, 556.

115. Christopher Dawson called Wells a "compiler," but one with historical vision and a talent for synthesis. Dawson, 359.

116. John K. A. Farrell, "H. G. Wells as an Historian," *University of Windsor Review* 2 (1967): 49. Farrell can himself be rather shallow in his assertions. On p. 47 he wrongly claims that Wells believed in inevitable progress to utopia before the First World War; actually Wellsian progressivism was always to some degree qualified.

117. Ibid., 48.

118. Arnold J. Toynbee, *A Study of History*, abridged by D. C. Somervell (New York: Oxford University Press, 1957), 1:238.

119. Wells, *Experiment*, 613.

120. In addition to discussing plagues and their effects on the Roman Empire, Wells notes of the Black Death that "never was there so clear a warning to seek knowledge and cease from bickering, to unite against the dark powers of nature." Wells, *The Outline*, 713. Modern mobility makes this even more pressing as epidemics can more easily become worldwide. Wells, *The Outline*, 1092. This is essentially the message in McNeill's *Plagues and Peoples*.

121. Warren W. Wagar, *Books in World History* (Bloomington: Indiana University Press, 1973), 21.

122. John Barker, *The Superhistorians; Makers of Our Past* (New York: Scribners, 1982), 300–310.

123. Wagar, *H. G. Wells*, 270.

124. As his son Anthony West said of Wells during his interwar period: "While my father was unquestionably boring the majority he was doing as much as any man then living to create the climate of opinion in the middle ground that was to make the creation of the United Nations and the establishment of the European Economic Community an inevitable part of the peace-keeping process at the end of World War Two." West, *H. G. Wells*, 132.

CHAPTER 3: THE PROBLEM OF
OSWALD SPENGLER

1. Walter Kaufmann, trans. and ed., *Goethe's Faust* (New York: Anchor, 1961), 1, 575–79.

2. Oswald Spengler, *The Decline of the West*, trans. Charles Francis Atkinson (New York: Knopf, 1926, 1928), 1:381.

3. Friedrich Nietzsche, *Ecco Homo*, *The Portable Nietzsche*, ed. Walter Kaufmann (New York: Viking, 1968), 660.

4. Spengler, *Decline*, 1:39.

5. Lewis Mumford, "Spengler's 'The Decline of the West,'" in *Books That Changed Our Minds*, ed. Malcolm Cowley and Bernard Smith (New York: Doubleday, 1939), 218.

6. Spengler, *Decline*, 1:xiii. Spengler's works as a whole are less empirical and more intuitive than those of any other historian examined in this volume. He explicitly admitted that he mined his personality for reflections of the Faustian culture-soul. Spengler's projection of his own personality into his writings on world history is reminiscent of Goethe's view of his own writings: "Everything of mine which has appeared so far consists only of fragments of a great confession." Quoted in Jeanne Ancelet-Hustache, *Goethe* (New York: Grove Press, 1960), 6.

7. Jurgen Naeher, *Oswald Spengler* (Rembeck: Rowohlt, 1984), 7–8.

8. Ibid., 7.

9. James Joll, "Two Prophets of the Twentieth Century: Spengler and Toynbee," *Review of International Studies* 11, no. 2 (1985): 91. Naeher, 8–13.

10. Naeher, 21–24. J. P. Stern, "The Weltangst of Oswald Spengler," *Times Literary Supplement*, Oct. 10, 1980, 1149.

11. Spengler, *Decline*, 1:79. Spengler claimed that *Weltangst* provided the deepest elements in conscious life, that it was a "secret melody not sensed by everyone" but that underlies all art and action in the world. See Naeher, 23.

12. Joll, 91. Stern, 1149.

13. Naeher, 28–29, 33. Joll, 92.

14. Naeher, 14.

15. Ibid., 11.

16. Spengler, *Decline*, 2:58.

17. Oswald Spengler, *Man and Technics: A Contribution to a Philosophy of Life* (1932; reprint, New York: Knopf, 1963), 71.

18. Ernst Haeckel, *Last Words on Evolution* (New York: Eckler, 1905), 16. Spengler, *Man and Technics*, 19.

19. Spengler, *Man and Technics*, 42, 43.

20. Stern, 1149. Naeher, 14.

21. Naeher, 25

22. Ibid., 140. Joll, 92. Stern, 1149.

23. Naeher, 140. Joll, 92.

24. Joll, 92. Stern, 1149. John F. Fennelly, *Twilight of the Evening Lands; Oswald Spengler a Half Century Later* (New York: Brookdale, 1972), 14.

25. Spengler, *Decline*, 1:46. Fennelly, 13.

26. Spengler, *Decline*, 1:50.

27. Oswald Spengler, "Pessimism," in *Selected Essays* (Chicago: Gateway, 1967), 147.

28. *Letters of Oswald Spengler, 1913–1936*, ed. Arthur Helps (New York: Knopf, 1966), Oct. 25, 1914, 27.

29. H. Stuart Hughes, *Oswald Spengler: A Critical Estimate* (New York: Scribners, 1952), 174.

30. Alistair Hamilton, *The Appeal of Fascism* (New York: Avon, 1973), 114–16.

31. Ernst Stutz, *Oswald Spengler als politischer Denker* (Bern: Francke, 1958), 239.

32. Spengler, *Decline*, 1:xiii, xv, 5.

33. Ibid., 1:16. According to Spengler, the "Faust-eye" of our culture is the only one that possesses the ability to see the whole picture of the world as "becoming." His role in this process could be seen as of messianic proportions in that he articulates the final and fulfilling expression of the Faustian vision. See *Decline*, 1:104.

34. Ibid., 1:22.

35. Ibid., 1:104.

36. Ibid., 1:21.

37. Ibid., 1:17–18.

38. Ibid., 1:5.

39. Ibid., 1:121. See G. A. Wells, "Herder's Two Philosophies of History," *Journal of the History of Ideas* 21, no. 4 (1960): 528–30.

40. Spengler, *Decline*, 2:12; 1:60, 67.

41. Ibid., 1:67.

42. Ibid., 1:54.

43. Ibid., 1:31.

44. Ibid.

45. Richard V. Pierard, "Culture versus Civilization: A Christian Critique of Oswald Spengler's Cultural Pessimism," *Fides et History* 14, no. 2 (1982): 39, 47. For an overview of the history of the juxtaposition of the two terms, see Norbert Elias, *The History of Manners*, vol.1 of *The Civilizing Process*

(New York: Pantheon, 1978), 8–31. For Hitler's use of the terms, see Adolf
Hitler, *Mein Kampf* (New York: Regnal and Hitchcock, 1939), 352.

46. Friedrich Nietzsche, *The Birth of Tragedy* and *The Genealogy of Morals*,
(Garden City: Doubleday, 1956), 136.

47. Spengler, *Decline*, 1:32.

48. Ibid., 1:352, 32.

49. Ibid., 1:351–55. The urban mind of civilization inevitably rejects
the religion of its springtime as it forms a liberal scientific world view.
Spengler, *Decline*, 2:97.

50. Spengler, *Decline*, 1:49n.

51. Ibid., 1:351.

52. Ibid., 2:103, 104.

53. Ibid., 2:435, 310–11.

54. Ibid., 2:430–31. Barthold Niebuhr, in his *Roman History* (1830),
had anticipated Spengler in holding that the West was in the position of Rome
in the third century B.C. heading toward the fall of liberal institutions and the
rise of a new despotism. Hans Kohn, ed., *The Mind of Germany* (New York:
Scribners, 1960), 46.

55. Houston Stewart Chamberlain, *Foundations of the Nineteenth Century* (New York: Fertig, 1968), 1:xxx. Gobineau argued the most extreme sort
of racist philosophy in his world history; in contradistinction to Spengler he
held that "Nations [races], whether progressing or stagnating, are independent
of the regions in which they live." Arthur comte de Gobineau, *The Inequality
of Human Races* (1853; reprint, New York: Fertig, 1967), 54.

56. John Godfrey Herder, *Outlines of a Philosophy of the History of Man*,
2d ed. (London: J. Johnson, 1803), 1:242–43, 427. Spengler, *Decline*, 2:119,
160, 165. On p. 160 Spengler asserts that a people is an aggregate that "feels
itself a unit," and later, on p. 165, he claims that a people is "a unit of the
soul. The great events of history were not really achieved by peoples. They
themselves created the peoples."

57. Herder, *Outlines*, 1:376, 298–99, 318, 427. "Language bears the
stamp of the mind and character of a people." Herder consequently sought a
"general physiognomy of nations from their languages" as the best "architecture of human ideas, the best logic and metaphysic of a found understanding"
(428). One can discern in Herder's physiognomic sense of the unity of a
people's character a methodology that passed on to Goethe and so inspired
Spengler both indirectly and directly.

58. Herder, *Outlines*, 2:46. Spengler, *Decline*, 2:114. Spengler's determinism, although not of a linear pattern, also parallels Herder's. According to
Herder (2:107), the principal law of history is "that everywhere on our Earth
whatever could be has been, according to the circumstances and occasions of
the times, and the nature or generated character of the people." William J.
Bossenbrook, *The German Mind* (Detroit: Wayne State University Press,
1961), 389, examines the sense of culture as a windowless monad with a
unique soul, as an influence of Herder on Spengler. G. A. Wells, "Herder's
Two Philosophies of History," *Journal of the History of Ideas* 21, no. 4 (1960):

528, evaluates Herder's determinism and, on 529, describes how Herder viewed the process by which mental characteristics are generated by historical and environmental conditions that determine future development. See also G. A. Wells, "Herder's Determinism," *Journal of the History of Ideas* 19, no. 1 (1958): 105–13. Like Herder, Spengler held that culture was an autochthonous product of its environmental setting; culture is rooted in a natural setting and as it develops it "renews and intensifies the intimacy of man and soil." Spengler, *Decline*, 2:90.

59. Spengler, *Decline*, 2:113, 139. In *Decline*, 1:302, Spengler describes the interconnections as follows:

> Clear thought, emancipated from all connection withseeing, presupposes as its organ a culture-language, which is created by the soul of the Culture as a part supporting other parts of its expression; and presently this language itself creates a "Nature" of word-meanings, a linguistic cosmos within which abstract notions, judgements and conclusions . . . can lead a mechanically deterministic existence. At any particular time, therefore, the current image of the soul is a function of the current language and its inner symbolism.

60. Chamberlain, *Foundations*, 1:502.
61. Spengler, *Decline*, 2:170.
62. Ibid., 2:170–72, 119–39, 165.
63. Ibid., 2:279. Spengler held that the foundations of culture were in its religious faith. The prime symbol is conceived in the religious youth of a people, as a sort of love.
64. Ibid., 1:174, 180.
65. Ibid., 1:189, 201.
66. See W. M. Flinders Petrie, *The Revolutions of Civilization* (London: Harper and Brothers, 1911), 5, 105, 114. Petrie held that all civilizations decay after reaching a maximal point in expressing themselves in a variety of successive cultural areas, after which they are too decadent to initiate anything; "there is no new generation without a mixture of blood."
67. Spengler, *Decline*, 1:174, 183, 132; 2:200.
68. Ibid., 2:233–43.
69. Ibid., 1:306.
70. Ibid., 2:243–61, 304.
71. Ibid., 1:134, 174, 183, 231, 263.
72. Ibid., 1:341–42.
73. Ibid., 1:264–67.
74. Ibid., 1:280–88, 291–93. He goes so far as to say that "what is practiced as art today . . . is impotence and falsehood."
75. Ibid., 2:180. "Strong Pessimism" comes from Nietzsche, *The Birth of Tragedy*, 4.
76. Pitirim Sorokin, *Social Philosophies of an Age of Crisis* (Boston: Beacon, 1950), 102–11. Spengler, *Decline*, 2:190. See also for further parallels

Nicholai Danilevsky, "The Slav Role in World Civilization," last chapter of *Russia and Europe* in *The Mind of Modern Russia*, ed. Hans Kohn (New York: Harper and Row, 1955), 195, 210. On p. 210 Danilevsky argues that it is a historical imperative to fight this element (which Spengler calls pseudomorphism) to allow the rise of Russian culture. The similarities of the two views are extraordinary, especially considering that Spengler probably had not read Danilevsky before he wrote. See Robert E. MacMaster, "Danilevsky and Spengler: A New Interpretation," *Journal of Modern History* 26 (1954): 154–61. Alfred L. Kroeber, *Style and Civilizations* (Ithaca: Cornell University Press, 1957), 109–17.

77. Spengler, *Decline*, 2:189.

78. Ibid., 2:192

79. Ibid., 2:196. See also Spengler, *Letters*, (Jul. 6, 1915), 34–38. Spengler described the prime symbol of the nascent Russian culture as a "plain without limit." Spengler, *Decline*, 1:201. On Marxism and tsarism see Oswald Spengler, "Prussianism and Socialism," in *Selected Essays* (Chicago: Gateway, 1967), 126–27. Dostoevsky is the prophet of the "immanent birth of a new religion in Russia"—the future will be dominated by Russia as it attempts to actualize its "sense of religious mission," its central cultural, social, and political expression.

80. Oswald Spengler, "The Two Faces of Russia and Germany's Eastern Problem," in *Selected Essays*, 171–72.

81. Spengler, *Decline*, 1:335–37.

82. Ibid., 2:330–31.

83. As he later put it, "we Germans will never again produce a Goethe, but indeed a Caesar." Spengler, "Pessimism," in *Selected Essays*, 154.

84. This is Spengler's transformation of Clausewitz's famous dictum. Spengler, *Decline*, 2:330.

85. Oswald Spengler, *Man and Technics; A Contribution to a Philosophy of Life* (1932; reprint, New York: Knopf, 1963), 10–11. "Every machine serves some process and owes its existence to *thought about this process.*"

86. Like Jacques Ellul, Spengler believed that "our technical thinking *must* have its actualization, sensible or senseless." Spengler, *Man and Technics*, 94.

87. Spengler, *Decline*, 2:501–4. Years later Spengler reiterated his contention that civilization had lost control of its tools: "The creature is rising up against its creator . . . the Lord of the World is becoming the slave of the Machine." Spengler, *Man and Technics*, 90.

88. Spengler, *Decline*, 2:505. Already in 1932, Spengler believed that the technicians were fleeing from machine dominance. Spengler, *Man and Technics*, 97–98.

89. Spengler, *Man and Technics*, 94.

90. Ibid., 101–3.

91. Spengler, "Prussianism," in *Selected Essays*, 17–18.

92. Ibid., 130.

93. Oswald Spengler, *The Hour of Decision* (New York: Knopf, 1934), ix.

94. Spengler, *The Hour*, xiii–xvi, 24.

95. Ibid., 230. He closed: "The ultimate decisions are waiting their man. . . . He whose sword compels victory here will be lord of the world. The dice are there ready for this stupendous game. Who dares to throw them."

96. Hamilton, 142–43.

97. Spengler, *Letters* (Mar. 15, 1927), 217.

98. Hamilton, 155, 117. Somewhat ironically Spengler considered Mussolini a greater leader; he was a "Lord of his country." See also T. W. Adorno, "Was Spengler Right?" *Encounter* 26, no. 148 (1966): 25–29. On February 14, 1933, Spengler wrote to a friend of the degeneration of the nationalist movement with the rise of Nazi dominance and the "grotesque incapacity of their leading clique." Spengler, *Letters*, 278.

99. Spengler, *Letters*, Goebbels to Spengler (Feb. 10, 1933), 289, Spengler's reply (Mar. 3, 1933), 290. Or in Anton M. Koktanek, ed., *Oswald Spengler, Briefe, 1913–1936* (München: C. H. Beck, 1963), 709–11.

100. Joll, 93.

101. On Moeller van den Bruck and Spengler see Fritz Stern, *The Politics of Cultural Despair* (Berkeley: Univ. of California Press, 1961), 238–39.

102. Gunther E. Grundel, *Jahre der Überwindung* (Breslau: Korn, 1934). The title is an obvious answer to Spengler's *The Hour of Decision*. The official world history of the regime was that set forth in *Mein Kampf* and in Rosenberg's *Der Mythus des 20. Jahrhunderts* (1930). Rosenberg sharply attacked Spengler's position on race, he rejected Spengler's perspective on what he saw as "heaven sent 'culture groups' " in favor of his own *Mythus* of blood, which precedes culture and determines it. Alfred Rosenberg, *Race and Race History and Other Essays*, ed. Robert Pois (New York: Harper and Row, 1970), 94–99.

103. Hamilton, 158.

104. Spengler, *Letters* (Oct. 15, 1935), to Spengler from Elizabeth Förster-Nietzsche, 304.

105. Spengler, *Decline*, 1:xiv.

106. The "hard Nietzscheans" were concerned less with the struggle of the individual for creation and self-overcoming (the central interest of the "soft Nietzscheans," like Kaufmann himself) as with the sense of life as a struggle between strong and weak in terms of worldly power. See Walter Kaufmann, *Nietzsche: Philosopher, Psychologist, Antichrist* (1950; reprint, Princeton: Princeton University Press, 1974), 414.

107. Spengler, *Man and Technics*, 16.

108. Oswald Spengler, "Nietzsche and His Century," in *Selected Essays*, 182–94.

109. Friedrich Nietzsche, *The Use and Abuse of History* (New York: Macmillan, 1986), 69–70. Nietzsche held that it was "high time to move forward with the whole battalion of satire and malice against the excesses of the 'historical sense,' the wanton love of the world process at the expense of life and existence" (60).

Notes to Pages 66–67

110. Ernst Stutz, *Oswald Spengler als politischer Denker* (Bern: Francke, 1958), 95.

111. See Hans Barth, *Truth and Ideology* (Berkeley: Univ. of California, 1976), 140n. See also Edmond Vermeil, *Doctrinaires de la Revolution allemande 1918–1938* (Paris: Sorlot, 1938), 84. Spengler relied on *The Will to Power*, which Elizabeth Förster-Nietzsche distorted with her own nationalism and racism. See also Kaufmann, *Nietzsche*, passim. Stern, *The Politics*, 286, 287, argues convincingly that Nietzsche warned against the transfer of the concept of 'will to power' from individual self-actualization to the state. This is the very misunderstanding of his work that Nietzsche most feared.

112. A useful view of Nietzsche's perspective is in Hayden White, "Nietzsche: The Poetic Defense of History in the Metaphorical Mode," in *Metahistory: The Historical Imagination in Nineteenth Century Europe* (Baltimore: Johns Hopkins University Press, 1973) 360–61 passim, 332–73.

113. Nietzsche, *The Birth of Tragedy*, 9–11, 33, 52.

114. Barth, *Truth and Ideology*, 178. Hamilton, 112, notes that Mann called Spengler an "ape" of Nietzsche. Eric Russell Bentley, *A Century of Hero-Worship* (Philadelphia: J. B. Lippincott, 1944), 210–11. Bentley holds that Spengler reduces Nietzsche to the male aspect of the will to power; his work is "relieved by no ray of Nietzschean sunshine."

115. On Goethe's impact on Spengler see Erich Heller, *The Disinherited Mind* (New York: Harcourt Brace Jovanovich, 1975), 91, 179–96 passim.

116. Christopher Dawson, *The Dynamics of World History*, ed. John J. Mulloy (New York: Sheed and Ward, 1957), 376.

117. Stephen Chant and Michael Joyce, "Spengler and the Anthropologists," *Contemporary Review* 131 (1927): 766.

118. Barth, *Truth and Ideology*, 182. Barth rejects the possibility that we can make a real comparison between historical expression and the underlying ground of the soul.

119. R. G. Collingwood, *The Idea of History* (1946; reprint, London: Oxford University Press, 1972), 163, 167, 169–70. R. G. Collingwood, "Oswald Spengler and the Theory of Historical Cycles," *Antiquity* 1 (1927): 311–25 passim. Alfred Kroeber called Spengler's denial of any viable diffusion "insolence." (86).

120. Don August Messer, *Oswald Spengler als Philosoph* (Stuttgart: Drud von Streder, 1922), 74, 88, 207.

123. Martin Brauun, "Bury, Spengler and the New Spenglerians," *History Today* 7 (1952): 528. Brauun noted that the "new Spenglerians"—Sorokin, Toynbee, and Kroeber—were really anti-Spenglerians who sought to free cycles from biological determinism.

124. Vermeil, 105, 125. Vermeil concluded that Spengler acted as a useful prelude to the Nazis, anticipating their doctrine "on the essential points." For further information on the two racisms and for an intriguing view of the importance of Spengler in British fascism, see Richard C. Thurlow,

"Destiny and Doom: Spengler, Hitler and 'British' Fascism," *Patterns of Prejudice* 15, no. 4 (1981): 23 passim.

125. Adorno, "Was Spengler Right?" 29.

126. Spengler, *Decline*, 1:421–24. The second law of thermodynamics symbolized for Spengler (just as it had for Henry Adams) "the world's end as completion of an inwardly necessary evolution." See also Bentley, 211.

127. Stutz, *Oswald Spengler*, 239. As Kroeber (65) noted, the idea "that science shares at least a degree of the relativity that is characteristic of all human culture, was first realized by Spengler."

128. Hughes, 165.

CHAPTER 4: THE RELIGIOUS PREMISES AND GOALS OF ARNOLD TOYNBEE'S WORLD HISTORY

1. Jacques Benigne Bossuet, *Discourse sur l'Histoire Universelle*, 3d ed. (Paris), pt. 3, chap. 1; quoted by Arnold J. Toynbee, *A Study of History* (London: Oxford University Press, 1933, 1939, 1954, 1961), 7:55. (Hereafter referred to as *Study*.)

2. Toynbee, *Study*, 10:112.

3. Arnold J. Toynbee, "A Study of History; What the Book Is for: How the Book Took Shape," in *Toynbee and History: Critical Essays and Reviews*, ed. A. Montague (Boston: Porter Sargent, 1956), 11.

4. Toynbee, *Study*, 7:245, 230.

5. Ibid., 3:235.

6. Ibid., 3:390.

7. Ibid., 3:383, and 1:194.

8. Ibid., 3:373.

9. Ibid., 12:569.

10. Ibid., 12:563.

11. Ibid., 10:87.

12. *Toynbee on Toynbee* (New York: Oxford University Press, 1974), 110. Arnold J. Toynbee, *Acquaintances* (London: Oxford University Press, 1967), 21–38.

13. *Toynbee on Toynbee*, 38.

14. William H. McNeill, *Arnold Toynbee; A Life* (New York: Oxford University Press, 1989), 9–24.

15. Arnold J. Toynbee, *Experiences* (New York: Oxford University Press, 1969), 127–47. Arnold J. Toynbee, *An Historian's Conscience: Correspondence of Arnold J. Toynbee and Columba Cary-Elwes, Monk of Ampleforth*, ed. Christian B. Peper (Boston: Beacon, 1986), Letter of August 5, 1938, 19.

16. Toynbee, *Experiences*, 36. See McNeill, *Arnold Toynbee*, 43, on mystical experiences, and 33–34, on his father's insanity.

17. *Toynbee on Toynbee*, 17. Toynbee, *Study*, 10:95.

18. *Toynbee on Toynbee*, 39, 110. In his autobiographical *Experiences* Toynbee discusses these deaths on at least eight separate occasions. In *Acquaintances* he mentions five individuals significant to him whose lives were cut

short by the war. In a letter to Father Columba (Jan. 25, 1972) in *An Historian's Conscience*, 537, Toynbee expressed wonder at his survival after the deaths of so many others. Lee E. Grugel, "In Search of a Legacy for Arnold Toynbee," *Journal of General Education* 31, no. 1 (1979): 39, also discusses Toynbee's sense of a survivor's mission.

19. McNeill, *Arnold Toynbee*, 65–68.

20. Toynbee, *Experiences*, 88.

21. Ibid., 81–84.

22. McNeill, *Arnold Toynbee*, 121. Toynbee, *Experiences*, 61–81.

23. Toynbee, *Study*, 10: passim, on "The Inspirations of Historians."

24. McNeill, *Arnold Toynbee*, 99.

25. Ibid., 168, 171–72, Toynbee, *Acquaintances*, 279.

26. Bodleian Library, Toynbee Papers, Memorandum to Foreign Office, Mar. 8, 1936, quoted by McNeill, *Arnold Toynbee*, 173.

27. Toynbee, *An Historian's Conscience* (Letters of June 23, 1940, and Oct. 10, 1940), 67, 77.

28. McNeill, *Arnold Toynbee*, 179, 189. Toynbee never joined the Catholic church because of what he saw as the intolerant exclusivity of church dogma and its curtailment of intellectual freedom. Toynbee, *An Historian's Conscience* (Letter of Jul. 21, 1919), 20.

29. McNeill, *Arnold Toynbee*, 149, 150, 184, 200. On Tony's suicide, Toynbee, *An Historian's Conscience* (Letter of Mar. 19, 1939), 32; on the breakup of his marriage (Letter of Feb. 25, 1943), 132; on psychoanalyst (Letter of May 26, 1944), 164.

30. McNeill, *Arnold Toynbee*, 184–200.

31. Toynbee, *Study*: In vol. 1, Toynbee assumes on pp. 159 and 194 that the goal of history is to produce supermen and plays with the notion that this goal includes a common consciousness (197). In vol. 2 Toynbee anticipates the fall of the modern West and suggests that Christianity "may conceivably become the living faith of a dying civilization for the second time" (220).

32. Toynbee, *Study*, 1:44–45.

33. Arnold J. Toynbee, *A Study of History*, abridged by D. C. Somervell (New York: Oxford University Press, 1946), 1:20. (Hereafter referred to as *A Study*.)

34. Toynbee, *Study*, 1:129. Toynbee later extended and revised his list up to twenty-six and then thirty civilizations.

35. Toynbee was familiar with and wrote in answer to the presentation of racial dogmas as world historical systems. He rejected the works of Gobineau, Chamberlain, Rosenberg, and Hitler, which posited the stimulus of "blood" in the origin of civilization. On the environmentalist side, Toynbee was both informed by and attempted to refute Ellsworth Huntington, whose *World Power and Evolution* (New Haven: Yale University Press, 1919), and *Civilization and Climate*, 2d ed. (New Haven: Yale University Press, 1922), took environmental arguments to an extremely determinative form. Toynbee included a note of criticism from Huntington as an appendix to vol. 1 (477–84).

36. Toynbee, *Study*, 1:253, 269.

37. Arnold J. Toynbee, "Can We Know the Pattern of the Past?" in Pieter Geyl, Arnold J. Toynbee, and Pitirim A. Sorokin, *The Pattern of the Past* (New York: Oxford University Press, 1948), 73–94.

38. Toynbee, *Study*, 1:301.

39. Toynbee constantly contradicted himself by positing universal patterns or laws of history but then denying the predictability of history. See Arnold J. Toynbee, *Change and Habit: The Challenge of Our Times* (New York: Oxford University Press, 1966), 7–9. Arnold J. Toynbee, *Civilization on Trial* (New York: Oxford University Press, 1948), 30.

40. Toynbee, *Study*, 12:255. Toynbee *does* owe a debt to Darwin through the influence of Winwood Reade's *The Martyrdom of Man* (New York: Butts, 1874), whose Darwinist challenge and response pattern of world history anticipated Toynbee's. See his perspectives on internal causation (6) and the challenge of the survival of the fittest (69).

41. Walter Kaufmann, trans. and ed., *Goethe's Faust* (New York: Anchor, 1961), lines 1336–37, 159.

42. Toynbee, *Study*, 1:303–6. Critics later changed Toynbee's mind about this process, which had actually begun in the desert oases: *Study*, 12:330. Toynbee relies here and in the Sumeric and Sinic cases on Wittfogel's famous hydraulic hypothesis.

43. Toynbee, *Study*, 1:229–30.

44. Ibid., 1:321.

45. Ibid., see 2:15, 65–73, on New England; 2:17, on Rome; 2:219–20 and 5:194, on black slavery, the Puritans, and Mormons; and 2:203, on Islam.

46. Ibid., 2:133, 1:31, 73, 112.

47. Ibid., 2:385–93.

48. Toynbee equivocated on the positive nature of civilization in an appendix to vol. 3, where he asked but did not answer the question: "Which are the true catastrophes: the Breakdowns of Civilizations or their Births?" (Toynbee, *Study*, 3:585).

49. Ibid., 6:275.

50. Ibid., 3:119.

51. Ibid., 3:88.

52. Ibid., 3:217.

53. Ibid., 3:232.

54. Ibid., 3:255. For a perspective on mass mimesis in progressive religious movement see 373.

55. Ibid., 3:383, 390.

56. Ibid., 3:235–37. The recreation of views of self in history that Toynbee postulates is similar to Erik Erikson's psychohistorical view of the role of the identity struggles of "great men" in history.

57. Ibid., 3:232.

58. Henri Bergson, *The Two Sources of Morality and Religion* (New York: Holt, 1935), 75.

59. Toynbee, *Study*, 3:234–37.

60. Bergson, 223. Toynbee, *Study*, 3:248. Toynbee here describes withdrawal and return as "the mystic's soul passing first out of action into ecstacy and then out of ecstacy into action again."

61. Toynbee, *Study*, 3:232–35.

62. Percival William Martin, *Experiment in Depth: A Study of the Work of Jung, Eliot and Toynbee* (London: Routledge and Paul, 1955), 14, 248, 254.

63. Toynbee, *Study*, 4:5, 6. Toynbee's long argument with Gibbon over the role of religion in the fall of civilizations is concluded in 10:105–7, where he asserts that Gibbon missed the boat by setting his field of study too small—the earth—"automatically ruling the supra-mundane dimension out of his reckoning."

64. Toynbee, *Study* 4:58, 78, 114. Toynbee claimed that civilizations do not fall from external violence. Other civilizations may provide a *coup de grace* and "devour his carcass after it has already become carrion," but death comes from within. He echoes Winwood Reade in this. (See n. 40 to this chapter).

65. Ibid., 5:63. "Proletarianization is a state of feeling rather than a matter of external circumstance."

66. Ibid., 5:31.

67. Ibid., 4:122–27.

68. Ibid., 4:260–61. This is the error of the Athenians in their anachronistic worship of the myth of the Periclean Age; Toynbee claims that their self-worship spelled Athens's failure to look beyond immediate interests toward a larger Hellenic unity and hence their loss of a larger hegemonic power. *Study*, 4:277. The Jews also failed to go beyond the worship of their "half truth" of monotheism, to embrace its logical culmination in Christ. In retaining the parochial worship of themselves as "God's Chosen People" they failed to open Judaism to Hellenism and were superseded by their internal proletariat (the Christians) and were left as a fossil of a dead and replaced civilization. *Study*, 4:262.

69. Ibid., 4:303–9. The present situation in the modern West is "philosophically contemporary." Western leadership is dominated by the "petrified devotees of the ideal of National Sovereignty" (4:320).

70. Ibid., 4:423.

71. Ibid., 4:505.

72. Ibid., 4:261.

73. Ibid., 6:284. See on Sinic society, 291; on Russia, 309; on the modern West, 314.

74. Ibid., 7:381. See also 7:56–239, on the ways in which civilizations act as conductors.

75. Ibid., 5:399, 384–85.

76. Ibid., 5:385.

77. Ibid., 5:527, 536, 540 (on Christianity and Mithraism).

78. Ibid., 5:359.

79. Ibid., 5:339–59.

80. Ibid., 5:374–75. Many critics have argued that the shift from civilization as the "intelligible field of study" to humanity as a whole and the higher religions wreaks havoc on the foundations of the whole work. See for example Raymond Aron, ed., *L'Histoire et ses interpretations: Entretiens autour de Arnold Toynbee* (Paris: Mouton, 1961), 43.

81. See Bergson, passim, and Toynbee, *Study*, 7:510.

82. Toynbee, *Study*, 7:425–26.

83. Ibid., 7:422.

84. Ibid., 7:443–44.

85. Ibid., 6:172–77. To Toynbee as to Bergson, the "higher" morality and religion come first to a set of saints who provide a model for the mimesis of the larger group. Bergson, 26.

86. Toynbee, *Study*, 7:423–25.

87. Ibid., 10:106.

88. Arnold J. Toynbee, *An Historian's Approach to Religion* (London: Oxford University Press, 1956), 128.

89. Toynbee, *Study*, 6:167.

90. Ibid., 6:278–79.

91. Ibid., 7:449, 470, 478. Later, on 701, he asserted that Christianity is the "highest" religion, that is, the most "open" and oriented to an external God, of any religion yet formed.

92. Ibid., 7:557–63.

93. Ibid., 7:558–66.

94. Bergson, 204. Toynbee, *Study*, 9:639; 10:39. "It is Man's task to execute, within the time that God allots him on Earth, a human mission to do God's will by working for the coming of God's Kingdom on Earth as it is in heaven." 10:26, Toynbee acknowledged his debt to Bergson for his teaching that the brotherhood of man requires the fatherhood of God.

95. Toynbee, *Study*, 10:3.

96. Ibid., 9:202–16.

97. Ibid., 10:36.

98. Ibid., 9:618–33.

99. Ibid., 9:634–35.

100. Toynbee, *An Historian's Conscience* (Letter of Aug. 5, 1938), 21.

101. Arnold J. Toynbee, "A Study of History: What I Am Trying to Do," *International Affairs* 31, no. 1–2 (Jan. 1955): 4. Toynbee, *Study*, 9:644, on Toynbee's quest to steer away from orthodox solutions and toward religious synthesis.

102. Toynbee, *Change and Habit*, 74, 189.

103. Toynbee, *Study*, 9:637.

104. Ibid., 10:139. McNeill, *Arnold Toynbee*, 90.

105. Toynbee, *Study*, 10:143.

106. Toynbee, *An Historian's Approach to Religion*, 212–16.

107. Toynbee, *An Historian's Conscience* (Letter of June 23, 1940), 67. Toynbee, *An Historian's Approach to Religion*, 274, 285.

108. Toynbee, *Study*, 10:93–95.
109. Toynbee, *Change and Habit*, 27–30.
110. Ibid., 176–79. Toynbee, *Civilization on Trial*, 39.
111. Toynbee, *An Historian's Approach to Religion*, 219.
112. Arnold J. Toynbee, *Surviving the Future* (London: Oxford University Press, 1971), 112, 118, 154. Arnold J. Toynbee, *The Present Day Experiment in Western Civilization* (London: Oxford University Press, 1962), 67.
113. Toynbee, *Change and Habit*, 112–42, 212, 224. Toynbee, *The Present Day Experiment*, 47. Toynbee, *An Historian's Approach to Religion*, 246.
114. Toynbee, *Change and Habit*, 226. Arnold J. Toynbee, *The World and the West* (New York: Oxford University Press, 1953), 98: on the "spiritual vacuum" and the nature of man that demands some belief fill it.
115. Toynbee, *Change and Habit*, 27–30.
116. Toynbee, *Surviving the Future*, 32–33.
117. *Toynbee on Toynbee*, 60. Arnold J. Toynbee, *Mankind and Mother Earth* (New York: Oxford University Press, 1976), 9, 17, 20, 596.
118. Toynbee, *An Historian's Approach to Religion*, 22. Toynbee, *An Historian's Conscience* (Letter of Jan. 20, 1974), 520.
119. *Toynbee on Toynbee*, 68.
120. McNeill, *Arnold Toynbee*, 252. Toynbee, *Experiences*, 379.
121. W. H. Walsh, "Toynbee Reconsidered," *Philosophy* 38 (1963): 74.
122. Pieter Geyl, *Debates with Historians* (New York: Meridian, 1958), 113. Crane Brinton, "Toynbee's City of God," *Virginia Quarterly Review* 32 (1956): 361. Rudolf Bultmann, *History and Eschatology* (Edinburgh: Edinburgh University Press, 1957), 120–21.
123. Geyl, *Debates*, 97, 148. See also, for example, Walter Kaufmann, "Toynbee: The Historian as False Prophet," *Commentary* 23: 344. Elie Kedourie, "Arnold Toynbee: History as Paradox," *Encounter* 42, 5 (1974): 59. G. J. Renier, "Toynbee's A Study of History," in Montague, 7. John Barker, *The Superhistorians: Makers of Our Past* (New York: Scribners, 1982), 298. William Dray, "Toynbee's Search for Historical Laws," *History and Theory* 1 (1960): 32–55, passim. McNeill, William H., "Some Basic Assumptions of Toynbee's *A Study of History*," in *The Intent of Toynbee's History*, ed. Edward T. Gargan (Chicago: Loyola University Press, 1961), 34.
124. Geyl, *Debates*, 131. Pitirim A. Sorokin, "Arnold J. Toynbee's Philosophy of History," *Journal of Modern History* 12 (1940): 381, 383. H. Mitchell, "Herr Spengler and Mr. Toynbee," in Montague, passim.
125. Geyl, *The Pattern*, 65, argues that Toynbee concludes from his analogies. Dray, 48, claims that the golden mean is tautological. Mitchell, passim, agrees. See also Franz Borkenau, "Toynbee and the Culture Cycle," *Commentary* 21, no. 3 (1956): 249. Sir Ernest Barker, "Dr. Toynbee's Study of History," in Montague, 96. On reification see Geyl, *Debates*, 133.
126. Kedourie, 59. Reinhold Niebuhr, *Faith and History* (New York: Scribners, 1949), 110. McNeill argues along a similar line in *Arnold Toynbee*, 102. Geyl, *Patterns*, 70. Christopher Dawson, "Toynbee's Study of History; The Place of Civilizations in History," in Montague, 131. José Ortega y

Gasset, *An Interpretation of Universal History* (New York: Norton, 1973), 220–21.

127. Geyl, *Debates*, 101, 111. Borkenau, 240. Niebuhr, 111.

128. Henry Lloyd Mason, *Toynbee's Approach to World Politics* (New Orleans: Tulane University Press, 1958), 9. Sorokin, 384. Mitchell, 83.

129. Bruce Mazlish, *The Riddle of History* (New York: Harper and Row, 1966), 354.

130. Kedourie, 61. Walter Kaufmann, "Toynbee and Superhistory," in Montague, 308–9. Frederick E. Robin, "The Professor and the Fossil," in Montague, passim. Abba Eban, "The Toynbee Heresy," in Montague, passim. Maurice Samuel, *The Professor and the Fossil* (New York: Knopf, 1956), passim. Borkenau, 242.

131. Trevor-Roper in Montague, 122. This is echoed by Kaufmann, "Toynbee: The Historian as False Prophet," who finds Toynbee "utterly unreliable" and lacking in "scholarly conscience" because he puts his own personality before history; 345. See also Barker in Montague, 110.

132. Lewis Mumford, "The Napoleon of Notting Hill," in Montague, 141. Mumford chastised Toynbee for his medieval withdrawal from and Manichaean rejection of this world. See also Hans Kohn, "Faith and Vision of a Universal World," in Montague, 357. Barker, *The Superhistorians*, 268. Hugh Trevor-Roper, "Arnold Toynbee's Millennium," in *Encounters*, ed. Stephen Spender et al. (New York: Basic Books, 1963), 132, on Toynbee's medieval aspirations; Trevor-Roper in Montague, 122, on regressive antimodernism.

133. Niebuhr, 110. Mazlish, 377. Geyl, *Debates*, 125, and then on 163: "Western Civilization . . . means nothing to Toynbee." Geyl, *The Pattern*, 58, rejects Toynbee's assertion that "all history is but a denouement to sixteenth century religious wars." George G. Iggers, "The Idea of Progress in Recent Philosophies of History," *Journal of Modern History* 30, no. 3 (1958): 222, explores the antidemocratic element in Toynbee. Geoffrey Barraclough, *An Introduction to Contemporary History* (New York: Penguin, 1967), 251, sees Toynbee as a last powerful exponent of "cultural pessimism." See also Kohn in Montague, 357.

134. Trevor-Roper, "Arnold Toynbee's Millennium," 141. Trevor-Roper beat a dead horse in 1989 by repeating his condemnations of Toynbee instead of reviewing McNeill's biography: Hugh Trevor-Roper, "The Prophet," *New York Times Review of Books*, Oct. 12, 1989, 28. Kedourie, 63–64. Brinton, 261. Brinton also describes Toynbee's paradigm as one of transcending history rather than describing it. Karl Popper, *The Open Society and Its Enemies* (Princeton: Princeton University Press, 1950), 436. Dray, 50, shows how in Toynbee's paradigm freedom can only occur in the transcendence of natural cycles. Walter A. McDougall, " 'Mais ce n'est pas l'histoire!' Some Thoughts on Toynbee, McNeill, and the Rest of Us," *Journal of Modern History* 58, no. 1 (1986): 24.

135. Popper, 436–39. Renier in Montague, 75.

136. On colossalism, see Kaufmann, "Toynbee: the Historian as False Prophet," 246. Mazlish, 353. On irresponsibility, see Isaiah Berlin, *Historical*

Inevitability (London: Oxford University Press, 1954), 77, 15–16. Trevor-Roper, "Arnold Toynbee's Millennium," 134, condemns Toynbee as the "intellectual ally of Hitler," who "spiritually hungers" for the downfall of the West.

137. Niebuhr, 242. Christopher Dawson, *The Dynamics of World History*, ed. John J. Mulloy (New York: Sheed and Ward, 1957), 386. Dawson, in Montague, 134. Kaufmann, "Toynbee: The Historian as False Prophet," 354. Edward Rochie Hardy, "The Validity of Toynbee's Universal Churches," in Gargan, 161–62.

138. Hardy in Montague, 154. Brinton, 261. McDougall, 24. Trevor-Roper, "Arnold Toynbee's Millennium," passim.

139. Toynbee, *Study*, 12:42, 52–54. On models as heuristic devices, 160. *Study*, 12:244: "When Trevor-Roper says that, in my work, 'the theories are not deduced from the facts,' the answer is that neither my theories nor anyone else's are or ever will be generated in that way." See also Toynbee, *Experiences*, 81.

140. Toynbee, *Experiences*, 90. Toynbee, "Can We Know the Pattern of the Past?" 91.

141. *Toynbee on Toynbee*, 110–12. On his fear of death as an impetus, see p. 54.

CHAPTER 5: THE IMPERATIVES OF SUPERSYSTEM TRANSITIONS

1. Pitirim A. Sorokin, *Social and Cultural Dynamics* (1937–41; reprint, New York: Bedminster, 1962), 4:778. (Hereafter, *S. and C. D.*).

2. Don Martindale, "Pitirim Sorokin: Soldier of Fortune," in *Sorokin and Sociology*, ed. G. C. Hallen (Motikatra: Satish Books, 1972), 16–19.

3. Pitirim A. Sorokin, *A Long Journey* (New Haven: College and University Press, 1963), 47.

4. Ibid., 12.

5. Pitirim A. Sorokin, *Hunger as a Factor in Human Affairs* (Gainesville: University Press of Florida, 1975), xiii.

6. Sorokin, *A Long Journey*, 14.

7. Pitirim A. Sorokin, "Sociology of My Mental Life," in *Pitirim Sorokin in Review*, ed. Philip J. Allen (Durham: Duke University Press, 1963), 15–19.

8. Sorokin, *A Long Journey*, 9. See also Carle C. Zimmerman, *Sociological Theories of Pitirim A. Sorokin* (Bombay: Thacker, 1973), 29.

9. Sorokin, *A Long Journey*, 29.

10. Ibid., 19.

11. Sorokin, "Sociology of My Mental Life," in Allen, 12.

12. Sorokin, *A Long Journey*, 40–41.

13. Sorokin, "Sociology of My Mental Life," in Allen, 14.

14. Sorokin, *A Long Journey*, 41.

15. Sorokin, "Sociology of My Mental Life," in Allen, 20.

16. Jacques Maquet, *The Sociology of Knowledge* (1951; reprint, Westport: Greenwood, 1973), 108–14, 205. Sorokin does sometimes assert claims

to the "cognitive value" or the "heuristic value" of his theory; but in this he is adopting, temporarily, the pragmatic style of Sensate social science. The vehemence of his defense of his statistical method (throughout and in response to his critics) and of the superiority of his theory to others gives support to Maquet's opinion. Sorokin, *S. and C. D.*, 2:423, 1:157.

17. Sorokin, *A Long Journey*, 160–69.
18. Ibid., 163.
19. Ibid., 160, 171, 173.
20. Ibid., 176.
21. Sorokin, *Hunger as a Factor in Human Affairs*, passim.
22. Sorokin, *A Long Journey*, 204–5.
23. Pitirim A. Sorokin, *Russia and the United States* (London: Stevers, 1950), 173.
24. Sorokin, *S. and C. D.*, 4:ix.
25. Sorokin, *A Long Journey*, 325.
26. Sigmund Freud, *Civilization and Its Discontents* (New York: Norton, 1961), 15.
27. Sorokin, *A Long Journey*, 268.
28. Sorokin, *S. and C. D.*, 1:ix-xi.
29. Ibid., 4:424.
30. Ibid., 1:xi.
31. Ibid., 1:19–35.
32. Pitirim A. Sorokin, "Reply to My Critics," in Allen, 483–85.
33. Sorokin, *S. and C. D.*, 1:45.
34. Ibid., 4:751–62.
35. Ibid., 1:55.
36. Ibid., 1:10.
37. Ibid., 1:67.
38. Ibid., 4:53.
39. Ibid., 4:95.
40. See Maquet, *The Sociology of Knowledge*, 116.
41. Sorokin, *S. and C. D.*, 4:763.
42. Ibid., 2:122.
43. Ibid., 2:475.
44. Sorokin, "Reply to My Critics," in Allen, 413.
45. Pitirim A. Sorokin, *Social Philosophies of an Age of Crisis* (Boston: Beacon, 1950), 216, 228.
46. Pitirim A. Sorokin, *The Crisis of Our Age* (New York: Dutton, 1941), 81.
47. Sorokin, *S. and C. D.*, 1:72–73.
48. Ibid., 1:91–95.
49. Ibid., 1:91–95.
50. Ibid., 1:75, 143.
51. Ibid., 1:285.
52. Ibid., 1:671.
53. Ibid., 1:270.

54. Ibid., 1:256–58.
55. Ibid., 1:256–58.
56. Sorokin, "Reply to My Critics," in Allen, 454.
57. Sorokin, *S. and C. D.*, 1:286–306.
58. Ibid., 1:310.
59. Ibid., 1:320–26.
60. Ibid., 1:327–52.
61. Sorokin, *The Crisis*, 52–68.
62. Sorokin, *S. and C. D.*, 1:402.
63. Ibid., 1:402.
64. Ibid., 1:382–502.
65. Sorokin concentrated his argument here against the system of W. M. Flinders Petrie, whose theory of cultural cycles asserted that the rise and "turning points" leading to the decline of particular arts were subject to extended chronological lags. For example, in our current civilizational cycle, the eighth to date, sculpture peaked in A.D. 1240, painting in 1400, mechanics in 1890, and wealth acquisition in 1910: this progression compares with that of the last cycle very closely. See W. M. Flinders Petrie, *The Revolutions of Civilization* (London: Harper and Brothers, 1911), 95. See also Sorokin, *S. and C. D.*, 1:200–210, and Sorokin, *Social Philosophies*, 12–33.
66. On architecture, see Sorokin, *S. and C. D.*, 1:517–68; on music, 1:593; on literature, 1:600–652.
67. Ibid., 2:46–50.
68. Ibid., 2:46–50.
69. 1 Cor. 111:18–19. Sorokin, *S. and C. D.*, 2:93.
70. Sorokin, *S. and C. D.*, 2:119.
71. Ibid., 2:51.
72. Ibid., 2:29–33.
73. Ibid., 2:160, 147, 149.
74. Ibid., 2:198.
75. Ibid., 2:229, 232.
76. Ibid., 2:511.
77. Ibid., 2:239.
78. Ibid., 2:254.
79. Ibid., 2:292–98. Cf. also Christopher Lasch's view of narcissistic culture, which contains broad parallels with Sorokin's view of the Sensate decadence of the modern West. Christopher Lasch, *The Culture of Narcissism* (New York: Norton, 1979).
80. Sorokin, *Social Philosophies*, 7, 280. Sorokin documents how, with the current breakdown of Sensate culture, there is a shift to cyclical perspective by major philosophers of history—himself included.
81. Sorokin, *S. and C. D.*, 2:446–48.
82. Ibid., 2:432.
83. Ibid., 3:60, 27–160.
84. Ibid., 3:162–208.

85. Ibid., 3:487, 492–96. These findings are sharply criticized by a friendly reviewer in Zimmerman, *Sociological Theories of Pitirim A. Sorokin*, 42–43.

86. Sorokin, *S. and C. D.*, 3:487.

87. Sorokin held that Hegel overgeneralized in his three-beat dialectic, as materialism and idealism always exist contemporaneously on a continuum. One form dominates at any particular stage in integration but there is no "monotonous uniformity" or exclusivity in their pattern. Sorokin, ibid., 2:203.

88. Ibid., 4:73. See also 4:481 on the principle of limits and disturbances.

89. Ibid., 2:52–53.

90. Ibid., 4:v.

91. Ibid., 4:775.

92. Ibid., 4:778.

93. Sorokin, *The Crisis*, 302.

94. Pitirim A. Sorokin, *The Reconstruction of Humanity* (Boston: Beacon, 1948), 142–45. Sorokin, *The Crisis*, 320. See also Pitirim A. Sorokin, *The American Sex Revolution, 1889–1968* (Boston: Sargent, 1956), and David R. Mace, "Sorokin's Theories on Sex and Society," in Allen, 140–59.

95. Sorokin, *The Crisis*, 302.

96. Sorokin, *S. and C. D.*, 4:778.

97. Pitirim A. Sorokin, *Man and Society in Calamity* (New York: Dutton, 1942), 178. Pitirim A. Sorokin and Walter A. Lunden, *Power and Morality* (Boston: Sargent, 1959), 174–82. Pitirim A. Sorokin, *Altruistic Love: A Study of American 'Good Neighbors' and Christian Saints* (1950; reprint, Boston: Beacon, 1969), 62.

98. Sorokin, *Man and Society*, 183.

99. Ibid., 180, 308, 309–16.

100. Ibid., 317.

101. Sorokin, *The Reconstruction*, 231.

102. Ibid., 231.

103. Sorokin, *S. and C. D.*, 4:778.

104. Sorokin, *A Long Journey*, 268. Sorokin, *The Reconstruction*, passim.

105. Sorokin, *The Crisis*, 315–18.

106. Sorokin, *The Reconstruction*, 190. "Freudianism . . . is one of the most insidious products of our decadent Sensate culture." *The Reconstruction*, 203. This idea of the divine in man as the source of creativity and morality is one that Sorokin shared with Berdyaev, whose ideas of "God-Manhood," "God-in-manity," and the "New Middle Ages" are strikingly close to Sorokin's perspective. Nikolai Berdyaev, *Christianity and Class War* (New York: Sheed and Ward, 1935), 91. Nikolai Berdyaev, *The Fate of Man in the Modern World* (Ann Arbor: Univ. of Michigan, 1961), 77, 114–15, 1.

107. Martindale in Allen, 15. Sorokin, *A Long Journey*, 273.

108. Bruce Mazlish, *The Meaning of Karl Marx* (New York: Oxford University Press, 1984).

109. Sorokin, *Russia and the United States*, 203.
110. Sorokin, *Altruistic Love*, 213. Sorokin, *A Long Journey*, 273.
111. Sorokin and Lunden, *Power*, 169. For Comte's view of the "reconstruction of spiritual power" see Gertrude Lenzer, ed., *Auguste Comte and Positivism: The Essential Writings* (Chicago: Univ. of Chicago, 1975), 310.
112. Pitirim A. Sorokin, ed., *Forms and Techniques of Altruistic and Spiritual Growth* (Boston: Beacon, 1954), vii.
113. Ibid., passim.
114. Sorokin, *The Reconstruction*, 215–20.
115. According to Mumford, in Sorokin's system "one cannot say . . . that a belief in demons is a sign of ignorance since, in terms of an ideational culture, it may represent the sum of wisdom." Lewis Mumford, "Insensate Ideologue," *New Republic*, July 14, 1937, 283–84. Alex Simirenko, "Social Origin, Revolution and Sociology: The Works of Timasheff, Sorokin and Gurvitch," *British Journal of Sociology* 24, no. 1 (1973): 88. Elton P. Guthrie, "Sorokin: Counselor to Reaction," *Science and Society* 3 (1939): 237. Crane Brinton, "Socio-Astrology," *Southern Review* 3 (1937): 243–66.
116. Sorokin, "Reply to My Critics," in Allen, 269–495. Pitirim A. Sorokin, "Is Accurate Social Planning Possible?" *American Sociological Review* 1 (Feb. 1936): 12–25. Pitirim A. Sorokin, "Comments on Schneider's Observations and Criticisms," in *Explorations in Social Change*, ed. George K. Zollschan and Walter Hirsch (New York: Houghton-Mifflin, 1964), 401–31. Pitirim A. Sorokin, "Histrionics," *Southern Review* 3 (Winter 1938): 554–64.
117. Though Sorokin notes, as in passing, that there is some accumulation in history, it is nowhere central to his system of *Dynamics*. Sorokin, *S. and C. D.*, 2:180.
118. Dean Keith Simonton, "Does Sorokin's Data Support His Theory? A Study of Generational Fluctuations in Philosophical Beliefs," *Journal for the Scientific Study of Religion* 15, no. 2 (1976): 197.
119. Arnold J. Toynbee, "Sorokin's Philosophy of History," in Allen, 91.
120. Sorokin, *The Reconstruction*, 47.
121. Martindale in Allen, 25.
122. Zimmerman, *Sociological Theories*, 34. Sorokin used the same description of himself in his autobiography. Sorokin, *A Long Journey*, 257–58.
123. Maquet, 214.
124. For example: Robert E. Park, "Review of *Social and Cultural Dynamics*, Vols. 1–3," *American Journal of Sociology* 43 (1938): 827. Simirenko, "Social Origin," 88.
125. Simirenko, "Social Origin," 84.

CHAPTER 6: CHRISTOPHER DAWSON

1. John Henry Newman, *The Idea of a University* (London: Longmans Green, 1902), 123.

2. Christopher Dawson, *The Judgement of the Nations* (New York: Sheed and Ward, 1942), 150.

3. Christopher Dawson, "The Life of Civilizations," *Sociological Review* 14 (1922): 53.

4. M. D. Knowles, "Christopher Dawson (1889–1970)," *Proceedings of the British Academy* 17 (1971): 442. Christina Scott, *A Historian and His World* (London: Sheed and Ward, 1984), 19. Scott is Dawson's daughter. "Dawson, Christopher Henry," in *Twentieth Century Authors*, ed. S. J. Kunitz (New York: H. W. Wilson, 1955), 266.

5. Daniel Callahan et al., "Christopher Dawson," *Harvard Theological Review* 66 (1973): 167.

6. Edward I. Watkins, "Christopher Dawson," *Commonweal* 18 (1933): 607. Scott, 28. Christopher Dawson, "Tradition and Inheritance," *The Wind and the Rain* (1949): 14.

7. Maisie Ward, "The Case of Christopher Dawson," *Catholic World* 169 (1949): 150. Dawson, "Tradition," 7, 16.

8. Scott, 28–30. Dawson, "Tradition," 8, 14, 17.

9. Dawson, "Tradition," 13, 15.

10. Ward, 150. Scott, 31–36.

11. Watkins, 608. Scott, 36–39. Knowles, 44.

12. Quoted by Scott, 49.

13. Christopher Dawson, *The Spirit of the Oxford Movement* (New York: Sheed and Ward, 1933), passim. Scott, 62–65.

14. Knowles, 444–45. Scott, 50–69.

15. Scott, 70–73. Ward, 151. "Christopher Henry Dawson," in *Catholic Authors*, ed. Matthew Hoehn (Detroit: Gale Research, 1981), 185.

16. Christopher Dawson, *Religion and the Modern State* (London: Sheed and Ward, 1936), 41–51. At one point Dawson noted that fascism, as an economic philosophy, "is not entirely groundless," that it "represents a genuine third alternative as against individualistic capitalism and communist socialism." Fascism as a faith system could satisfy its adherents in a way that the liberalism of the West does not. He claimed that there was no fundamental reason the passing of parliamentary democracy must be opposed on Christian principles, and that a loss of economic and political freedom might accord with an increase in spiritual freedom. See Scott, 126, on its reception.

17. Christopher Dawson, *Beyond Politics* (London: Sheed and Ward, 1939), 83.

18. Dawson, *Religion and the Modern State*, 135, 51. His most serious criticism of fascism was that it had no spiritual element; it substituted religious emotion for spirituality and it embraced a national rather than a universal orientation. But, in itself, "Catholicism is by no means hostile to the authoritarian ideal of the state." In 1944 he echoed this authoritarianism in Christopher Dawson, "Peace Aims and Power Politics," *Dublin Review* 213 (1944): 99.

19. Scott, 104. Callahan, 168.

20. Knowles, 445–47. Scott, on his view of fascism, 126.

21. Hilaire Belloc, *Europe and the Faith* (New York: Paulist Press, 1920), ix, passim. Alexander Calvert, S.J., *The Catholic Literary Revival* (1935; reprint, Port Washington: Kennikat Press, 1968), 301–16.

22. Christopher Dawson, "T. S. Eliot on the Meaning of Culture," in *The Dynamics of World History*, ed. John J. Mulloy (New York: Sheed and Ward, 1957), 108–14.

23. Scott, 178–88. Callahan, 167.

24. Callahan, 173.

25. Scott, 205.

26. Christopher Dawson, *Religion and Culture* (New York: Sheed and Ward, 1948), 47, 48. In 1949 he described all great cultures as "theogamies" where the human and divine came together in a sacred tradition. See Christopher Dawson, "The Relationship between Religion and Culture," *Commonweal* 49 (1949): 490.

27. Christopher Dawson, *The Age of the Gods* (Boston: Houghton Mifflin, 1928), xix.

28. John J. Mulloy, "Continuity and Development in Dawson's Thought," in Dawson, *The Dynamics of World History*, 407. Mulloy quotes a private letter from Dawson (Jan. 1, 1955).

29. Christopher Dawson, "Sociology and the Theory of Progress," in *American Conservative Thought in the Twentieth Century*, ed. William F. Buckley, Jr. (Indianapolis: Bobbs-Merrill, 1970), 434.

30. Dawson, *The Age of the Gods*, xiii-xx.

31. Dawson, *Religion and Culture*, 48.

32. Dawson, "The Life of Civilizations," 51, 54, 55. Watkins, 609. Watkins, Dawson's best friend, testifies that Dawson did not read Spengler until much later.

33. Ernst Troeltsch, *Absoluteness of Christianity and the History of Religions* (Richmond: John Knox, 1971), 53, 162. With Newman, Dawson rejected liberal invocations to a relativity based upon the spirit of the age. See Dawson, *The Spirit of the Oxford Movement*, 42.

34. Dawson, *The Age of the Gods*, 40–155. Christopher Dawson, *Religion and the Rise of Western Culture* (Garden City: Doubleday, 1958), 35, 53, 17.

35. Christopher Dawson, *Progress and Religion* (New York: Sheed and Ward, 1938), 118.

36. Dawson, *The Age of the Gods*, 382–83.

37. Dawson, "The Life of Civilizations," 58–60.

38. Christopher Dawson, "Civilization and Morals," in *Dynamics*, 60.

39. Dawson, *Progress and Religion*, 125.

40. Ibid., 155–60.

41. Dawson, *Religion and the Rise of Western Culture*, 23.

42. Dawson, "The Life of Civilizations," 62.

43. Christopher Dawson, "Civilization in Crisis," *Catholic World* 182, no. 2 (1956): 248.

44. Dawson, *Progress and Religion*, 44.

45. Dawson, "The Life of Civilizations," 62–64.

46. Christopher Dawson, *The Historic Reality of Christian Culture* (New York: Harper and Brothers, 1960), 47–67. Christopher Dawson, *Medieval Essays* (New York: Sheed and Ward, 1954), 57.

47. Dawson, *Medieval Essays*, 57.

48. Christopher Dawson, *The Dividing of Christendom* (New York: Sheed and Ward, 1965), 62–78.

49. Dawson, *Progress and Religion*, 241. Christopher Dawson, "The Historic Origins of Liberalism," *Review of Politics* 16 (1954): 271.

50. Dawson, *Religion and Culture*, 212.

51. Dawson, "The Life of Civilizations," 68.

52. Ibid., 68.

53. Dawson, "Civilization in Crisis," 251.

54. Christopher Dawson, "The Evolution of the Modern City," in *Dynamics*, 193–96. Christopher Dawson, "Catholicism and the Bourgeois Mind," in *Dynamics*, 201, 215. See also Christopher Dawson, "The Significance of Bolshevism," *American Review* 1 (1933): 44; and Christopher Dawson, "The World Crisis and the English Tradition," in *Dynamics*, 217.

55. Dawson, "Sociology and the Theory of Progress," 437. See also Christopher Dawson, "The Recovery of Spiritual Unity," *Catholic World* 143 (1936): 350.

56. Charles A. Ellwood, *The Reconstruction of Religion* (New York: Macmillan, 1922), 285.

57. Christopher Dawson, "Sociology as a Science," in *Dynamics*, 38, 39.

58. Christopher Dawson, "The Christian View of History," in *Dynamics*, 232–55. "There is no law of history by which we can predict the future." Christopher Dawson, "Christianity and Contradiction in History," in *Dynamics*, 280.

59. Dawson, *Religion and Culture*, 62–87, 153. Dawson's view is close to Troeltsch's on "personalism" as the history-transforming element of Christianity. See Troeltsch, *The Absoluteness*, passim.

60. Dawson, *Religion and Culture*, 191–207.

61. Christopher Dawson, "Vitalization or Standardization in Culture," in *Dynamics*, 95.

62. Christopher Dawson, "Stages in Man's Religious Experience," in *Dynamics*, 187.

63. To Dawson, world history as a field was itself only a broad application of the Christian world view, whatever its guise, be it Marxian or Comtean progress or a cyclical pattern; it can only be approached through the Western tradition. Christopher Dawson, "The Relevance of European History," *History Today* 6, no. 9 (1956): 607.

64. Dawson, "Vitalization or Standardization in Culture," in *Dynamics*, 95.

65. Dawson, "Catholicism and the Bourgeois Mind," in *Dynamics*, 210.

66. Dawson, *Beyond Politics*, 135.

67. Dawson, "Christianity and Contradiction in History," in *Dynamics*, 258–64. See also Christopher Dawson, "The Kingdom of God and History," in *Dynamics*, 280; and Christopher Dawson, "Saint Augustine and the City of God," in *Dynamics*, 315.

68. Christopher Dawson, *The Movement of World Revolution* (New York: Sheed and Ward, 1959), 22.

69. Dawson, *Progress and Religion*, 259. Dawson, *Religion and Culture*, 216.

70. Dawson, "Civilization in Crisis," 249. Dawson, *Religion and Culture*, 212–18.

71. Dawson, *Religion and Culture*, 212–18.

72. Dawson, "Sociology and the Theory of Progress," 434.

73. Dawson, "The Relevance of European History," 608–12.

74. Christopher Dawson, "Toynbee's Odyssey of the West," *Commonweal* 61 (1954): 62–67. Christopher Dawson, "Toynbee's Study of History: The Place of Civilizations in History," in *Toynbee and History*, ed. A. Montague (Boston: Porter Sargent, 1956), 133–35.

75. Dawson, "Stages in Man's Religious Experience," in *Dynamics*, 188. Dawson, *The Movement of World Revolutions*, 176.

76. Dawson, "Civilization in Crisis," 252.

77. Dawson, *Religion and Culture*, 106. Dawson, *The Judgement of the Nations*, 124.

78. Dawson, *Beyond Politics*, 135.

79. Dawson, *Religion and the Modern State*, 106, 113, 123.

80. Dawson, "Peace Aims and Power Politics," 102, 107.

81. Christopher Dawson, "Religion and Mass Civilization—The Problem of the Future," *Dublin Review* 214 (1944): 8. Also see Dawson, *The Historic Reality of Christian Culture*, 27.

82. Christopher Dawson, *America and the Secularization of Modern Culture* (Houston: Univ. of St. Thomas, 1960), 18–25. See also Dawson, *The Judgement of the Nations*, 154. In 1940 Dawson distinguished between the tyrannies of the past and the ultimate nature of modern totalitarianism; the new masters "are engineers of the mechanism of world power: a mechanism that is more formidable than anything the ancient world knew because it is not confined to external means like the despotisms of the past, but uses all the resources available from modern psychology to make the human soul the motor of its dynamic purpose." Christopher Dawson, "The Threat to the West," *Commonweal* 31 (1940): 317. On his agreement with Mumford on his view of the megalopolis, see C. J. McNaspy, "Chat with Christopher Dawson," *America* 106 (1961): 120.

83. Dawson, *Beyond Politics*, 78–79. He says further: "It seems that a new society was arriving which will acknowledge no hierarchy of values, no intellectual authority, and no social or religious tradition, but will live for the moment in a chaos of pure sensation." Dawson, *Progress and Religion*, 240.

84. Christopher Dawson, "The Foundations of Unity," *Dublin Review* 211 (1942): 104.

85. Dawson, *The Historic Reality of Christian Culture*, 27.

86. Dawson, *The Judgement of the Nations*, 157, 164. See also Dawson, *Religion and the Modern State*, 58, on the totalitarian machine order as the Antichrist predicted in Revelation.

87. Dawson, "The Threat to the West," 317–18.

88. Dawson, *The Historic Reality of Christian Culture*, 79, 119.

89. Christopher Dawson, "What the World Needs," *Catholic World* 137 (1933): 93.

90. Dawson, *The Historic Reality of Christian Culture*, 113. John R. E. Bliese, "Christopher Dawson: His Interpretation of History," *Modern Age* 23 (1979): 265. Bliese felt that Dawson's educational solution was "hopelessly inadequate." V. A. Demant, "The Importance of Christopher Dawson," *Nineteenth Century* 129 (1951): 75, agrees with Bliese.

91. Christopher Dawson, "The Challenge of Secularism," *Catholic World* 182 (1956): 326.

92. Dawson, *The Judgement of the Nations*, 128.

93. Ibid., 123.

94. Paul, 1 Cor. 12:7. See 1 Cor. 12:4–27. "Now you are the body of Christ and individually members of it" (12:27). Christopher Dawson, "Freedom and Vocation," *Dublin Review* 420 (1942): 6–11. And see Dawson, *Religion and the Rise of Modern Culture*, 169–72, for Dawson's view of the ideal of the Middle Ages and for his conception of a new order based upon it. "In every aspect of Medieval culture we find this conception of a hierarchy of goods and values and a corresponding hierarchy of estates and vocations which bind the whole range of human relations together in an ordered spiritual structure that reaches from earth to heaven" (177).

95. See his comments on agriculture in Dawson, "The World Crisis and the English Tradition," in *Dynamics*, 218–19; also his frequent references in his articles for the *Sociological Review* to Geddesian Neotechnic society and New Towns.

96. Dawson, *Medieval Essays*, 57.

97. Christopher Dawson, "The Institutional Forms of Christian Culture," *Religion in Life* 24 (1954–55): 379.

98. Dawson, *The Movement of World Revolutions*, 65.

99. Ibid., 102–5.

100. See letter to John J. Mulloy (Sept. 25, 1954), quoted in Scott, 163. See also Dawson in Montague, 131–32.

CHAPTER 7: LEWIS MUMFORD

1. George Perkins Marsh, *Man and Nature, or, Physical Geography as Modified by Human Action* (1864; reprint, New York: Scribner, 1874), 42–43.

2. Nikolai Berdyaev, *The Fate of Man in the Modern World* (Ann Arbor: Univ. of Michigan, 1961), 71.

3. Lewis Mumford, *Sketches from Life* (New York: Dial Press, 1982), 448–49. See also Lewis Mumford, *My Work and Days: A Personal Chronicle* (New York: Harcourt Brace Jovanovich, 1979), 97.

4. Lewis Mumford, *The Conduct of Life* (1951; reprint, New York: Harcourt Brace Jovanovich, 1970), 39. Mumford believed that his view of human nature was, in a sense, a natural extension of Bergson's philosophy: "My own philosophy could be treated as a modification of his, for whereas he draws a distinction between intuition, which is vital, and reason, which is mechanized . . . I go on to point out that the mechanical itself is a creation of life," one that only becomes antivital when divorced from life. Letter to Van Wyck Brooks, Aug. 17, 1935, in Robert E. Spiller, ed., *The Van Wyck Brooks Lewis Mumford Letters* (New York: Dutton, 1970), 117.

5. Lewis Mumford, *In the Name of Sanity* (New York: Harcourt Brace, 1954), 197.

6. Emerson, quoted in Roderick Nash, *Wilderness and the American Mind* (New Haven: Yale University Press, 1973), 85.

7. Lewis Mumford, *The Urban Prospect* (New York: Harcourt Brace and World, 1968), 209.

8. Lewis Mumford, "The Automation of Knowledge," *Vital Speeches* 30 (May 1, 1964): 442.

9. Lewis Mumford, *Faith for Living* (New York: Harcourt Brace, 1940), 296.

10. Mumford, *My Work and Days*, 26. Lewis Mumford, *Findings and Keepings: Analects for an Autobiography* (New York: Harcourt Brace Jovanovich, 1975), 7.

11. Mumford, *Sketches*, 25–32. Martin Filler, "Lewis Mumford: The Making of an Architectural Critic," *Architectural Record* 170 (Apr. 1982): 116.

12. Mumford, *Sketches*, 12, 42, 56, 73. Wilfred M. McClay, "Lewis Mumford," *American Scholar* 57 (Winter 1988): 112.

13. Mumford, *Sketches*, 3, 4, 13, 86. Mumford, *Findings*, 156.

14. Mumford, *Findings*, 155.

15. Mumford, *Sketches*, 65, 94, 98.

16. Ibid., 177.

17. Lewis Mumford, "What I Believe," *Forum* 83 (Nov. 1930): 263.

18. Mumford, *Sketches*, 199.

19. Ibid., 129.

20. Ibid., 131.

21. Mumford, *Findings*, 9, 17. Mumford, *Sketches*, 137.

22. Filler, 118.

23. Mumford, *My Work and Days*, 374. Mumford, "What I Believe," 363.

24. Mumford, *Sketches*, 212–13.

25. Mumford, *Sketches*, 214–20.

26. Filler, 118. Mumford, *Sketches*, 234, 248, 285.

27. Mumford, *Findings*, 202–6.

28. Donald L. Miller, *Lewis Mumford; A Life* (New York: Weidenfeld and Nicholson, 1989), 296.

29. Filler, 120. See also Miller, 164.

30. Lewis Mumford, *The Story of Utopias* (1922; reprint, New York: Harcourt Brace, 1962), 2, 95–96, 268.

31. Mumford, *The Story of Utopias*, 304–5. In his later work he would repudiate this third category.

32. Ibid.

33. Lewis Mumford, *The Golden Day* (New York: Boni and Liverright, 1926), 280. As he put it later, "the very ability to dream is the first condition for the dream's realization." Mumford, *The Conduct of Life*, 120.

34. Mumford, *The Conduct of Life*, 131.

35. Mumford, *Findings*, 353.

36. Mumford, *Sketches*, 242.

37. Mumford, *Findings*, 101. See also Mumford, *The Urban Prospect*, 209.

38. Mumford, *Sketches*, 322. Abbie Ziffren, "Biography of Patrick Geddes," in *Patrick Geddes: Spokesman for Man and the Environment*, ed. Marshall Stalley (New Brunswick: Rutgers University Press, 1972), 96.

39. Mumford, *Findings*, 99–100.

40. Ibid., 100, and *Sketches*, 329–32.

41. Mumford, *My Work and Days*, 118.

42. Mumford, *The Urban Prospect*, 211–12. Mumford, *Sketches*, 232.

43. Lewis Mumford, "Cities Fit to Live In," *Nation*, May 15, 1948, 531–32.

44. Mumford, *My Work and Days*, 374–400.

45. Lewis Mumford, "The Corruption of Liberalism," *New Republic*, Apr. 29, 1940, 568–73. Mumford broke with many of his old personal friends at this time (like F. L. Wright) over irreconcilable positions on isolation. Mumford, *Sketches*, 436.

46. Mumford, *Faith*, 42–46, 81.

47. Ibid., 106, 111.

48. Lewis Mumford, *The Culture of Cities* (New York: Harcourt Brace, 1938), 11. See also Mumford, *Faith*, 122, 123; and Mumford, "What I Believe," 268.

49. Lewis Mumford, *Green Memories; The Story of Geddes Mumford* (1947; reprint, Westport: Greenwood, 1973), 256, 257, 91.

50. Peter Shaw, "Mumford in Retrospect," *Commentary* 56 (Sept. 1973): 73. For Mumford's view of the Beard affair see his letter to Van Wyck Brooks (Dec. 3, 1947) in Spiller, 323–27.

51. Mumford, *Green Memories*, passim.

52. Mumford, *Faith*, 233.

53. Ibid., 196.

54. Lewis Mumford, *The Myth of the Machine: The Pentagon of Power* (New York: Harcourt Brace Jovanovich, 1970), 248–51.

55. Mumford, *My Work and Days*, 456–60.

56. Lewis Mumford, "Morals of Extermination," *Atlantic*, Oct. 1959, 39–44.

57. Mumford, *The Urban Prospect*, 235.

58. Lewis Mumford, *The Myth of the Machine: Technics and Human Development* (New York: Harcourt Brace Jovanovich, 1967), 225. Miller, 513.

59. Mumford, *Myth: Pentagon*, 311. Lewis Mumford, "Prize or Lunacy," *Newsweek*, July 7, 1969, 61.

60. McClay, 111. R. Dahlin, "Harper and Row Signs Lewis Mumford," *Publisher's Weekly*, Oct. 22, 1979, 52. "Lewis Mumford Wins National Literature Medal," *Publisher's Weekly*, Jan. 1, 1973, 32–33.

61. Mumford, *Findings*, 98. Mumford, *The Golden Day*, 13.

62. Mumford, *The Golden Day*, 25–27.

63. Ibid., 104.

64. Emerson, quoted by Mumford, *The Golden Day*, 100. Mumford admitted in a letter to Van Wyck Brooks (Dec. 23, 1925) that he embraced an "instinctive Platonism" and transcendentalism. Spiller, 37.

65. Mumford, *The Conduct of Life*, bibliographic note on Emerson, 298.

66. Lewis Mumford, *Herman Melville* (New York: Literary Guild, 1929), passim.

67. Henry Adams, *The Education of Henry Adams* (1918; reprint, Boston: Houghton Mifflin, 1961), passim. Mumford shared Adams's view of the gilded age or, as he called these years, "the Brown Decades." He pointed out the degenerative pattern of American culture as the Paleotechnic economy transformed it in its own image. See Lewis Mumford, *The Brown Decades* (New York: Harcourt Brace, 1931), passim. Also Mumford, *The Golden Day*, 136, 166, 204.

68. Lewis Mumford, "Downfall or Renewal: Review of *The Decline of the West*," *New Republic*, May 12, 1926, 368–69.

69. Lewis Mumford, "Spengler's Des Untergang des Abendlands," in *Books That Changed Our Minds*, ed. Malcolm Cowley and Bernard Smith (New York: Doubleday, 1939), 222. See also Lewis Mumford, *The Condition of Man* (New York: Harcourt Brace, 1973), 372–76.

70. Lewis Mumford, *Technics and Civilization* (New York: Harcourt Brace, 1934), 283, 273, 353.

71. Mumford, *Technics*, 355–56.

72. Ibid., 358, 386, 382.

73. Mumford, *Faith*, 390–406.

74. Patrick Geddes, *Cities in Evolution* (1913; reprint, New York: Fertig, 1968), 63.

75. Mumford, *Technics*, 110–23.

76. Ibid., 134–35.

77. Ibid., 88–93.

78. Ibid., 41–50.

79. Lewis Mumford, *The Culture of Cities* (New York: Harcourt Brace, 1938), 94.

80. Mumford, *Technics*, 38, 52.

81. Ibid., 156–63.
82. Ibid., 176–83.
83. Mumford, *In the Name of Sanity*, 119.
84. Mumford, *Technics*, 212–63.
85. Ibid., 279. See also Herbert Marcuse, *Eros and Civilization* (Boston: Beacon, 1966), passim.
86. Mumford, *Technics*, 363–65.
87. Ibid., 426, 367. Mumford, *The Culture of Cities*, 9, 218.
88. Mumford, *The Culture of Cities*, 74. Mumford later claimed precedence over Toynbee in his theory of withdrawal and return. Mumford, *Sketches*, 449. See also Miller, 420.
89. Mumford, *In the Name of Sanity*, 163.
90. Mumford, *The Conduct of Life*, 252.
91. Mumford, *The Culture of Cities*, 55, 151.
92. Ibid., 488.
93. ibid., 3.
94. Ibid., 262.
95. Henry Adams, *The Tendency of History* (New York: Book League of America, 1929), 29, 71. Mumford, *My Work and Days*, 259. Mumford, *In the Name of Sanity*, 100–101, 61. Mumford, *The Conduct of Life*, 393.
96. Adams, 119 passim.
97. Lewis Mumford, "Anticipations and Social Adjustments in Science," *Bulletin of the Atomic Scientists* 10 (Feb./Mar. 1954): 35–36.
98. Mumford, *Sketches*, 274. See also Mumford, *The Urban Prospect*, 235, where Mumford claimed that the optimistic rhetoric of his early works was hollow: the "Second World War blasted these naive hopes," that is, of an imminent coming of a Biotechnic culture.
99. Lewis Mumford, "The Napoleon of Notting Hill," in *Toynbee and History*, ed. A. Montague (Boston: Porter Sargent, 1956), 143, 144. Mumford rejected Toynbee's dualism as naive.
100. Lewis Mumford, "Apology to Henry Adams," *Virginia Quarterly Review* 38, no. 2 (1962): 211.
101. Mumford, *Myth: Pentagon*, 59.
102. Mumford, *The Conduct of Life*, 218.
103. Lewis Mumford, *The City in History* (New York: Harcourt Brace and World, 1961), 184.
104. Mumford, *The Conduct of Life*, 67–72.
105. Ibid., 57.
106. Ibid., 211–12.
107. Ibid., 116–19.
108. Mumford, *The City in History*, 216–17. Lewis Mumford, *The Transformations of Man* (New York: Harper and Row, 1972), 28.
109. Lewis Mumford, "Utopia, the City and the Machine," *Daedalus* 94, no. 2 (Winter 1965): 272–73.
110. Mumford, *Myth: Technics*, 214.
111. Ibid., 139–50.

112. Mumford, *The Transformations*, 16.
113. Mumford, *The City in History*, 37.
114. Ibid., 113. Growth is not, as Mumford believed Toynbee posited, "a single process of de-materialization, a transposition of earthly life into a heavenly simalcrum."
115. Ibid., 35, 41.
116. Ibid., 92–109. Mumford compared this urban specialization to the "polymorphism of the insect hive." See also Mumford, *The Transformations of Man*, 47–49, where he stated that the reason for the "acceptance of this 'civilized' hierarchical order remains undiscoverable until we allow for the irrational and the supernatural."
117. Mumford, *Myth: Technics*, 190.
118. Ibid., 216.
119. Ibid., 186
120. Ibid., 191, 212.
121. Mumford, *Myth: Pentagon*, 315–16. Teilhard de Chardin is, in effect, "playing God."
122. Mumford, *Myth: Technics*, 228–36, 253.
123. Mumford, *The City in History*, 203. Mumford, *Myth: Technics*, 255.
124. Mumford, *Myth: Technics*, 281. Mumford, *Myth: Pentagon*, 24.
125. Jacques Ellul, *The Technological Society* (New York: Knopf, 1964), 430, 19, 79, 177. See also E. T. Chase, "Man, Machines and Mumford," *Commonweal* 87 (May 8, 1968): 694–95.
126. Mumford, *Myth: Pentagon*, 278. Ellul, 426, 434.
127. Mumford, *Myth: Pentagon*, 350. Christopher Lasch, *The Culture of Narcissism* (New York: Norton, 1979), passim.
128. Mumford, *Myth: Pentagon*, 408.
129. Allan Temko, "Lewis Mumford at Seventy-Two," *Harper's*, Oct. 1967, 107. Shaw, 74, rejects what he sees as Mumford's misuse of empty rhetoric.
130. William Kuhns, *Post Industrial Prophets* (New York: Weybright and Talley, 1971), 33, 63.
131. McClay, 118. Morton White and Lucia White, *The Intellectual versus the City* (New York: New American Library, 1972), 205. The Whites held that Mumford's work is the "most thorough, unrelenting contemporary expression of anti-urbanism." Geoffrey Bruun, "Metropolitan Strait Jacket," *Saturday Review of Literature*, Apr. 15, 1961, 17. Bruun rejected Mumford's "organ notes of doom."
132. David R. Conrad, *Education for Transformation: Implications in Lewis Mumford's Ecohumanism* (Palm Springs: ETC, 1976), 79. Conrad, though a supporter of Mumford, condemned his delusions of an all-inclusive transformation. A good example of Mumford's holistic approach to reform can be observed in his confrontational testimony before the Ribicoff Committee in 1967, where he rejected massive new federal funds for housing as a dead end. Instead of supporting low-income housing programs, Mumford chastised

the panel, especially Ribicoff, for their faith in American industrial civilization. "You accept, I take it, the current American faith in the necessity for an expanded, machine-centered economy, as if this were one of the great laws of nature, or if not, then America's happiest contribution to human prosperity and freedom." Urban renewal within such a "power-obsessed, machine-oriented economy" could not produce positive results. Mumford, *The Urban Prospect*, 223.

133. White, 235. Conrad, 80. J. Bronowski, "Strategy for the Next Plateau," *Nation*, June 14, 1956, 42, 43.

134. Roger Starr, "Mumford's Utopia," *Commentary* 61 (June 1976): 62.

135. White, 235. Van R. Halsey, Jr., "Lewis Mumford's Golden Day," *New Republic*, Aug. 12, 1957, 21. Heinz Eulau, "Mumford: Not Guide but Lantern," *New Republic*, Apr. 22, 1946, 583–84.

136. P. Shaw, 73.

137. See Henry Adams, "Mont St. Michel and Chartres," in *Adams*, ed. Ernest Samuels and Jayne N. Samuels (New York: Library of America, 1983), 337–714 passim.

138. Mumford, *In the Name of Sanity*, 183.

CHAPTER 8: WILLIAM H. MCNEILL'S ECOLOGICAL MYTHISTORY

1. William H. McNeill, *Mythistory and Other Essays* (Chicago: Univ. of Chicago, 1986), 16.

2. William H. McNeill, *The Human Condition: An Ecological and Historical View* (Princeton: Princeton University Press, 1980), 74.

3. William H. McNeill, "*The Rise of the West* after Twenty-Five Years," *Journal of World History* 1 (Spring 1990): 2.

4. William H. McNeill, "Review Essay: *The Nature of History* by Arthur Marwick and Comment on *Ecrit L'Histoire* by Paul Veyne," *History and Theory* 11 (1972): 106. Also William H. McNeill, *The Shape of European History* (New York: Oxford University Press, 1974), 30.

5. R. Walters, "McNeill, William H., His Own History," *New York Times Book Review*, Oct. 6, 1963, 30. Cf. John T. McNeill, *The History and Character of Calvinism* (New York: Oxford University Press, 1954), passim. See also McNeill's dedication to his father in William H. McNeill, *Venice: The Hinge of Europe, 1081–1797* (Chicago: Univ. of Chicago, 1974). McNeill, in correspondence with the author (Dec. 15, 1989) noted that "we have a very similar cast of mind, always looking for the commonality that connects human beings and groups."

6. William H. McNeill, "The View from Greece," in *Witnesses to the Origins of the Cold War*, ed. Thomas T. Hammond (Seattle: Univ. of Washington, 1982), note before pagination, 98.

7. Walters, 30. William H. McNeill, *The Greek Dilemma: War and Aftermath* (Philadelphia: Lippincott, 1947), passim.

8. McNeill, *Mythistory*, 186.

9. See McNeill's subsequent article, "The Introduction of the Potato into Ireland," *Journal of Modern History* 21 (1949): 218–22; and "McNeill, William H., 1917," in *Contemporary Authors*, ed. Ann Avory, Rev. Ed. (Detroit: Gale Research, 1981), 2:459.

10. William H. McNeill, "Carl Becker, Historian," *History Teacher* 19 (1985): 89–100. McNeill called *Modern History* his early "gospel," 97.

11. McNeill, *Mythistory*, 157.

12. See McNeill's later exposition of the problem in William H. McNeill, "The American War of Independence in World Perspective," in *Reconsiderations on the Revolutionary War; Selected Essays*, ed. Don Higginbotham (Westport: Greenwood, 1978), 3, 8. McNeill's view of the American Revolution situates it as but one of many rebellious responses, most unsuccessful, to the worldwide advance of European "centralized bureaucratic administration."

13. McNeill, *Mythistory*, 162–70. McNeill, "Carl Becker," 99.

14. McNeill, *Mythistory*, 183. Robert Redfield, *The Primitive World and Its Transformations* (Ithaca: Great Seal Books, 1953), 22.

15. McNeill correspondence with the author, Dec. 15, 1989. In his recent article, William H. McNeill, "Control and Catastrophe in Human Affairs," *Daedalus* 118, no. 1 (1989): 11, McNeill takes Redfield's view a step further with an assertion that every gain in coordination and efficiency is offset by an increased vulnerability. A good example of McNeill's view on the ambiguous path of progress is found in his study of Greek modernization: William H. McNeill, "Dilemmas of Modernization," *Massachusetts Review* 9 (1968): 141. Here growth since World War II, prosperity, and urbanization have led to a psychological break with traditional peasant culture, amoralism and a pervasive materialism have resulted, and the accumulation of goods has become the highest moral priority. See also McNeill's conclusions in William H. McNeill, "The Making of Modern Times," *Harper's*, Nov. 1984, 17.

16. McNeill, *The Shape of European History*, 40.

17. McNeill, *The Human Condition*, 28.

18. McNeill, *Mythistory*, 174–78.

19. McNeill, correspondence with the author, Dec. 15, 1989.

20. McNeill, *Mythistory*, 177, 178.

21. Ibid., 181.

22. Ibid., 186–97.

23. William H. McNeill, *America, Britain and Russia: Their Cooperation and Conflict, 1941–1946* (1953; reprint, New York: Johnson Reprint, 1970), 766–68.

24. McNeill, *America, Britain and Russia*, see 361 and 755 on the importance of leaders; 760–63 on the role of ideas; and 756 passim on the predominant power of underlying patterns.

25. McNeill, *Mythistory*, 57.

26. William H. McNeill, *Arnold Toynbee; A Life* (New York: Oxford University Press, 1989), 286.

27. McNeill, *Venice*, xv.

28. McNeill, *The Shape of European History*, 37–39.

29. William H. McNeill, *Europe's Steppe Frontier, 1500–1800* (Chicago: Univ. of Chicago Press, 1964), 32.

30. McNeill, *Mythistory*, 183.

31. Ralph Linton, *The Tree of Culture* (New York: Knopf, 1955), 662–70.

32. Alfred L. Kroeber, *Configurations of Cultural Growth* (Berkeley and L.A.: Univ. of California Press, 1944), 828.

33. Kroeber, *Configurations*, 761. On the similarity of his perspective to Sorokin's see 21, 67, 91, and also the appendix on Sorokin in Alfred L. Kroeber, *Style and Civilizations* (Ithaca: Cornell University Press, 1957).

34. Kroeber, *Configurations*, 763.

35. Kroeber, *Style and Civilizations*, 160. See also Eric R. Wolf, "Understanding Civilizations," *Comparative Studies in Society and History* 9 (1966–67): 446–65, on McNeill's debt to Kroeber and his school.

36. Carroll Quigley, *The Evolution of Civilizations* (New York: Macmillan, 1961), 68.

37. Quigley, *Evolution*, 69.

38. McNeill, *Mythistory*, 59. See also William H. McNeill, *Plagues and Peoples* (Garden City: Anchor, 1976), passim.

39. William H. McNeill, *The Rise of the West: A History of the Human Community* (Chicago: Univ. of Chicago Press, 1963), 597.

40. William H. McNeill, *Past and Future* (Chicago: Univ. of Chicago Press, 1954), 8.

41. Ibid., 14, 67.

42. Ibid., 67–68, 79, 111.

43. Ibid., 67, 91. McNeill documented this process in World War II in his work on *America, Britain and Russia*. He considered the two world wars as points of punctuation within an overall trend in this direction: "During the two world wars millions of individuals submitted their daily activities to the control of government officials—a control which, I think, it is not fantastic to compare with the control engineers are accustomed to exercise over inanimate machines." Ibid., 50.

44. Ibid., 14, 67.

45. Ibid., 179, 211.

46. See Walters, 30. Perhaps most symbolic of the positive reception that *The Rise of the West* received was Hugh Trevor-Roper's *New York Times Book Review*, "Barbarians Were Often at the Gate", Oct. 6, 1963, 1. His perspective of McNeill's work was in sharp contrast to his ridicule of Toynbee's metahistory: "This is not only the most learned and the most intelligent, it is also the most stimulating and fascinating book that has ever set out to recount and explain the whole history of mankind."

47. McNeill, *Mythistory*, 62.

48. McNeill, *The Rise*, 1, 18, 42, 81, 103. See also William H. McNeill, *A World History* (New York: Oxford University Press, 1967), 99.

49. McNeill, *The Rise*, 254, 267, 273.

50. McNeill, *A World History*, 121–24.
51. McNeill, *The Rise*, 379. McNeill follows Toynbee and the Western historiographical tradition in his evaluation of Greece as a key milestone and center of diffusion in history: "It may be a confession of my own culture-boundness to say that the classical Greek style of civilization seems to excel all its contemporaries." McNeill, *The Shape of European History*, 57.
52. McNeill, *The Rise*, 391–93.
53. Ibid., 399, 502.
54. Ibid., 515, 545.
55. Ibid., 584.
56. Ibid., 614, 707–8.
57. Ibid., 877.
58. McNeill, *Mythistory*, 53.
59. McNeill, *The Rise*, 794.
60. Ibid., 801–14. See also William H. McNeill, "The Complex Web of International Relations," in *The Twentieth Century: A Promethean Age*, ed. Alan Bullock (New York: McGraw-Hill, 1971), 50.
61. McNeill, *The Rise*, 868.
62. Ibid., 875–76. In his later work on *The Human Condition*, 72, McNeill retained this view of the military industrial machine dominance of world society: "It is easy to imagine a time not far in the future when existing public and private bureaucracies might come together into a self-perpetuating structure aimed first and foremost at keeping things as nearly stable as possible by guarding the privileges and power of existing managerial elites around the globe."
63. McNeill, *Mythistory*, 64, 65. McNeill has recently published an evaluation of his "great book": McNeill, *"The Rise of the West* after Twenty-Five Years," 1–22.
64. McNeill, *Past and Future*, 14, 30. McNeill, *Venice*, 145–46, 218.
65. McNeill, *Plagues and Peoples*, 20–22.
66. Alfred W. Crosby, *The Columbian Exchange: Biological and Cultural Consequences of 1492* (Westport: Greenwood, 1972). McNeill deals with these die-offs in *Plagues and Peoples*, 203–8. Both authors are forced to use statistics that measure population loss without empirical means of detailing the escape movement of people from disease centers.
67. Alfred W. Crosby, *Ecological Imperialism: The Biological Expansion of Europe, 900–1900* (New York: Cambridge University Press, 1986), 21.
68. McNeill, *Plagues and Peoples*, 30–32, 37, 50–53.
69. Ibid., 69–71.
70. Ibid., 109, 76.
71. McNeill, *The Rise*, 322–46. McNeill, *Plagues and Peoples*, 111.
72. McNeill, *The Human Condition*, 31.
73. McNeill, *Plagues and Peoples*, 114–16, 126–27. See also McNeill, *The Human Condition*, 36, on the role of adaptation to ecological conditions in the rise of the higher religions. William H. McNeill, "Disease in History," *Social Science and Medicine* 12, no. 2 (1978): 80 (special issue).

74. Ibid., 80–81.
75. McNeill, *Plagues and Peoples*, 182–85.
76. Ibid., 215.
77. Ibid., 256.
78. Ibid., 256.
79. McNeill, *The Human Condition*, 17.
80. Ibid., 22–25.
81. William H. McNeill, *The Pursuit of Power: Technology, Armed Force and Society since .. 1000* (Chicago: Univ. of Chicago Press, 1982).
82. McNeill, *The Human Condition*, 70–72. McNeill, *The Pursuit of Power*, 116.
83. William H. McNeill, "The Industrialization of War," *Southern Humanities Review* 13 (1979): 152.
84. McNeill, "The American War of Independence," 10.
85. McNeill, *Mythistory*, 199, 201, 210, 233. Cf. also Fernand Braudel, *The Mediterranean and the Mediterranean World in the Age of Philip II*, 2 vols. (New York: Harper, 1976); and Fernand Braudel, *Afterthoughts on Material Civilization and Capitalism* (Baltimore: Johns Hopkins University Press, 1977), for a sense of his perspective on deep structure in the long duration. For an excellent brief analytical evaluation of Braudel's model see Samuel Kinser, "Annaliste Paradigm? The Geohistorical Structuralism of Fernand Braudel," *American Historical Review* 86, no. 1 (1987): 63–102.
86. William H. McNeill, "Religion in the Modern World: An Historian's Reflections," *Papers in Comparative Studies* 3 (1984): 23.
87. McNeill, "Religion," 25. There is a close commonality here with Erik Erikson's view of religious change in response to the requirements of identity shifts of individual leaders and their widespread adoption among populations undergoing the same macrohistorical tensions. See Erik Erikson, *Young Man Luther: A Study in Psychoanalysis and History* (New York: Norton, 1958), 254.
88. McNeill, "Religion," 26–28.
89. McNeill, *The Rise*, 383.
90. McNeill, "Religion," 31–32.
91. McNeill, *Past and Future*, 175.
92. Ibid., 202.
93. Ibid., 190.
94. William H. McNeill, "The Decline of the West," in *Solzhenitsyn at Harvard*, ed. Ronald Berman (Washington: Ethics and Public Policy Center, 1980), 127–28.
95. McNeill, "The Decline of the West," 129.
96. McNeill, *The Rise*, vii.
97. McNeill, *Mythistory*, 16, 37.
98. McNeill, correspondence with the author, Dec. 15, 1989: "So I am a missionary too: maybe a little less flamboyant than Toynbee was."
99. William H. McNeill, "On National Frontiers: Ethnic Homogeneity and Pluralism," in *Small Comforts for Hard Times: Humanists on Public Policy*,

ed. Michael Mooney and Florian Stuber (New York: Columbia University Press, 1977), 207–19.

100. McNeill, *Arnold Toynbee*, 286.

101. William H. McNeill, Editor's Introduction to *The Liberal Interpretation of History*, by Lord Acton (Chicago: Univ. of Chicago Press, 1967), xii–xvii.

102. McNeill, Introduction, xix.

103. Walter A. McDougall, " 'Mais ce n'est pas l'histoire!' Some Thoughts on Toynbee, McNeill, and the Rest of Us," *Journal of Modern History* 58, no. 1 (1986): 40, Letter of Dec. 11, 1984.

104. McNeill, *The Shape of European History*, 3. William H. McNeill, "What's Happening to European History in the United States?" *Proceedings of the American Philosophical Society* 123 (1979): 343.

105. McNeill, "On National Frontiers," 214.

106. McNeill, *The Pursuit of Power*, 254. William H. McNeill, *The Great Frontier: Freedom and Hierarchy in Modern Times* (Princeton: Princeton University Press, 1983), 58. McNeill notes here that "the rewards of interdependence and exchange are too great to be foregone."

107. William H. McNeill, "A Cartesian Historian," *World Politics* 8 (1955): 127, 132.

108. Alvin H. Bernstein, "The Arms Race in Historical Perspective," *Orbis* 27 (1983): 761–66.

109. It may be that McNeill has, consciously or not, reacted against Toynbee's emphasis on creative change in individuals as a mystical inspiration that leads in the processes at the origin and growth of civilization.

110. McNeill, correspondence with the author, Dec. 15, 1989.

111. McNeill, *The Rise*, 876.

112. Ibid., 876.

113. Ibid. As far back as 1953 McNeill made similar avowals hoping that "a stubborn residuum of human psychology . . . [may] always continue to limit the managers." McNeill, *America, Britain and Russia*, 767.

114. McNeill, *The Rise*, 877.

115. William H. McNeill, "July 1914–July 1964," *Foreign Affairs* 42 (1964): 567, 561.

116. McNeill, *A World History*, vi.

117. McNeill, "Control and Catastrophe," 9. "Intelligence and ingenuity . . . run a race with all the nasty eventualities that interfere with human hopes and purposes; it is far from clear which is winning."

118. William H. McNeill, "The Making of Modern Times," *Harper's*, November 1984, 14, 16.

119. McNeill, "July 1914–July 1964," 567.

120. McNeill, "Disease in History," 81.

121. McNeill, *Plagues and Peoples*, 291. McNeill, *The Human Condition*, 72.

122. McNeill, "Control and Catastrophe," 12.

123. Ibid.

124. McNeill, *The Human Condition*, 74. "What we believe about our past, after all, does much to define how we behave in the present and what we do towards making up the future." See also William H. McNeill, "The Relevance of World History," *Sir Herbert Butterfield, Cho Yun Hsu and William H. McNeill on Chinese and World History*, ed. Noah Edward Fehl (Hong Kong: Chinese Univ. of Hong Kong, 1971), 47–48.

125. William H. McNeill, "Democracy Faces a Global Dilemma," *New York Times Magazine*, Nov. 17, 1963, 123. McNeill claims that "the wise . . . rejoice in their ignorance [of the future], for foreknowledge of anything important to us would in fact be utterly crushing . . . it would deprive us of all that makes living worthwhile." See also McNeill, *A World History*, 415, 495.

CHAPTER 9: WORLD HISTORY AND ESCHATOLOGY

1. Ralph Waldo Emerson, *Representative Men*, vol. 5 of *The Complete Works of Ralph Waldo Emerson* (Boston and New York: Houghton Mifflin, 1876), 113.

2. Nikolai Berdyaev, *The Divine and the Human* (London: Geoffrey Bles, 1944), 168–69. Berdyaev located the origin of this cultural predisposition in the Western religious heritage. "History is created by the expectation that in the future there will be a great manifestation, and that this manifestation will be a disclosure of Meaning in the life of the nations. It is the expectation of the appearance of the Messiah or of the Messianic kingdom" (167).

3. Rudolf Bultmann, *History and Eschatology* (Edinburgh: Edinburgh University Press, 1957), 133. Bultmann makes this claim in review of Collingwood's sense of history as a means of "human self knowledge."

4. Bultmann, 7.

5. Robert Nisbet, *History of the Idea of Progress* (New York: Basic Books, 1980), 357.

6. Mircea Eliade, *The Myth of the Eternal Return; or Cosmos and History* (Princeton: Princeton University Press, 1954), 152–53 passim. In Robert J. Lifton, *History and Human Survival* (New York: Random House, 1970), 335, Lifton echoes this sense from the perspective of the writer of history: "One may speak of a reaching back to prehistory—to a state in which imagined and actual events could not be distinguished—in order to reassemble symbolic elements that might revitalize both imagination and history."

7. Erich Kahler, in his "biography of humanity" written during World War II, also predicted a world state and new religious age. Erich Kahler, *Man the Measure* (New York: Pantheon, 1943). Eric Voegelin's profound multivolumed exploration of *Order and History* (Baton Rouge: Louisiana State University Press, 1956–87) charts a world history of periods closed to the perception of transcendental reality (order) and those open to it. Voegelin believed that

the modern West was at the end of a closed period. Also see Voegelin's comments in Raymond Aron, ed., *L'Histoire et ses interpretations: Entretiens autour de Arnold Toynbee* (Paris: Mouton, 1961) 140.

8. Pitirim A. Sorokin, *The Crisis of Our Age: Social and Cultural Outlook* (New York: Dutton, 1941), 14.

9. Pitirim A. Sorokin, *Social Philosophies of an Age of Crisis* (Boston: Beacon, 1950), 7.

10. F. Chatelet, like Sorokin and Toynbee, holds that philosophies of history are born when a civilization is menaced by crisis and that all such systems offer utopian solutions. Aron, *L'Histoire et ses interpretations*, 112.

11. Pierre Teilhard de Chardin, *The Phenomenon of Man* (New York: Harper, 1959), 27, 271. "Thus, something in the cosmos escapes from entropy, and does so more and more."

12. John T. Marcus, *Heaven, Hell and History: A Survey of Man's Faith in History from Antiquity to the Present* (New York: Macmillan, 1967), xx.

13. Marcus, xx–xxiv.

14. Fernand Braudel, *On History* (Chicago: Univ. of Chicago, 1980), 7.

15. Lifton's major works include his theoretical opus: Robert J. Lifton, *The Broken Connection* (New York: Simon and Schuster, 1979), and applications of his psychology to world history, including Robert J. Lifton, *Death in Life: Survivors of Hiroshima* (New York: Random House, 1968); Robert J. Lifton, *The Nazi Doctors: Medical Killing and the Psychology of Genocide* (New York: Basic Books, 1986); and Lifton, *History and Human Survival*. In *The Broken Connection*, 283, he asserts that "we can understand much of human history as the struggle to achieve, maintain and affirm a collective sense of immortality under constantly changing psychic and material conditions."

16. Of the seven authors examined, Spengler, Wells, Dawson, and Mumford were all, to one extent or another, outsiders to any standard academic milieu. It is also noteworthy that major insights in metahistory have come, as often as not, from academic disciplines other than history; Sorokin and Wallerstein exemplify two perspectives from sociology. Kroeber, Linton, Redfield, and Wolf have employed anthropological insights. Of the two other major historians considered only McNeill has pursued a standard academic teaching career; Toynbee held a rather singular post at Chatham House. Also, Wells and Mumford, and to a lesser extent Sorokin and Spengler, were autodidacts whose creativity came in part from their propensity to strike out alone upon fresh intellectual paths.

17. William H. McNeill, *Mythistory and Other Essays* (Chicago: Univ. of Chicago, 1986), 21–22.

18. Immanuel Wallerstein, *Historical Capitalism* (London: Verso, 1983), 98.

19. Wallerstein, *Historical Capitalism*, 90. The quote is from Immanuel Wallerstein, "Crisis as Transition," in *Dynamics of Global Crisis* (New York: Monthly Review, 1982), 50, 54.

20. Wallerstein, "Crisis," 50–51.

21. Wallerstein, *Historical Capitalism*, 109.

22. Immanuel Wallerstein, *The Capitalist World Economy* (New York: Cambridge University Press, 1979), 52, 65.

23. See Wallerstein's exposition of his theory in Immanuel Wallerstein, *The Modern World System*, 2 vols. to date (New York: Academic Press, 1974, 1980). Braudel's work also contains invaluable insights on the "limits of the possible" set by structures of everyday life and the conjunctures between these structures and the major events of the political and economic history of the modern world. Braudel's work centers, however, on the origins of capitalism and the past four centuries of European history.

24. Immanuel Wallerstein, "The Rise and Future Demise of the World Capitalist System: Concepts for Comparative Analysis," *Comparative Studies in Society and History* 16 (1974): 392.

25. Wallerstein, *Historical Capitalism*, 98.

26. Eric Wolf, *Europe and the People without History* (Berkeley: Univ. of California, 1982).

27. For a detailed critique of Wallerstein's work from a Marxist perspective, see Robert Brenner, "On the Origins of Capitalist Development: A Critique of Neo-Smithian Marxism," *New Left Review* 104 (1977): 25–92. There are considered reviews of the logical premises and coherence of Wallerstein's system in Stanley Aronowitz, "A Metahistorical Critique of Immanuel Wallerstein's The Modern World System," *Theory and Society* 10 (1981): 503–20; and in Haldun Gulalp, "Frank and Wallerstein Revisited: A Contribution to Brenner's Critique," *Journal of Contemporary Asia* 11, no. 2 (1981): 169–88.

28. Jawaharlal Nehru, *Glimpses of World History* (1934; reprint, London: Asia Publishing House, 1962).

29. See K. M. Panikkar, *Asia and Western Dominance* (Northhampton: George Allen, 1959).

30. Sorokin, *Social Philosophies*, 137.

31. A. Z. Manfred, ed., *A Short History of the World*, 2 vols. (Moscow: Progress Publishers, 1974). The focus here, as one might expect, is on the successes of the Soviet Union; even in this, however, there is a blatant distortion. Stalin is mentioned only four times while Lenin receives forty-six citations. Trotsky's name appears only twice, once as wanting to exploit the peasantry to build industry (2:73) and earlier as one among other European centrists "posing as revolutionaries" (1:577–78).

32. William H. McNeill, *Arnold Toynbee: A Life* (New York: Oxford University Press, 1989), 286.

33. Leopold von Ranke, "Weltgeschichte," in *The Secret of World History: Selected Writings on the Art and Source of History*, ed. Roger Wines (New York: Fordham University Press, 1981), 1:vi–ix, 250. "The goal is to bring to life the whole truth. . . . The facts are thus: the idea is infinite; the achievement by its very nature, limited. Fortunate enough, when one sets forth on the correct path and attains a result which can withstand further research and criticism" (243).

34. McNeill, *Mythistory*, 32. One need look no further than Chamberlain and Rosenberg.

35. Peter Gay, *Freud for Historians* (New York: Oxford University Press, 1985), 6.

BIBLIOGRAPHY

Adams, Brooks. *The Law of Civilization and Decay.* 1896. Reprint. New York: Macmillan, 1921.

Adams, Henry. *The Education of Henry Adams.* 1918. Reprint. Boston: Houghton Mifflin, 1961.

————. "Mont St. Michel and Chartres." In *Adams,* edited by Ernest Samuels and Jayne N. Samuels, 337–714. New York: Library of America, 1983.

————. *The Tendency of History.* New York: Book League of America, 1929.

Adorno, T. W. "Was Spengler Right?" *Encounter* 26, no. 148 (1966): 25–29.

Allen, Philip J., ed. *Pitirim Sorokin in Review.* Durham: Duke University Press, 1963.

Ancelet-Hustache, Jeanne. *Goethe.* New York: Grove, 1960.

Aron, Raymond. *The Dawn of Universal History.* New York: Praeger, 1961.

Aron, Raymond, ed. *L'Histoire et ses interpretations: Entretiens autour de Arnold Toynbee.* Paris: Mouton, 1961.

Aronowitz, Stanley. "A Metahistorical Critique of Immanuel Wallerstein's The Modern World System." *Theory and Society* 10 (1981): 503–20.

Augustine. *The City of God.* London and Toronto: T. M. Dent and Sons, 1931.

Baltzer, Armin. *Philosoph oder Prophet? Oswald Spengler's Vermächtnis und Voraussagen.* Göttingen: Nicklaus, 1962.

Barker, John. *The Superhistorians: Makers of Our Past.* New York: Scribners, 1982.

Barker, Sir Ernest. "Dr. Toynbee's Study of History." *International Affairs* 31 (1955): 5–16.

Barraclough, Geoffrey. *An Introduction to Contemporary History.* New York: Penguin, 1967.

Barth, Hans. *The Idea of Order.* Dordrect: D. Reidel, 1960.

————. *Truth and Ideology.* Berkeley: Univ. of California, 1976.

Belgion, Montgomery. *H. G. Wells.* 1953. Reprint. London: Longmans, Green, 1964.

Belloc, Hilaire. *Europe and the Faith.* New York: Paulist Press, 1920.

Bentley, Eric Russell. *A Century of Hero-Worship.* Philadelphia: J. B. Lippincott, 1944.

Berdyaev, Nikolai. *Christianity and Class War.* New York: Sheed and Ward, 1935.

————. *The Destiny of Man.* London: Geoffrey Bles, 1937.

————. *The Divine and the Human.* London: Geoffrey Bles, 1944.

————. *Dream and Reality: An Essay in Autobiography.* London: Geoffrey Bles, 1950.

————. *The Fate of Man in the Modern World.* Ann Arbor: Univ. of Michigan, 1961.

————. *The Meaning of History.* London: Geoffrey Bles, 1936.

Bergson, Henri. *The Two Sources of Morality and Religion.* New York: Holt, 1935.

Berlin, Isaiah. *Historical Inevitability.* London: Oxford University Press, 1954.
———. *Vico and Herder.* London: Hogarth, 1976.
Bernstein, Alvin H. "The Arms Race in Historical Perspective." *Orbis* 27 (1983): 761–68.
Bliese, John R. E. "Christopher Dawson: His Interpretation of History." *Modern Age* 23 (1979): 259–65.
Bodin, Jean. *Method for the Easy Comprehension of History.* 1583, 1595. Reprint. New York: Columbia University Press, 1945.
Borkenau, Franz. "Toynbee and the Culture Cycle." *Commentary* 21, no. 3 (1956): 239–49.
Borrello, Alfred. *H. G. Wells: Author in Agony.* Carbondale: Southern Illinois University Press, 1972.
Bossenbrook, William J. *The German Mind.* Detroit: Wayne State University Press, 1961.
Bossuet, Jacques Benigne. *Discourse on Universal History.* 1681. Reprint. Chicago: Univ. of Chicago, 1976.
Bozeman, Adda B. "Decline of the West? Spengler Reconsidered." *Virginia Quarterly Review* 59, no. 2 (1983): 181–207.
Braudel, Fernand. *Afterthoughts on Material Civilization and Capitalism.* Baltimore: Johns Hopkins University Press, 1977.
———. *The Mediterranean and the Mediterranean World in the Age of Philip II.* 2 vols. New York: Harper, 1976.
———. *On History.* Chicago: Univ. of Chicago, 1980.
Brauun, Martin. "Bury, Spengler and the New Spenglerians." *History Today* 7 (1952): 525–99.
———. "The Idea of Progress in Recent Philosophies of History." *Journal of Modern History* 30, no. 3 (1958): 215–26.
Brenner, Robert. "On the Origins of Capitalist Development: A Critique of Neo-Smithian Marxism." *New Left Review* 104 (1977): 25–92.
Brinder, Leonard. "The Natural History of Development Theory." *Comparative Studies in Society and History* 28 (1986): 3–33.
Brinton, Crane. "Socio-Astrology." *Southern Review* 3 (1937): 243–66.
———. "Toynbee's City of God." *Virginia Quarterly Review* 32 (1956): 361–75.
Bronowski, J. "Strategy for the Next Plateau." *Nation,* June 14, 1956, 41–42.
Brooks, Van Wyck. "Lewis Mumford: American Prophet." *Harper's,* June 1952, 46–53.
Bruun, Geoffrey. "Metropolitan Strait Jacket." *Saturday Review of Literature,* Apr. 15, 1961, 17.
Bryan, G. McLeod. "The 'Kingdom of God' Conception in Sorokin and Toynbee." *Social Forces* 26: 288–92.
Bultmann, Rudolf. *History and Eschatology.* Edinburgh: Edinburgh University Press, 1957.
Burckhardt, Jakob. *Judgements on History and Historians.* Boston: Beacon, 1958.
Bury, John B. *The Idea of Progress.* 1932. Reprint. New York: Dover, 1955.

Callahan, Daniel et al. "Christopher Dawson." *Harvard Theological Review* 66 (1973): 167–70.

Calvert, Alexander, S.J. *The Catholic Literary Revival.* 1935. Reprint. Port Washington: Kennikat Press, 1968.

Calvocoressi, Peter. "Arnold Toynbee, 1889–1975: A Memorial Lecture." *International Affairs* 52, no. 1 (1976): 1–10.

Chamberlain, Houston Stewart. *Foundations of the Nineteenth Century.* 2 vols. New York: Fertig, 1968.

Chant, Stephen, and Joyce, Michael. "Spengler and the Anthropologists." *Contemporary Review* 131 (1927): 765–69.

Chase, E. T. "Man, Machines and Mumford." *Commonweal* 87 (May 8, 1968): 694–95.

"Christopher Henry Dawson." In *Catholic Authors,* edited by Matthew Hoehn. Detroit: Gale Research, 1981, 185.

Cohn, Norman. *Pursuit of the Millennium: Revolutionary Millenarians and Mystical Anarchists of the Middle Ages.* New York: Oxford University Press, 1970.

Collingwood, R. G. *The Idea of History.* 1946. Reprint. London: Oxford University Press, 1972.

———. "Oswald Spengler and the Theory of Historical Cycles." *Antiquity* 1 (1927): 311–25.

Collins, Christopher. "Zamyatin, Wells and the Utopian Tradition." *Slavonic and East European Review* 44, no. 103 (1966): 351–60.

Condorcet, Jean-Antoine-Nicholas de Caritat. *Sketch for a Historical Picture of the Progress of the Human Mind.* London: Weidenfeld and Nicholson, 1955.

Conrad, David R. *Education for Transformation: Implications in Lewis Mumford's Ecohumanism.* Palm Springs: ETC, 1976.

Cowell, Frank Richard. *History, Civilization and Culture: An Introduction to the History and Sociology of Pitirim A. Sorokin.* London: Black, 1952.

———. *Values in Human Society.* Boston: Sargent, 1970.

Cowley, Malcolm. "Outline of Wells' History." *New Republic,* Nov. 14, 1934, 22–23.

Cowley, Malcolm, and Smith, Bernard, eds. *Books That Changed Our Minds.* New York: Doubleday, 1939.

Craig, Gordon A. "Review of William H. McNeill: *The Pursuit of Power.*" *American Historical Review* 88, no. 5 (1983): 1239–40.

Crosby, Alfred W. *The Columbian Exchange; Biological and Cultural Consequences of 1492.* Westport: Greenwood, 1972.

———. *Ecological Imperialism: The Biological Expansion of Europe, 900–1900.* New York: Cambridge University Press, 1986.

Dahlin, R. "Harper and Row Signs Lewis Mumford." *Publisher's Weekly,* Oct. 22, 1979, 52.

Danilevsky, Nicholai. "The Slav Role in World Civilization." Last chapter of *Russia and Europe.* In *The Mind of Modern Russia,* edited by Hans Kohn, 195–212. New York: Harper and Row, 1955.

Davis, Eric. "Gide's L'Immoraliste and the Crisis of Historical Thought." *Historical Reflections* 14 (1987): 329–44.

"Dawson, Christopher Henry." In *Twentieth Century Authors*, edited by S. J. Kunitz. New York: H. W. Wilson, 1955, 266-67.

Dawson, Christopher. *The Age of the Gods*. Boston: Houghton Mifflin, 1928.

———. *America and the Secularization of Modern Culture*. Houston: Univ. of St. Thomas, 1960.

———. *Beyond Politics*. London: Sheed and Ward, 1939.

———. "The Challenge of Secularism." *Catholic World* 182 (1956): 326.

———. "Christianity and the Humanist Tradition." *Dublin Review* 226 (1952): 1–11.

———. "Civilization in Crisis." *Catholic World* 182, no. 2 (1956): 246–52.

———. *The Dividing of Christendom*. New York: Sheed and Ward, 1965.

———. *The Dynamics of World History*. Edited by John J. Mulloy. New York: Sheed and Ward, 1957.

———. "Education and Christian Culture." *Commonweal* 59 (1953): 216–20.

———. "The European Revolution." *Catholic World* 179 (1954): 86–95.

———. "The Foundations of Unity." *Dublin Review* 211 (1942): 97–104.

———. "Freedom and Vocation." *Dublin Review* 420 (1942): 1–11.

———. "Future of Christian Culture." *Commonweal* 59 (1954): 595–98.

———. *The Gods of Revolution*. New York: New York University Press, 1972.

———. "The Historic Origins of Liberalism." *Review of Politics* 16 (1954): 267–82.

———. *The Historic Reality of Christian Culture*. New York: Harper and Brothers, 1960.

———. "The Institutional Forms of Christian Culture." *Religion in Life* 24 (1954–55): 373–80.

———. *The Judgement of the Nations*. New York: Sheed and Ward, 1942.

———. "The Life of Civilizations." *Sociological Review* 14 (1922): 51–68.

———. *The Making of Europe*. 1932. Reprint. London: Sheed and Ward, 1948.

———. *Medieval Essays*. New York: Sheed and Ward, 1954.

———. Introduction to *The Mongol Missions*, edited by Christopher Dawson, vii–xxxvii. New York: Sheed and Ward, 1955.

———. *The Movement of World Revolution*. New York: Sheed and Ward, 1959.

———. "New Decline and Fall." *Commonweal* 15 (1932): 32022.

———. "Not Pacifists but Peacemakers." *Catholic World* 145 (1937): 102–4.

———. "Peace Aims and Power Politics." *Dublin Review* 213 (1944): 97–108.

———. "The Problem of Christ and Culture." *Dublin Review* 226 (1952): 64–69.

———. "The Problem of Metahistory." *History Today* 1 (1951): 9–12.

———. *Progress and Religion*. New York: Sheed and Ward, 1938.

———. "The Recovery of Spiritual Unity." *Catholic World* 143 (1936): 349–50.

———. "The Relationship between Religion and Culture." *Commonweal* 49 (1949): 488–90.

———. "The Relevance of European History." *History Today* 6, no. 9 (1956): 606–15.

———. *Religion and Culture*. New York: Sheed and Ward, 1948.

———. "Religion and Mass Civilization—The Problem of the Future." *Dublin Review* 214 (1944): 1–8.

———. *Religion and the Modern State*. London: Sheed and Ward, 1936.

———. *Religion and the Rise of Western Culture*. Garden City: Doubleday, 1958.

———. "The Significance of Bolshevism." *American Review* 1 (1933): 36–49.

———. "Sociology and the Theory of Progress." In *American Conservative Thought in the Twentieth Century*, edited by William F. Buckley Jr., 427–38. Indianapolis: Bobbs-Merrill, 1970.

———. *The Spirit of the Oxford Movement*. New York: Sheed and Ward, 1933.

———. "The Threat to the West." *Commonweal* 31 (1940): 317–18.

———. "Toynbee's Odyssey of the West." *Commonweal* 61 (1954): 62ff.

———. "Tradition and Inheritance." *The Wind and the Rain* (1949): 7–17.

———. "What the World Needs." *Catholic World* 137 (1933): 92–94.

———. "Why I Am a Catholic." *Chesterton Review* 9, no. 2 (1983): 110–13.

De Beus, J. G. *The Future of the West*. New York: Harper and Brothers, 1953.

Demant, V. A. "The Importance of Christopher Dawson." *Nineteenth Century* 129 (1951): 66–75.

Dray, William. "Toynbee's Search for Historical Laws." *History and Theory* 1 (1960): 32–55.

Dubos, René. "Despairing Optimist." *American Scholar* 42 (Summer 1973): 378–80.

Eliade, Mircea. *The Myth of the Eternal Return; Or Cosmos and History*. Princeton: Princeton University Press, 1954.

Elias, Norbert. *The History of Manners*. Vol. 1 of *The Civilizing Process*. New York: Pantheon, 1978.

Ellul, Jacques. *The Technological Society*. New York: Knopf, 1964.

Ellwood, Charles A. *The Reconstruction of Religion*. New York: Macmillan, 1922.

Emerson, Ralph Waldo. *Representative Men*. Vol. 5. of *The Complete Works of Ralph Waldo Emerson*. Boston and New York: Houghton Mifflin, 1876.

Erikson, Erik. *Young Man Luther: A Study in Psychoanalysis and History*. New York: Norton, 1958.

Eulau, Heinz. "Mumford: Not a Guide but a Lantern." *New Republic*, Apr. 22, 1946, 583–85.

Farrell, John K. A. "H. G. Wells as an Historian." *University of Windsor Review* 2 (1967): 47–57.

Fennelly, John F. *Twilight of the Evening Lands: Oswald Spengler a Half Century Later*. New York: Brookdale, 1972.

Ferguson, Adam. *The History of Civil Society*. 1767. Reprint. Edinburgh: Edinburgh University Press, 1966.

Filler, Martin. "Lewis Mumford: The Making of an Architectural Critic." *Architectural Record* 170 (Apr. 1982): 116–23.

Frank, Waldo. "Views on Human Nature; Review of *The Conduct of Life.*" *Saturday Review of Literature* 34 (Sept. 22, 1951): 11–12.

Freud, Sigmund. *Civilization and Its Discontents.* New York: Norton, 1961.

———. *New Introductory Lectures on Psychoanalysis.* Standard ed. Edited by James Strachey. 1933. Reprint. New York: Norton, 1965.

———. *Totem and Taboo.* New York: Moffat, Yard, 1919.

Frye, Northrop. "The Decline of the West by Oswald Spengler." *Daedalus* 103, no. 1 (1974): 1–13.

Gargan, Edward T., ed. *The Intent of Toynbee's History: A Cooperative Appraisal.* Chicago: Loyola University Press, 1961.

Gay, Peter. *Freud for Historians.* New York: Oxford University Press, 1985.

Geddes, Patrick. *Cities in Evolution.* 1913. Reprint. New York: Fertig, 1968.

Geyl, Pieter. *Debates with Historians.* New York: Meridian, 1958.

Geyl, Pieter; Toynbee, Arnold J.; and Sorokin, Pitirim A. *The Pattern of the Past.* Oxford: Oxford University Press, 1948.

Ghosh, Oroon K. "Some Theories of Universal History." *Comparative Studies in Society and History* 8 (1964–65): 1–20.

Gill, Brendan. "The Sky Line." *New Yorker,* Feb. 23, 1987, 106–9.

Gobineau, Arthur comte de. *The Inequality of Human Races.* 1853. Reprint. New York: Fertig, 1967.

Goddard, E. H., and Gibbons, P. A. *Civilization or Civilizations: An Essay in the Spenglerian Philosophy of History.* London: Constable, 1921.

Gottfried, Paul. "Oswald Spengler and the Inspiration of the Classical Age." *Modern Age* 26, no. 1 (1982): 68–75.

Grugel, Lee E. "In Search of a Legacy for Arnold Toynbee." *Journal of General Education* 31, no. 1 (1979): 35–43.

Grundel, Gunther E. *Jahre der Überwindung.* Breslau: Korn, 1934.

Grutzmacher, Richard Heinrich. "Spengler und Nietzsche." *Sammlung* 50 Jg. 5, 590–608.

Gulalp, Haldun. "Frank and Wallerstein Revisited: A Contribution to Brenner's Critique." *Journal of Contemporary Asia* 11, no. 2 (1981): 169–88.

Guthrie, Elton P. "Sorokin: Counselor to Reaction." *Science and Society* 3 (1939): 229–38.

Haeckel, Ernst. *Last Words on Evolution.* New York: Eckler, 1905.

Hale, William Harlan. *Challenge to Defeat: Modern Man in Goethe's World and Spengler's Century.* New York: Harcourt Brace, 1932.

Hallen, G. C., ed. *Sorokin and Sociology.* Motikatra: Satish Books, 1972.

Halsey, Van R. Jr. "Lewis Mumford's Golden Day." *New Republic,* Aug. 12, 1957, 21.

Hamilton, Alistair. *The Appeal of Fascism: A Study of Intellectuals and Fascism, 1919–1945.* New York: Avon, 1973.

Hart, Hornell. "Sorokin's Data Versus His Conclusions." *American Sociological Review* 4 (1939): 635–46.

Hayden, J. Michael. " 'New' History: New Bottles and Old Wine." *Canadian Journal of History* 15, no. 3 (1980): 409–11.

Hegel, G. W. F. *Lectures on the Philosophy of World History*. Edited by D. Forbes. Cambridge: Cambridge University Press, 1975.

———. *Reason in History: A General Introduction to the Philosophy of History*. New York: Liberal Arts Press, 1953.

Heller, Erich. "Oswald Spengler and the Predicament of the Historical Imagination." In *The Disinherited Mind*, 179–96. New York: Harcourt Brace Jovanovich, 1975.

Hellman, John. "Christopher Dawson and Eastern Europe." *Ukrainian Quarterly* 20 (1965): 236–51.

Herder, John Godfrey. *Outlines of a Philosophy of the History of Man*. 2d ed. 2 vols. London: J. Johnson, 1803.

Heylyn, Peter. *Cosmographie in Four Books: Containing the Chorographie and Historie of the Whole World*. London: Philip Chetwind, 1666.

H. G. Wells: A Comprehensive Bibliography. London: H. G. Wells Society, 1968.

Hillegas, Mark Robert. *The Future as Nightmare: H. G. Wells and the Anti-Utopians*. New York: Oxford University Press, 1967.

Hitler, Adolf. *Mein Kampf*. New York: Regent and Hitchcock, 1939.

Hook, Sidney. "Man's Destiny: A Scientific View." *New York Times Book Review*, Aug. 17, 1947, 4, 22.

Horkheimer, Max. "Vico and Mythology." *New Vico Studies* 5 (1988): 63–78.

Hughes, H. Stuart. *Oswald Spengler: A Critical Estimate*. New York: Scribners, 1952.

Huntington, Ellsworth. *Civilization and Climate*. 2d ed. New Haven: Yale University Press, 1922.

———. *World Power and Evolution*. New Haven: Yale University Press, 1919.

Huxley, Thomas Henry. *Evolution and Ethics and Other Essays*. New York: Appleton, 1905.

Huxtable, Ada Louise. "The Sage of the Skyline." *New York Times Book Review*, Nov. 26, 1989, 3, 24–25.

Hyde, William J. "The Socialism of H. G. Wells in the Early Twentieth Century." *Journal of the History of Ideas* 17, no. 2 (1956): 217–34.

Iggers, George G. "The Idea of Progress in Recent Philosophies of History." *Journal of Modern History* 30, no. 3 (1958): 215–26.

Ingle, Steven J. "The Political Writing of H. G. Wells." *Queens's Quarterly Review* 81, no. 3 (1974): 396–411.

———. "Politics and Literature: An Unconventional Relationship." *Political Studies* 25, no. 4 (1977): 549–62.

Issawi, Charles, ed. *An Arab Philosopher of History: Selections from the Prolegomena of Ibn Khaldun of Tunis*. 1950. Reprint. London: Murray, 1969.

Jacoby, Russell. *The Last Intellectuals*. New York: Basic Books, 1987.

Jaspers, Karl. *The Origin and Goal of History*. New Haven: Yale University Press, 1953.

John of Sleidan. *De Quatour Summis Impiris (The Key to History, or, A Most Methodicall Abridgement of the Four Cheife Monarchies)*. London: University Microfilms/Nathaniel Rolls, 1695 ed.

Joll, James. "Two Prophets of the Twentieth Century: Spengler and Toynbee." *Review of International Studies* 11, no. 2 (1985): 91–104.

Jones, Eric L. "Economic History at the Species Level." *History of European Ideas* 3, no. 1 (1982): 95–105.

Kahler, Erich. *Man the Measure*. New York: Pantheon, 1943.

Kant, Immanuel. "Ideas towards a Universal History from a Cosmopolitan Point of View." In *On History*, edited by Lewis White Beck, 11–27. Indianapolis: Bobbs-Merrill, 1963.

———. "Prolegomena to Any Future Metaphysics." *Classics of Western Philosophy*, edited by Stephen M. Cahn, 764–839. Indianapolis: Hackett, 1977.

Kaufmann, Walter, trans. and ed. *Goethe's Faust*. New York: Anchor, 1961.

———. *Nietzsche: Philosopher, Psychologist, Antichrist*. 1950. Reprint. Princeton: Princeton University Press, 1974.

———. "Toynbee: The Historian as False Prophet." *Commentary* 23: 344–55.

Kedourie, Élie. "Arnold Toynbee: History as Paradox." *Encounter* 42, no. 5 (1974): 57–66.

Kellner, Hans. "Figures in the Rumpelkammer: Goethe, Faust, Spengler." *Journal of European Studies* 13 (1983): 142–67.

Kinser, Samuel. "Annaliste Paradigm? The Geohistorical Structuralism of Fernand Braudel." *American Historical Review* 86, no. 1 (1987): 63–102.

Knowles, M. D. "Christopher Dawson (1889–1970)." *Proceedings of the British Academy* 17 (1971): 439–52.

Kohn, Hans, ed. *The Mind of Germany: The Education of a Nation*. New York: Scribners, 1960.

Koktanek, Anton M., ed. *Oswald Spengler, Briefe, 1913–1936*. München: C. H. Beck, 1963.

Kroeber, Alfred L. *Configurations of Cultural Growth*. Berkeley and Los Angeles: Univ. of California Press, 1944.

———. "The Delimination of Civilizations." *Journal of the History of Ideas* 14 (1953): 264–75.

———. *Style and Civilizations*. Ithaca: Cornell University Press, 1957.

Kuhn, Thomas. *The Structures of Scientific Revolutions*. Chicago: Univ. of Chicago, 1962.

Kuhns, William. *Post Industrial Prophets*. New York: Weybright and Talley, 1971.

Lampert, Eugueny. *Nicholas Berdyaev and the New Middle Ages*. London: James Clark, n.d.

Lasch, Christopher. *The Culture of Narcissism*. New York: Norton, 1979.

Lattimore, Owen. "Spengler and Toynbee." *Atlantic Monthly*, April 1948, 104–5.

Lenzer, Gertrude, ed. *Auguste Comte and Positivism: The Essential Writings*. Chicago: Univ. of Chicago, 1975.

Le Play, Frederic. *On Family, Work, and Social Change*. Edited by Catherine Bodard Silver. Chicago: Univ. of Chicago, 1982.

Lessing, Gotthold Ephraim. "Education of the Human Race." In *Literary and Philosophical Essays*, 185–209. New York: Collier, 1961.

"Lewis Mumford Wins National Literature Medal." *Publisher's Weekly*, Jan. 1, 1973, 32–33.

Liebel, Helen P. "The Historian and the Idea of World Civilization." *Dalhousie Review* 47, no. 4 (1968): 455–66.

Lifton, Robert J. *The Broken Connection*. New York: Simon and Schuster, 1979.

———. *Death in Life; Survivors of Hiroshima*. New York: Random House, 1968.

———. *History and Human Survival*. New York: Random House, 1970.

———. *The Nazi Doctors: Medical Killing and the Psychology of Genocide*. New York: Basic Books, 1986.

Linton, Ralph. *The Tree of Culture*. New York: Knopf, 1955.

Locas, Claude. "Christopher Dawson: A Bibliography." *Harvard Theological Review* 66 (1973): 177–206.

Löwith, Karl. *Meaning in History: The Theological Implications of the Philosophy of History*. Chicago: Univ. of Chicago, 1949.

Machiavelli, Niccolo di Bernando. *The Discourses, The Portable Machiavelli*. Edited by Peter Bondanella and Mark Musa. New York: Penguin, 1979.

McClay, Wilfred M. "Lewis Mumford." *American Scholar* 57 (Winter 1988): 111–18

McConnell, Frank D. "H. G. Wells: Utopia and Doomsday." *Wilson Quarterly* 4, no. 3 (1981): 176–86.

McDougall, Walter A. " 'Mais ce n'est pas l'histoire!' Some Thoughts on Toynbee, McNeill, and the Rest of Us." *Journal of Modern History* 58, no. 1 (1986): 19–42.

MacMaster, Robert E. "Danilevsky and Spengler: A New Interpretation." *Journal of Modern History* 26 (1954): 154–61.

McNaspy, C. J. "Chat with Christopher Dawson." *America* 106 (1961): 120–22.

———. "Christopher Dawson: In Memoriam." *America* 122 (1972): 634.

———. "Dawson at Eighty." *America* 121 (1969): 302.

———. "Dawson's New Contribution to Dialogue." *America* 112 (1965): 432.

McNeill, John T. *The History and Character of Calvinism*. New York: Oxford University Press, 1954.

"McNeill, William H., 1917." In *Contemporary Authors*, edited by Ann Avory. Rev. ed. Detroit: Gale Research, 1981, 2: 459.

McNeill, William H. *America, Britain and Russia: Their Cooperation and Conflict 1941–1946*. 1953. Reprint. New York: Johnson Reprint, 1970.

———. "The American War of Independence in World Perspective." In *Reconsiderations on the Revolutionary War: Selected Essays*, edited by Don Higginbotham, 3–13. Westport: Greenwood, 1978.

———. *Arnold Toynbee: A Life*. New York: Oxford University Press, 1989.

———. "Carl Becker, Historian." *History Teacher* 19 (1985): 89–100.

———. "A Cartesian Historian." *World Politics* 8 (1955): 124–33.

———. "The Complex Web of International Relations." In *The Twentieth Century: A Promethean Age*, edited by Alan Bullock, 31–54. New York: McGraw-Hill, 1971.

———. "Control and Catastrophe in Human Affairs." *Daedalus* 118, no. 1 (1989): 1–16.

———. "The Decline of the West." In *Solzhenitsyn at Harvard*, edited by Ronald Berman, 123–30. Washington: Ethics and Public Policy Center, 1980.

———. "Democracy Faces a Global Dilemma." *New York Times Magazine*, Nov. 17, 1963, 21, 131–32.

———. "Dilemmas of Modernization." *Massachusetts Review* 9 (1968): 133–46.

———. "Disease in History." *Social Science and Medicine* 12, no. 2 (1978): 79–81. Special Issue.

———. "The Draft in the Light of History." In *The Draft: A Handbook of Facts and Alternatives*, edited by Sol Tax, 117–21. Chicago: Univ. of Chicago Press, 1967.

———. Editor's Introduction to *The Liberal Interpretation of History*, by Lord Acton. Chicago: Univ. of Chicago Press, 1967.

———. *Europe's Steppe Frontier, 1500–1800*. Chicago: Univ. of Chicago Press, 1964.

———. *The Great Frontier: Freedom and Hierarchy in Modern Times*. Princeton: Princeton University Press, 1983.

———. *The Greek Dilemma: War and Aftermath*. Philadelphia: Lippincott, 1947.

———. "Historical Patterns of Migration." *Current Anthropology* 20 (1979): 95–98.

———. *The Human Condition: An Ecological and Historical View*. Princeton: Princeton University Press, 1980.

———. "The Industrialization of War." *Southern Humanities Review* 13 (1979): 139–56.

———. "The Introduction of the Potato into Ireland." *Journal of Modern History* 21 (1949): 218–22.

———. "July 1914–July 1964." *Foreign Affairs* 42 (1964): 559–68.

———. "The Making of Modern Times." *Harper's*, Nov. 1984, 14–15, 17.

———. *The Metamorphosis of Greece since World War Two*. Chicago: Univ. of Chicago Press, 1978.

———. "Modern European History." In *The Past before Us: Contemporary Historical Writing in the U.S.*, edited by Michael Kammen, 95–112. Ithaca: Cornell University Press, 1980.

———. *Mythistory and Other Essays*. Chicago: Univ. of Chicago Press, 1986.

———. "On National Frontiers: Ethnic Homogeneity and Pluralism." In *Small Comforts for Hard Times: Humanists on Public Policy*, edited by Michael Mooney and Florian Stuber, 207–19. New York: Columbia University Press, 1977.

———. *Past and Future*. Chicago: Univ. of Chicago Press, 1954.

————. "The Peasant Revolt of Our Times." In *Changing Perspectives on Man*, edited by Ben Rothblatt, 227–42. Chicago: Univ. of Chicago Press, 1968.

————. *Plagues and Peoples*. Garden City: Anchor, 1976.

————. *Polyethnicity and National Unity in World History*. Toronto: Univ. of Toronto, 1986.

————. "The Pursuit of Power: An Historian Reflects." *Bulletin of the Atomic Scientists* 38, no. 4 (1982): 19–23.

————. *The Pursuit of Power: Technology, Armed Force and Society since A.D. 1000*. Chicago: Univ. of Chicago Press, 1982.

————. "The Relevance of World History." In *Sir Herbert Butterfield, Cho Yun Hsu and William H. McNeill on Chinese and World History*, edited by Noah Edward Fehl, 44–55. Hong Kong: Chinese Univ. of Hong Kong, 1971.

————. "Religion in the Modern World: An Historian's Reflections." *Papers in Comparative Studies* 3 (1984): 23–32.

————. "Review Essay: *The Nature of History* by Arthur Marwick and Comment on *Ecrit L'Histoire* by Paul Veyne." *History and Theory* 11 (1972): 103–9.

————. *The Rise of the West; A History of the Human Community*. Chicago: Univ. of Chicago Press, 1963.

————. "*The Rise of the West* after Twenty-Five Years." *Journal of World History* 1 (Spring 1990): 1–22.

————. *The Shape of European History*. New York: Oxford University Press, 1974.

————. *Venice: The Hinge of Europe, 1081–1797*. Chicago: Univ. of Chicago, 1974.

————. "The View from Greece." In *Witnesses to the Origins of the Cold War*, edited by Thomas T. Hammond, 98–122. Seattle: Univ. of Washington, 1982.

————. "What's Happening to European History in the United States?" *Proceedings of the American Philosophical Society* 123 (1979): 341–43.

————. *A World History*. New York: Oxford University Press, 1967.

————. "World History in the Schools." In *New Movements in the Study and Teaching of History*, edited by Martin Ballard, 16–25. London: Temple Smith, 1970.

Manfred, A. Z., ed. *A Short History of the World*. 2 vols. Moscow: Progress Publishers, 1974.

Manuel, Frank E. *Shapes of Philosophical History*. Stanford: Stanford University Press, 1965.

Maquet, Jacques. *The Sociology of Knowledge*. 1951. Reprint. Westport: Greenwood, 1973.

Marcus, John T. *Heaven, Hell and History: A Survey of Man's Faith in History from Antiquity to the Present*. New York: Macmillan, 1967.

Marcuse, Herbert. *Eros and Civilization: A Philosophical Inquiry into Freud*. Boston: Beacon, 1966.

————. *One Dimensional Man*. Boston: Beacon, 1964.

Marsh, George Perkins. *Man and Nature, or, Physical Geography as Modified by Human Action*. 1864. Reprint. New York: Scribner, 1874.

Martin, Percival William. *Experiment in Depth: A Study of the Works of Jung, Eliot and Toynbee*. London: Routledge and Paul, 1955.

Marx, Karl, and Engels, Friedrich. *The Communist Manifesto*. New York: Washington Square, 1964.

Mason, Henry Lloyd. *Toynbee's Approach to World Politics*. New Orleans: Tulane University Press, 1958.

Matter, Joseph Allen. *Love, Altruism, and the World Crisis: The Challenge of Pitirim Sorokin*. Chicago: Nelson-Hall, 1974.

Mazlish, Bruce. *The Meaning of Karl Marx*. New York: Oxford University Press, 1984.

————. *The Riddle of History*. New York: Harper and Row, 1966.

Meiland, Jack W. *Skepticism and Historical Knowledge*. New York: Random House, 1965.

Mencken, H. L. "The Late Mr. Wells." In *Prejudices, First Series*, 22–35. New York: Knopf, 1919.

Messer, Don August. *Oswald Spengler als Philosoph*. Stuttgart: Drud von Streder, 1922.

Miller, Donald L. *Lewis Mumford: A Life*. New York: Weidenfeld and Nicholson, 1989.

Montague, A., ed. *Toynbee and History: Critical Essays and Reviews*. Boston: Porter Sargent, 1956.

Mumford, Lewis. "Anticipations and Social Adjustments in Science." *Bulletin of the Atomic Scientists* 10 (Feb./Mar. 1954): 34–36.

————. "Apology to Henry Adams." *Virginia Quarterly Review* 38, no. 2 (1962): 196–217.

————. "Authoritarian and Democratic Technics." *Technology and Culture* 5, no. 1 (1964): 1–8.

————. "The Automation of Knowledge: Address of April 19, 1964." *Vital Speeches* 30 (May 1, 1964): 441–46.

————. *The Brown Decades*. New York: Harcourt Brace, 1931.

————. "Cities Fit to Live In." *Nation*, May 15, 1948, 530–33.

————. *The City in History*. New York: Harcourt Brace and World, 1961.

————. *The Condition of Man*. New York: Harcourt Brace, 1973.

————. *The Conduct of Life*. 1951. Reprint. New York: Harcourt Brace Jovanovich, 1970.

————. "The Corruption of Liberalism." *New Republic*, Apr. 29, 1940, 568–73.

————. *The Culture of Cities*. New York: Harcourt Brace, 1938.

————. "Downfall or Renewal: Review of *The Decline of the West*." *New Republic*, May 12, 1926, 367–69.

————. "Enemy Within." *Forbes*, Nov. 15, 1971, 46.

————. *Faith for Living*. New York: Harcourt Brace, 1940.

————. *Findings and Keepings; Analects for an Autobiography*. New York: Harcourt Brace Jovanovich, 1975.

————. *The Golden Day*. New York: Boni and Liverright, 1926.

————. *Green Memories: The Story of Geddes Mumford*. 1947. Reprint. Westport: Greenwood, 1973.

————. *Herman Melville*. New York: Literary Guild, 1929.

————. "History: Neglected Clue to Technological Change." *Technology and Culture* 2, no. 3 (1961): 230–36.

————. "Insensate Ideologue." *New Republic*, July 14, 1937, 282–84.

————. *In the Name of Sanity*. New York: Harcourt Brace, 1954.

————. Introduction to *The Ecological Basis of Planning*, by Artur Glickson. Edited by Lewis Mumford, Ed. The Hague: Nijhoff, 1971.

————. "Letter to the President." *New Republic*, Dec. 30, 1936, 363–65.

————. "Menace to the American Promise." *New Republic*, Nov. 8, 1939, 64–65.

————. "Morals of Extermination." *Atlantic*, Oct. 1959, 38–44.

————. *The Myth of the Machine: The Pentagon of Power*. New York: Harcourt Brace Jovanovich, 1970.

————. *The Myth of the Machine: Technics and Human Development*. New York: Harcourt Brace Jovanovich, 1967.

————. *My Work and Days: A Personal Chronicle*. New York: Harcourt Brace Jovanovich, 1979.

————. "The Napoleon of Notting Hill." In *Toynbee and History*, edited by A. Montague. Boston: Porter Sargent, 1956.

————. "New Regional Plan to Arrest Megalopolis." *Architectural Record* 137 (Mar. 1965): 147–54.

————. "Prize or Lunacy?" *Newsweek*, July 7, 1969, 61.

————. "Restoration of Sex." *New Republic*, Apr. 15, 1936, 281–82.

————. *Sketches from Life*. New York: Dial Press, 1982.

————. "Spengler's 'The Decline of the West.'" In *Books that Changed Our Minds*, edited by Malcolm Cowley and Bernard Smith, 217–38. New York: Doubleday, 1939.

————. *The Story of Utopias*. 1922. Reprint. New York: Harcourt Brace, 1962.

————. *Technics and Civilization*. New York: Harcourt Brace, 1934.

————. *The Transformations of Man*. New York: Harper and Row, 1972.

————. *The Urban Prospect*. New York: Harcourt Brace and World, 1968.

————. "Utopia, the City and the Machine." *Daedalus* 94, no. 2 (Winter 1965): 271–92.

————. "What I Believe." *Forum* 83 (Nov. 1930): 263–68.

Naeher, Jurgen. *Oswald Spengler*. Rembeck: Rowohlt, 1984.

Nash, Roderick. *Wilderness and the American Mind*. New Haven: Yale University Press, 1973.

Nehru, Jawaharlal. *Glimpses of World History*. 1934. Reprint. London: Asia Publishing House, 1962.

Neill, Thomas P. "Toynbee and Dawson on the Meaning of Contemporary History." In *Christianity and Culture*, edited by J. Stanley Murphy, 21–30. Montreal: Palm, 1960.

Newman, John Henry. *The Idea of a University*. London: Longmans Green, 1902.

Nicholas, M-P. *De Nietzsche à Hitler*. Paris: Fasquelle, 1936.

Niebuhr, Reinhold. *Faith and History*. New York: Scribners, 1949.

Nietzsche, Friedrich. *The Birth of Tragedy* and *The Genealogy of Morals*. Garden City: Doubleday, 1956.

———. *The Portable Nietzsche*. Edited by Walter Kaufmann. New York: Viking, 1968.

———. *The Use and Abuse of History*. New York: Macmillan, 1986.

Nisbet, Robert. *History of the Idea of Progress*. New York: Basic Books, 1980.

Ortega y Gasset, José. *An Interpretation of Universal History*. New York: Norton, 1973.

Orwell, George. "Wells, Hitler and the World State." In *Collected Essays, Journalism and Letters of George Orwell*. 4 vols. Edited by Sonia Orwell and Ian Angus, 2:139–44. London: Secker and Warburg, 1968.

Panikkar, K. M. *Asia and the Western Dominance*. Northhampton: George Allen, 1959.

Park, Robert E. "Review of *Social and Cultural Dynamics*, Vols. 1–3." *American Journal of Sociology* 43 (1938): 824–32.

Parrinder, Patrick. "H. G. Wells and the Fiction of Catastrophe." *Renaissance and Modern Studies* 28 (1984): 40–58.

Partenhenner, David. "Henry Adams' Weltanschauung." *Journal of the History of Ideas* 41 (1988): 339–45.

Perry, Marvin. *Arnold Toynbee and the Crisis of the West*. Washington: University Press of America, 1982.

Petrie, W. M. Flinders. *The Revolutions of Civilization*. London: Harper and Brothers, 1911.

Pierard, Richard V. "Culture versus Civilization: A Christian Critique of Oswald Spengler's Cultural Pessimism." *Fides et History* 14, no. 2 (1982): 37–49.

Plato's Republic. Translated by G. M. A. Grube. Indianapolis: Hackett, 1974.

Pois, Robert A. "Spengler, Oswald (Arnold Gottfried)." In *Thinkers of the Twentieth Century*, edited by Elizabeth Devine et al., 534–36. Detroit: Gale Research, 1983.

Pomper, Philip. "McNeill, William Hardy, 1917–." In *Thinkers of the Twentieth Century*, edited by Elizabeth Devine et al., 379–80. Detroit: Gale Research, 1983.

Popper, Karl. *The Open Society and Its Enemies*. Princeton: Princeton University Press, 1950.

Priestley, J. B. "Light in a Thousand Dark Places." *Horizon* 8, no. 1 (1966): 33–37.

Quigley, Carroll. *The Evolution of Civilizations*. New York: Macmillan, 1961.

———. "Power Politics of Human History." *Saturday Review of Literature*, Aug. 24, 1963, 41–42.

Raleigh, Sir Walter. *The History of the World*. 1614. Reprint. London: Thomas Basset et al., 1687.

Ranke, Leopold Von. *The Secret of World History: Selected Writings on the Art and Science of History*. Edited by Roger Wines. New York: Fordham University Press, 1981.

Reade, Winwood. *The Martyrdom of Man*. New York: Butts, 1874.

Redfield, Robert. *The Primitive World and Its Transformations*. Ithaca: Great Seal Books, 1953.

Reed, John Robert. *The Natural History of H. G. Wells*. Athens: Ohio University Press, 1982.

Richard, Michael P. "Sorokin's Scenarios for the West: Implications for Third World Development." *Journal of Asian and African Studies* 14, nos. 3–4 (1979): 274–83.

Robinson, James Harvey. *Mind in the Making*. New York: Harper, 1921.

Rosenberg, Alfred. *Race and Race History and Other Essays*. Edited by Robert Pois. New York: Harper and Row, 1970.

Rule, John C., and Crosby, Barbara Stevens. "Bibliography of Works on A. J. Toynbee, 1946–1960." *History and Theory* 4, 2 (1965): 212–33.

Ryan, Alan. "The Master of Mish Mash." *New Republic*, Aug. 7 and 14, 1989, 29ff.

Samuel, Maurice. *The Professor and the Fossil*. New York: Knopf, 1956.

Sandoz, Ellis, ed. *Eric Voegelin's Significance for the Modern Mind*. Baton Rouge: Louisiana State University Press, 1991.

Schapiro, J. Salwyn. "Mr. Wells Discovers the Past." *Nation*, 112 (1921): 224–31.

Schneider, Louis. "Toward Assessment of Sorokin's View of Change." In *Explorations in Social Change*, edited by George K. Zollschan and Walter Hirsch, 371–400. New York: Houghton Mifflin, 1964.

Scott, Christina. *A Historian and His World*. London: Sheed and Ward, 1984.

Shaw, George Bernard. *Complete Plays*. London: Odham, 1937.

Shaw, Peter. "Mumford in Retrospect." *Commentary* 56 (Sept. 1973): 71–74.

Shotwell, James T. "Spengler, a Poetic Interpreter of History." *Current History* 30 (1929): 283–87.

Simirenko, Alex. "Social Origin, Revolution and Sociology: The Works of Timasheff, Sorokin and Gurvitch." *British Journal of Sociology* 24, no. 1 (1973): 84–92.

Simonton, Dean Keith. "Does Sorokin's Data Support His Theory?: A Study of Generational Fluctuations in Philosophical Beliefs." *Journal for the Scientific Study of Religion* 15, no. 2 (1976): 187–98.

Slosson, Edwin Emery. "H. G. Wells." In *Six Major Prophets*, 56–128. Boston: Little, Brown, 1917.

Smith, David C. *H. G. Wells: Desperately Mortal*. New Haven: Yale University Press, 1986.

Smith, Page. "The Millennial Vision of H. G. Wells." *Journal of Historical Studies* 2 (1968–1970): 23–24.

Soper, David Wesley. "Christopher Dawson." In *Exploring the Christian World Mind*, 15–21. New York: Philosophical Library, 1964.

Sorokin, Pitirim A. "Arnold J. Toynbee's Philosophy of History." *Journal of Modern History* 12 (1940): 374–87.

———. *Altruistic Love: A Study of American 'Good Neighbors' and Christian Saints*. 1950. Reprint. Boston: Beacon, 1969.

———. *The American Sex Revolution, 1889–1968*. Boston: Sargent, 1956.

———. "Comments on Schneider's Observations and Criticisms." In *Explorations in Social Change*, edited by George K. Zollschan and Walter Hirsch, 401–31. New York: Houghton-Mifflin, 1964.

———. *The Crisis of Our Age*. New York: Dutton, 1941.

———. "Histrionics." *Southern Review* 3 (Winter 1938): 554–64.

———. *Hunger as a Factor in Human Affairs*. Gainesville: University Press of Florida, 1975.

———. "Is Accurate Social Planning Possible?" *American Sociological Review* 1 (Feb. 1936): 12–25.

———. *A Long Journey*. New Haven: College and University Press, 1963.

———. *Man and Society in Calamity*. New York: Dutton, 1942.

———. *The Reconstruction of Humanity*. Boston: Beacon, 1948.

———. *Russia and the United States*. London: Stevens, 1950.

———. *Social and Cultural Dynamics*. 4 vols. 1937–41. Reprint. New York: Bedminster, 1962.

———. *Social Philosophies of an Age of Crisis*. Boston: Beacon, 1950.

———. *The Ways and Power of Love*. Chicago: H. Regnery, 1967.

Sorokin, Pitirim A., ed. *Forms and Techniques of Altruistic and Spiritual Growth*. Boston: Beacon, 1954.

Sorokin, Pitirim A., and Lunden, Walter A. *Power and Morality*. Boston: Sargent, 1959.

Spengler, Oswald. *The Decline of the West*. 2 vols. Translated by Charles Francis Atkinson. New York: Knopf, 1926, 1928.

———. *The Hour of Decision*. New York: Knopf, 1934.

———. *Letters of Oswald Spengler, 1913–1936*. Edited by Arthur Helps. New York: Knopf, 1966.

———. *Man and Technics: A Contribution to a Philosophy of Life*. 1932. Reprint. New York: Knopf, 1963.

———. *Selected Essays*. Chicago: Gateway, 1967.

Spiller, Robert E., ed. *The Van Wyck Brooks Lewis Mumford Letters*. New York: Dutton, 1970.

Stalley, Marshall, ed. *Patrick Geddes; Spokesman for Man and the Environment*. New Brunswick: Rutgers University Press, 1972.

Starr, Roger. "Mumford's Utopia." *Commentary* 61 (June 1976): 59–62.

Steiner, Rudolph. *Oswald Spengler: Prophet of World Chaos*. New York: Anthroposophic Press, 1949.

Stern, Fritz. *The Politics of Cultural Despair*. Berkeley: Univ. of California, 1961.

Stern, J. P. "The Weltangst of Oswald Spengler." *Times Literary Supplement*, Oct. 10, 1980, 1149–51.

Stromberg, Roland C. *Arnold J. Toynbee: Historian for an Age of Crisis*. Carbondale: Southern Illinois University Press, 1972.

Stutz, Ernst. *Oswald Spengler als politischer Denker*. Bern: Francke, 1958.

Talbutt, Palmer. *Reanimation in Philosophy*. New York: Univ. Press of America, 1986.

Tate, Allen. "Fundamentalism; Review of 'Decline of the West' Vol. 1." *Nation*, May 12, 1926, 532–34.

Teilhard de Chardin, Pierre. *The Phenomenon of Man*. New York: Harper, 1959.

Temko, Allan. "Lewis Mumford at Seventy-Two." *Harper's*, Oct. 1967, 106–11.

———. "Which Guide to the Promised Land: Fuller or Mumford?" *Horizon* 10 (Summer 1968): 24–31.

Thomson, Kenneth W. *Toynbee's Philosophy of World History and Politics*. Baton Rouge: Louisiana University Press, 1972.

Thurlow, Richard C. "Destiny and Doom: Spengler, Hitler, and 'British' Fascism." *Patterns of Prejudice* 15, no. 4 (1981): 17–33.

Toynbee, Arnold J. *Acquaintances*. London: Oxford University Press, 1967.

———. *America and the World Revolution and Other Lectures*. New York: Oxford University Press, 1962.

———. *Change and Habit: The Challenge of Our Times*. New York: Oxford University Press, 1966.

———. *Civilization on Trial*. New York: Oxford University Press, 1948.

———. *Experiences*. New York: Oxford University Press, 1969.

———. *An Historian's Approach to Religion*. London: Oxford University Press, 1956.

———. *An Historian's Conscience: Correspondence of Arnold J. Toynbee and Columba Cary-Elwes, Monk of Ampleforth*. Edited by Christian B. Peper. Boston: Beacon, 1986.

———. *Mankind and Mother Earth*. New York: Oxford University Press, 1976.

———. *The Present Day Experiment in Western Civilization*. London: Oxford University Press, 1962.

———. *A Study of History*. 12 vols. London: Oxford University Press, 1933, 1939, 1954, 1961.

———. *A Study of History*. 2 vols. Abridged by D. C. Somervell. New York: Oxford University Press, 1946, 1957.

———. *A Study of History*. Revised and abridged with Jane Caplan. Oxford: Oxford University Press, 1972.

———. "A Study of History; What I Am Trying to Do." *International Affairs* 31, nos. 1–2 (Jan. 1955): 1–4.

———. *Surviving the Future*. London: Oxford University Press, 1971.

———. *Toynbee on Toynbee*. New York: Oxford University Press, 1974.

———. *The World and the West*. New York: Oxford University Press, 1953.

Trevor-Roper, Hugh R. "Arnold Toynbee's Millennium." In *Encounters*, edited by Stephen Spender et al. New York: Basic Books, 1963.

———. "Barbarians Were Often at the Gate: Review of *The Rise of the West*." *New York Times Book Review*, Oct. 6, 1963, 1, 30.

———. "The Prophet." *New York Times Review of Books*, Oct. 12, 1989, 28.

Troeltsch, Ernst. *Absoluteness of Christianity and the History of Religions*. Richmond: John Knox, 1971.

Turgot, Anne-Robert-Jacques. "On Universal History." In *Turgot on Progress, Sociology and Economics*, edited by Ronald L. Meek, 61–119. Cambridge: Cambridge University Press, 1973.

Vermeil, Edmond. *Doctrinaires de la Revolution allemande 19181938*. Paris: Sorlot, 1938.

Vico, Giambattista. *The New Science*. 1744. Reprint. Garden City: Doubleday, 1961.

Voegelin, Eric. *Autobiographical Reflections*. Baton Rouge: Louisiana University Press, 1989.

———. *Order and History*. 5 vols. Baton Rouge: Louisiana University Press, 1956–1987.

Voltaire, François Marie Arouet de. *Essai sur les moeurs et l'esprit des nations*. 2 vols. Paris: Garnier Frères, 1963.

Wade, Mason. "A Catholic Spengler." *Commonweal* 22 (1935): 6057.

Wagar, W. Warren. *Books in World History*. Bloomington: Indiana University Press, 1973.

———. *The City of Man: Prophesies of a World Civilization in Twentieth Century Thought*. Boston: Houghton Mifflin, 1963.

———. *H. G. Wells and the World State*. Freeport: Yale University Press, 1961.

Wagar, W. Warren, ed. *Science, Faith and Man*. New York: Walker, 1968.

Wallerstein, Immanuel. *The Capitalist World Economy*. New York: Cambridge University Press, 1979.

———. "Crisis as Transition." In *Dynamics of Global Crisis*, edited by Samir Amin, Giovanni Arrighi, Andre Gunder Frank, and Immanuel Wallerstein, 11–54. New York: Monthly Review, 1982.

———. *Historical Capitalism*. London: Verso, 1983.

———. *The Modern World System*. 2 vols. New York: Academic Press, 1974, 1980.

———. "The Rise and Future Demise of the World Capitalist System: Concepts for Comparative Analysis." *Comparative Studies in Society and History* 16 (1974): 387–415.

Walsh, W. H. "Toynbee Reconsidered." *Philosophy* 38 (1963): 7177.

Walters, R. "McNeill, William H., His Own History." *New York Times Book Review*, Oct. 6, 1963, 30.

Ward, Leo R. "Dawson on Education in Christian Culture." *Modern Age* 17 (1973): 399–407.

Ward, Maisie. "The Case of Christopher Dawson." *Catholic World* 169 (1949): 150ff.

Watkins, Edward I. "Christopher Dawson." *Commonweal* 18 (1933): 607–9.

Weber, Max. *On Capitalism, Bureaucracy and Religion*. Edited by Stanislaw Andreski. London: George Allen and Unwin, 1983.

Weigart, Hans W. "Oswald Spengler, Twenty-Five Years After." *Foreign Affairs* 21 (1942): 120–31.

Wells, G. A. "Herder's Determinism." *Journal of the History of Ideas* 19, no. 1 (1958): 105–13.

———. "Herder's Two Philosophies of History." *Journal of the History of Ideas* 21, no. 4 (1960): 527–37.

Wells, Herbert George. *Anticipations of the Reaction of Mechanical and Scientific Progress on Human Life and Thought*. London: Chapman and Hall, 1902.

———. *The Definitive Time Machine*. Edited by Harry M. Gedulds. Blooming-ton: Indiana University Press, 1987.

———. *Experiment in Autobiography*. 1934. Reprint. Boston: Little Brown, 1984.

———. *The Fate of Homo Sapiens*. London: Secker and Warburg, 1939.

———. *God the Invisible King*. New York: Macmillan, 1917.

———. *Interviews and Recollections*. Edited by J. R. Hammond. Totowa: Barnes and Noble, 1980.

———. *Men like Gods*. New York: Grossett and Dunlop, 1922.

———. *Mind at the End of Its Tether*. London: William Heinemann, 1945.

———. *A Modern Utopia*. London: Chapman and Hall, 1905.

———. "My Auto-Obituary." In *Interviews and Recollections*, edited by J. R. Hammond. Totowa: Barnes and Noble, 1980.

———. *The New World Order*. New York: Knopf, 1940.

———. *The Open Conspiracy*. Garden City: Doubleday, 1928.

———. *The Outline of History*. Garden City: Garden City Publishing, 1920.

———. *The Salvaging of Civilization; The Probable Future of Mankind*. New York: Macmillan, 1922.

———. *The Shape of Things to Come*. New York: Macmillan, 1934.

———. *A Short History of the World*. Rev. ed. Edited by Raymond Postgate and G. P. Wells. New York: Penguin, 1965.

———. *The Way the World is Going*. London: Ernest Benn, 1928.

———. *World Brain*. Garden City: Doubleday, Doran, 1938.

———. *The World Set Free*. New York: Dutton, 1914.

West, Anthony. "H. G. Wells." *Encounter* 7 (Feb. 1957): 52–59.

———. *H. G. Wells: Aspects of a Life*. New York: Random House, 1984.

White, Hayden. *Metahistory: The Historical Imagination in Nineteenth Century Europe*. Baltimore: Johns Hopkins University Press, 1973.

White, Morton, and White, Lucia. *The Intellectual versus the City*. New York: New American Library, 1972.

Wilhelmson, Frederick D. "The Vision of Christopher Dawson." *Commonweal* 67 (1958): 355–58.

"William H. McNeill, Bibliography." *Journal of Modern History* 58 (1986): 3–18.

Williamson, Jack. *H. G. Wells: Critic of Progress*. Baltimore: Mirage, 1973.

Winetrout, Kenneth. *Arnold Toynbee: The Ecumenical Vision*. Boston: Twayne, 1975.

Wolf, Eric R. *Europe and the People without History*. Berkeley: Univ. of Califor-nia, 1982.

———. "Materialists vs. Mentalists." *Comparative Studies in Society and History* 4 (1982): 148–52.

———. "Understanding Civilizations." *Comparative Studies in Society and History* 9 (1966–67): 446–65.

Zimmerman, Carle C. *Sociological Theories of Pitirim A. Sorokin*. Bombay: Thacker, 1973.

———. *Sorokin—The World's Greatest Sociologist*. Saskatoon: Univ. of Saskatch-ewan, 1968.

INDEX